easy Adobe Photoshop® 6

See it done

Do it yourself

que®

Part 1: Getting Started

Part 2: Opening and Saving Files

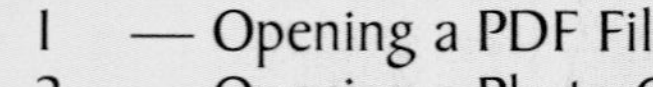

Part 3: Making and Saving Selections

Part 4: Working with Colors and Patterns

Part 5: Painting Images

Part 6: Editing Images

Part 7: Adjusting Colors and Tones

Part 8: Working with Layers

Part 9: Creating and Editing Type

Part 10: Creating Special Effects

Part 11: Creating Artistic Effects

Part 12: Creating Images for the Web

International Standard Book Number: 0-7897-2423-5

Library of Congress Catalog Card Number: 00-101760

Printed in the United States of America

First Printing: October, 2000

02 01 4 3 2

Trademarks

Warning and Disclaimer

About the Author

Kate Binder is a production artist and freelance writer living in southern New Hampshire. The author of *Teach Yourself QuarkXPress 4 in 14 Days* and co-author of *Photoshop 4 Complete*, she also writes articles on desktop production tools and techniques for *Publish* magazine. She can be reached at **easyps@prospecthillpub.com**, and her Web page is at **http://www.prospecthillpub.com/**. She recommends that her readers not attempt these techniques without at least one retired racing greyhound on the premises—she finds that she requires four greyhounds to keep her going. For more information, see **http://www.adopt-a-greyhound.org/**.

Dedication

This book is for my partner and best friend: my husband Don.

Acknowledgments

Belated thanks to Jack Doucette and Richard Binder, who graciously provided many of the photos used in this book.

Associate Publisher
Greg Wiegand

Acquisitions Editor
Beth Millett

Development Editor
Beth Millett

Managing Editor
Thomas Hayes

Project Editor
Tonya Simpson

Indexer
Aamir Burki

Proofreader
Benjamin Berg

Technical Editor
Kevin Darbro

Team Coordinator
Julie Otto

Interior Designer
Jean Bisesi

Cover Designer
Anne Jones

Illustrations
Bruce Dean

How to Use This Book

It's as Easy as 1-2-3

Each part of this book is made up of a series of short, instructional lessons, designed to help you understand basic information that you need to get the most out of your computer hardware and software.

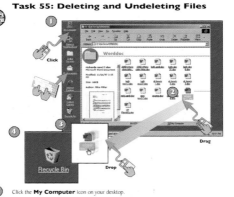

Click: Click the left mouse button once.

Double-click: Click the left mouse button twice in rapid succession.

Right-click: Click the right mouse button once.

Pointer Arrow: Highlights an item on the screen you need to point to or focus on in the step or task.

Selection: Highlights the area onscreen discussed in the step or task.

Click & Type: Click once where indicated and begin typing to enter your text or data.

1 Each step is fully illustrated to show you how it looks onscreen.

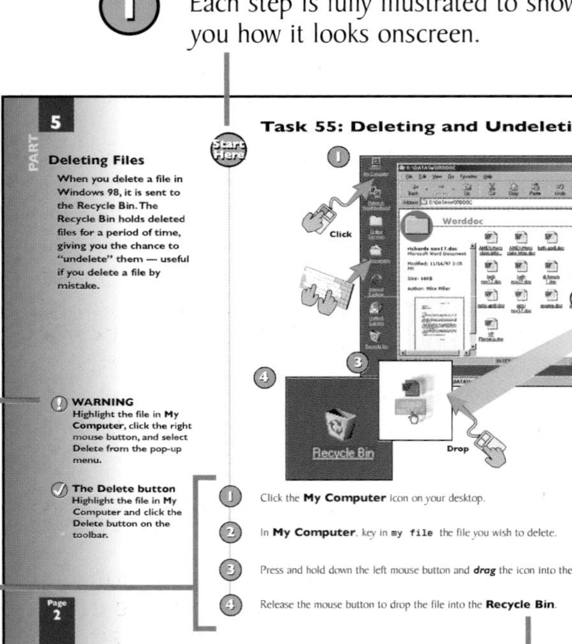

PART
5
Task 55: Deleting and Undeleting Files
Deleting Files
When you delete a file in Windows 98, it is sent to the Recycle Bin. The Recycle Bin holds deleted files for a period of time, giving you the chance to "undelete" them — useful if you delete a file by mistake.
WARNING
Highlight the file in My Computer, click the right mouse button, and select Delete from the pop-up menu.
The Delete button
Highlight the file in My Computer and click the Delete button on the toolbar.
Click
Drag
Drop
Recycle Bin
1 Click the My Computer icon on your desktop.
2 In My Computer, key in my file the file you wish to delete.
3 Press and hold down the left mouse button and drag the icon into the Recycle Bin.
4 Release the mouse button to drop the file into the Recycle Bin.
Page 2

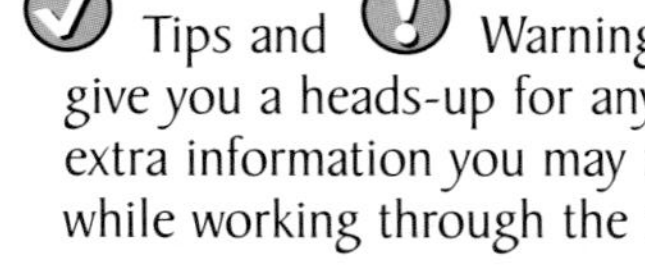

Tips and Warnings give you a heads-up for any extra information you may need while working through the task.

2 Each task includes a series of quick, easy steps designed to guide you through the procedure.

3 Items that you select or click in menus, dialog boxes, tabs, and windows are shown in **bold**. Information you type is in a `special font`.

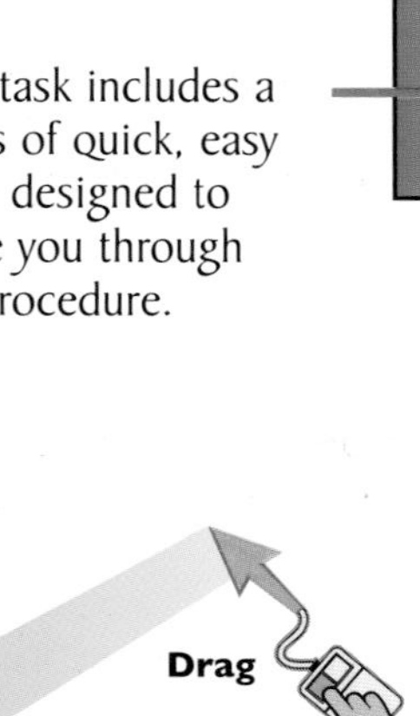

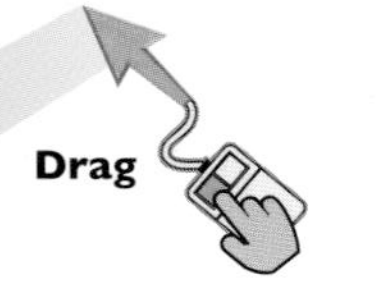

How to Drag: Point to the starting place or object. Hold down the mouse button (right or left per instructions), move the mouse to the new location, then release the button.

Next Step: If you see this symbol, it means the task you're working on continues on the next page.

End Task: Task is complete.

Introduction to *Easy Adobe Photoshop 6*

Adobe Photoshop 6 is a big, complex program—it's an image editor, a paint program, a Web graphics design tool, and more. It can do a lot for you, but first you must tame it and make it your own. Learning to use its basic tools will allow you to explore further on your own.

That's why *Easy Adobe Photoshop 6* provides concise, visual, step-by-step instructions for handling all the tasks you'll need to accomplish. You'll learn how to get started in Photoshop 6, how to choose the right color mode for each project, how to adjust scanned images to look their best, how to paint new images with your choice of tools, how to apply filters that can completely transform an image with a single click, and more.

The images shown in this book come from various sources—some of them are included with your copy of Photoshop. These images appear as examples; you can complete all the tasks in the book using your own iamges. Have fun experimenting!

You can choose to read the book cover to cover or to use it as a reference when you encounter a piece of Photoshop 6 that you don't know how to use. Either way, *Easy Adobe Photoshop 6* lets you see it done and do it yourself.

Tell Us What You Think!

As the reader of this book, *you* are our most important critic and commentator. We value your opinion and want to know what we're doing right, what we could do better, what areas you'd like to see us publish in, and any other words of wisdom you're willing to pass our way.

As an associate publisher for Que, I welcome your comments. You can fax, email, or write me directly to let me know what you did or didn't like about this book—as well as what we can do to make our books stronger.

Please note that I cannot help you with technical problems related to the topic of this book, and that due to the high volume of mail I receive, I might not be able to reply to every message.

When you write, please be sure to include this book's title and author as well as your name and phone or fax number. I will carefully review your comments and share them with the author and editors who worked on the book.

Fax: 317-581-4666

Email: **desktop_pub@macmillanusa.com**

Mail: Que
201 West 103rd Street
Indianapolis, IN 46290 USA

PART I

Getting Started

Photoshop is a powerful program with so many features that very few users explore them all. Like any program, though, Photoshop has basic functions that you'll use in almost every project: printing, zooming in and out to view an image, changing an image's print size, undoing commands, and so on. In addition, Photoshop includes features borrowed from page layout programs that help you position elements and measure areas precisely within images.

Part I shows you how to create files, view images in different ways, measure distances and place objects on images, and change an image's size and shape. Also included in this part are ways to automate your work, undo one or more commands you've already executed, and apply a series of steps to an entire group of images at one time.

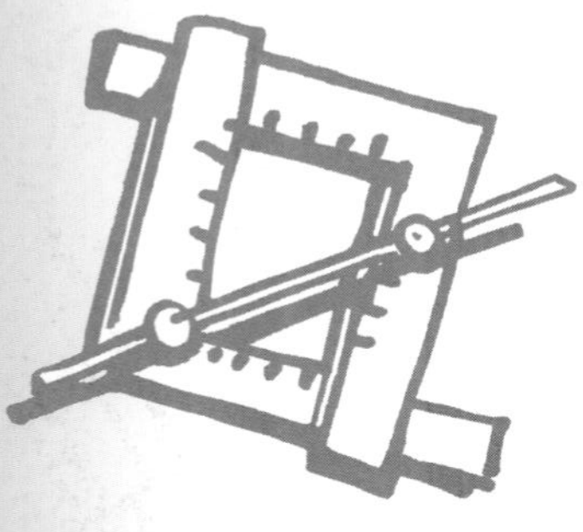

Tasks

Each Photoshop image you create begins with a new file. When you create the file, you specify its dimensions, *resolution*, and *color mode*, depending on the file's ultimate destination (print or onscreen display).

Task 1: Creating a New File

Start Here

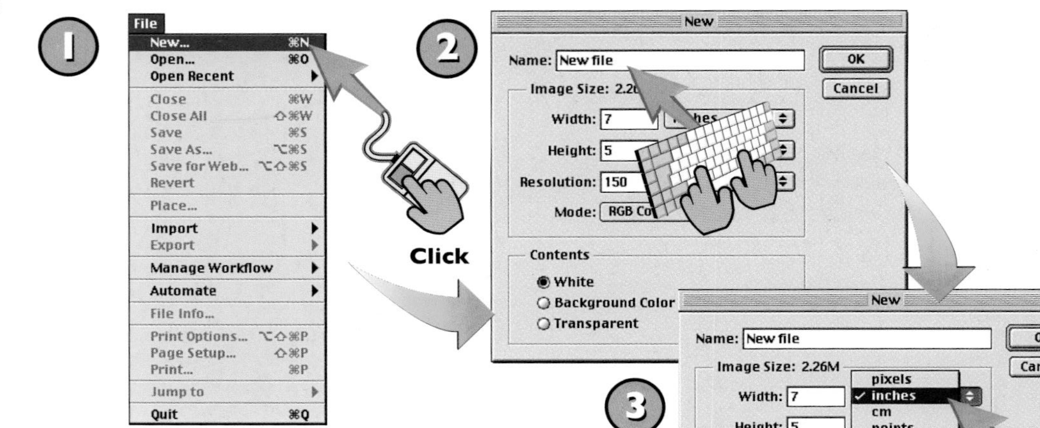

1. Choose **File**, **New**.
2. Enter a name for the file in the **New** dialog box.
3. Choose measurement units and enter dimensions for the file's width and height.
4. Enter a resolution for the file.

Next Step

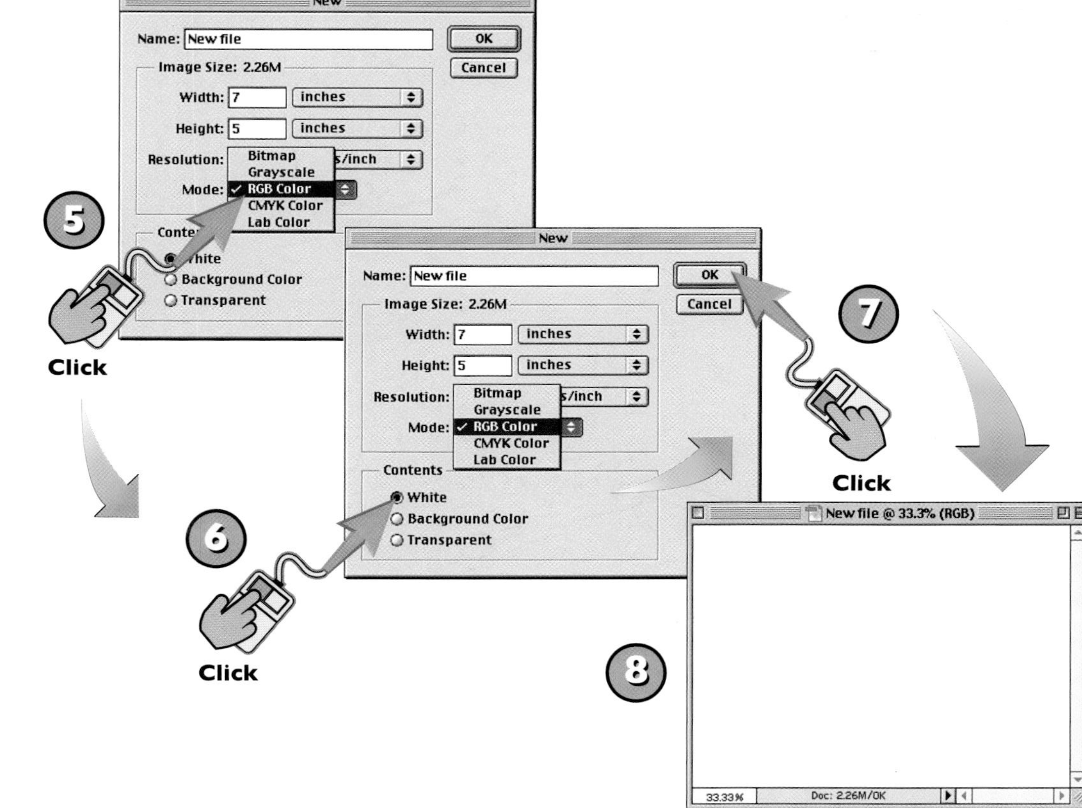

5 Choose a color mode from the **Mode** pop-up menu.

6 Choose a background color for the file.

7 Click **OK**.

8 Begin working in the new file's window.

Use *Bitmap* for black-and-white line art images; *Grayscale* for images with shades of gray, such as black-and-white photos; *RGB* for Web and screen presentation images; and *CMYK* for color images that will be printed on a press.

End Task

Task 2: Moving an Image

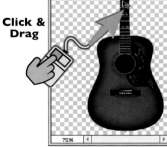

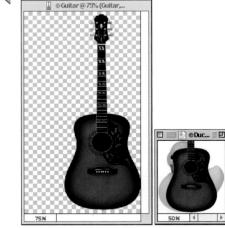

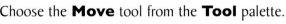

Start Here

With the **Move** tool, you can move an image within its window or drag it into another image window. For images without multiple *layers*, the **Move** tool moves the entire image; if an image contains multiple layers, the **Move** tool works on individual layers or on linked layers. (For more information about layers, see **Part 8, "Working with Layers."**)

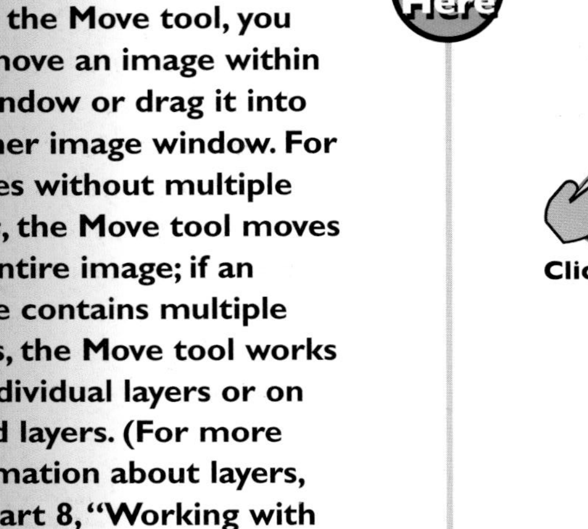

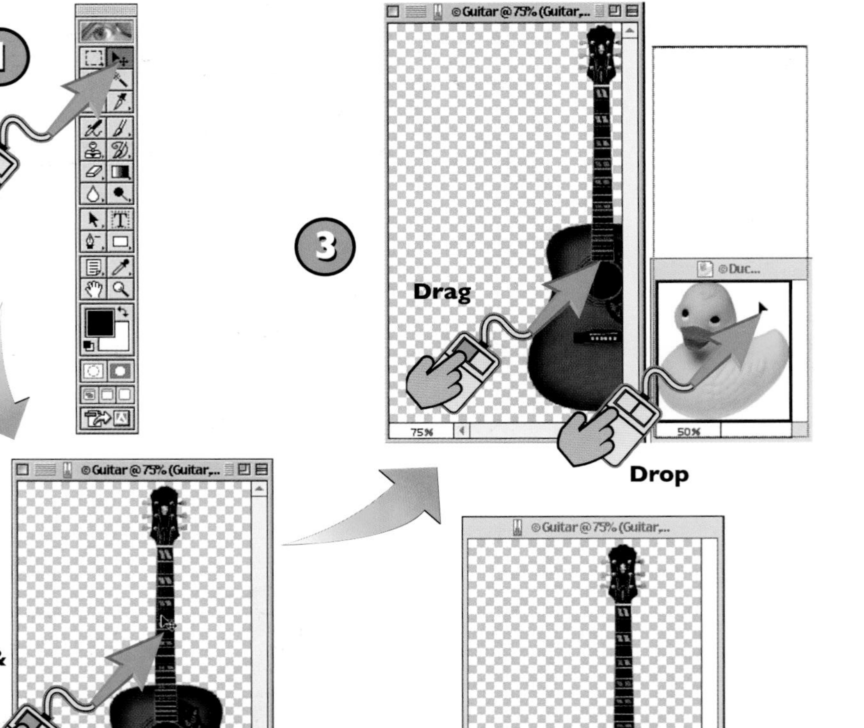

- Hold down the **Shift** key as you drag to move the image straight up and down or left and right.

- Using the **Move** tool on an image without layers changes the Background into a layer. To save the file in a format other than Photoshop, choose **Layer**, **Flatten Image** first to change the layer back into a Background.

1. Choose the **Move** tool from the **Tool** palette.
2. Click and drag the image to move it around on its own canvas.
3. Drag the image into another window to copy it into another file.

End Task

Task 3: Changing the Zoom Percentage

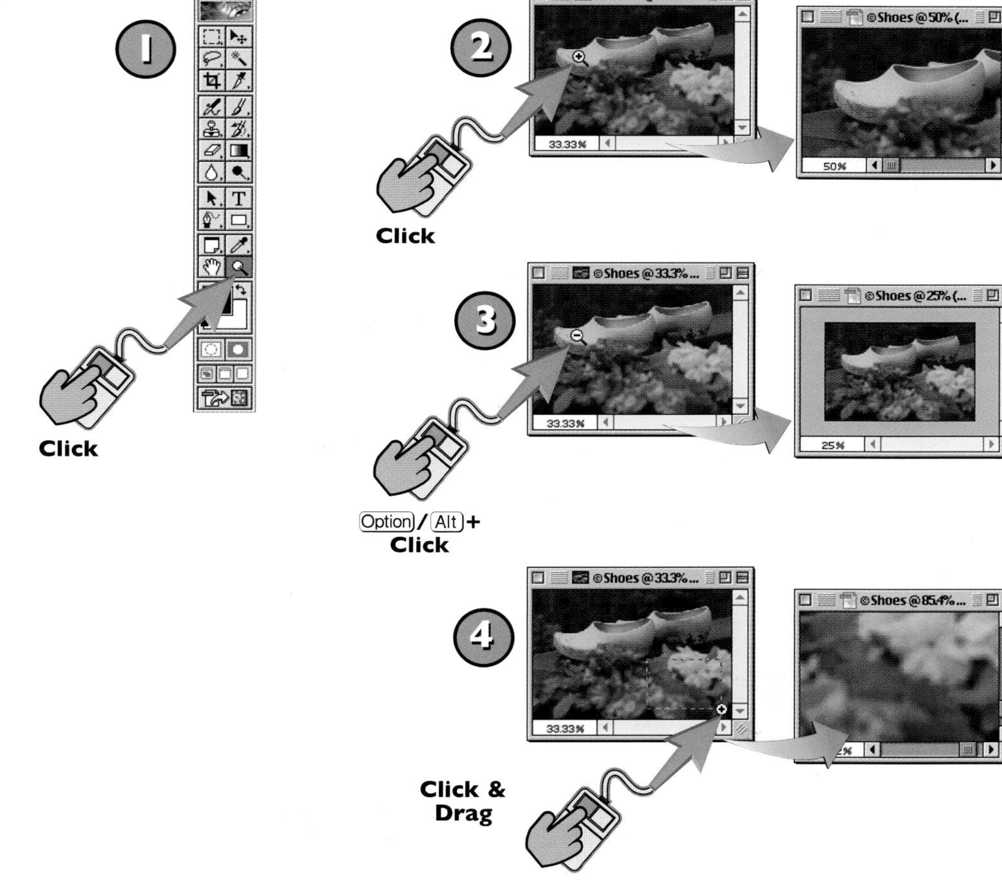

1. Choose the **Zoom** tool from the **Tool** palette.
2. Click in the image to enlarge it (zoom in).
3. **Option+click/Alt+click** in the image to reduce it (zoom out).
4. If you want to enlarge a specific area, click and drag to draw a marquee around the area you want to enlarge.

Photoshop enables you to view images at any size from .15% to 1600% of their actual size. As you work in Photoshop, you'll find that you switch zoom percentages often, zooming in to work on details and zooming out to get "the big picture."

The Zoom tool's magnifying glass cursor will contain a plus sign when you're zooming in and a minus sign when you're zooming out.

To zoom to a specific percentage, click in the zoom percentage box in the lower-left corner of the window, type a new percentage, and press Enter.

Start Here

Task 4: Viewing Image Windows in Different Ways

Screen clutter is a constant problem for digital artists. To get rid of the distracting extra windows and backgrounds on your screen, you can view Photoshop images in alternative modes.

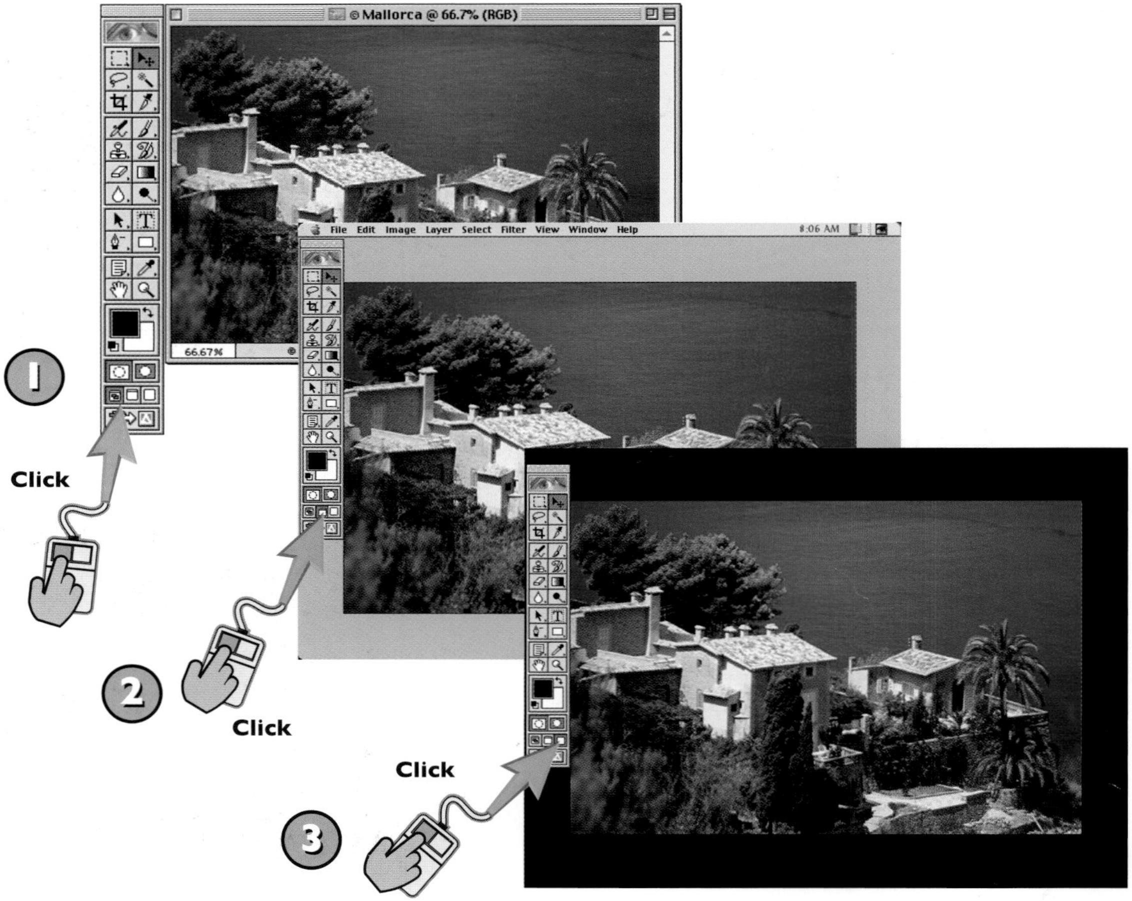

- If the image is too small to fill the entire screen, a gray background will show around it in Full Screen Mode with Menu Bar.
- If the image is too small to fill the entire screen, a black background will show around it in Full Screen Mode. Palettes will still be displayed.
- If palettes start cluttering up your screen, press **Tab** to hide any open palettes; press **Tab** again to bring them back. Press **Shift+Tab** to hide all palettes except the **Tool** palette.

1 Click

2 Click

3 Click

1. Click the **Standard Screen Mode** button on the **Tool** palette to view the image in a standard window.
2. Click the **Full Screen Mode with Menu Bar** button on the **Tool** palette to center the image on the entire screen without hiding the menu bar.
3. Click the **Full Screen Mode** button on the **Tool** palette to fill the screen with the image and hide the menu bar.

Start Here

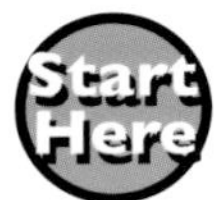

Task 5: Viewing Different Parts of an Image

1
Window
Show Tools
Show Options
Show Navigator
Show Info
Show Color
Show Swatches
Show Styles
Show History
Show Actions
Show Layers
Show Channels
Show Paths
Show Character
Show Paragraph
Reset Palette Locations
Click
2
Hands @ 150% (Gray)
Navigator
150%
Click &
Drag
3
Hands @ 286% (Gray)
285.77%
Click &
Drag
4
Hands @ 100% (Gray)
100%
Click

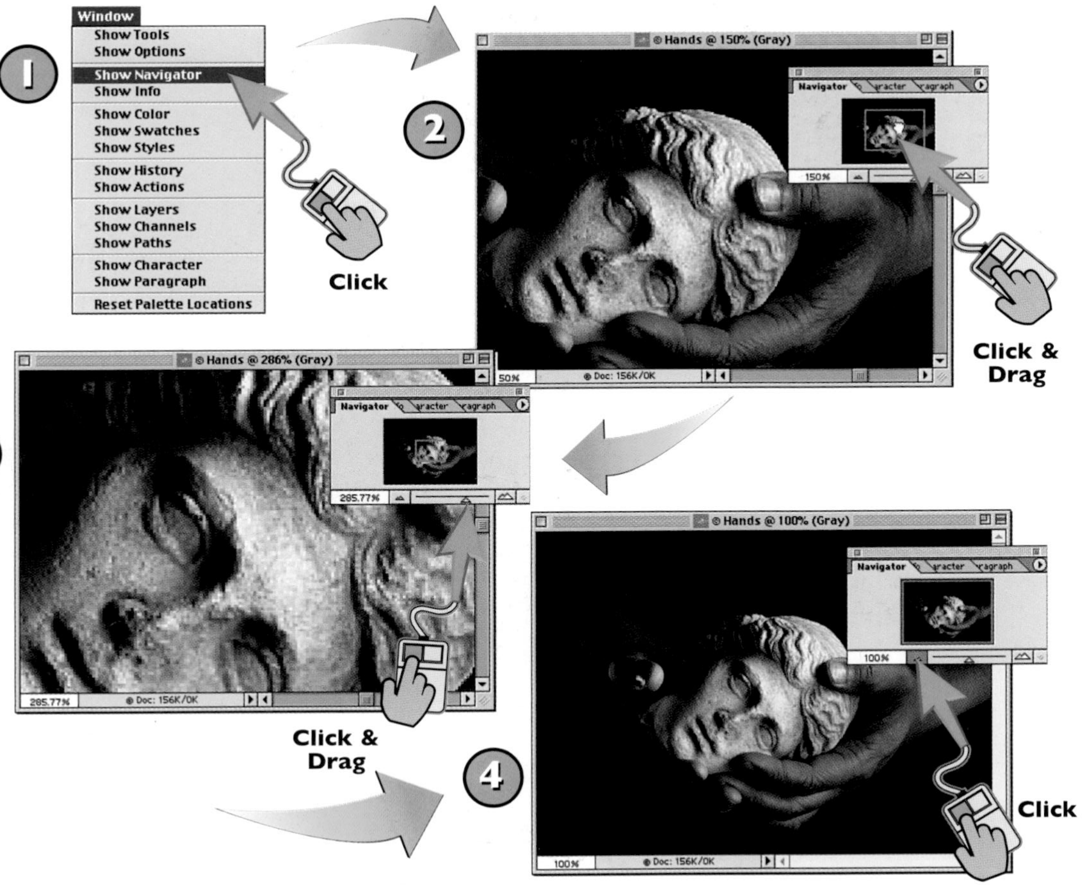

1. Choose **Window**, **Show Navigator**.
2. Click in the **Navigator** palette's red rectangle and drag it to show a different part of the image.
3. Drag the slider to change the zoom percentage.
4. Click the **Zoom In** and **Zoom Out** buttons to change the zoom percentage in specific increments from .15% up to 1600%.

The Navigator palette is a handy way to move around a large image quickly and to zoom in and out of the image. Its controls offer several alternative ways to navigate through an image.

If you find you can't drag the red rectangle, it's because the entire image is already showing in the window. You might need to move or hide palettes to see all of it.

For a specific percentage, click in the zoom percentage box in the lower-left corner of the palette, type a new percentage, and press Enter.

The *Grabber Hand* is the easiest (but not always the most efficient) way to view different parts of an image. Hold down the Spacebar in the image window and drag the image around with the hand cursor. With larger images, you'd be dragging forever with the Grabber Hand, so try the Navigator palette instead.

End Task

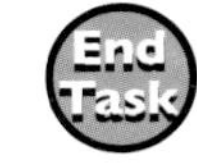

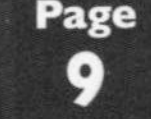

Task 6: Viewing Information About an Image's Size and Colors

The Info palette is Photoshop's clearinghouse location for information about the colors and distances in images. It can display *pixel* colors in eight different ways—including two at the same time—and show measurements in six different units.

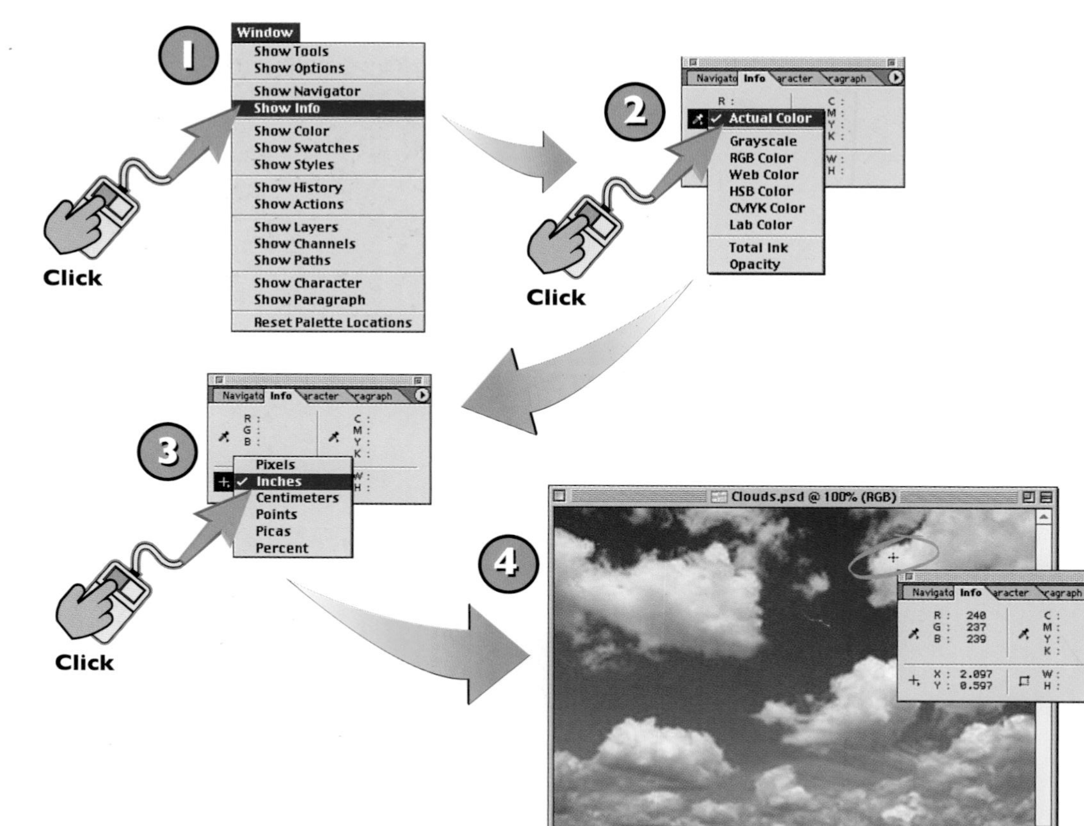

When you move the cursor over the image, the color and coordinates of the pixel under the cursor are displayed in the palette.

The Actual Color option in the eyedropper icon's pop-up menu uses the color system corresponding to the image's color mode: *RGB* for an RGB image, *CMYK* for a CMYK image, and so on.

For more information about color modes, see Part 4, "Working with Colors and Patterns."

1. Choose **Window**, **Show Info**.
2. Click and hold the palette's eyedropper icons and choose a color mode from each pop-up menu.
3. Click and hold the palette's crosshairs icon and choose measurement units from the pop-up menu.
4. Move the cursor over the image to display information about each pixel's color and position.

End Task

Task 7: Comparing Different Points in an Image

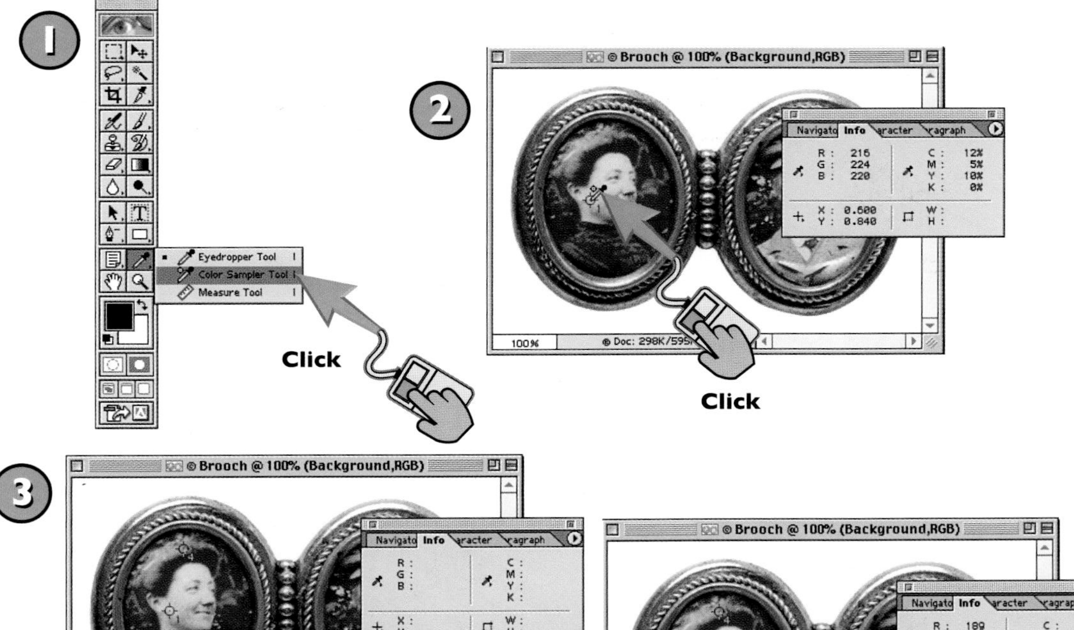

The Color Sampler tool lets you view information on the Info palette about multiple points in an image. For example, you can determine whether one section of the image is darker or whether two points are at the same vertical position.

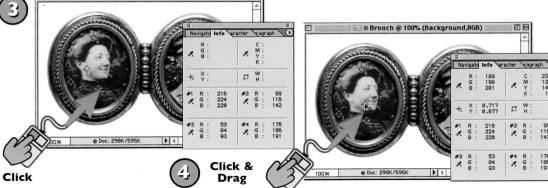

1. Click and hold the **Eyedropper** tool in the **Tool** palette, and slide the mouse over to choose the **Color Sampler Tool**.
2. Click in the image; the **Info** palette pops up if it wasn't already open.
3. Click at one, two, or three more points; their colors appear on the **Info** palette.
4. Click and drag any point to compare a different location in the image.

To change the color mode or measurement units displayed on the Info palette, see Task 6, "Viewing Information About an Image."

Task 8: Measuring a Distance

Start Here

Photoshop provides a special tool that you can use to find the size of objects in an image. Like the Color Sampler tool, the Measure tool uses the Info palette to display the results of its calculations, and you can choose to view measurements in different units.

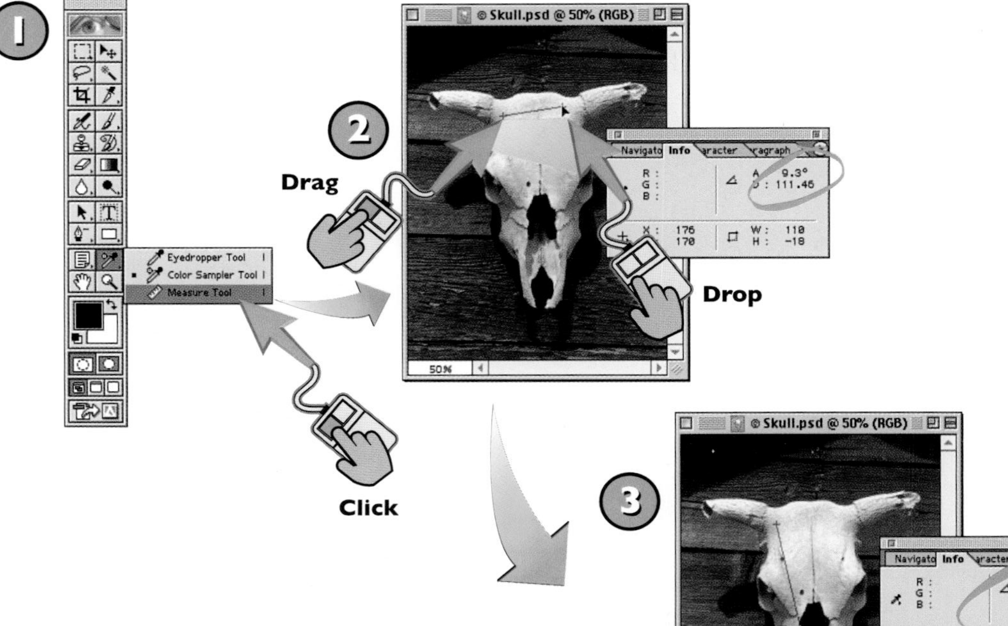

- The distance and angle of the line you drew are displayed in the **Info** palette.
- To turn the measuring line into a protractor, **Option+click/Alt+click** on either end and drag out another line. The angle between the two segments of the measurement line is displayed on the **Info** palette.
- To change the measurement units displayed in the **Info** palette, see Task 6, "Viewing Information About an Image."

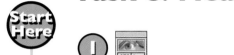

1. Click and hold the **Eyedropper** tool in the **Tool** palette, and slide the mouse over to choose the **Measure** tool.
2. Click and hold at the point where you want to start measuring. Drag to the point where you want to stop measuring.
3. Click either end of the measuring line, and drag to measure a different distance.

Task 9: Adding Rulers and Nonprinting Guides

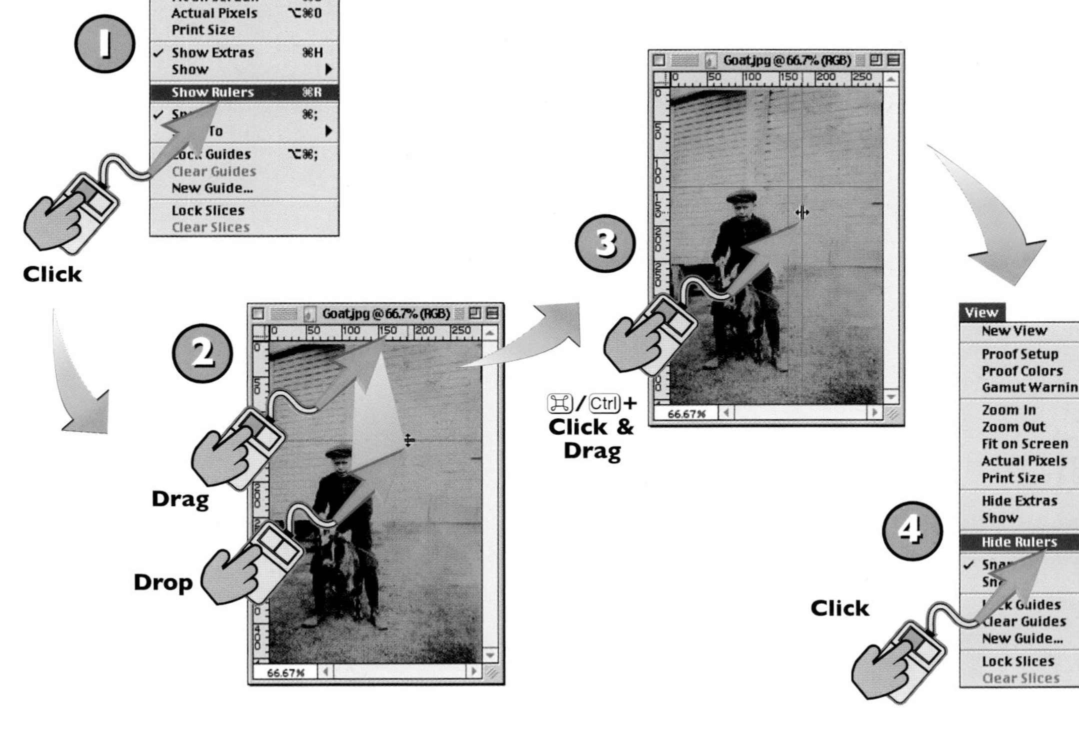

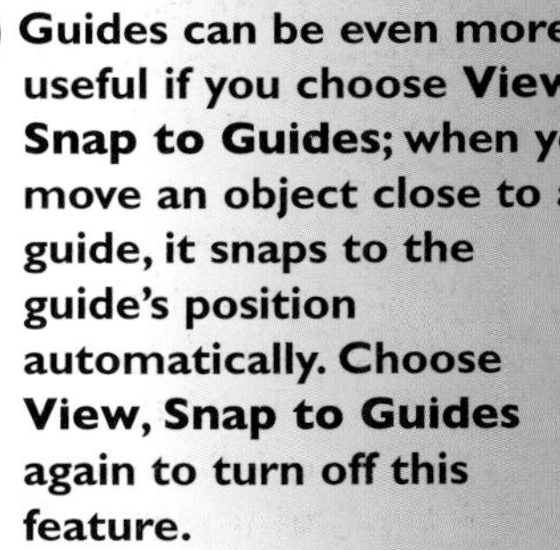

1. Choose **View**, **Show Rulers** or press **Cmd+R/Ctrl+R** to display the rulers.
2. Click a ruler, and drag to make a guide.
3. **Cmd+click/Ctrl+click** and drag to move a guide; drag all the way to the ruler to delete it.
4. Choose **View**, **Hide Rulers**, or press **Cmd+R/Ctrl+R** again to hide the rulers.

You can position elements in an image more precisely with the aid of rulers and guidelines, like those found in page layout and drawing software. The *rulers* and *guides* don't print, and they don't show onscreen if you view an image in any program other than Photoshop.

To change the ruler's units, double-click the ruler and choose a different option from the Units pop-up menu in the Units & Rulers Preferences dialog box.

Guides can be even more useful if you choose View, Snap to Guides; when you move an object close to a guide, it snaps to the guide's position automatically. Choose View, Snap to Guides again to turn off this feature.

Task 10: Displaying a Nonprinting Grid

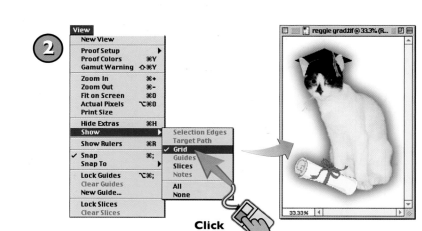

Start Here

In addition to movable guides, Photoshop can display a *grid* overlaid on an image. This feature is especially useful when other elements—such as lines or text—will be combined with the image. Like guides, gridlines don't print, and they won't be displayed if you view a Photoshop file in any other program.

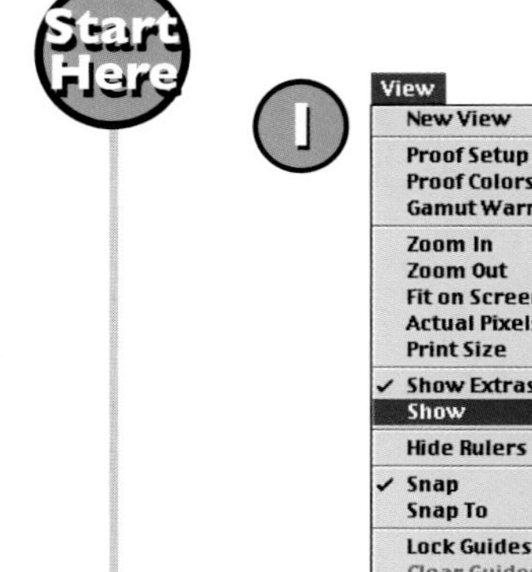

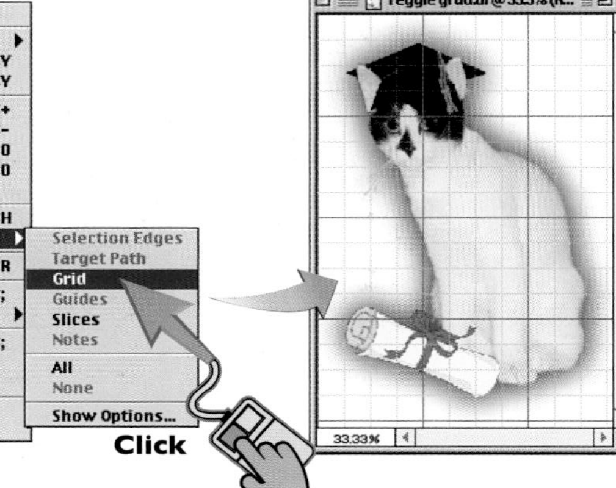

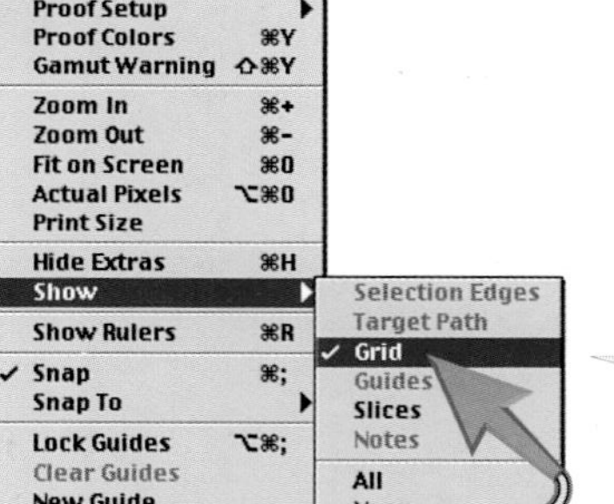

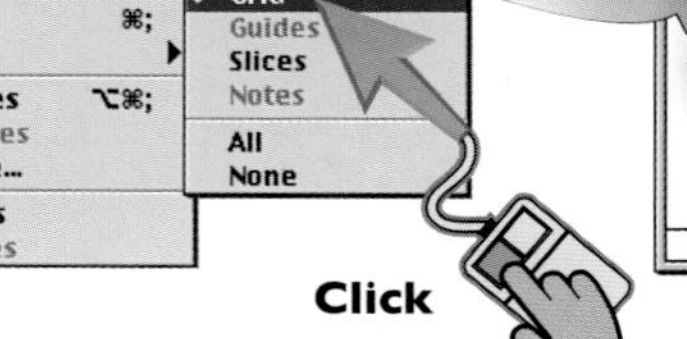

reggie grad.tif @ 33.3% (R...
33.33%

✓ You can choose the color, style, and frequency of the gridlines in the Guides & Grid Preferences dialog box. Choose Edit, Preferences, Guides & Grid.

✓ The grid can be even more useful if you choose View, Snap to Grid; when you move an object close to a gridline, it snaps to the gridline's position automatically. Choose View, Snap to Grid again to turn off this feature.

1. Choose **View**, **Show**, **Grid** to display the grid.

2. Choose **View**, **Show**, **Grid** again to hide the grid.

Task 11: Cropping an Image

Start Here

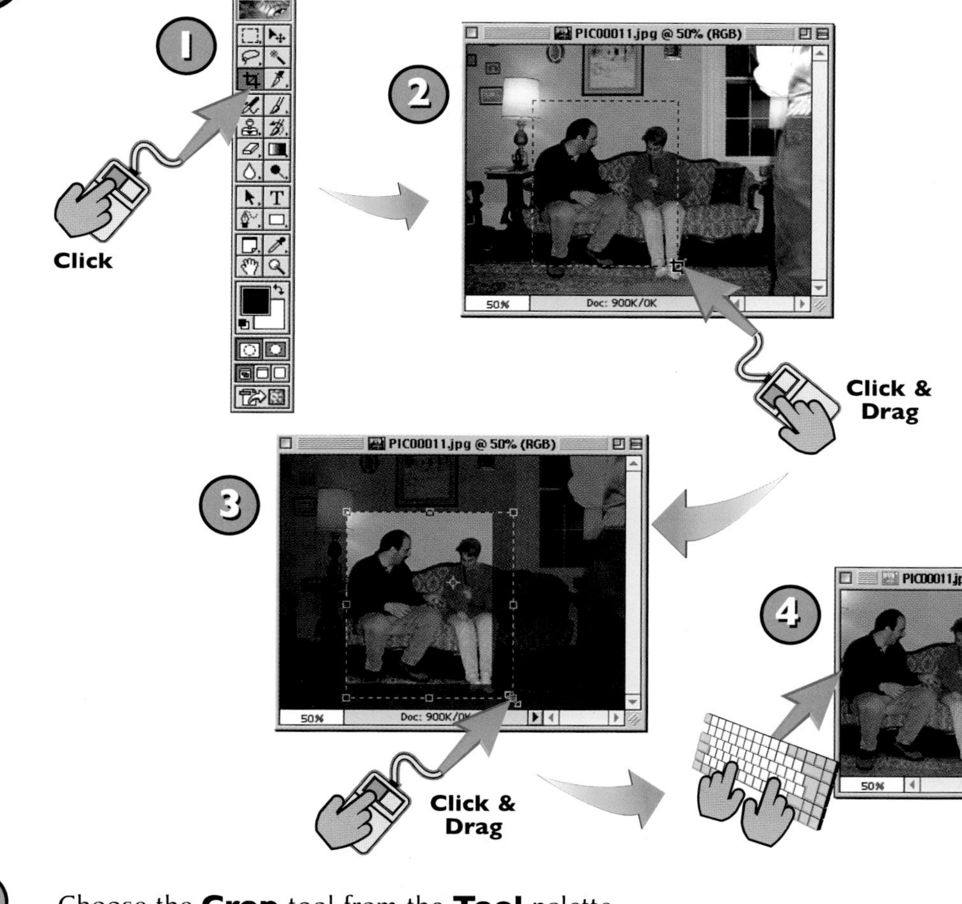

1. Choose the **Crop** tool from the **Tool** palette.
2. Click and drag in the image to define the area you want to keep.
3. Click and drag on the points to adjust the size and shape of the cropping rectangle.
4. Press **Enter** to crop the image, or press **Esc** to cancel the operation.

Cropping **is a procedure familiar to any professional photographer. In cropping, you remove the extraneous portions of an image so that it shows only what you want it to show. Photoshop makes cropping much easier than it is in the darkroom.**

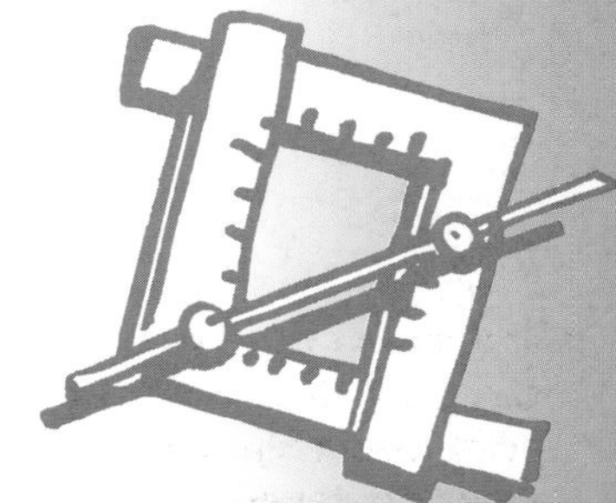

If you change your mind about what part of the image you want to feature, you can move the entire cropping rectangle by clicking within it and dragging.

Task 12: Changing an Image's Size or Resolution

Size and *resolution* are closely related in Photoshop, so these two image attributes are controlled through the same dialog box. You can choose to resize an image with or without *resampling* its resolution. If you allow resampling, the resolution of the image doesn't change, and if you don't, the image resolution increases or decreases in inverse proportion to the image's size.

Start Here

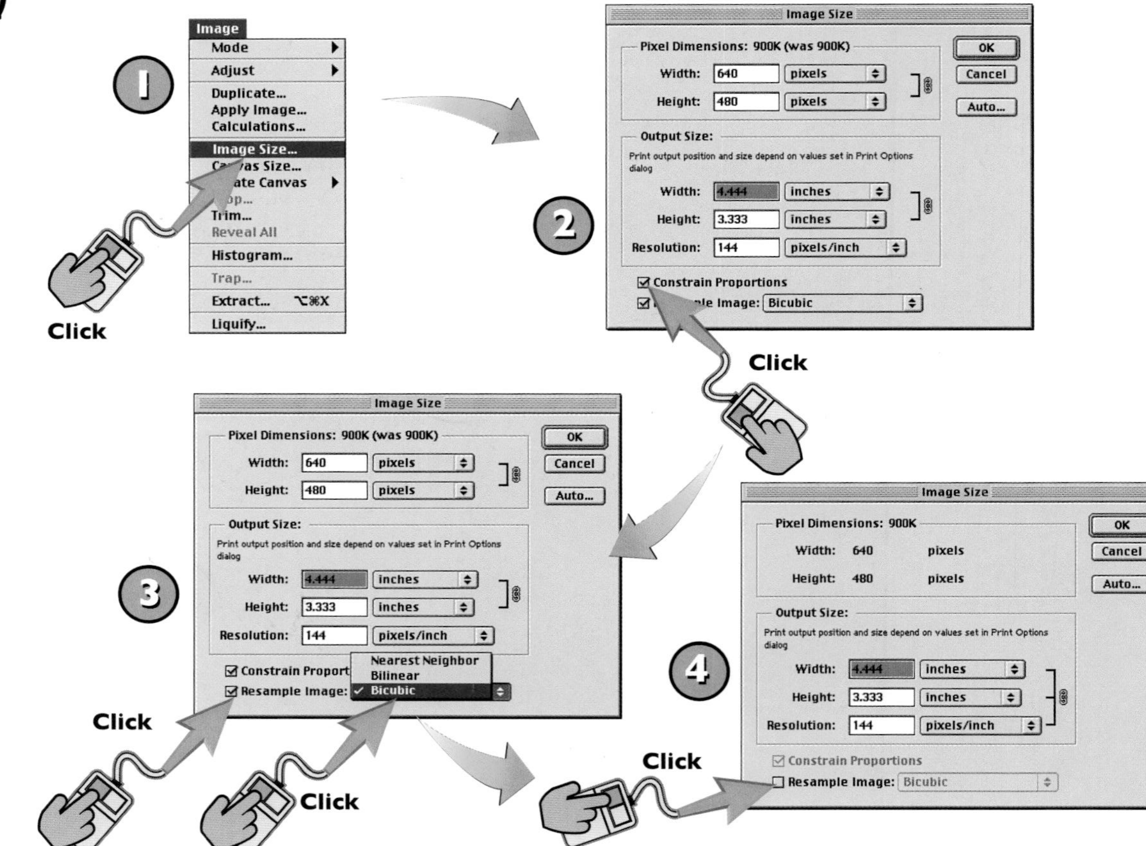

1. Choose **Image**, **Image Size**.
2. Click **Constrain Proportions** to make sure the image's proportions stay the same.
3. Click **Resample Image** to change the size but not the resolution; choose **Bicubic** from the **Method** pop-up menu.
4. Click **Resample Image** off to tie the resolution to the image size.

✓ When Photoshop resamples an image, the software adds or subtracts pixels and reassigns pixel colors to create the same image with more or fewer pixels.

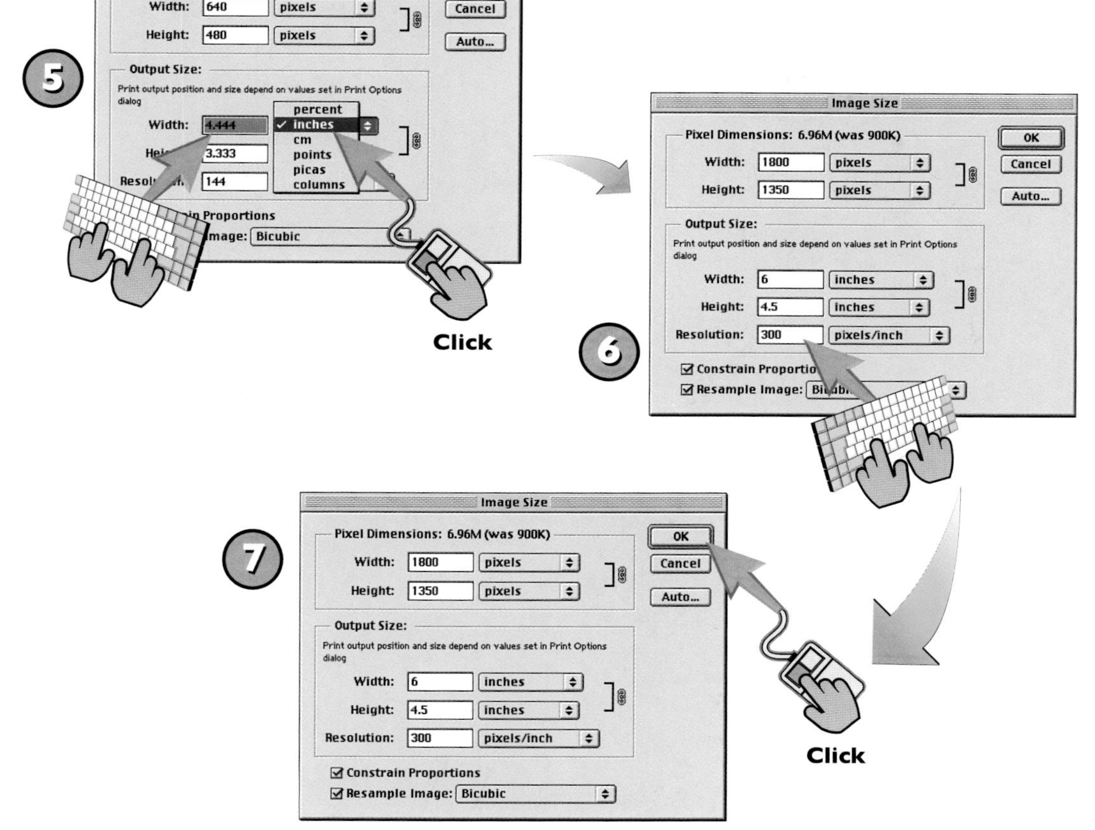

5. To change the size, choose **Output Size** units from the pop-up menus and enter a new width or height in the **Output Size** area.

6. If **Resample Image** is on, enter a new resolution.

7. Click **OK**.

With Resample Image off, if the image is enlarged, the resolution will decrease, and vice versa.

Avoid enlarging an image or increasing its resolution if possible. To accomplish this, Photoshop must create new pixels in the image, and the software can only guess what color each new pixel should be. Enlarged images are often blurry, with out-of-focus details.

Task 13: Changing the Canvas Size

Start Here

If an image is the right size but you need more room around the edges to work in, you can add that space by increasing the image's *canvas size*. This operation increases the size of the file without enlarging the existing image elements, filling the new space with the current *background color*.

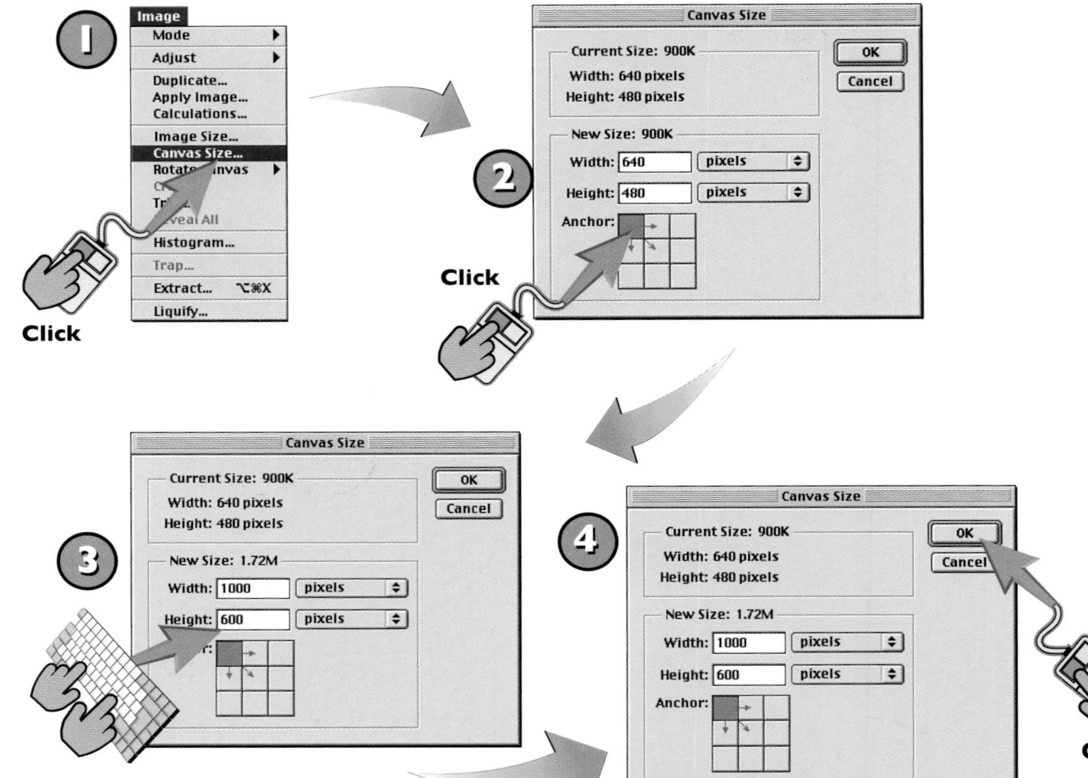

To change the color of the added canvas area, choose a different background color before changing the canvas size. (See Part 4, "Working with Colors and Patterns," to change the foreground and background colors.)

1. Choose **Image**, **Canvas Size**.
2. Click a box in the **Anchor** grid to determine where the extra space will be added.
3. Enter new measurements in the **Width** and **Height** fields.
4. Click **OK** to change the Canvas size.

Task 14: Undoing the Last Command

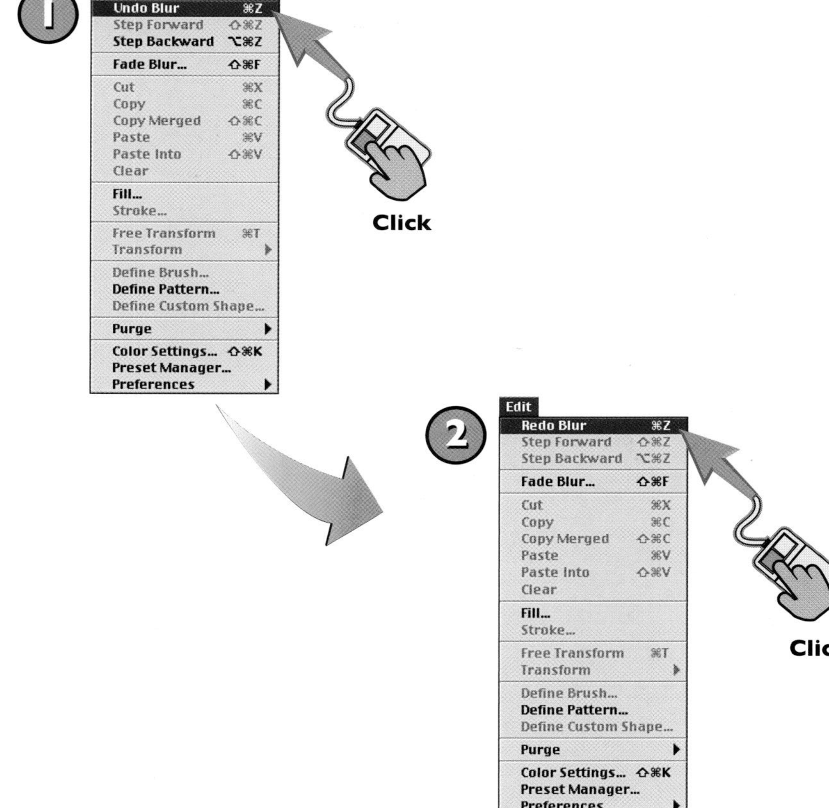

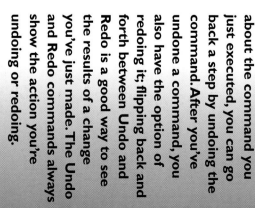

If you change your mind about the command you just executed, you can go back a step by undoing the command. After you've undone a command, you also have the option of redoing it; flipping back and forth between Undo and Redo is a good way to see the results of a change you've just made. The Undo and Redo commands always show the action you're undoing or redoing.

1. Choose **Edit**, **Undo**.
2. If you change your mind, choose **Edit**, **Redo**.

✓ If you need to undo more than one operation, see the next task.

✓ The **Undo** and **Redo** commands also contain the name of the operation you're undoing or redoing—for example, **Undo Gaussian Blur** or **Redo Levels**.

✓ You can't undo operations that don't affect the image, such as making changes to the preferences, using the **Measure** tool, or changing the foreground and background colors.

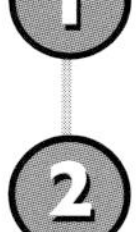

Task 15: Undoing More Than One Command

Using Photoshop's History palette, you can step back through the creation process to an image's original state or stop at any point along the way. It's a good way to create several variations on an image or to go back to an earlier stage of the image when you're experimenting with new techniques.

Start Here

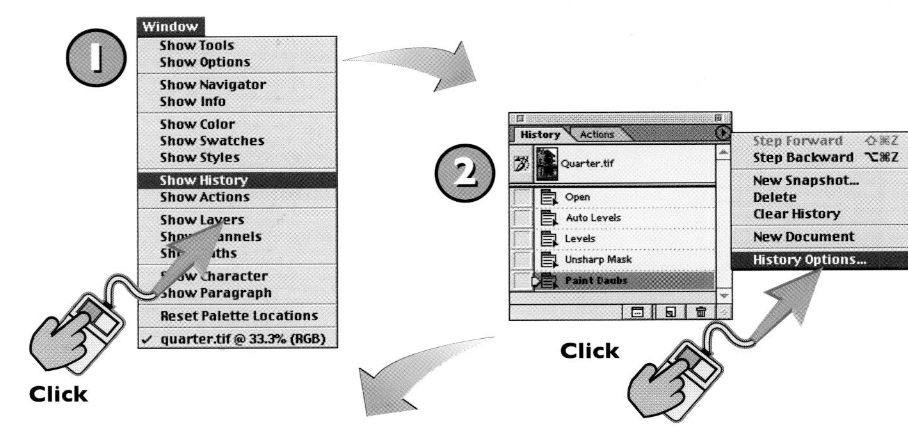

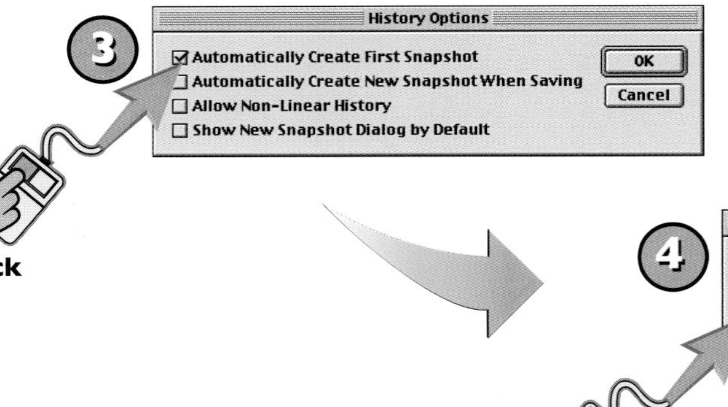

1. Choose **Window**, **Show History**.
2. From the **History** palette menu, choose **History Options**.
3. Click on **Automatically Create First Snapshot**.
4. To delete steps in the **History** palette without affecting adjacent steps, click **Allow Non-Linear History**.

You aren't restricted to reverting the entire image to a previous stage; you can "paint" in the reversion by using the History Brush tool. See Part 6, Task 15, "Restoring Part of the Image to an Earlier Stage," to learn how to restore part of an image.

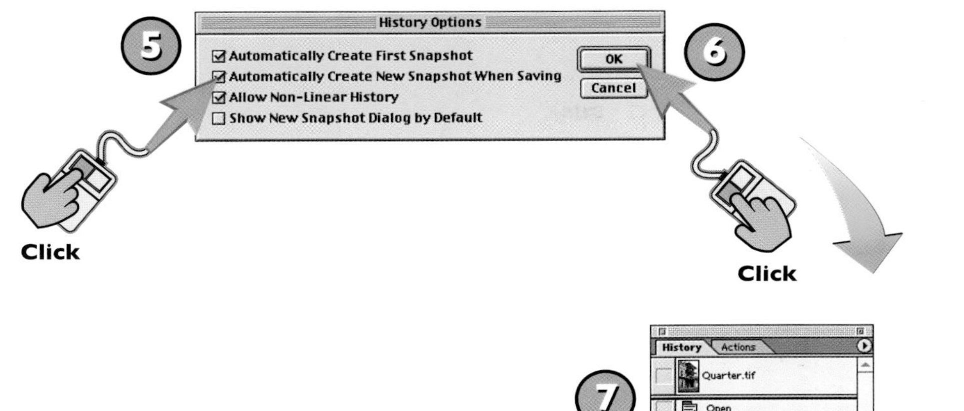

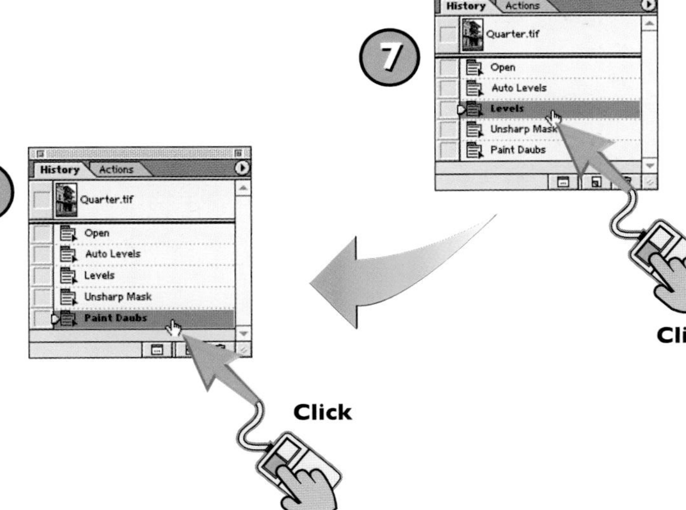

5. If you want snapshots whenever you save, check **Automatically Create New Snapshot When Saving**.
6. Click **OK**.
7. Click a command in the list to return the image to its state right after that command.
8. Click a later command to reapply the intervening operations to the image.

If you're using the **Non-Linear History** option and you go back to an earlier state of the image and make a change, that change is added to the list of changes at the end. Without **Non-Linear History**, all the other changes after the point to which you went back would be deleted. Although **Non-Linear History** clutters the **History** palette a bit, it is a way to leave all your options open.

You can create a new document based on any step in the **History** palette by dragging that step to the **New Document** icon, the left-hand icon at the bottom of the palette. The new document will show the image as it appeared at the completion of that step.

Task 16: Automating a Series of Steps

If you find yourself performing the same steps over and over again, you can save a lot of time and effort by creating an Action that will perform those steps for you any time you invoke it. Actions are listed in the Actions palette, which has a Button mode that lets you play an action just by clicking its name.

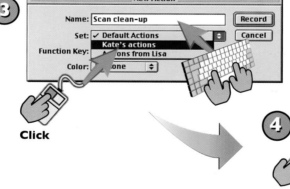

Start Here

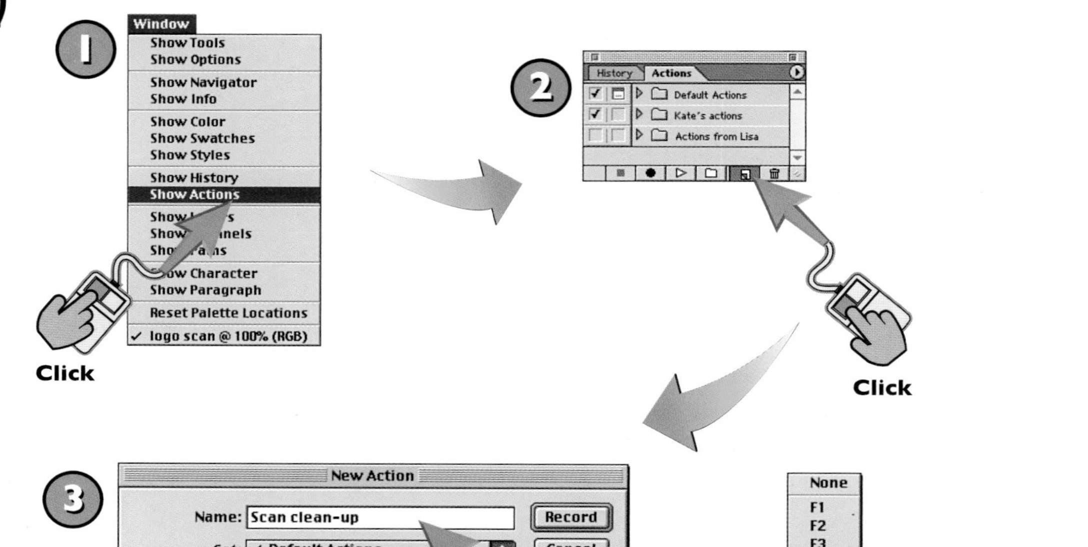

1. Choose **Window**, **Show Actions**.
2. Click the **New Action** button.
3. Enter a name for the Action, and choose a set to which it should belong.
4. Choose a function key that can trigger the action, and click to add modifier keys to the function key.

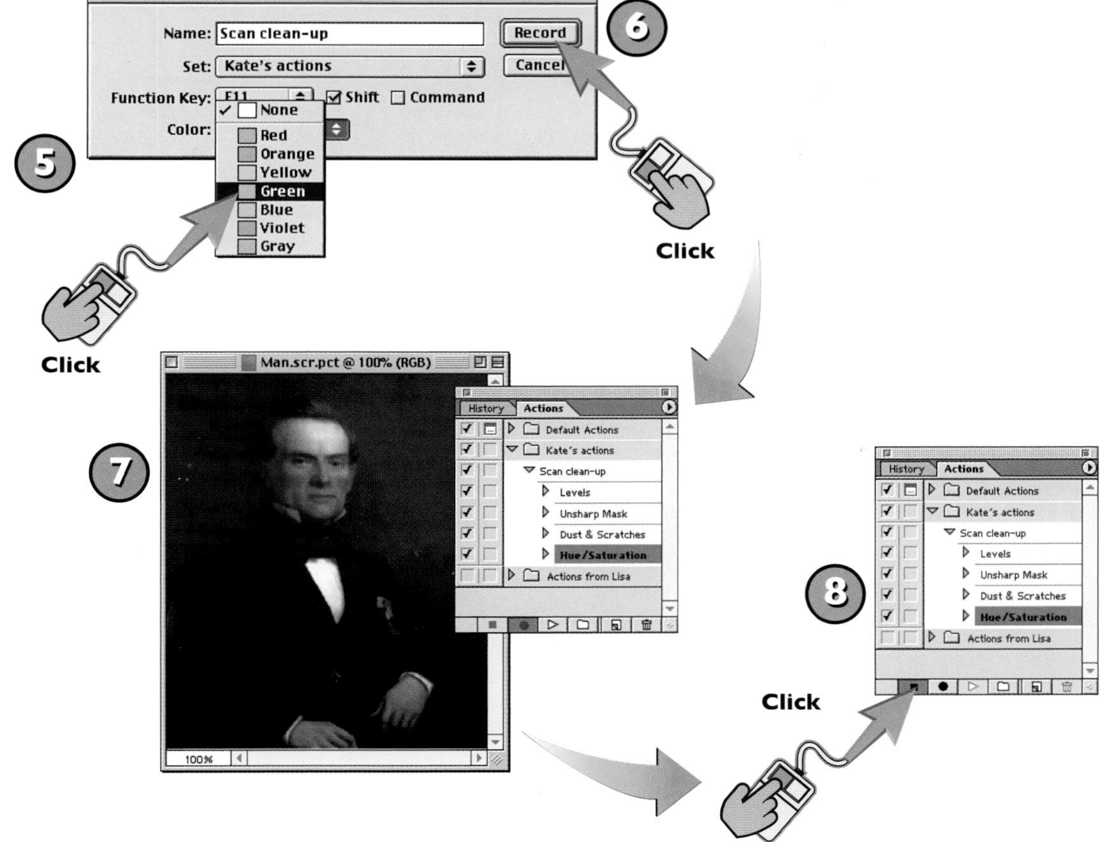

5 Choose a color for the Action's button.

6 Click **Record**.

7 Perform all the steps you want to add to the Action.

8 Click the **Stop** button on the **Actions** palette when you're finished recording the Action.

To play an Action, click its name, and then click the triangular Play button on the Actions palette. An alternative method: From the Actions palette menu, choose Button Mode; in Button mode, you can play actions just by clicking their names in the palette.

You can trade Actions with other Photoshop users. To save Actions, click the set name in the Actions palette and choose Actions palette menu, Save Actions. To load an Actions file, choose Actions palette menu, Load Actions.

The other buttons on the Actions palette enable you to do the following, in order from left to right: stop playing or recording an Action; record more steps within an Action; play an Action; create a new set of Actions; create a new Action; delete an Action.

Task 17: Batch Processing Multiple Images

Start Here

Batch processing enables you to perform the same *Action* on a group of images without having to open each one and set the Action in motion. First you must create an Action to be applied to each image (see Task 16, "Automating a Series of Steps").

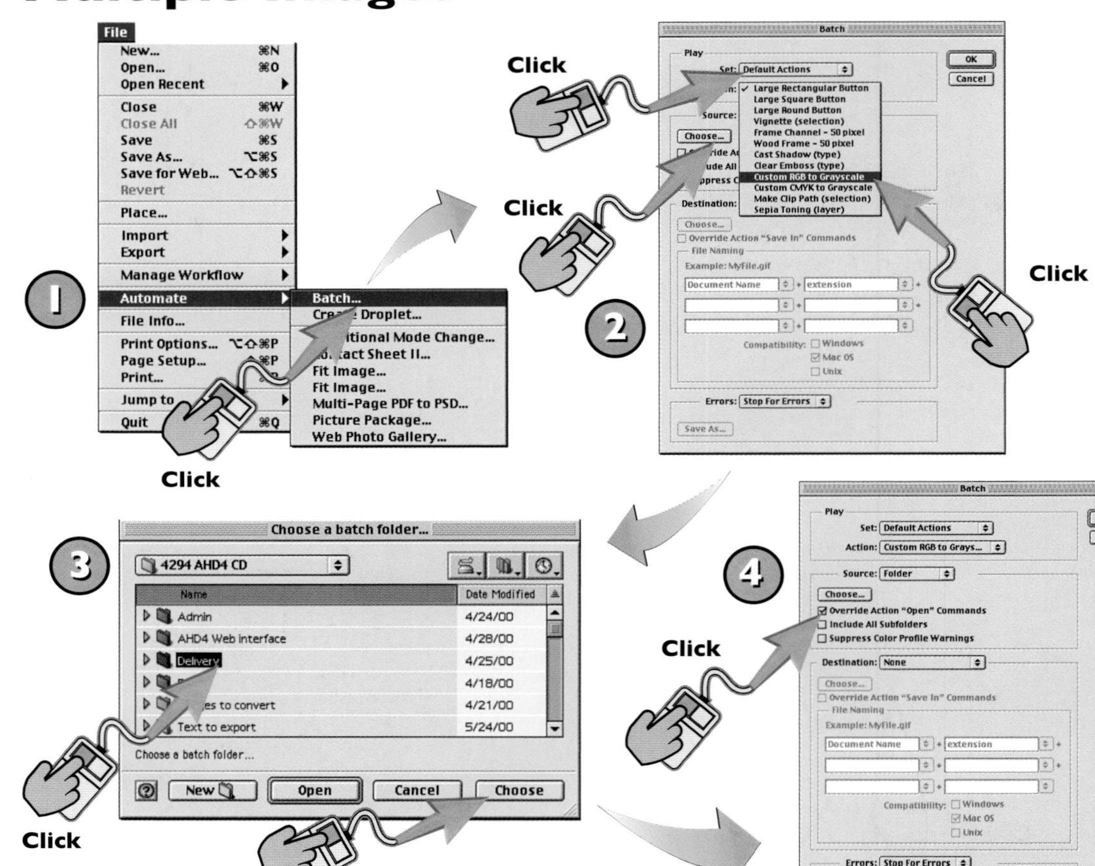

1. Choose **File**, **Automate**, **Batch**.
2. Choose an Action set from the **Set** pop-up menu and an Action from the **Action** menu, and then click the **Choose** button.
3. Find the folder of images you want to process, and then click **Choose**.
4. Click **Override Action "Open" Commands** to make sure that Photoshop opens only the images in the batch folder.

If your batch images are always located in the same place and saved in the same place, you can incorporate the **Open** and **Save** commands in the Action. In this case, you'll need to click off **Override Action "Open" Commands** and **Override Action "Save In" Commands.**

Next Step

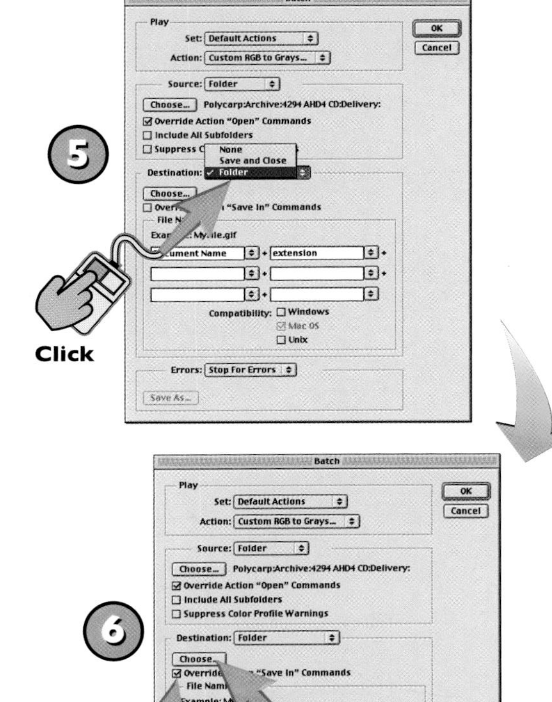

5 Choose **Save and Close** or **Folder** from the **Destination** pop-up menu.

6 If you chose **Folder**, click **Choose**, locate the folder in which to save, and then click **Override Action "Save In" Commands**.

7 Choose **Stop For Errors** from the **Errors** pop-up menu.

8 Click **OK** to begin processing.

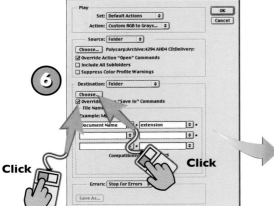

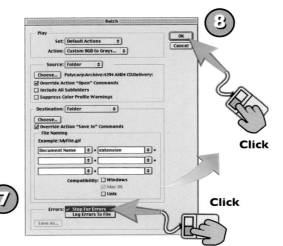

Photoshop can automatically rename modified files during batch processing. In the Batch dialog's File Naming area, choose the filename elements you want to use from the pop-up menus; Photoshop displays an example of the resulting filename above the menus. To ensure that the resulting filenames are compatible with another platform, check one of the check boxes at the bottom of the File Naming area.

To keep the original versions of the images and save new versions with the changes, choose Folder from the Destination pop-up menu; then click Choose and select a folder in which to save the modified images.

End Task

Task 18: Making a Contact Sheet

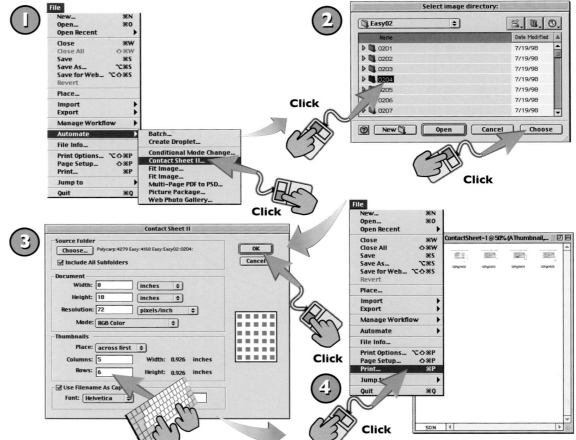

Images have a way of accumulating, whether they're stock images or ones you've created with Photoshop. A good way to get a look at all of your stored images is to make printed contact sheets, a process that Photoshop can automate for you.

✓ You can change the size of the contact sheets by entering different width and height values in the **Document** area; if your printer can handle legal- or tabloid-sized paper, you might want to create contact sheets in those sizes.

✓ Other options for contact sheets include whether images are placed in order from left to right or from top to bottom, as well as whether the contact sheets are created in color or grayscale. You can also choose to have each thumbnail accompanied by its filename.

Start Here

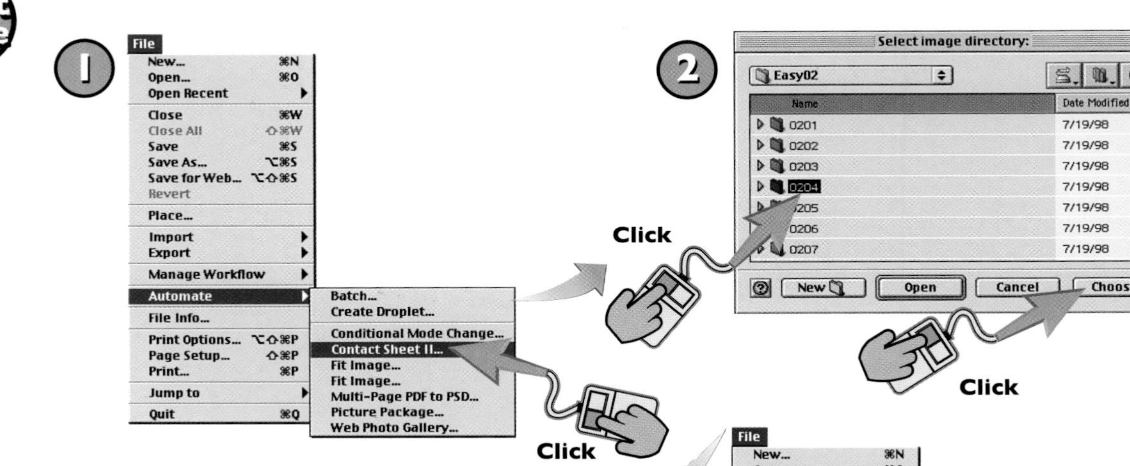

1. Choose **File**, **Automate**, **Contact Sheet II**.
2. Click **Choose** and select a folder of images, and then click **Choose**.
3. Enter the number of columns and rows for the contact sheets, and click **OK**.
4. Print the contact sheet documents Photoshop creates.

Task 19: Freeing Up Memory

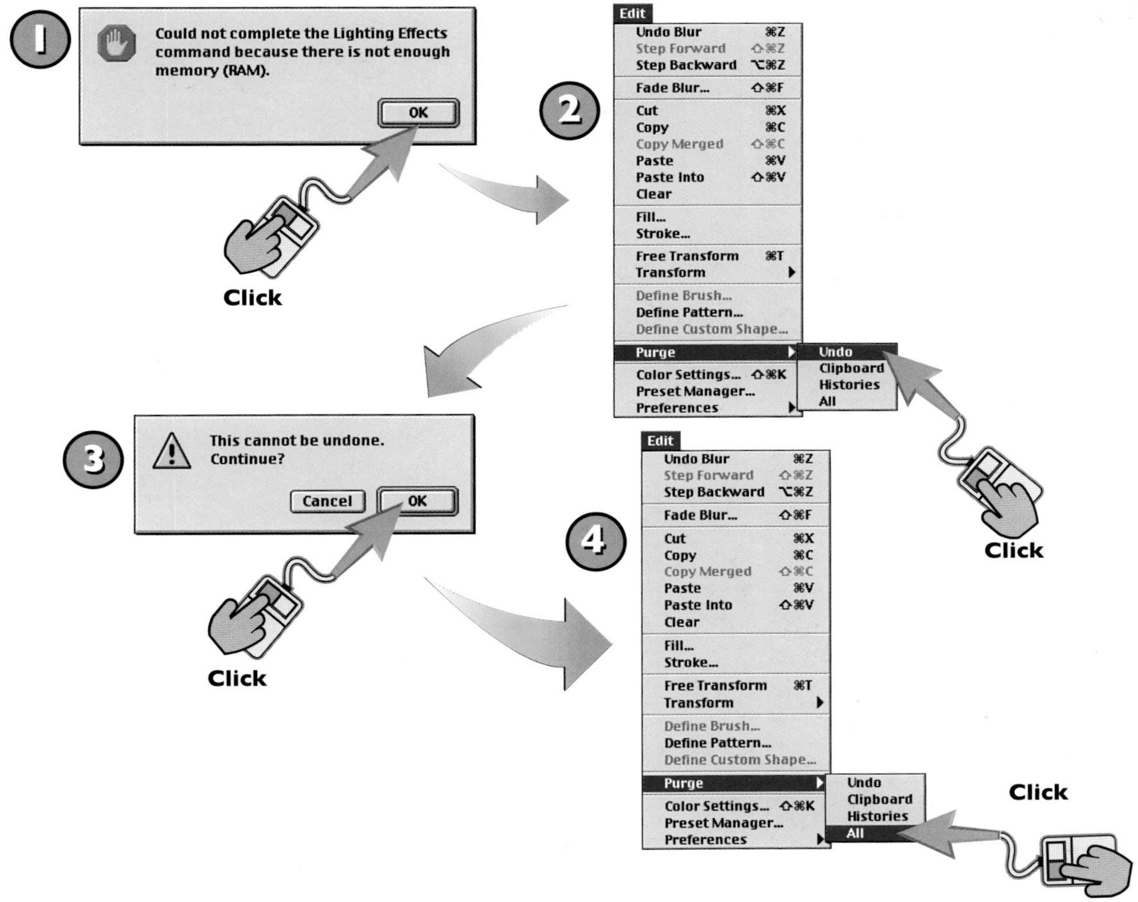

Anyone who has used Photoshop knows that it takes a lot of memory, or *RAM*, to run. Because Photoshop stores the image you're working on in memory, you can run out of memory if you try to work on a large image or apply a complex *filter*. Here's how to free up some of that memory so you can proceed.

1. When Photoshop warns you that you've run out of RAM, click **OK**.
2. Choose **Edit**, **Purge** and choose from among the first four options.
3. Photoshop warns you that you can't undo this operation; click **OK**.
4. If you still don't have enough memory to perform the desired command, choose **Edit**, **Purge**, **All**.

✓ **Edit, Purge, All** clears all four options at once: **Undo**, **Clipboard**, **Pattern**, and **Histories**.

✓ Photoshop's **Purge** options do have a drawback—you lose access to whatever you're purging. Therefore, you shouldn't purge the Clipboard if you'll need to paste whatever's on it later. Also, after you've purged the Undo buffer, you won't be able to undo the action immediately before the purge except by using the **History** palette (see Task 15).

Task 20: Printing a File

Sooner or later, everyone—even Web designers—needs to print a file. Photoshop offers sophisticated printing options side-by-side with the capability to simply press Cmd+P/Ctrl+P and hit Enter.

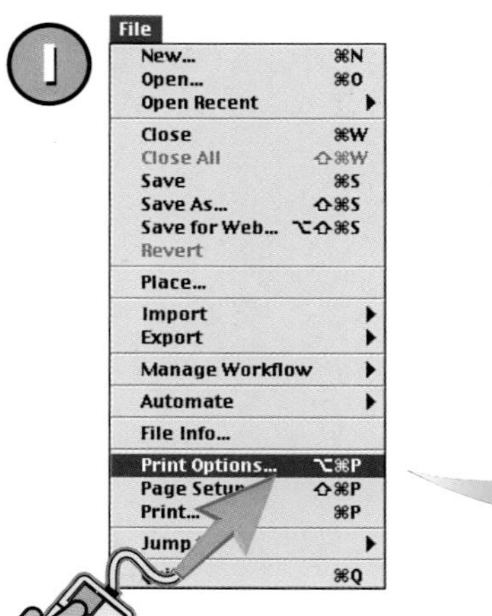

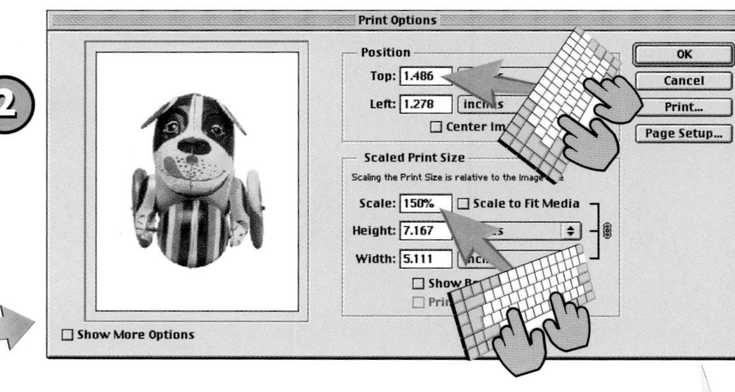

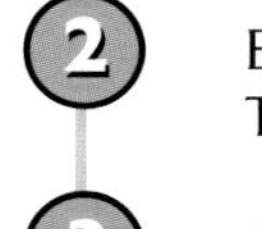

1. Choose **File**, **Print Options** or press **Cmd+Option+P/Ctrl+Alt+P**.

2. Enter measurements in the **Position** area to control where the image will print on the paper. To print the image at a different size, enter measurements in the **Scaled Print Size** area.

3. Click **Show Bounding Box** to display the paper's edges in the dialog box's preview area.

4. Click **Center Image** to center the printout on the paper, and click **Scale to Fit Media** to enlarge or reduce the printout to match the paper size.

Photoshop offers many complex printing options; for special printing needs, check the Photoshop manual or a more advanced Photoshop book such as *Special Edition Using Adobe Photoshop 6*.

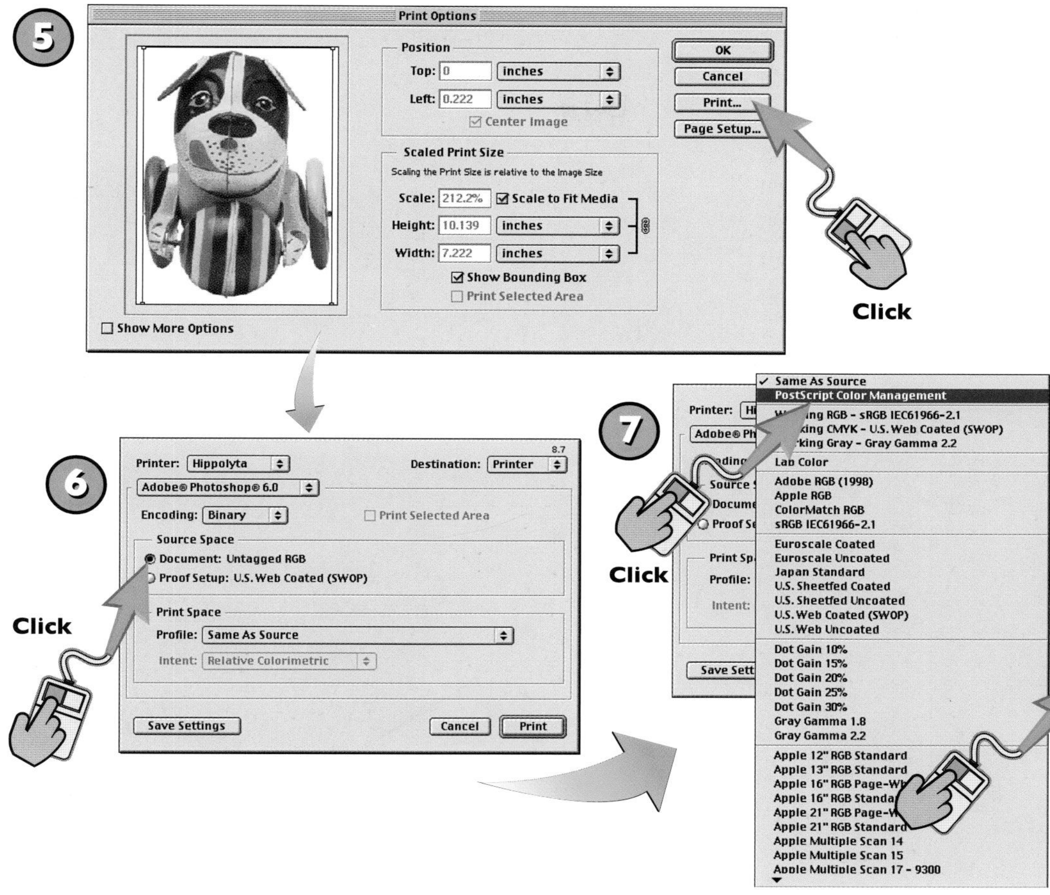

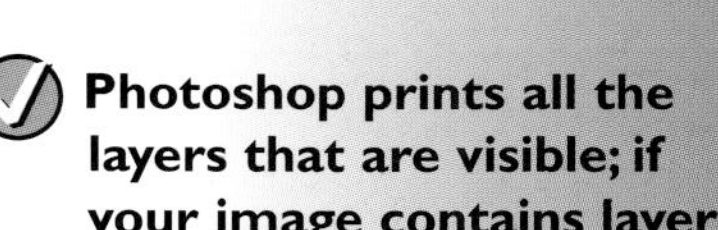

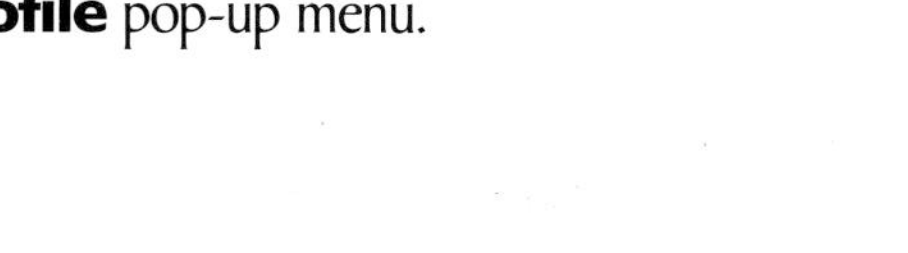

5 Click the **Print** button to switch to the **Print** dialog box.

6 Switch to the **Adobe Photoshop 6.0** panel of the **Print** dialog box and click on the **Document** option button in the **Source Space** area.

7 Choose **PostScript Color Management** (to use color management) or **Same as Source** (to avoid using color management) from the **Profile** pop-up menu.

8 Click **Print**.

Photoshop prints all the layers that are visible; if your image contains layers that you don't want to print, make them invisible before choosing the Print command (see Part 8, "Working with Layers," for more information on making layers visible and invisible).

Always save before printing, in case there's a printing problem that causes your computer to crash. This tip is a good idea when working with any program, not just Photoshop!

Photoshop can save textual information about an image within an image file—notes that can include the image's creator, copyright information, keywords for image cataloging software, and other useful information. Stock images you buy (or acquire along with Photoshop) might contain some of this information, and you can add it to your own images.

Start Here

Task 21: Viewing Information About an Image

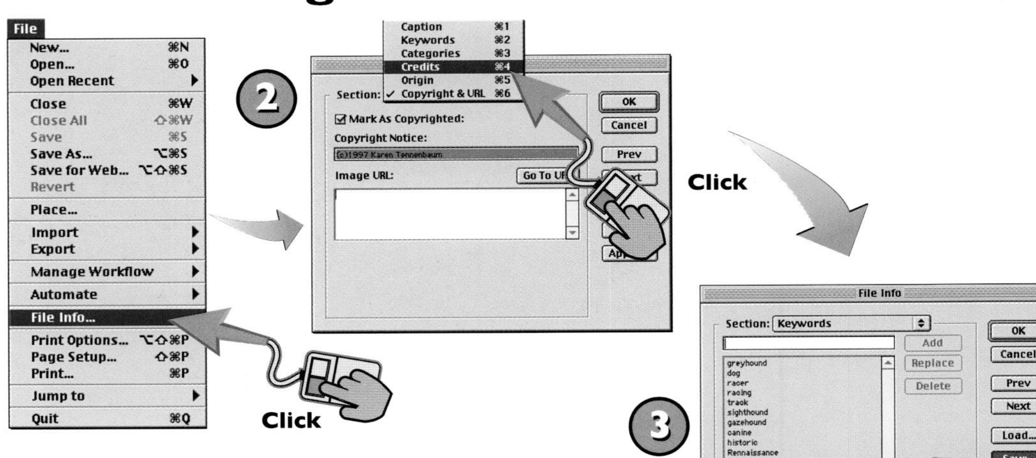

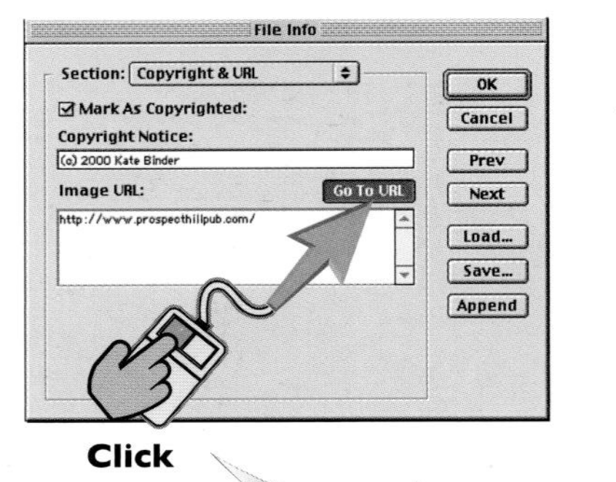

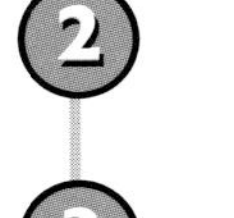

1. Choose **File**, **File Info**.
2. Choose an option from the pop-up menu at the top of the **File Info** dialog box to view various kinds of information.
3. To save information to use it in other images, click **Save**; click **Load** to insert your information or click **Append** to add it to the info that's already there.
4. To go to an image creator's Web page, click **Go to URL** in the dialog box's **Copyright and URL** panel.

Be sure you don't change the copyright information for an image that doesn't belong to you. Likewise, if you'll be distributing your own images, be sure to insert your own copyright information to help protect your intellectual property rights.

Task 22: Duplicating an Image

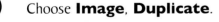

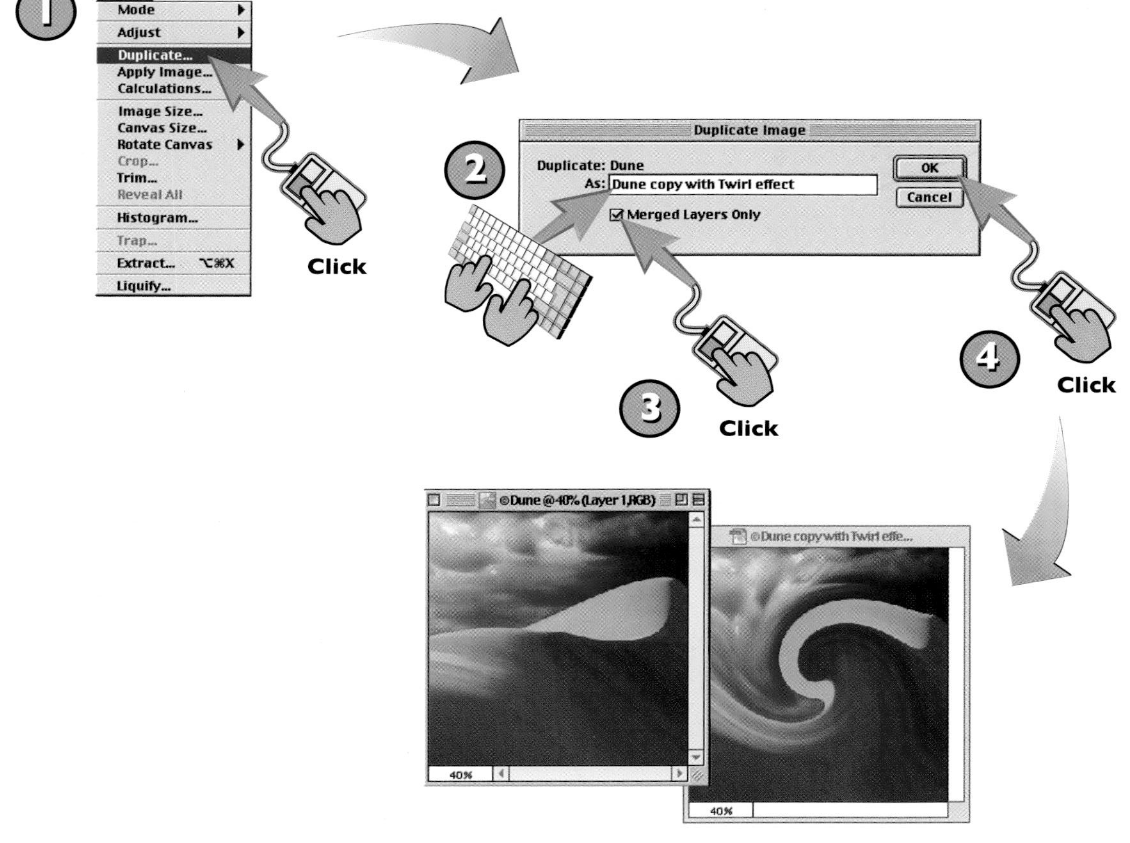

Sometimes your ideas for an image go in two directions—at that point, it's useful to be able to copy an image to create an identical file that you can start working on with your new ideas. The Duplicate command does this without requiring you to close the image, duplicate the file, and rename it manually.

1. Choose **Image**, **Duplicate**.
2. Enter a name for the new image file.
3. Click **Merged Layers Only** to merge the original image's layers into a single layer in the duplicate image.
4. Click **OK** to create the new image.

When you save the new image, Photoshop fills in the name that you gave the image in the Save dialog box. You can change it at this time if you want to, or you can choose to keep it.

PART 2

Opening and Saving Files

All computer files are created equal in one sense: They're all made up of electronic "bits" that can be turned on or off to make a pattern that a computer can read. The tricky part is in knowing which pattern, or ***file format***, to use for a given purpose. Photoshop supports dozens of file formats, but most of the time you'll need to use only five or six of these. For print designs, EPS and TIFF are preferred; for Web designs, GIF and JPEG are your best bet. (To save images in these Web formats, see Part 12, "Creating Images for the Web.")

This part shows you how to open different kinds of files and how to save files in different formats. In addition, Part 2 explains how to change filenames, use filename extensions to identify file formats, and add previews to images so you'll be able to view the images when you import them into other programs.

Tasks

Task 1: Opening a PDF File

Photoshop is famous for its capability to open files in any format, and that includes Adobe Acrobat's Portable Document Format (*PDF*). This is a great way to turn logos or other graphics used in a PDF file into Photoshop images that you can use in creating new documents.

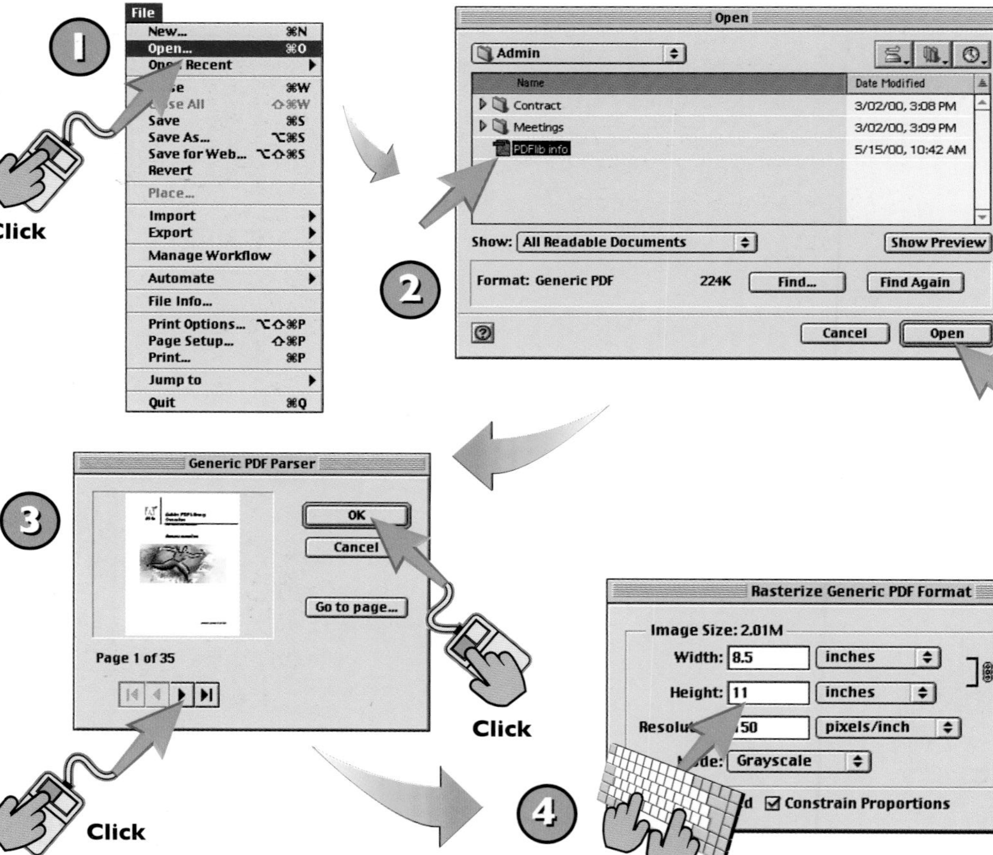

- Photoshop can open only one PDF page at a time.
- By default, Photoshop enters the document's original measurements in the **Rasterize Generic PDF Format** dialog box.

1. Choose **File**, **Open**.
2. Select a PDF file and click **Open**.
3. Click the arrow buttons to choose the page of this document you want to open, and click **OK**.
4. Enter the width and height to which you want the page to be converted.

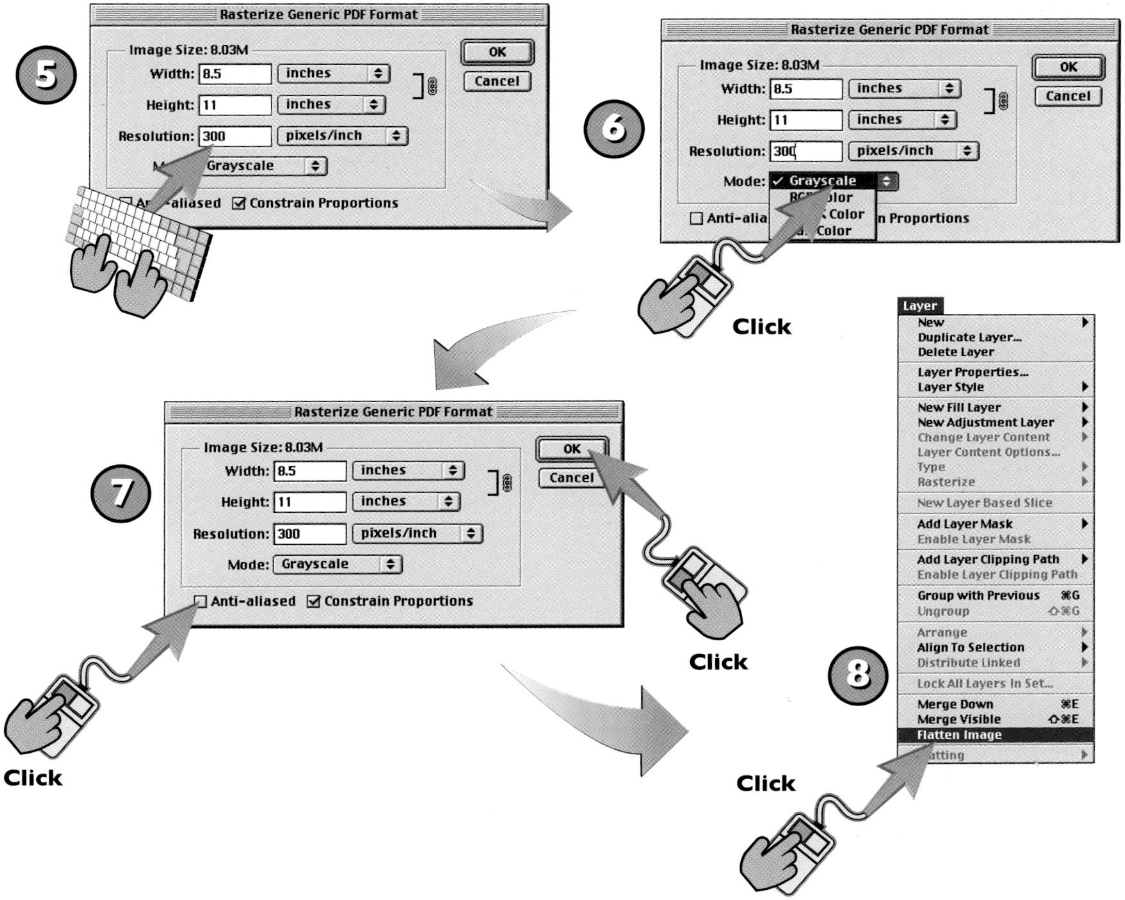

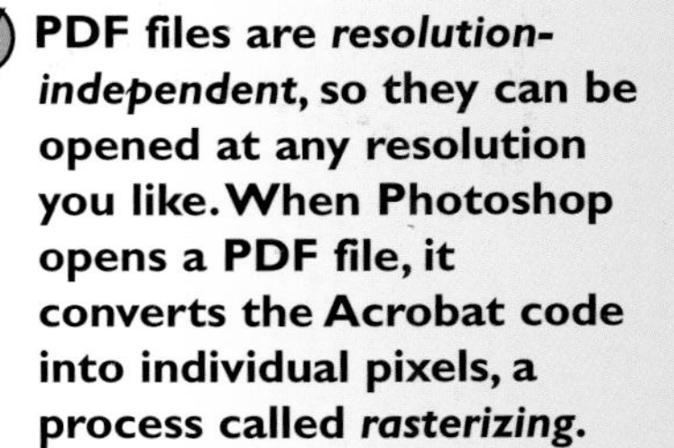

- **5** Enter a resolution—**72** for onscreen use, **300** or more for print use.
- **6** Choose a color mode—**Grayscale** for print or onscreen, **CMYK** for print, or **RGB** for onscreen.
- **7** Click **Anti-aliased** on if the image will be used onscreen, or off if the image will be used in print, and click **OK**.
- **8** Choose **Layer**, **Flatten Image**.

PDF files are *resolution-independent*, so they can be opened at any resolution you like. When Photoshop opens a PDF file, it converts the Acrobat code into individual pixels, a process called *rasterizing*.

Photoshop places rasterized EPS and PDF files on a layer; before you can save them in a format other than Photoshop's own, you must flatten the layers.

Task 2: Opening a Photo CD Image

Many stock photography companies supply their images in *Photo CD* format. This multi-resolution format stores several different versions in each image file, so you can choose which one you want when you open a Photo CD file.

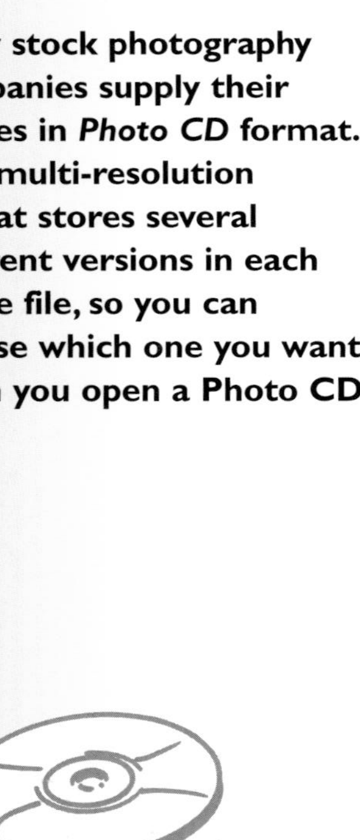

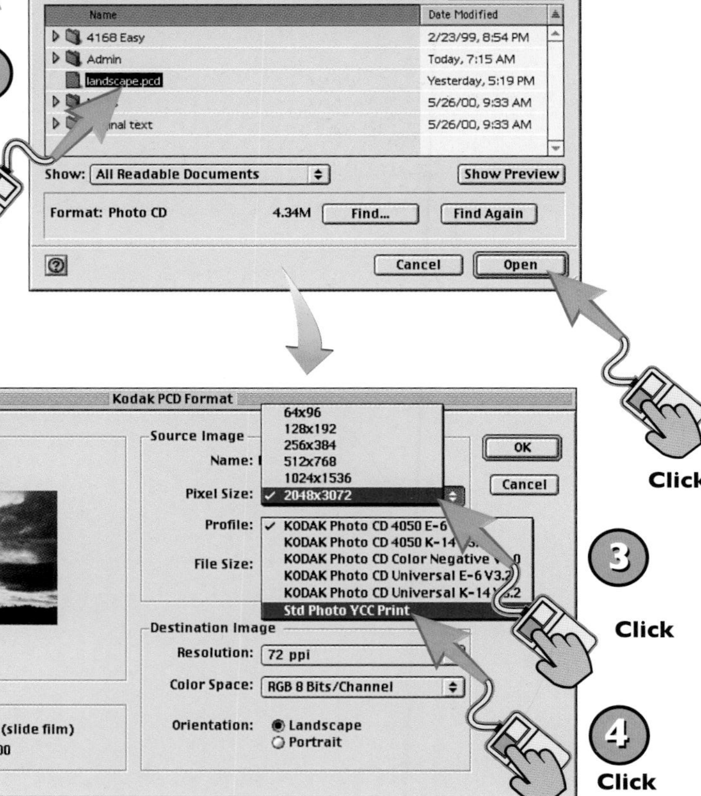

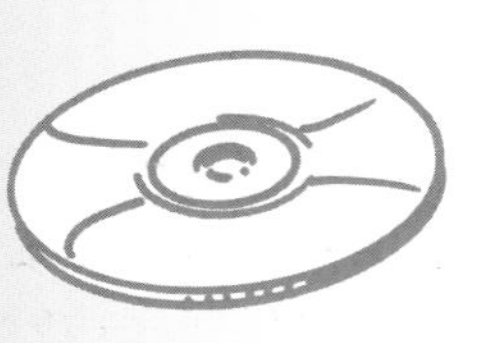

1. Choose **File**, **Open**.

2. Find the Photo CD file you want to open, and click **Open**.

3. In the **Source Image** area, choose a **Pixel Size**.

4. Choose a **Source Image** profile to match the original film used; if you don't know which profile to use, just leave the default.

✓ Each Photo CD file contains up to six images, from a tiny thumbnail to a full-page high-resolution image.

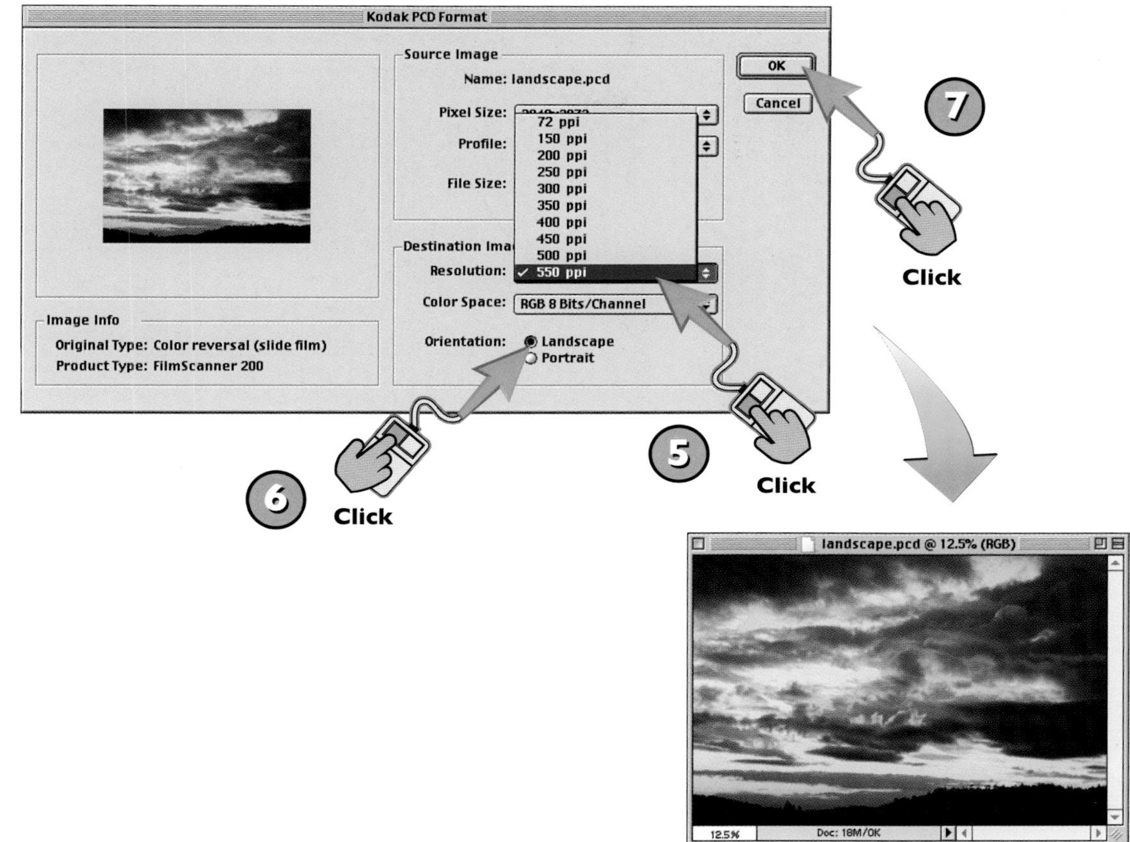

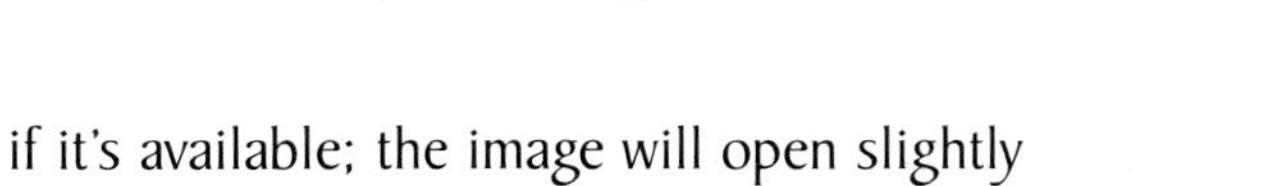
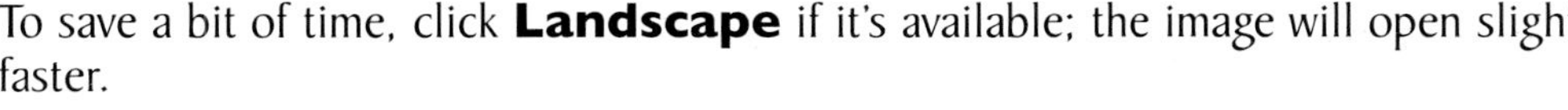

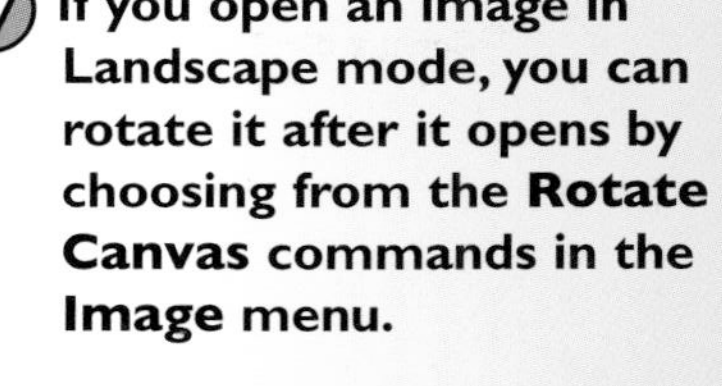
If you open an image in Landscape mode, you can rotate it after it opens by choosing from the **Rotate Canvas** commands in the **Image** menu.

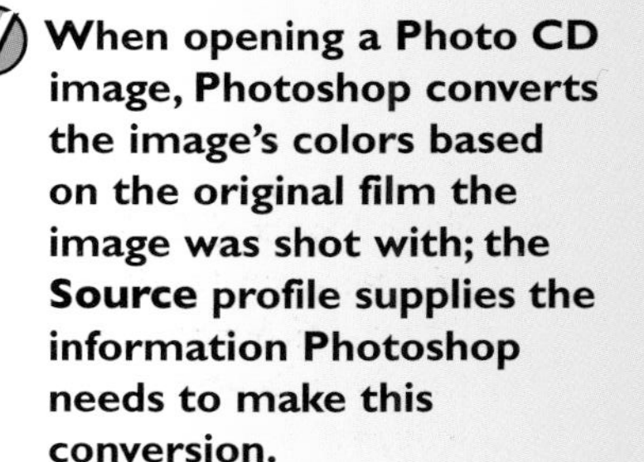
When opening a Photo CD image, Photoshop converts the image's colors based on the original film the image was shot with; the **Source** profile supplies the information Photoshop needs to make this conversion.

5 In the **Destination** area, choose a resolution for the opened image.

6 To save a bit of time, click **Landscape** if it's available; the image will open slightly faster.

7 Click **OK** to open the image.

Photoshop enables you to convert vector EPS files, such as those created by CorelDRAW or Adobe Illustrator, to pixel-based images so you can work with them in Photoshop. This is a good way to incorporate EPS images into a Photoshop collage or to use Photoshop to edit images in ways that you can't do in CorelDRAW or Illustrator.

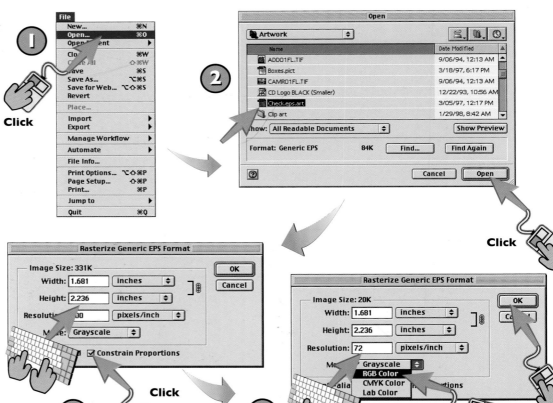

Task 3: Opening a Vector EPS Image

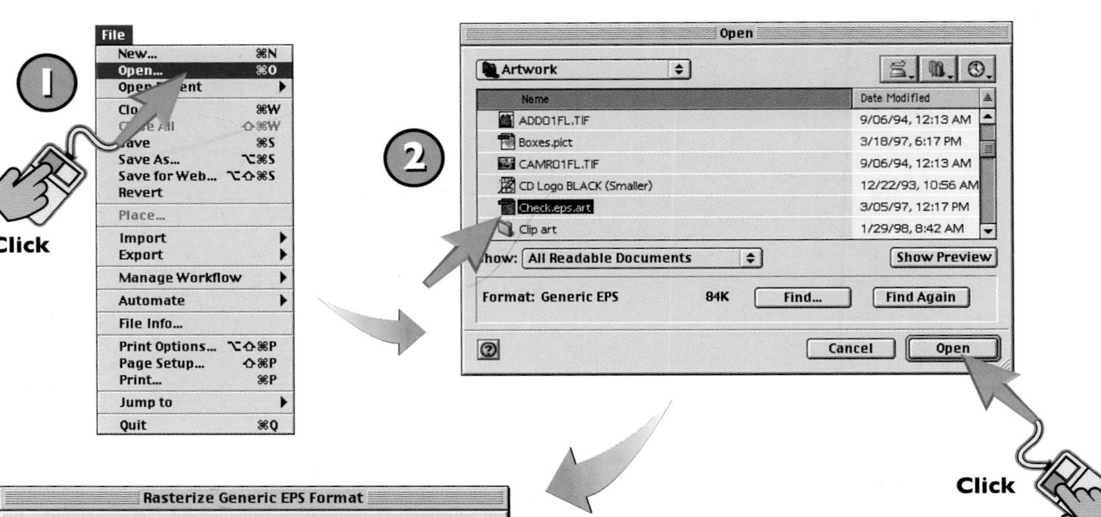

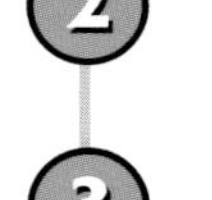

1. Choose **File**, **Open** or press **Cmd+O/Ctrl+O**.
2. Locate the file you want to open, and click **Open**.
3. Click **Constrain Proportions** and enter the desired **Width** or **Height** of the image.
4. Enter the **Resolution**; then choose a color **Mode** and click **OK** to open the file.

✓ If the image you're converting is intended for onscreen use, you'll want to choose a low *resolution*—probably 72—and click **Anti-aliased.** *Anti-aliasing* blurs the edges within the image slightly to make them appear smoother at low resolutions.

Task 4: Placing an Image Within Another Image

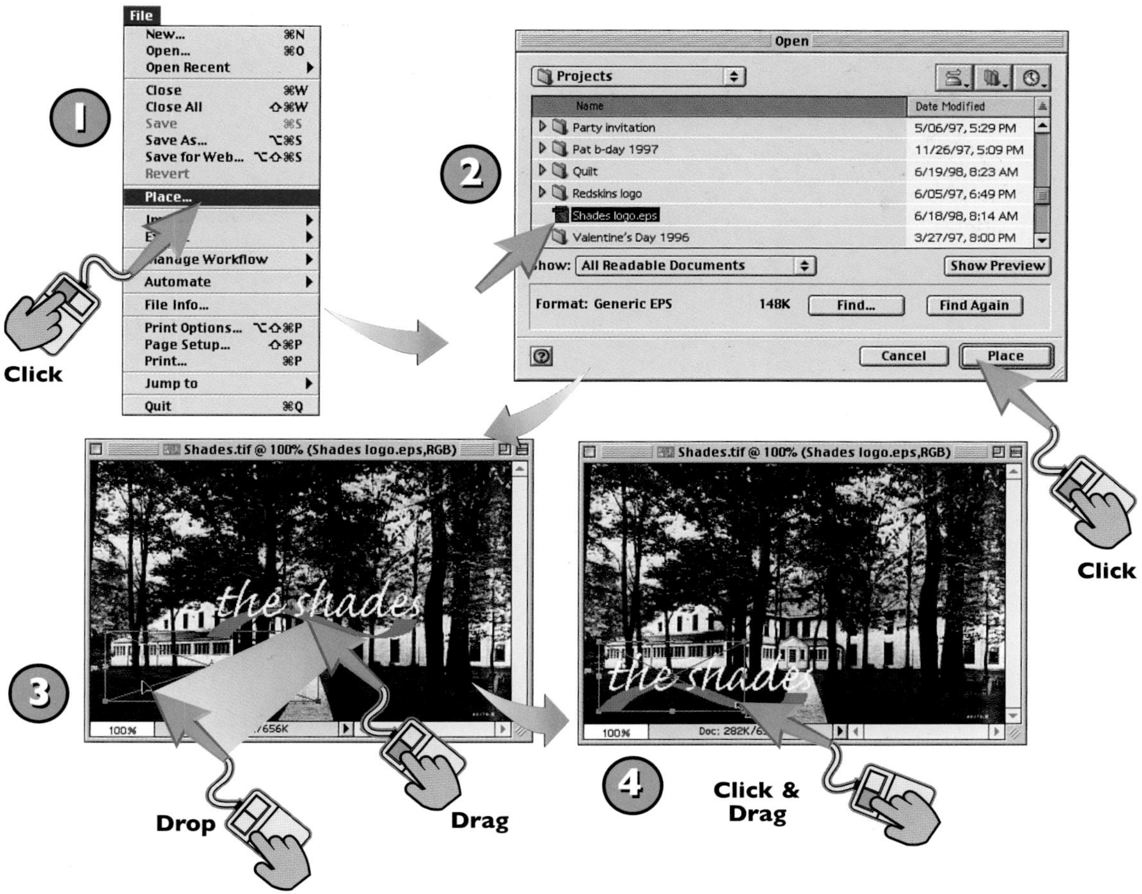

If you want to incorporate *EPS* or *PDF* images into an existing Photoshop image, use the Place command. When you place an image, Photoshop inserts it into the existing image on a new layer and enables you to move it and resize it before it's *rasterized*.

1 With an existing Photoshop image open, choose **File**, **Place**.

2 Locate the file you want to insert, and click **Place**.

3 Click and drag to move the placed image.

4 Click and drag on its corners to resize it. When the image is positioned and sized correctly, press **Enter** to rasterize it.

✓ Hold down **Shift** as you drag the corners of the placed image to resize it proportionally.

✓ You can rotate the image by placing the cursor outside a corner until the cursor turns into a curved double-headed arrow; click and drag to rotate.

Task 5: Saving a File with a New Name or Format

In addition to saving changes as you go along, Photoshop enables you to change the name and format of a file while you're working on it. The Save As dialog box is the same one you see the first time you save a brand new file.

Click

Click

Click

Click

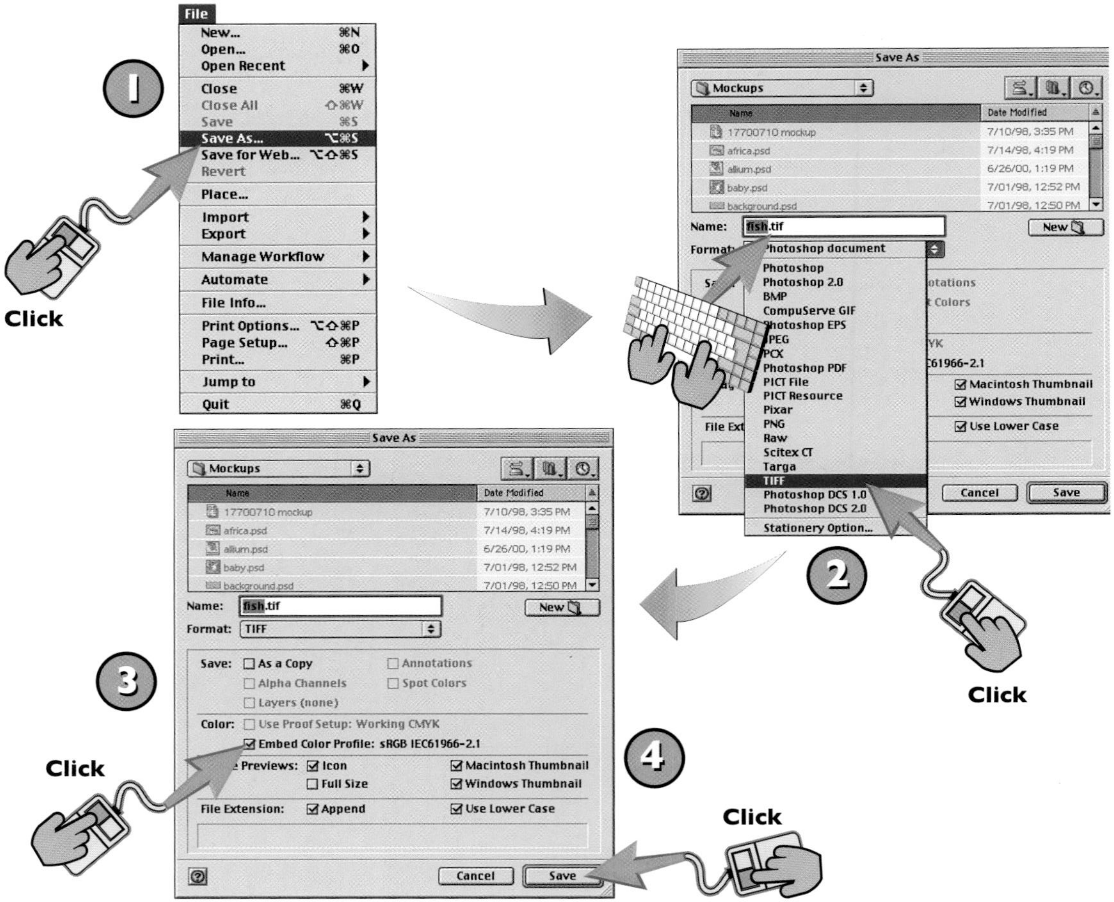

1. Choose **File**, **Save As**.
2. Choose a new location for the file and enter its new name, and then choose a new format from the **Format** pop-up menu.
3. Choose the information you want saved with the image by checking the appropriate boxes in the lower half of the dialog box.
4. Click **Save** to save the file.

Depending on the format you choose when you use the Save As command, you might see another dialog box with additional options after you click Save.

Task 6: Automatically Adding Filename Extensions to Saved Images

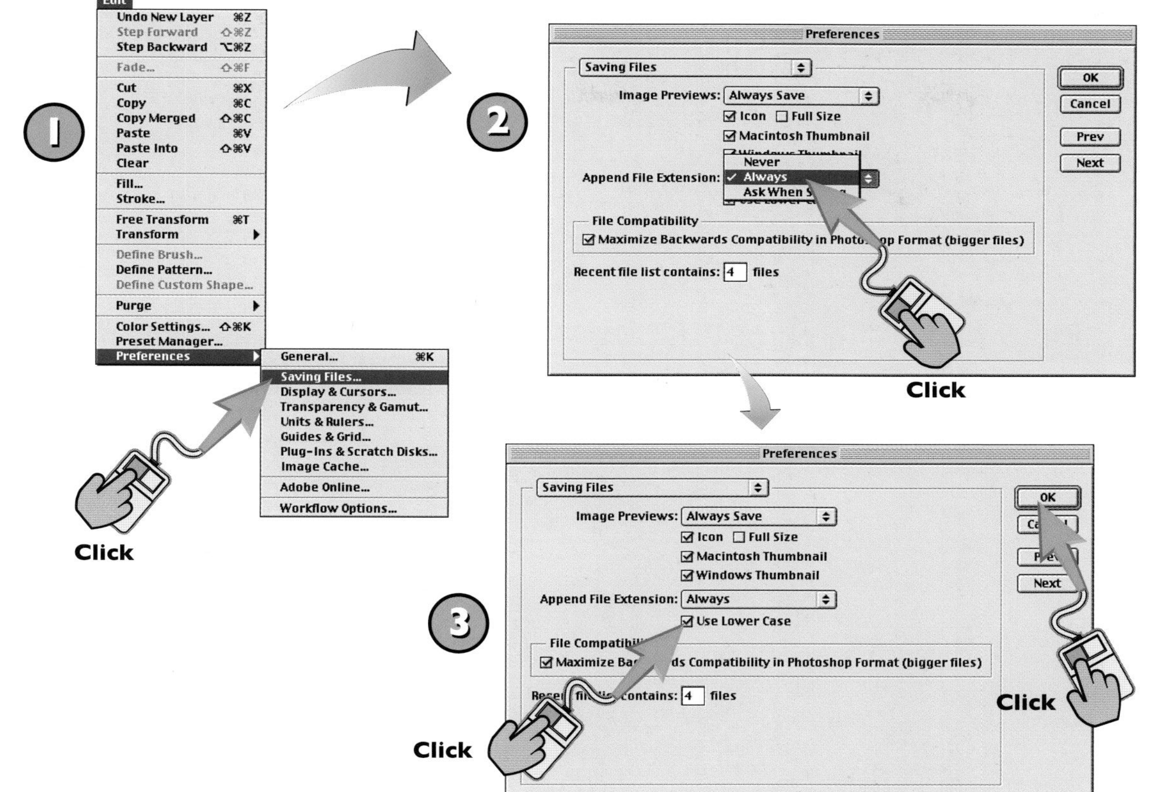

Filename extensions are vital in the Windows/DOS world and can be useful to Mac OS users as well. If you're a Mac OS user, it's a good idea to set your Photoshop preferences so that you can have filename extensions added automatically when you save files. Then Windows systems will be able to identify those files.

If you choose Ask When Saving, the Save dialog box will have a check box labeled Append; just click this check box and Photoshop adds the extension to the Name field.

The Use Lower Case option in the Preferences dialog box isn't irrevocable; if you choose Ask When Saving, a Use Lower Case check box is also added to the Save dialog box, so you can change your mind about lowercase extensions when you save each file.

1. Choose **Edit**, **Preferences**, **Saving Files**.
2. In the **Append File Extension** pop-up menu, choose **Always** to add extensions automatically or **Ask When Saving** to add a check box to the **Save** dialog box.
3. Click **Use Lower Case** if you want extensions to be lowercase letters, and click **OK**.

Task 7: Saving a TIFF File

Start Here

In print production, the most commonly used file format is *TIFF*. It incorporates *lossless compression*, meaning you can compress a TIFF file without losing any image data, and it's supported by almost every graphics program.

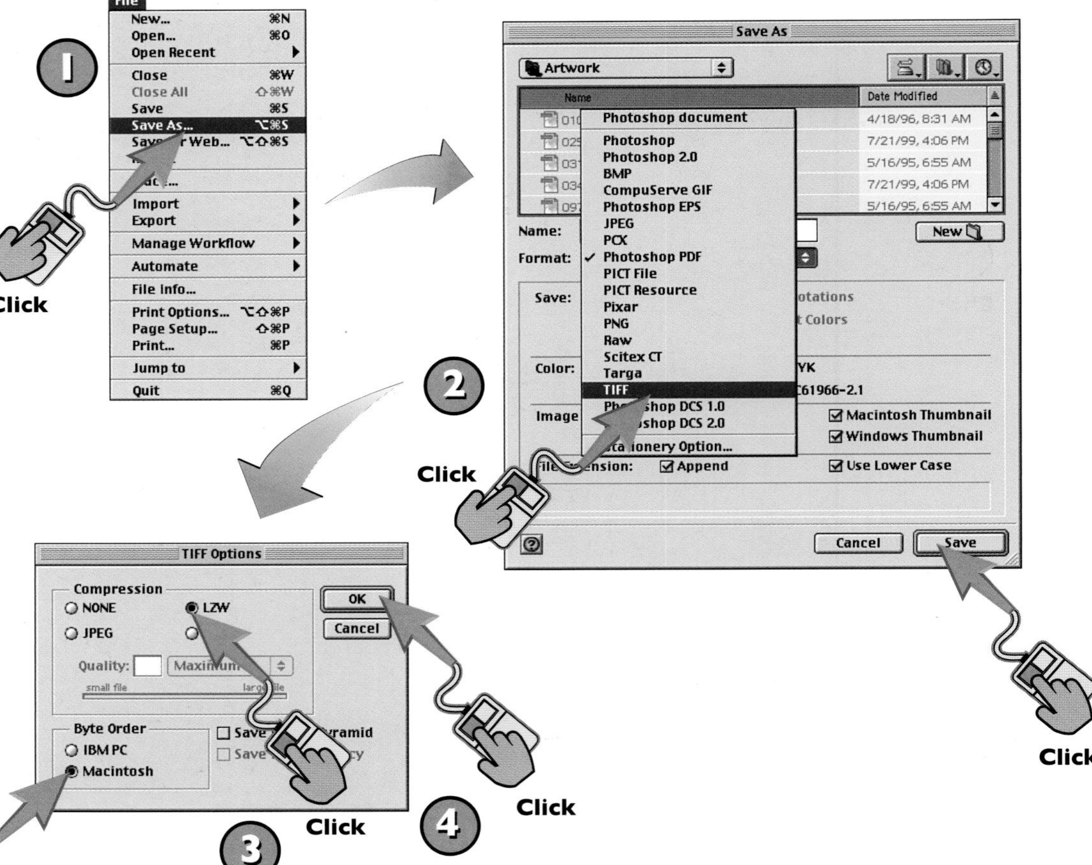

1. Choose **File**, **Save As**.
2. Give the file a name, choose **TIFF** from the **Format** pop-up menu, and then click **Save**.
3. Click **LZW** compression and choose the destination platform: **Macintosh** or **IBM PC**.
4. Click **OK** to save the file.

If you're not sure on what platform a file will be used, or if it will be used on both Macintoshes and PCs, choose **PC** in the **TIFF Options** dialog box. Macintoshes can handle files saved either way, but PCs aren't so forgiving.

Occasionally, an older *RIP* will refuse to print images saved with *LZW* compression; in this case, you'll need to resave TIFF files without compression. This is more and more rare, however, so it's best to use **LZW** as a matter of course.

Task 8: Saving an EPS File

In addition to TIFF, EPS files are very common in print production. The name stands for Encapsulated *PostScript*, which means that these files are precoded for PostScript printers.

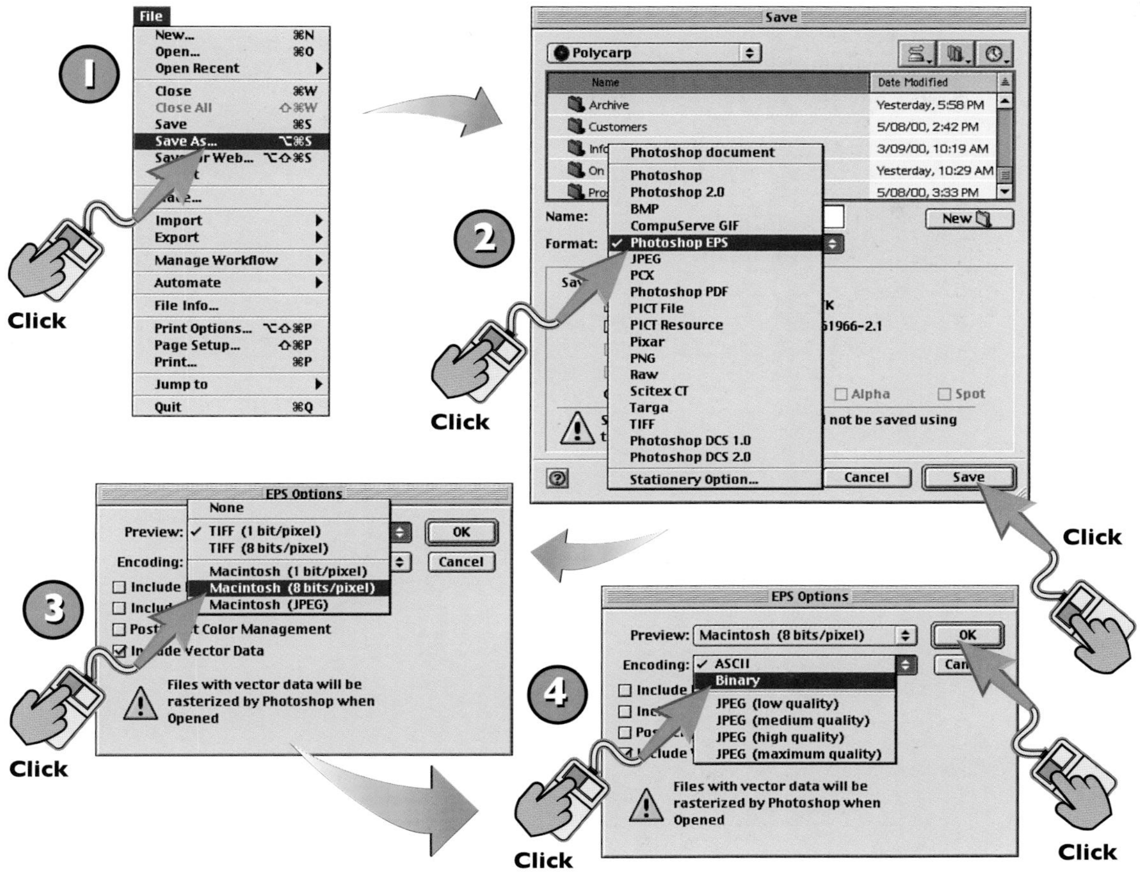

1. Choose **File**, **Save As**.

2. Give the file a name, choose **Photoshop EPS** from the **Format** pop-up menu, and then click **Save**.

3. Choose a **Preview** type: **Macintosh** for use on Macintoshes or **TIFF** for use on Windows systems.

4. Choose **Binary** from the **Encoding** pop-up menu, and click **OK** to save the file.

When choosing a *preview* type, use 1-bit for black-and-white images and 8-bit for *grayscale* or color images.

If an EPS file will be used only on Macintoshes, you can try *JPEG* encoding. It will reduce the size of the file, but it can't be read by some Windows systems (it requires Apple's QuickTime).

Task 9: Saving a Pre-Separated DCS EPS File

Start Here

DCS stands for Desktop Color Separations; it's a precolor-separated format, which means that *color-separated* film outputs faster when you use this format because images don't have to be separated in the *RIP*. DCS images are contained in five files, one for each *process color* and a composite that you can import into a page layout program.

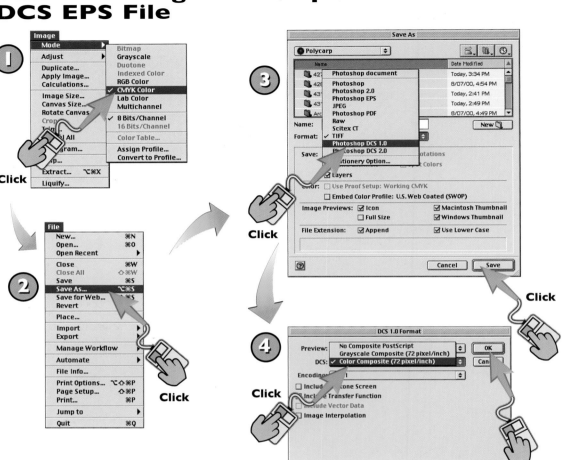

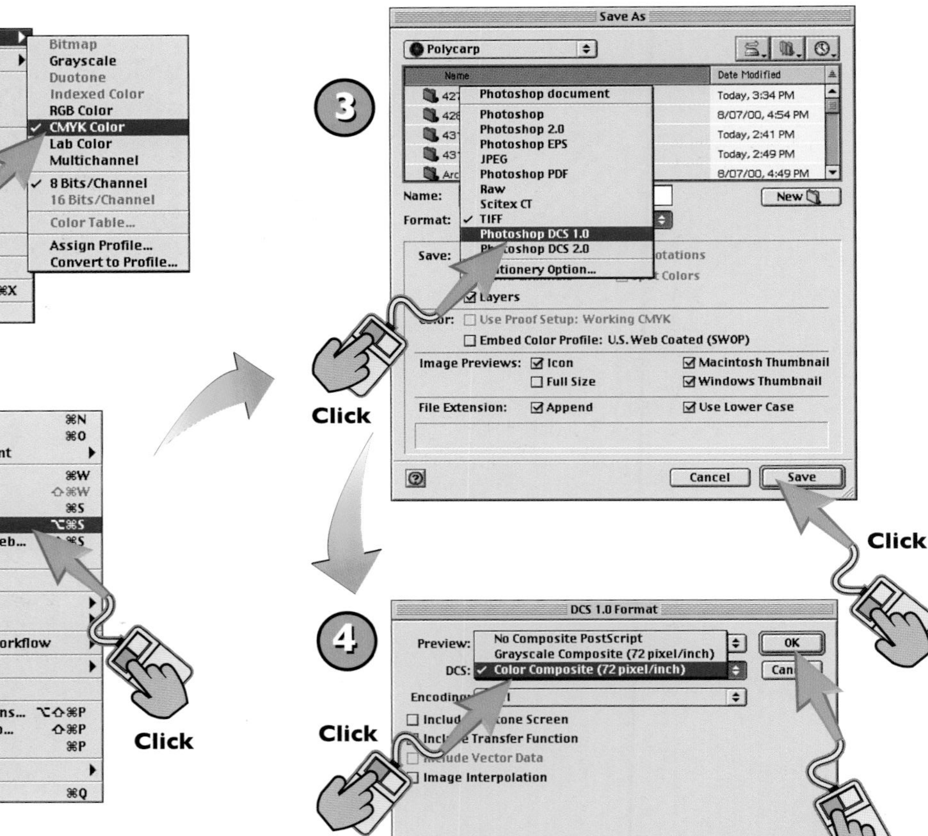

1. Make sure the image is in CMYK mode by choosing **Image**, **Mode**, **CMYK Color**.
2. Choose **File**, **Save As**.
3. Give the file a name and choose **Photoshop DCS 1.0** from the **Format** pop-up menu, and then click **Save**.
4. Choose a DCS composite option—none, grayscale, or color—and click **OK** to save the file.

✓ Other than the DCS composite options, the other choices in the **DCS 1.0 Format** dialog box are just like those in the **EPS Options** dialog box (see Task 8, "Saving an EPS File").

✓ Photoshop DCS 2.0 is a more sophisticated version of the DCS format that supports spot colors and can create a smaller single file, as opposed to the multiple files of DCS 1.0.

Task 10: Adding Previews to Saved Images

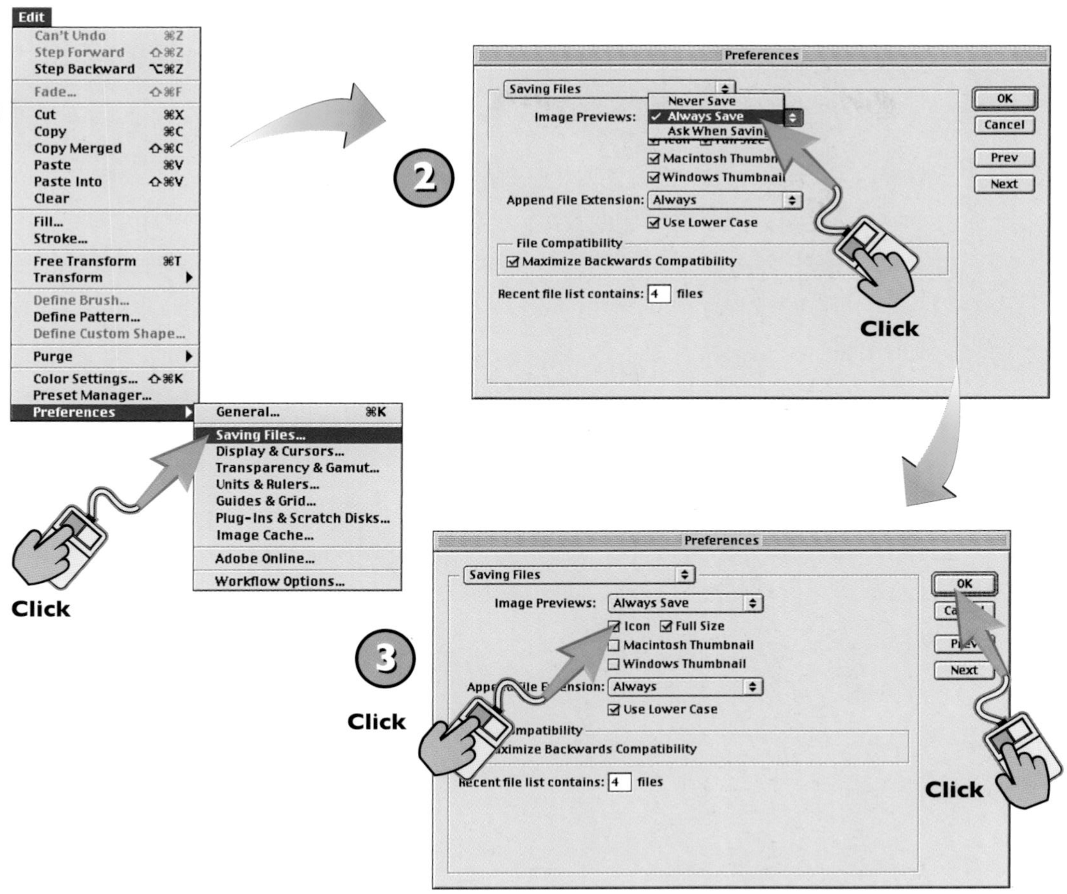

Image previews enable you to see what files look like before you open them. *Icon previews* are icons on the desktop that show a tiny representation of the image; *thumbnail previews* are viewable in Photoshop's Open dialog box; and *full-size previews* are low-resolution versions of the image for applications that can't open high-resolution files.

1. Choose **Edit**, **Preferences**, **Saving Files**.
2. Choose an option from the **Image Previews** pop-up menu: **Never Save**, **Always Save**, or **Ask When Saving**.
3. On Mac OS, choose the types of preview you want to include, and click **OK**.

For Windows users, the Ask When Saving option adds a check box to the Save dialog box; check the box if you want to add a preview. For Mac OS users, three check boxes are displayed, one for each type of preview.

If file size is a concern, you might want to skip adding previews and icons—they can make your Photoshop files much bigger. Files without previews and icons can still be placed in other applications such as QuarkXPress, and they can still be opened and edited in Photoshop.

PART 3

Making and Saving Selections

Most operations in Photoshop start with a *selection*. Any time you want to apply an effect to part of an image rather than the entire image, you must select the portion of the image on which you want to work. Photoshop enables you to select parts of the image that don't touch each other, and you can combine selections in various ways. You can make selections in several ways, such as by painting over the area you want to select or by using the Pen tool to draw a precise outline of the area to be selected. You can also save selections for future use.

Part 3 shows you how to create selections with Photoshop's selection tools, how to save and restore selections by using channels and paths, and how to select areas based on their color. This part also covers ways to modify selections after they're created.

Tasks

To apply changes to a single area of a Photoshop image, first you must select that area. Photoshop's Marquee tool offers the simplest, quickest way to select an area, and it comes in both rectangular and elliptical versions.

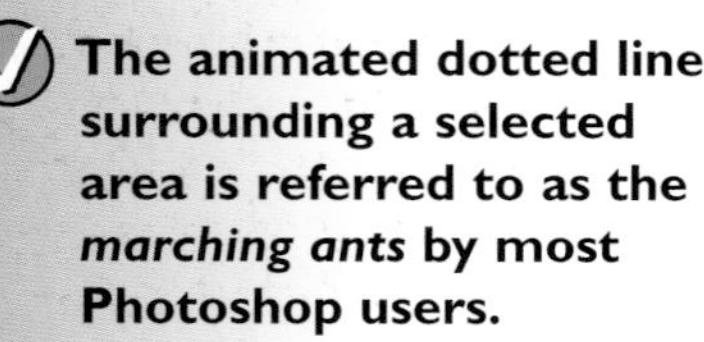
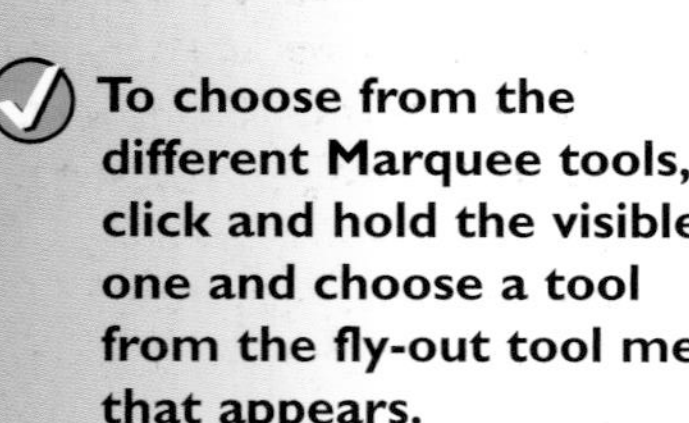

✓ The animated dotted line surrounding a selected area is referred to as the *marching ants* by most Photoshop users.

✓ To choose from the different Marquee tools, click and hold the visible one and choose a tool from the fly-out tool menu that appears.

Task 1: Selecting a Geometric Area

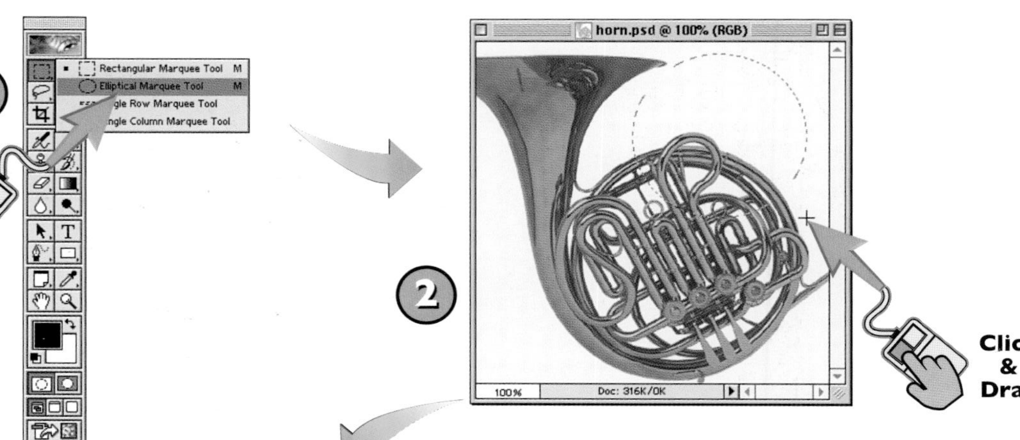

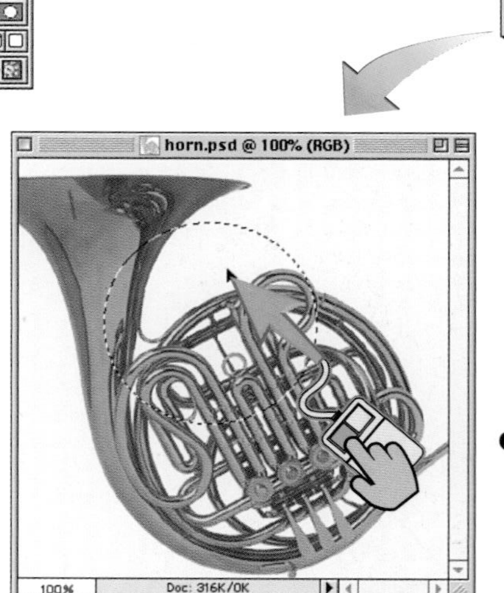

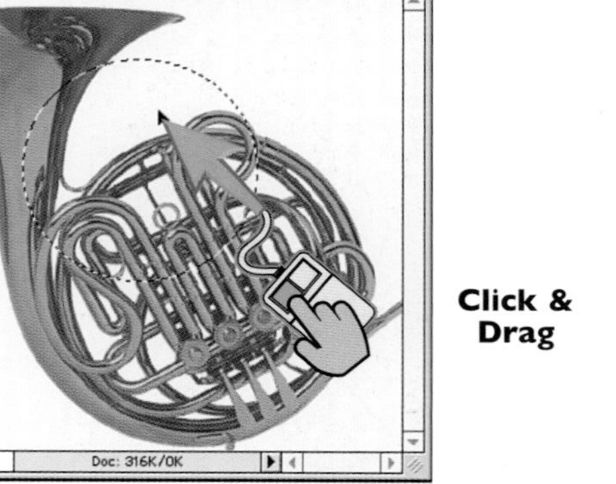
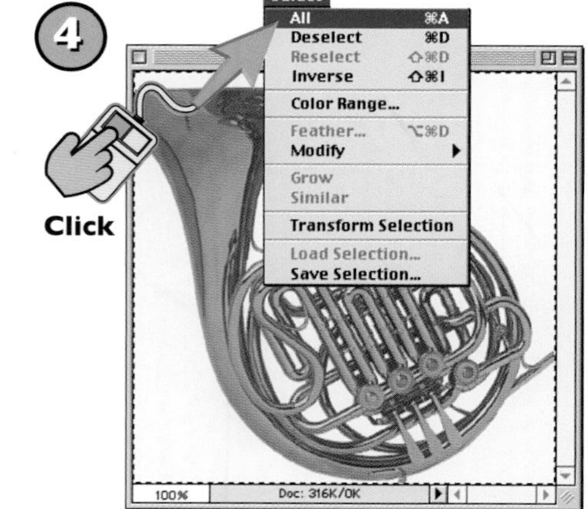

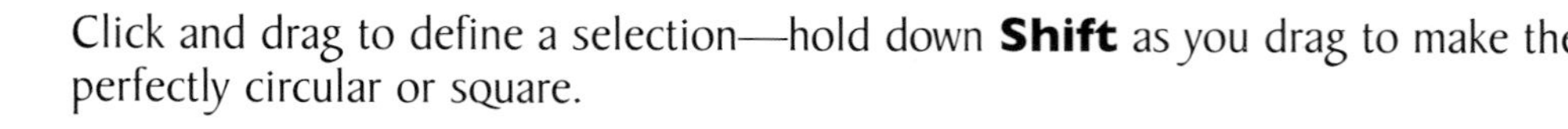

1. Choose the elliptical or rectangular **Marquee** tool from the **Tool** palette.
2. Click and drag to define a selection—hold down **Shift** as you drag to make the selection perfectly circular or square.
3. Click and drag in the selection to move it.
4. To select the entire image, choose **Select**, **All** or press **Cmd+A/Ctrl+A**.

End Task

Task 2: Selecting an Irregular Area

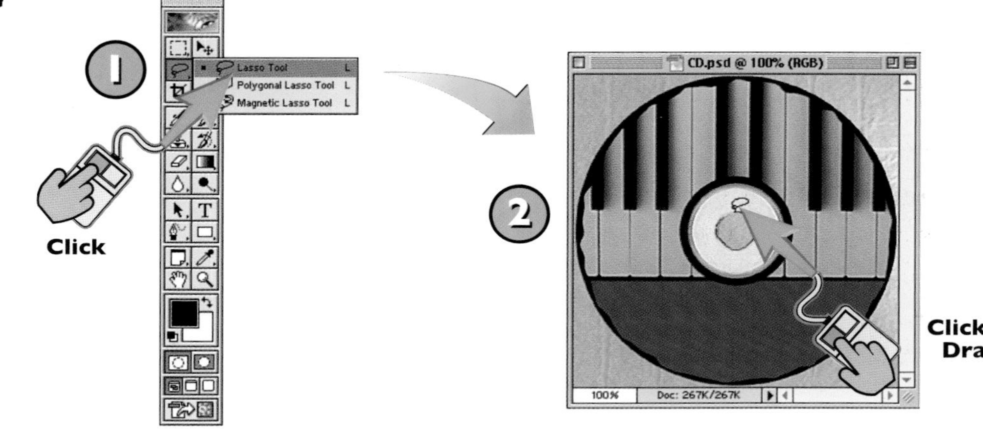

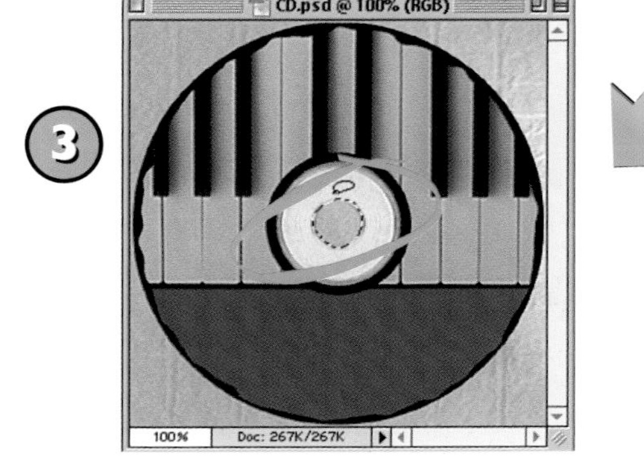

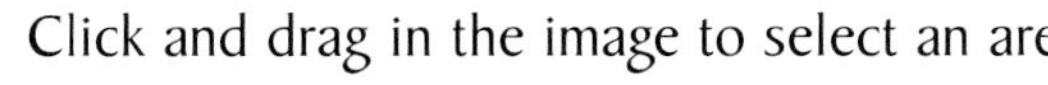

1. Choose **Lasso Tool** from the **Tool** palette.

2. Click and drag in the image to select an area.
3. Release the mouse button to create the selection—Photoshop connects your starting and ending points with a straight line.

You can select an irregular shape by using the Lasso tool to draw around the area you want to select. The bottom end of the lasso's "rope" is the tip of the tool.

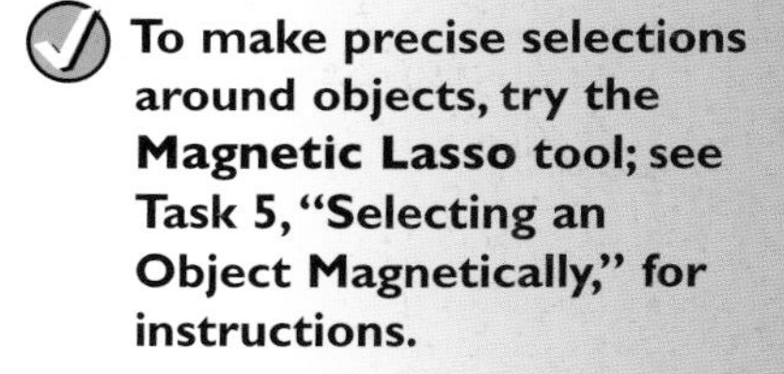

To make precise selections around objects, try the Magnetic Lasso tool; see Task 5, "Selecting an Object Magnetically," for instructions.

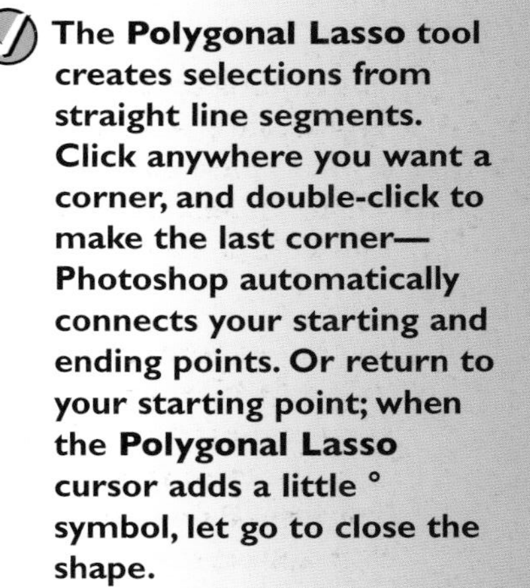

The Polygonal Lasso tool creates selections from straight line segments. Click anywhere you want a corner, and double-click to make the last corner—Photoshop automatically connects your starting and ending points. Or return to your starting point; when the Polygonal Lasso cursor adds a little ° symbol, let go to close the shape.

Task 3: Selecting an Area of a Fixed Size or Shape

To make a *selection* of a specific size or shape, you use the Marquee tools, modifying them so that they can select only that size or shape when you click in the image.

Start Here

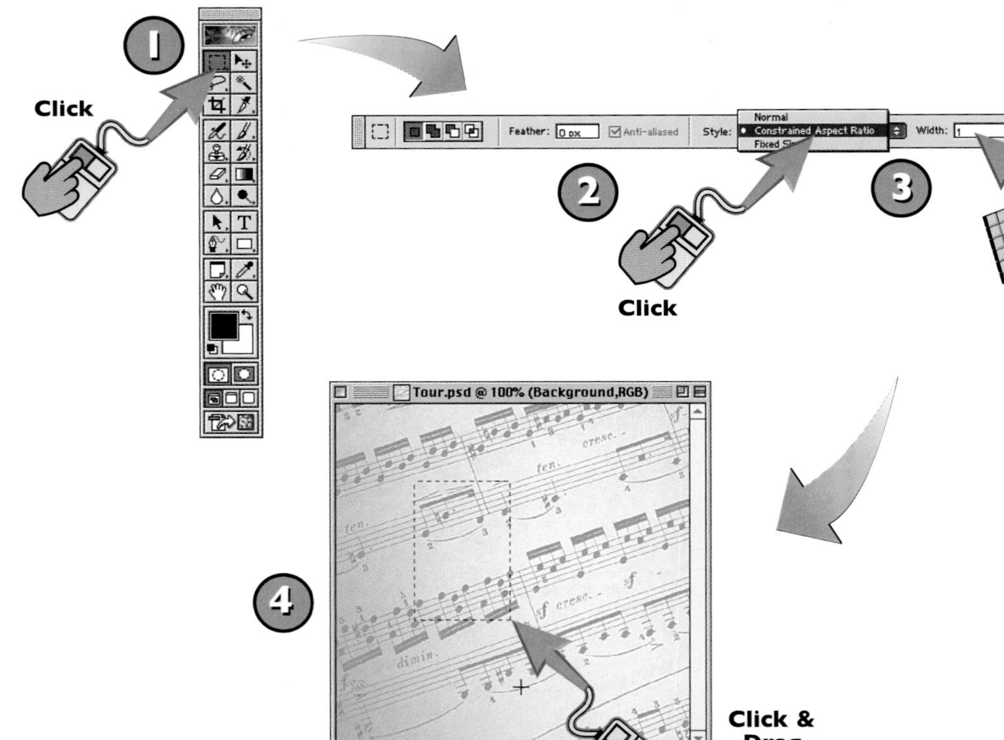

1. Double-click the **Marquee** tool in the **Tool** palette to display the **Marquee Options** bar.
2. To select an area with specific proportions, choose **Constrained Aspect Ratio** in the bar's **Style** pop-up menu.
3. Enter a ratio for the **Width** and **Height** of the selection.
4. Click and drag in the image to make the selection.

Fixed-size selections are useful as measuring tools, too; to make sure objects in an image are all within a certain size, set the Marquee tool to that size and click each object to make sure it falls within the *marching ants*.

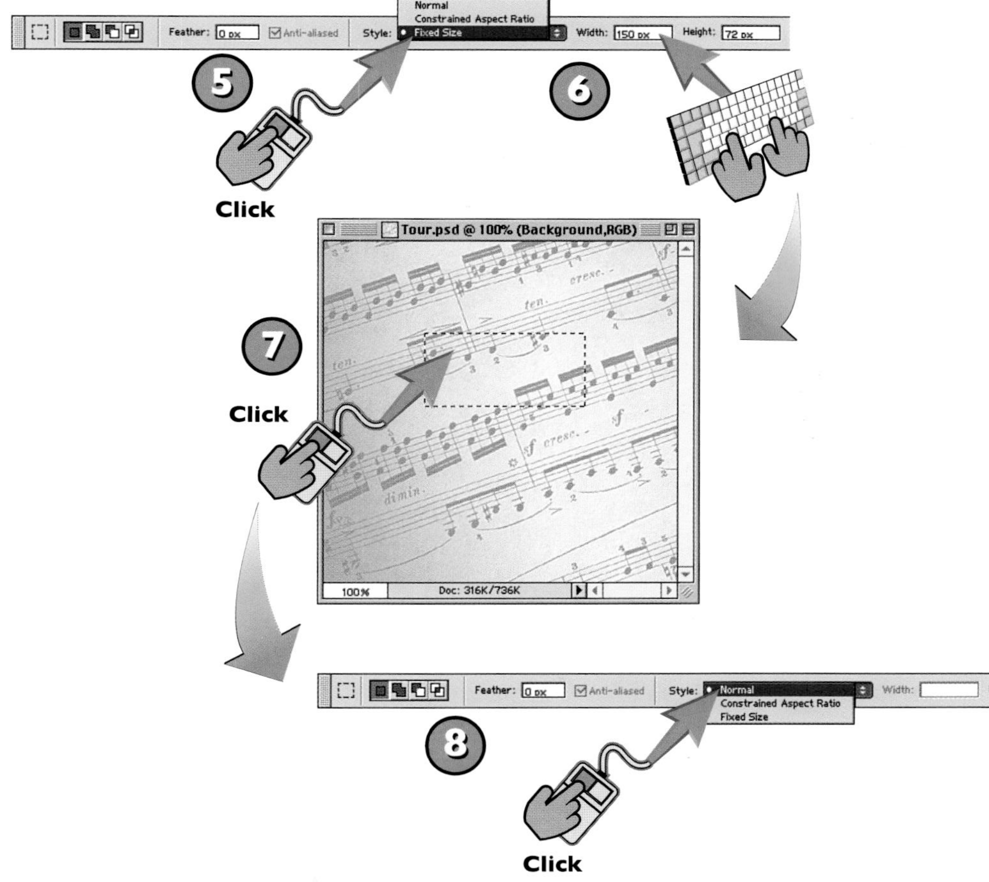

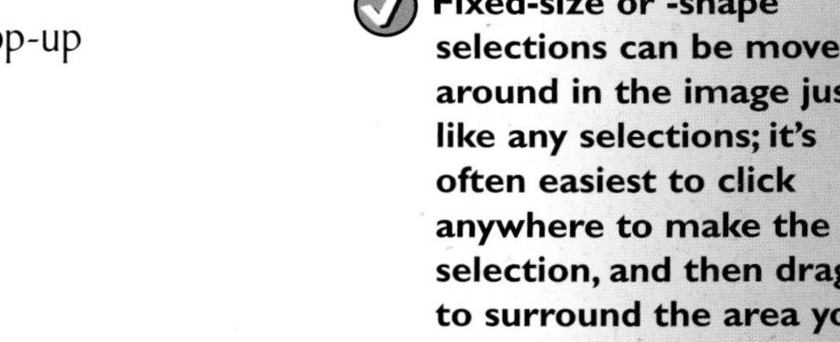

5. To select an area of a specific size, choose **Fixed Size** in the bar's **Style** pop-up menu.

6. Enter the **Width** and **Height** of the selection in pixels.

7. Click in the image to make the selection.

8. Choose **Normal** to return the **Marquee** tool to its normal behavior.

Fixed-size or -shape selections can be moved around in the image just like any selections; it's often easiest to click anywhere to make the selection, and then drag it to surround the area you want selected.

Task 4: Selecting One Column or Row of Pixels

You don't often need this capability, but when the need arises to make stripes, or to delete just a fringe of pixels along the edge of an object, Photoshop provides a tool to let you do it. The single-column and single-row Marquee tools select just what their names imply.

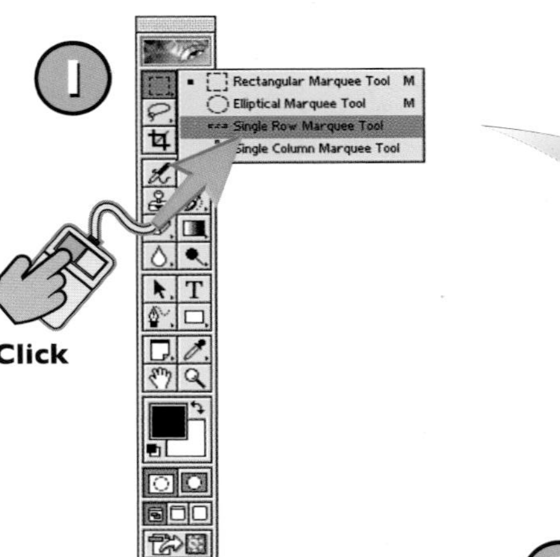

Dragging with the single-column or single-row Marquee tool moves the *selection* rather than enlarges it, because you can't select more than one column or row with these tools.

1. Click the **Marquee** tool in the **Tool** palette and slide the mouse over to select the single-column or single-row **Marquee** tool.
2. Click in the image to make the selection.

Task 5: Selecting an Object Magnetically

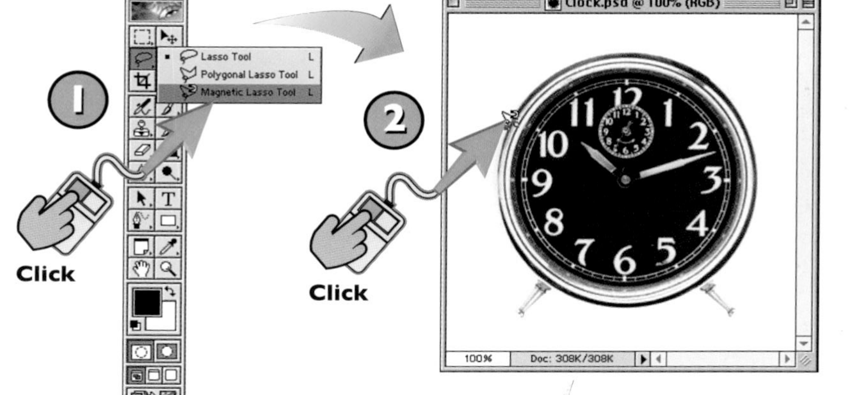

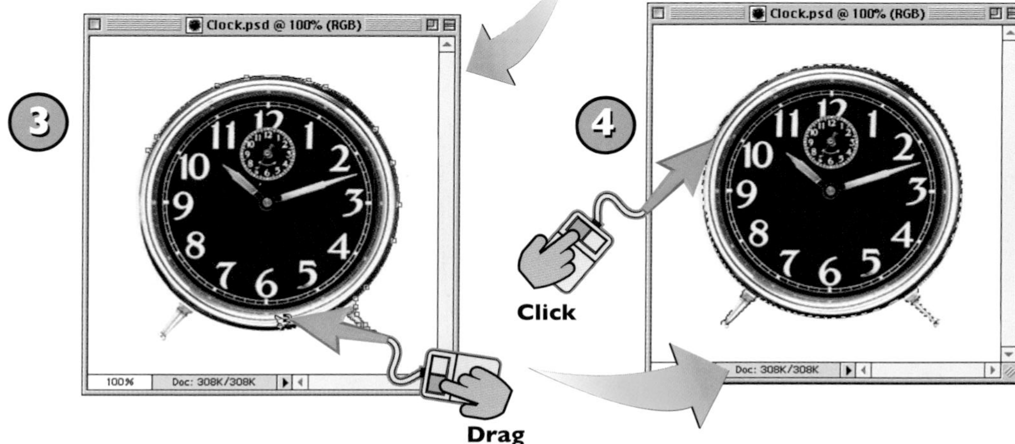

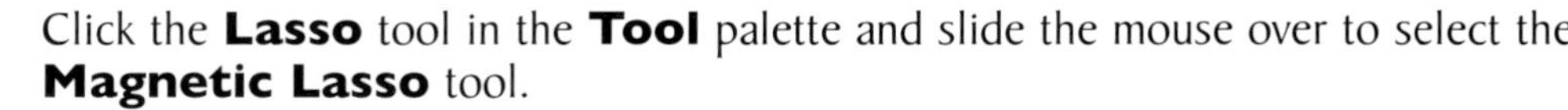

1 Click the **Lasso** tool in the **Tool** palette and slide the mouse over to select the **Magnetic Lasso** tool.

2 Click (without holding down the mouse button) near an edge of the object you want to select.

3 Drag the cursor around the edge of the object.

4 Click again at the starting point to create the selection.

Selecting hard-edged objects is easier than it used to be with Photoshop's Magnetic Lasso tool. This tool finds the edges between areas of different colors and draws *selections* along those edges.

You can override the Magnetic Lasso's choice of where to place its selection line at any point by clicking where you want the selection to go; the selection won't be created until you double-click or click again on your starting point.

If the Magnetic Lasso seems to be rounding off corners, double-click the Lasso tool in the Tool palette to bring up the Magnetic Lasso Options palette and make sure Anti-aliased isn't checked.

You'll know you've reached your starting point when the Magnetic Lasso's cursor adds a °. Click to close the selection.

Task 6: Creating a Selection by Painting

Based on an analogy with the prepress technician's rubylith, Photoshop's Quick Mask feature enables you to paint a transparent reddish image over your existing image that can then be converted to a *selection*. Because you can paint in Quick Mask mode with less than 100% opacity, pixels selected this way can be partially selected, so that whatever effect you apply to them is only partially applied.

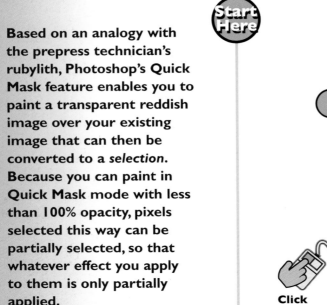

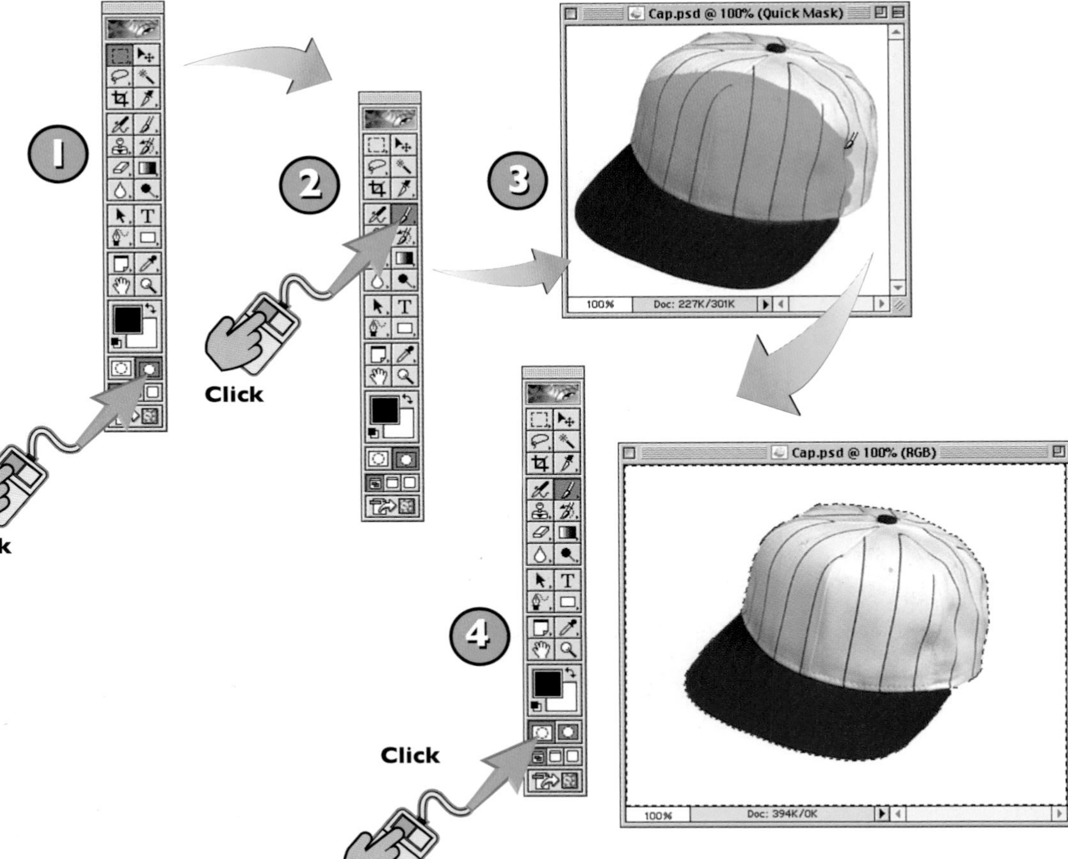

To begin using Quick Mask with part of the image already masked out, select the portion of the image you want to keep before entering Quick Mask mode.

1. Click the **Quick Mask Mode** button on the **Tool** palette, or press **Q**.
2. Choose a painting tool from the **Tool** palette.
3. Paint over the portions of the image that should not be included in the selection.

4. Click the **Standard Mode** button or press **Q** again to return to normal selection mode.

Task 7: Selecting the Inverse of a Selection

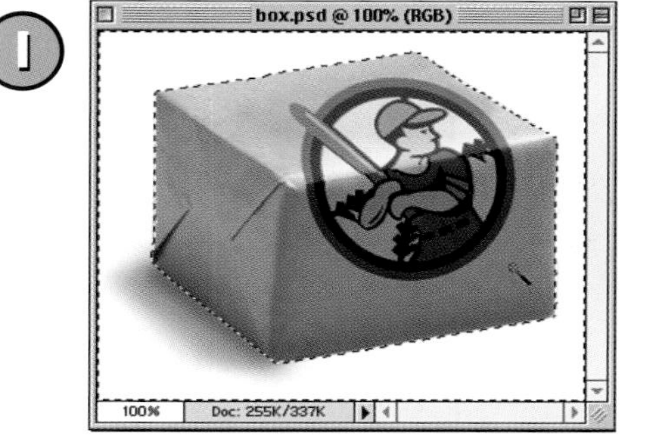

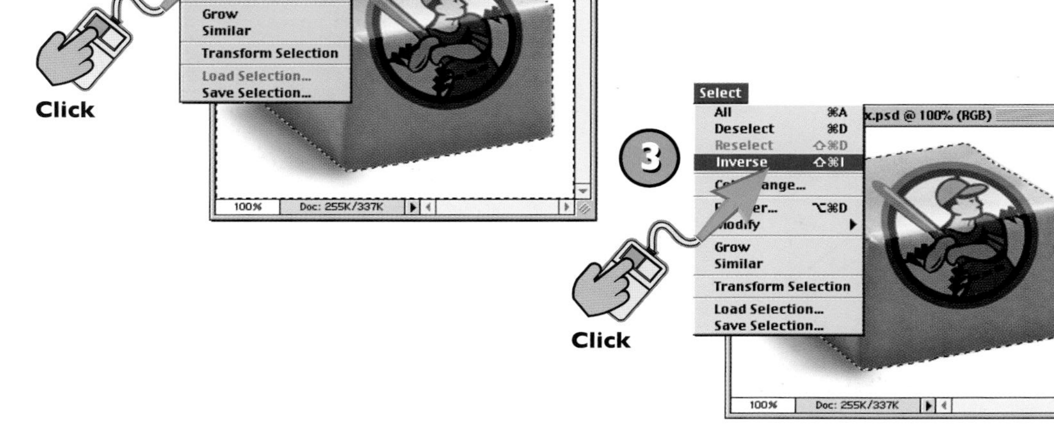

Probably one of the most confusing commands in Photoshop, the Inverse command is very different from the Invert command (which reverses the colors in the image to create a negative). The Inverse command inverts a selection instead, selecting the parts of an image that were not included in the original selection.

1. Make a selection by using any method.
2. Choose **Select**, **Inverse** or press **Cmd+Shift+I/Ctrl+Shift+I**.
3. Click **Select**, **Inverse** again, or press **Cmd+Shift+I/Ctrl+Shift+I** to return to the original selection.

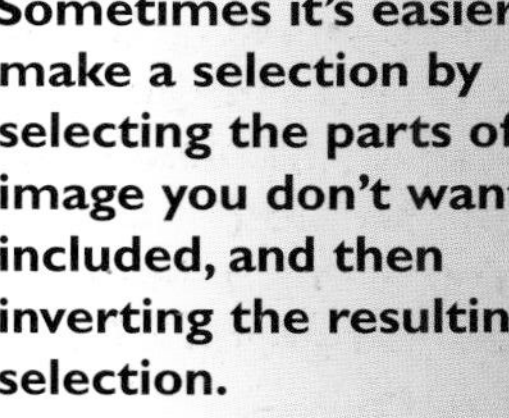

Sometimes it's easier to make a selection by selecting the parts of the image you don't want included, and then inverting the resulting selection.

Task 8: Selecting an Area of the Same Color

Start Here

Using the Magic Wand tool really does feel like doing magic. Clicking with this tool selects all the pixels in an area that are the same—or nearly the same—color as the pixel on which you directly click.

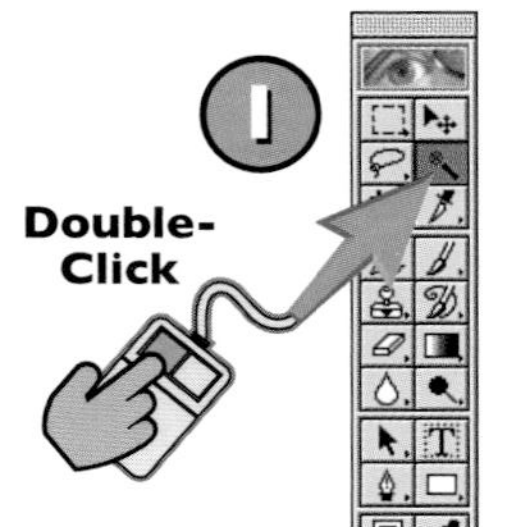

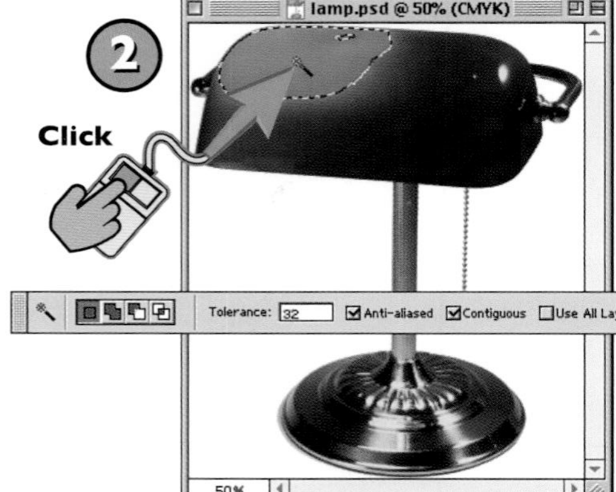

Use the Magic Wand together with the Inverse command to select objects on a plain background. First select the background with the Magic Wand, and then press Cmd+Shift+I to invert the selection so that the object itself is selected.

1. Double-click the **Magic Wand** tool in the **Tool** palette to select the Magic Wand and display the **Magic Wand Options** toolbar.
2. Click in the image to select a group of pixels of the same color range.

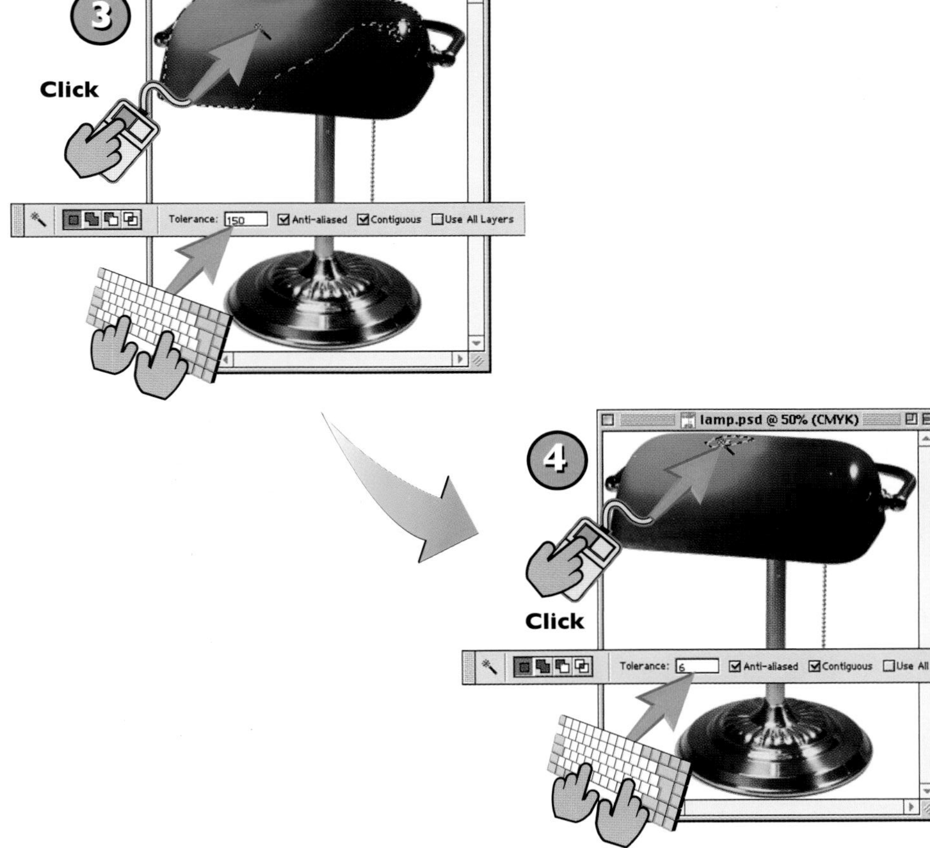

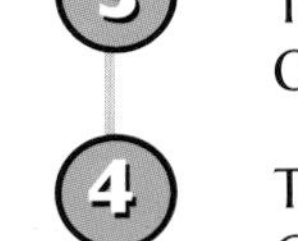

3 To broaden the color range to select more pixels, adjust the **Tolerance** setting on the Options bar upward, and then click again in the image.

4 To narrow the color range to select fewer pixels, adjust the **Tolerance** setting on the Options bar downward, and then click again in the image.

After you select an area with the Magic Wand, choose Select, Similar to select other areas of the same color throughout the image.

Task 9: Selecting Multiple Areas of the Same Color

When you need to select the same color all over an image, the Magic Wand tool isn't enough. Photoshop gives you a way to do this: the Color Range command. You can adjust the tolerance of the selection using a preview, so that the final selection is just what you want.

Start Here

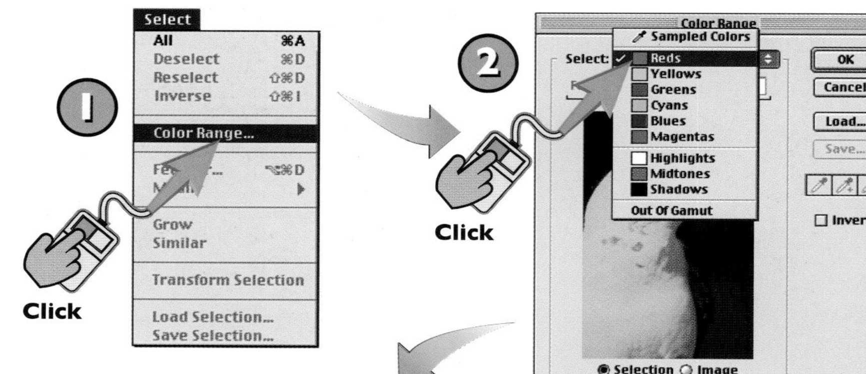

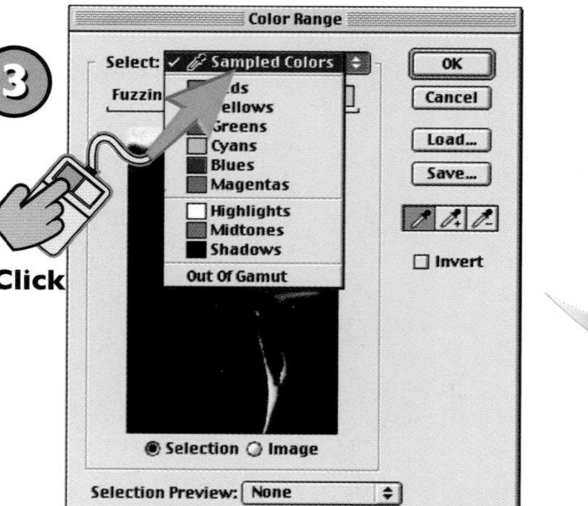

Color Range
Select: Sampled Colors
Fuzziness: 72
OK
Cancel
Load...
Save...
Invert
Selection
Image
Selection Preview: None
Click
parrot.psd @...
50%

1. Choose **Select**, **Color Range**.
2. To select a specific range of colors, choose a color from the **Select** pop-up menu.
3. To select a color chosen from the image, choose **Sampled Colors** from the **Select** menu.
4. Click the **Selection** radio button to preview the selected area in the dialog box.

The Fuzziness slider performs the same function as the Magic Wand's Tolerance setting; it determines how close to the original color a pixel must be for it to be included in the selection.

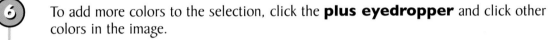

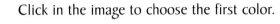

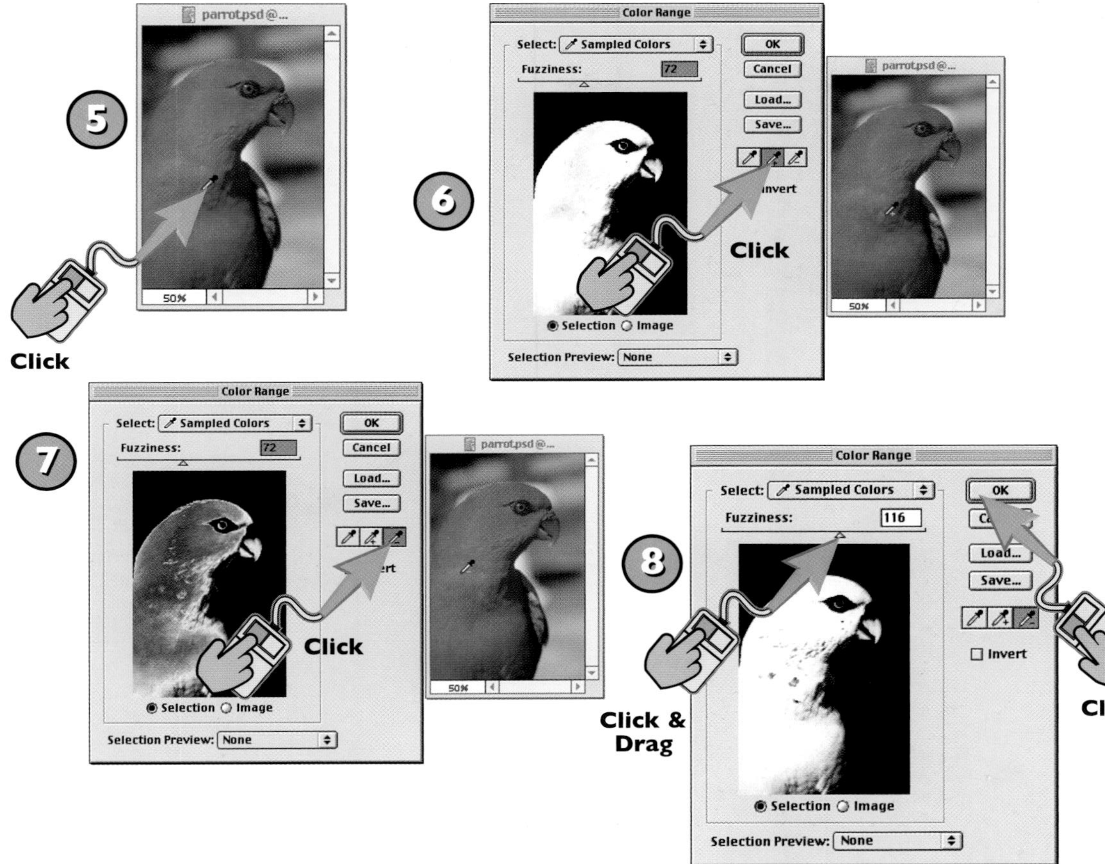

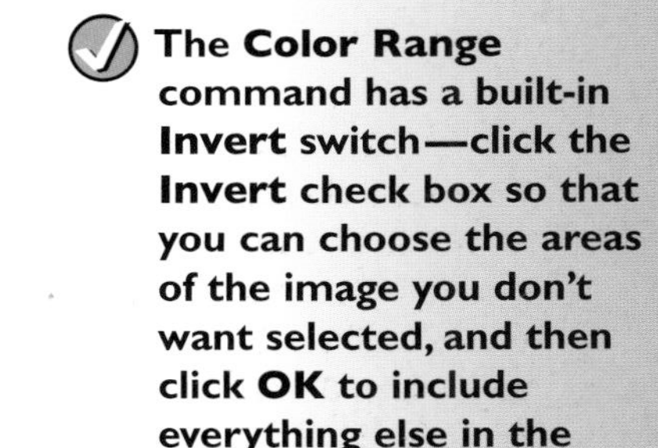

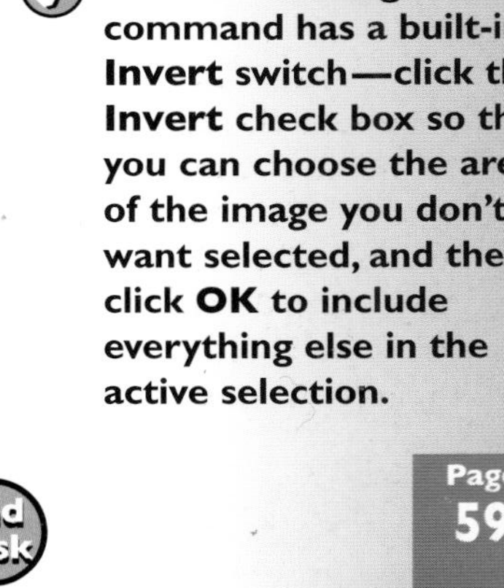

5 Click in the image to choose the first color.

6 To add more colors to the selection, click the **plus eyedropper** and click other colors in the image.

7 To remove colors from the selection, click the **minus eyedropper** and click other colors in the image.

8 To select more or fewer pixels, drag the **Fuzziness** slider right or left respectively, and then click **OK** to create the selection.

You can click the eyedropper tools in the image or in the dialog box preview—whichever shows more clearly the area of the selection that you want to affect.

The **Color Range** command has a built-in **Invert** switch—click the **Invert** check box so that you can choose the areas of the image you don't want selected, and then click **OK** to include everything else in the active selection.

Task 10: Creating a Selection from Type

In Photoshop, sometimes type is more than just text—you can make it glow, spin, tremble, or just about anything else. Some type effects start out with a type-shaped selection rather than actual type, so Photoshop lets you choose whether to create actual type or just a selection when you use the Type tool.

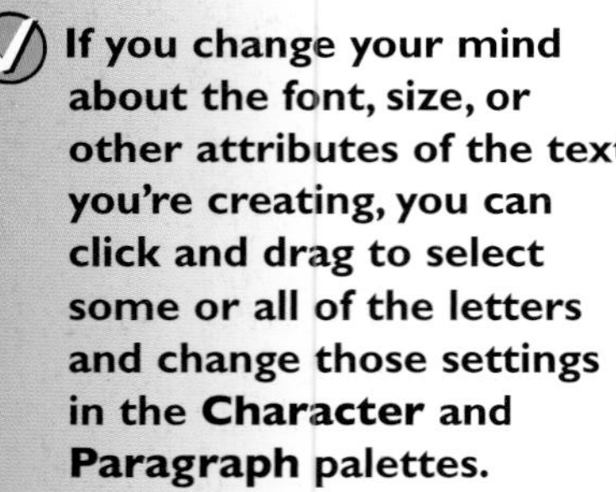

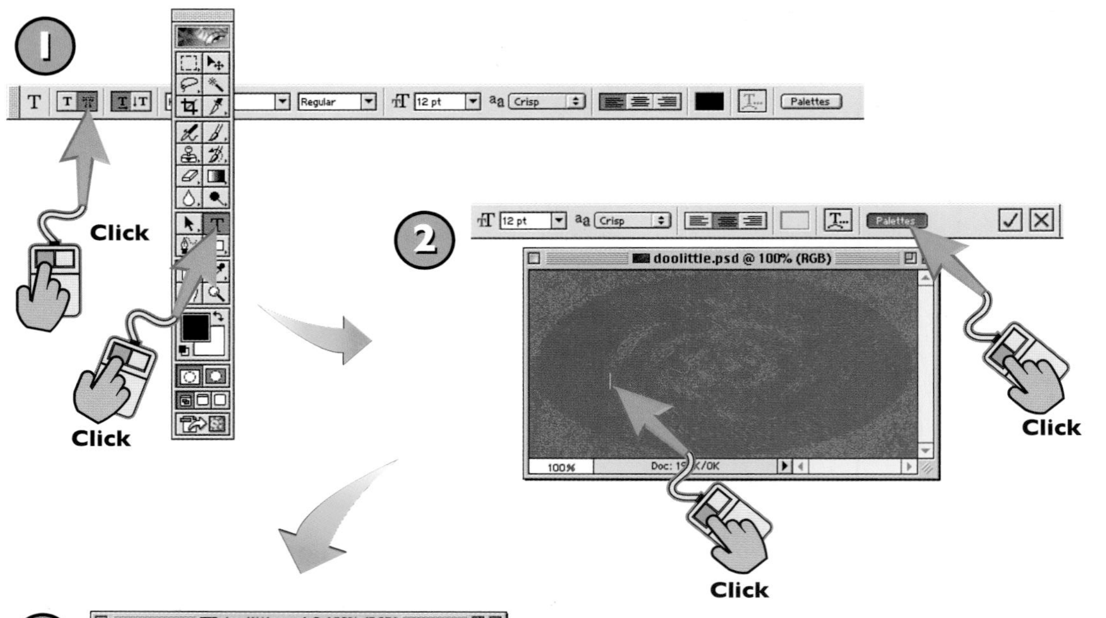

✓ If you change your mind about the font, size, or other attributes of the text you're creating, you can click and drag to select some or all of the letters and change those settings in the **Character** and **Paragraph** palettes.

✓ For more information about creating type and using the options in the **Character** and **Paragraph** palettes and the **Type Options** bar, see Part 9, "Creating and Editing Type."

1. Double-click the **Type** tool in the **Tool** palette, and click the **Type Mask** button on the **Type Options** bar.
2. Click in the image to begin typing, and then click the **Palettes** button on the **Type Options** bar.
3. In the **Character** palette, choose a font and size for the type, and then enter the text.
4. Press **Enter** to create the selection.

Task 11: Adding to a Selection

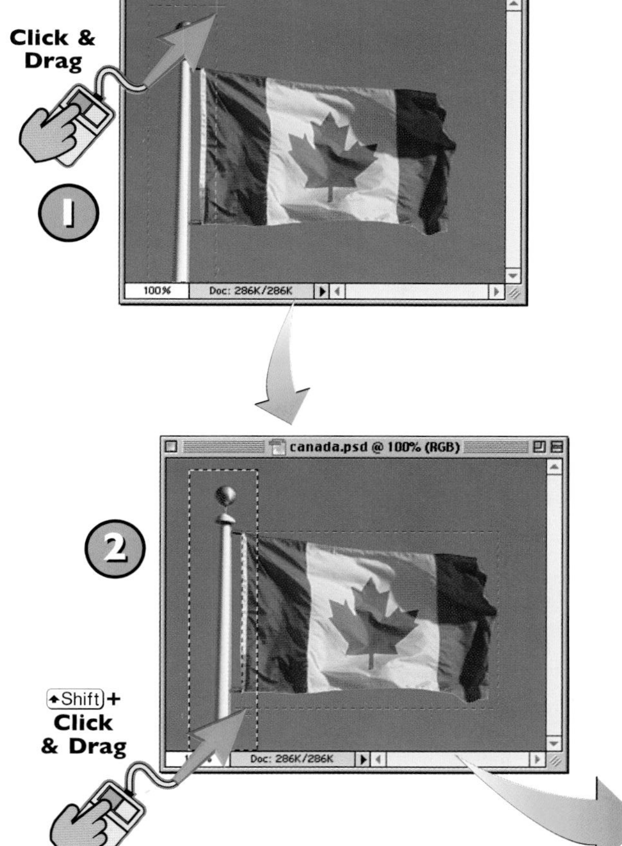

In Photoshop, the Shift key almost always means "add." That holds true when creating selections as well; with a selection active, holding down the Shift key enables you to add more selected areas to the selection.

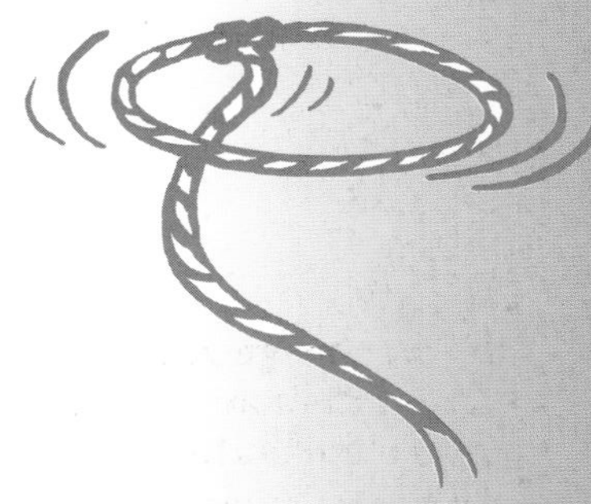

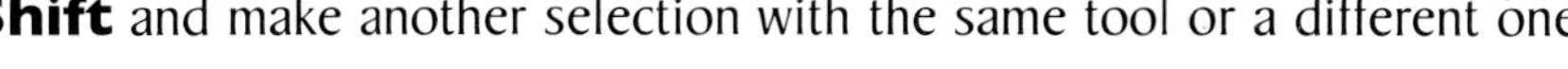

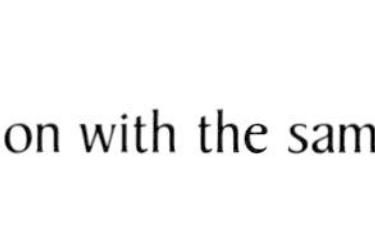

1. Create a selection by using any method.
2. Press **Shift** and make another selection with the same tool or a different one.

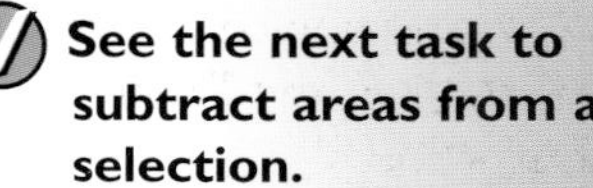

Using the **Shift** key enables you to mix and match different selection methods; try starting a selection with the **Magic Wand** tool, and then adding to it by using **Shift** and the **Lasso** tool, for example.

See the next task to subtract areas from a selection.

Task 12: Subtracting from a Selection

If things get out of hand when making a selection, you don't need to start all over again. You can deselect portions of a selected area by holding down the Option/Alt key.

Start Here

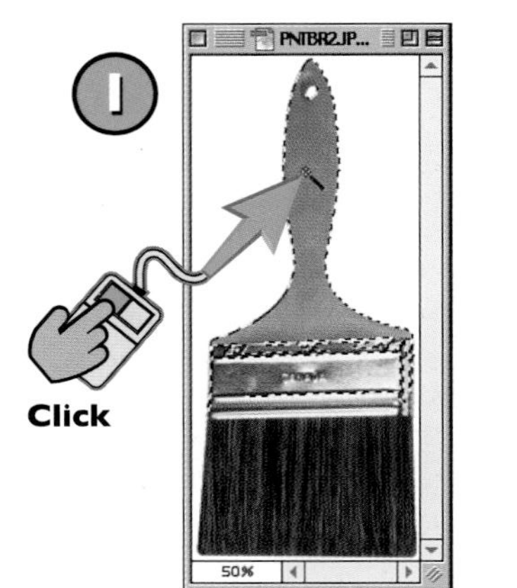

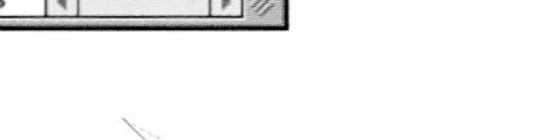

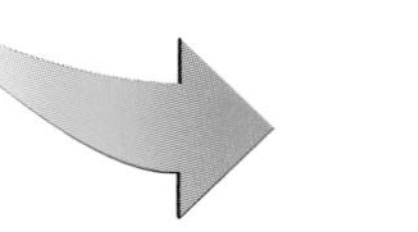

The Magic Wand tool often selects a larger area than you really want; use the Option key to clip off those unwanted portions of the selection with another selection tool, such as the Lasso.

By alternating among different selection tools and by using the Shift and Option keys, you can quickly select any area of an image; don't be afraid to mix and match these different selection techniques.

1. Create a selection by using any method.
2. Press **Option/Alt** and deselect the "extra" area with the same tool or a different one.

End Task

Task 13: Making a Selection Smaller or Larger

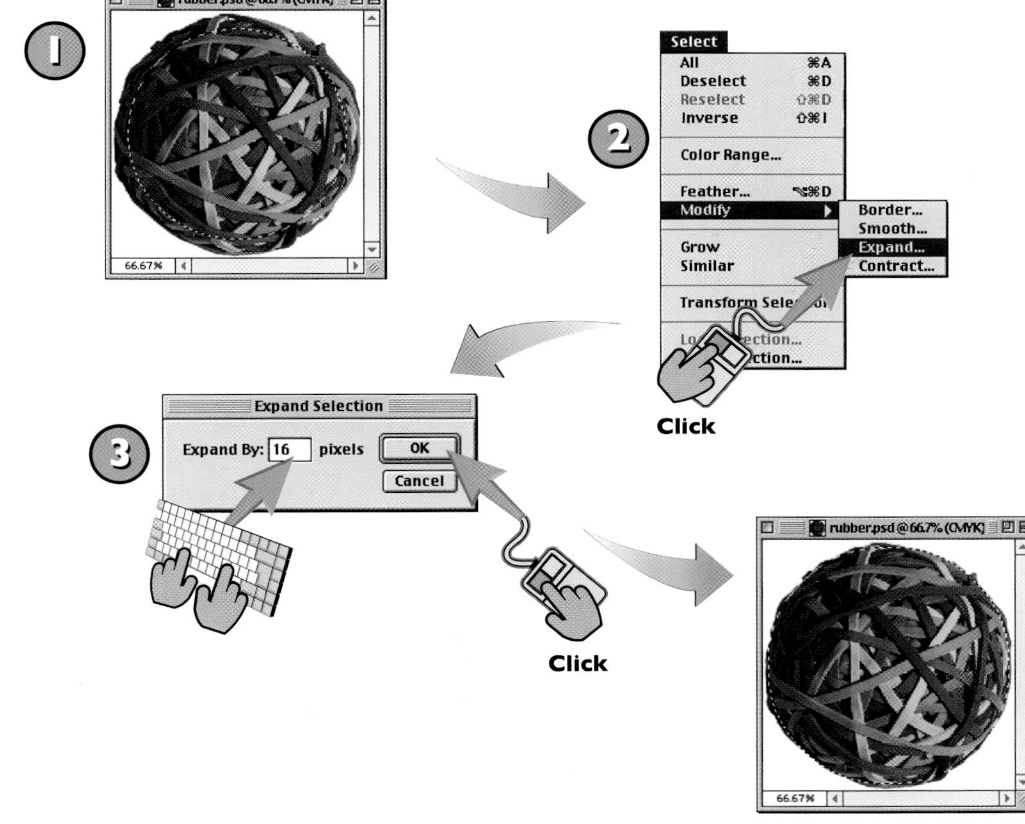

Sometimes a selection is perfectly shaped but not the correct size. In this case, adding a bit around the edges or shrinking the selection a bit is easy. The Expand and Contract commands work with selections created by using any method, and you can use them as many times as you need to adjust the selection perfectly.

1. Create a selection by using any method.
2. Choose **Select**, **Modify**, **Expand** to enlarge the selection or **Select**, **Modify**, **Contract** to shrink it.
3. Enter a number between 1 and 100 pixels, and click **OK** to adjust the selection.

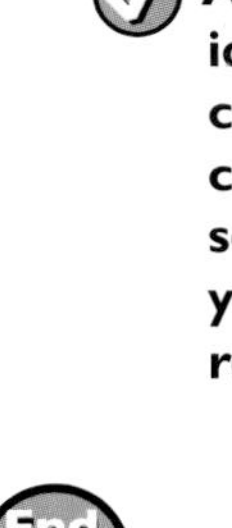

An unfortunate idiosyncrasy of the **Expand** command is that it cuts off corners of rectangular selections, so if you use it, you no longer have a rectangular selection.

Task 14: Selecting the Non-Transparent Areas of a Layer

A selection made up of a layer's opaque *pixels* is called that layer's *transparency mask*. You can select a layer's transparency mask even if that layer isn't currently active or visible, so it's a good way to duplicate a shape on another layer. You can also combine transparency masks from more than one layer into a selection.

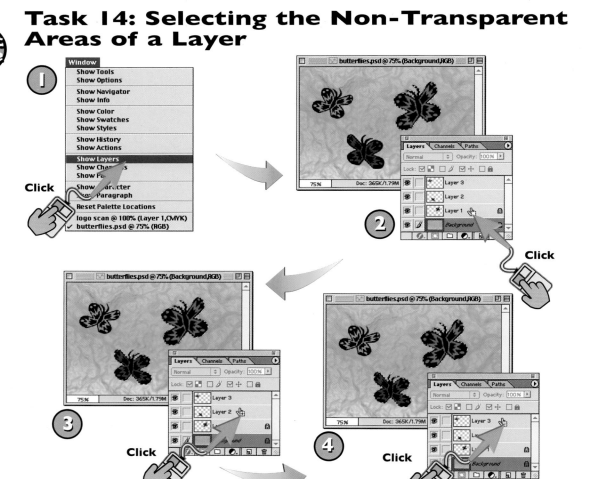

This procedure works only for rasterized layers. Be sure to rasterize shape layers to load their transparency masks.

If an image's background layer is not made transparent when the image is created, you can't select that layer's transparency mask.

Start Here

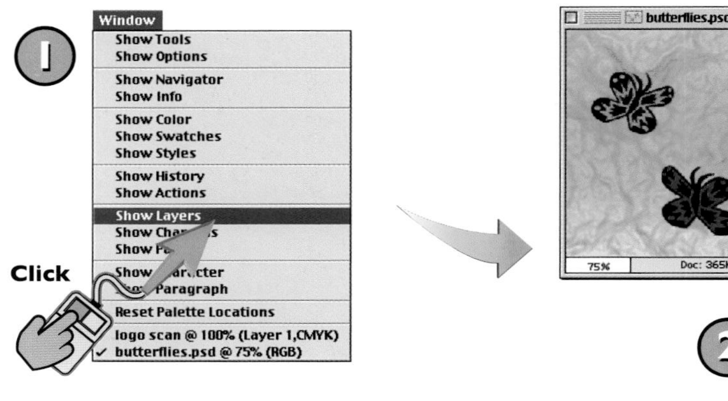

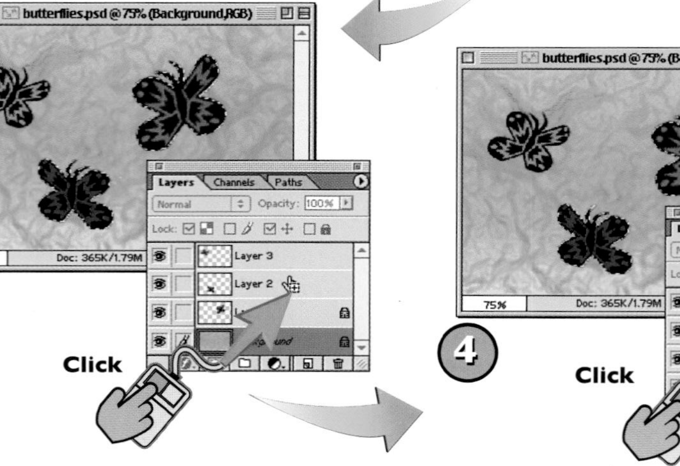

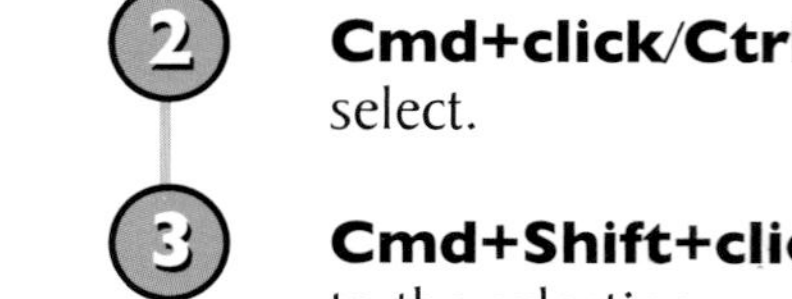

1. Choose **Window**, **Show Layers**.
2. **Cmd+click/Ctrl+click** on the name of the layer whose transparency mask you want to select.
3. **Cmd+Shift+click/Ctrl+Shift+click** a layer name to add that layer's transparency mask to the selection.
4. **Cmd+Option+click/Ctrl+Alt+click** a layer name to remove that layer's transparency mask from the selection.

Task 15: Selecting a Border Area

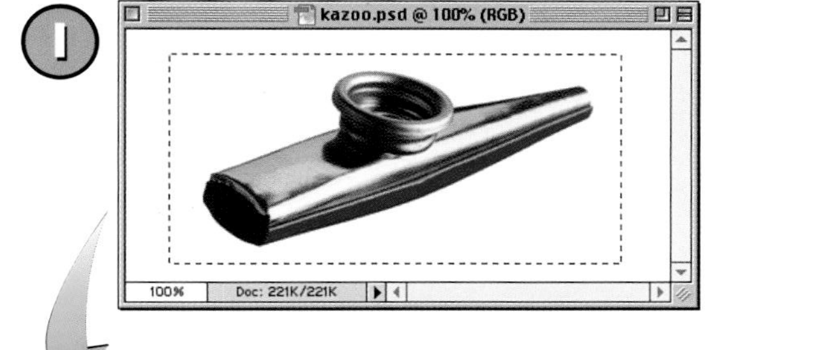

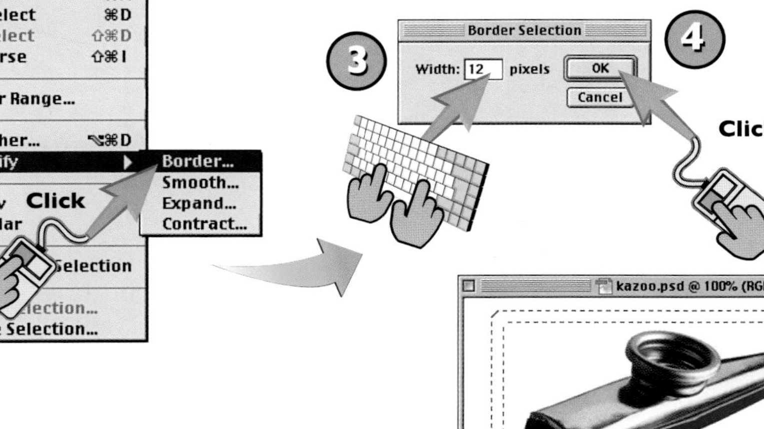

Suppose you don't want to apply a change to an entire selected area—just to the edges of it. Photoshop enables you to do this by changing the selection to a border selection.

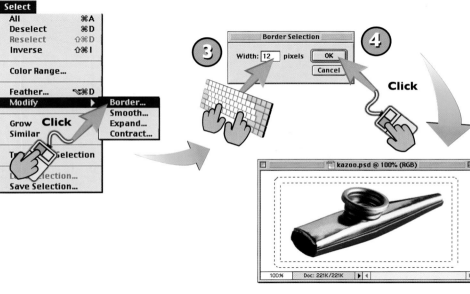

1. Make a selection by using any method.
2. Choose **Select**, **Modify**, **Border**.
3. Enter a number of pixels between 1 and 200 for the border **Width**.
4. Click **OK** to select the border area.

A border selection is automatically *feathered*, meaning that the pixels along its edges are only partially selected. Effects you apply to a feathered selection will gradually fade out from the center.

For more information about feathered selections, see Task 18, "Feathering the Edges of a Selection."

Task 16: Transforming a Selection

After a selection is made, you can resize and reshape it in many ways by *transforming* it. To transform the pixels in the selected area of the image, you use the Transform commands in the Edit menu. However, to transform the shape of selection marquees themselves, you use the Transform Selection command in the Select menu.

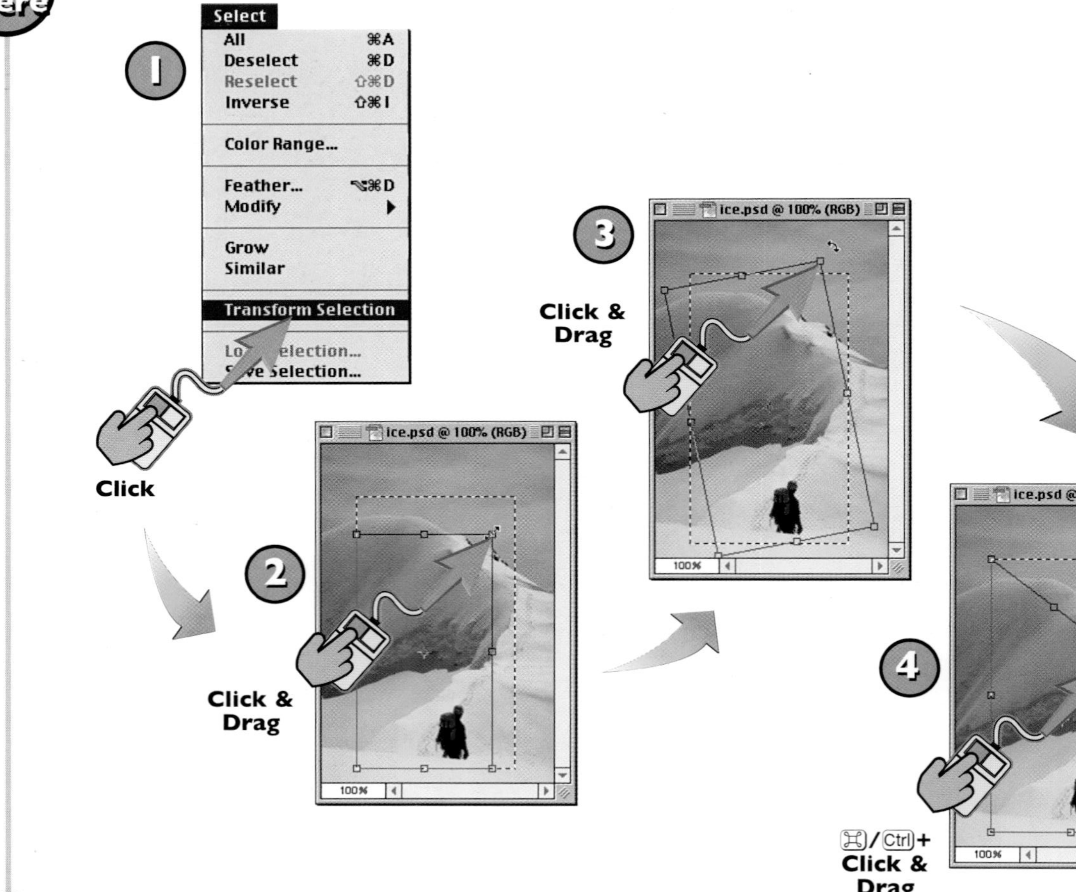

1. Create a selection by using any method and choose **Select**, **Transform Selection**.
2. To scale the selection, click any handle and drag.
3. To rotate the selection, click and drag outside the selection border.
4. To reshape the selection, **Cmd+click/Ctrl+click** and drag any handle.

The cursor changes as you hold down modifier keys and move over different handles. A black arrowhead means you're about to move the selection, a gray one means you're applying perspective or skewing, a double arrow indicates resizing, and a curved double arrow indicates rotating.

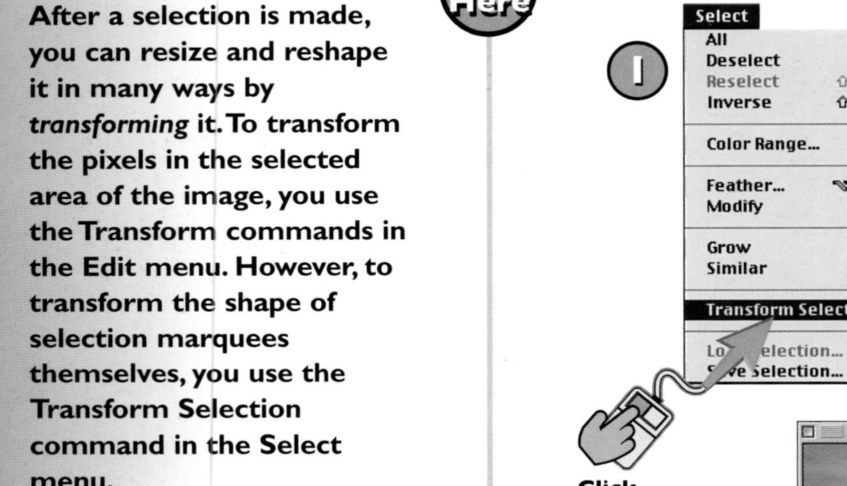

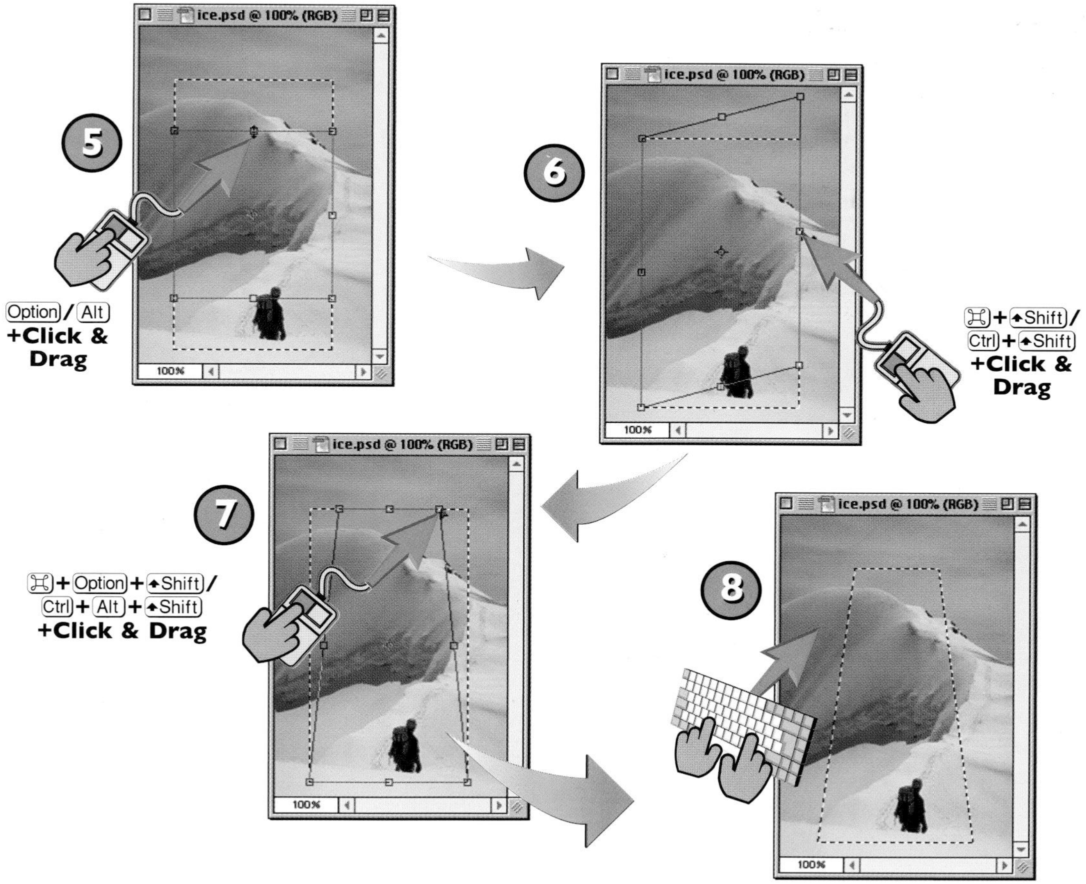

5 To reshape the selection symmetrically, **Option+click/Alt+click** and drag any handle.

6 To skew the selection, **Cmd+Shift+click/Ctrl+Shift+click** a side handle and drag.

7 To apply perspective to the selection, **Cmd+Option+Shift+click/Ctrl+Alt+Shift+click** a corner handle and drag.

8 Press **Enter** to apply the changes or **Esc** to cancel them.

It's usually hard to picture the effect of these transformations on a selection without trying it; a good exercise is to make a selection and experiment with the different transformations until they make sense.

For more information on transforming a selected area, see Part 6, "Editing Images."

Task 17: Smoothing a Selection

Start Here

Selections—especially those made with the Magic Wand tool or the Color Range command—often have rough edges and little "bubbles" of unselected pixels within selections. An easy way to fix this problem is to use the Smooth command, which removes small extraneous selections outside the main selection as well.

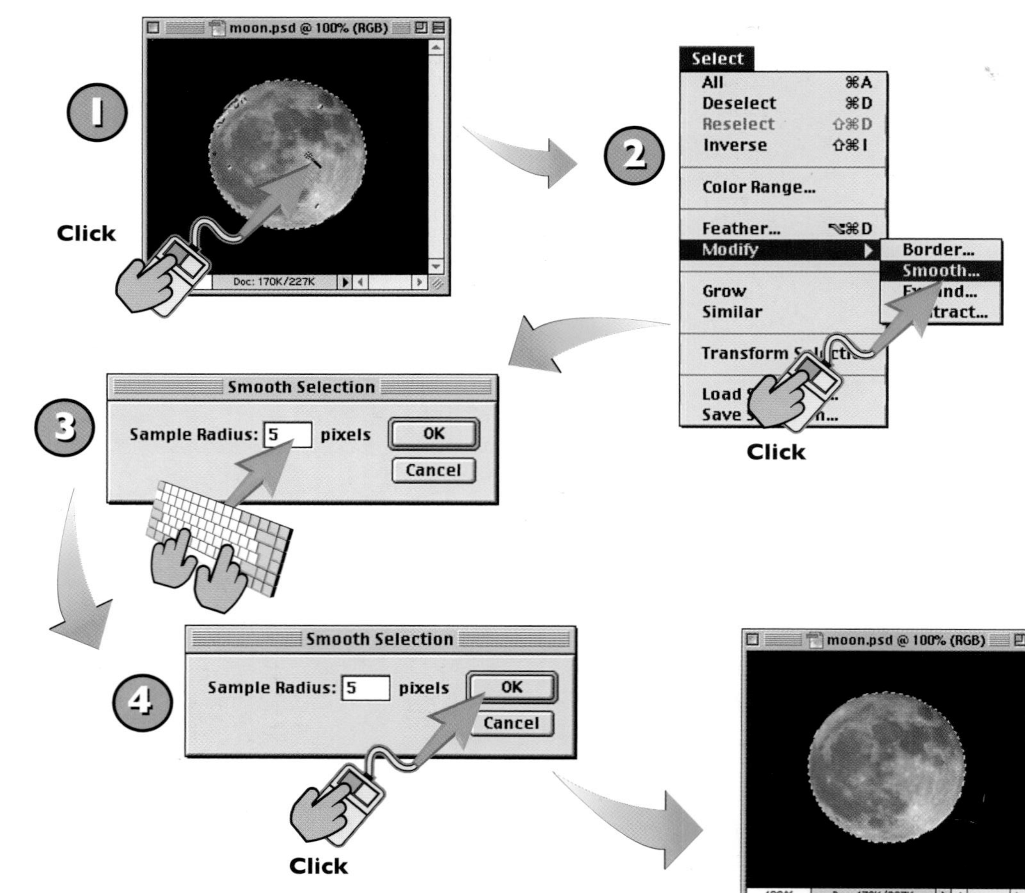

1. Make a selection by using any method.
2. Choose **Select**, **Modify**, **Smooth**.
3. Enter a number of pixels between 1 and 100 for the **Sample Radius**—this is the smallest "bubble" that will be smoothed out.
4. Click **OK** to smooth the selection.

The **Smooth** command works with any selection, not just those made with the **Magic Wand** or **Color Range** methods. It's a good way to smooth the edges of a selection made with the **Lasso** tool, too.

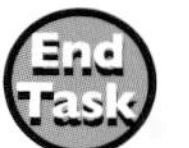

End Task

Task 18: Feathering the Edges of a Selection

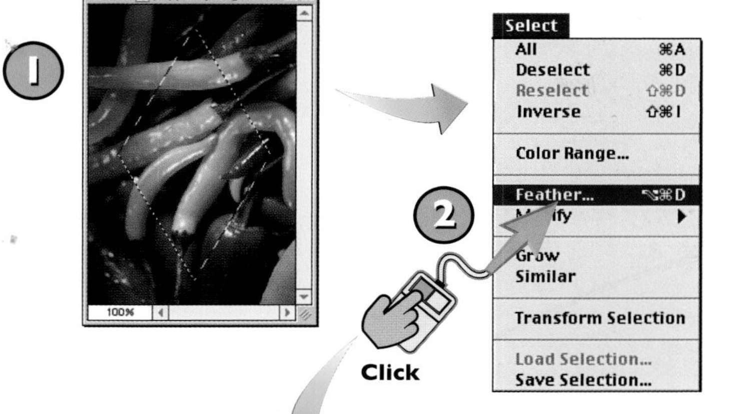

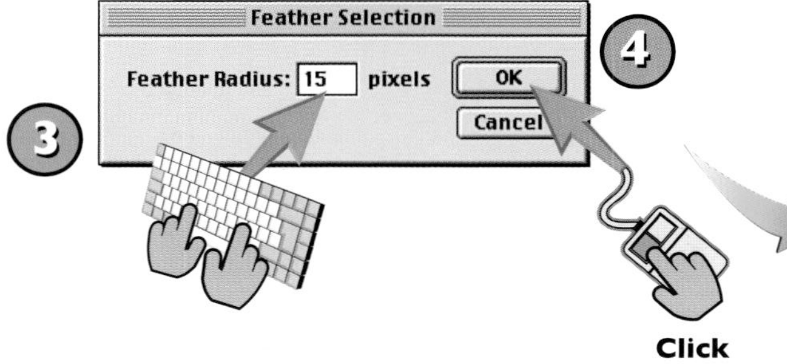

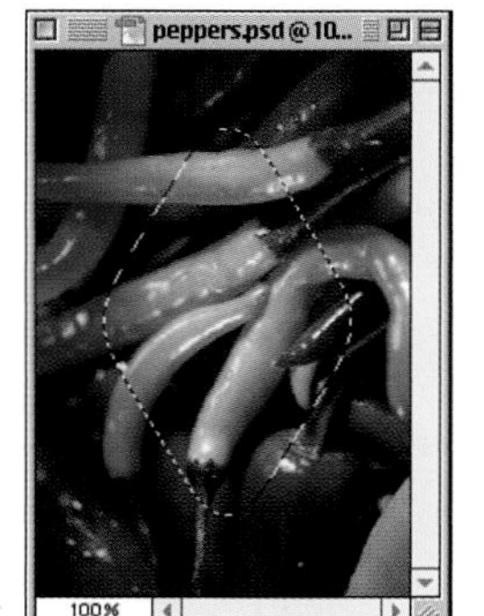

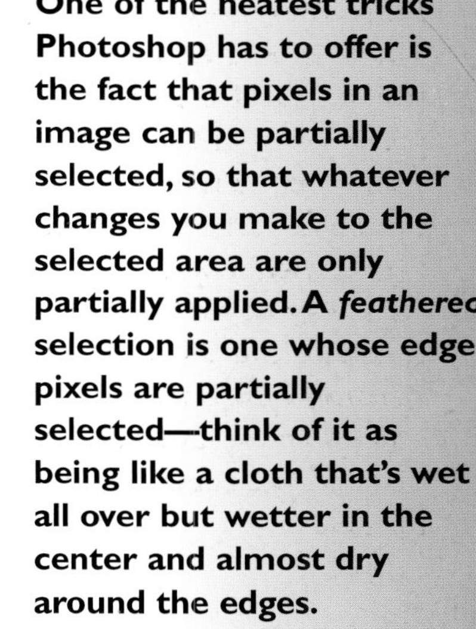

One of the neatest tricks Photoshop has to offer is the fact that pixels in an image can be partially selected, so that whatever changes you make to the selected area are only partially applied. A *feathered* selection is one whose edge pixels are partially selected—think of it as being like a cloth that's wet all over but wetter in the center and almost dry around the edges.

1. Make a selection by using any method.
2. Choose **Select**, **Feather** or press **Cmd+Option+D/Ctrl+Alt+D**.
3. Enter a **Feather Radius** in pixels—the possible range is from .2 to 250.
4. Click **OK** to feather the selection.

✓ The Feather Radius determines how deep the feathered area is—how far it extends from the edge of the selection.

✓ After you apply a feather to it, the selection might appear to shrink and become more rounded, but you won't really see the effect until you make a change to the selected area, such as filling it with a color.

Photoshop's *marching ants* are helpful in defining the selected area, but they can be distracting when you're trying out changes for that area. Hiding the selection marquee can help. You also must remember to deselect, or drop, a selection when you're finished with it.

Task 19: Hiding and Deselecting a Selection

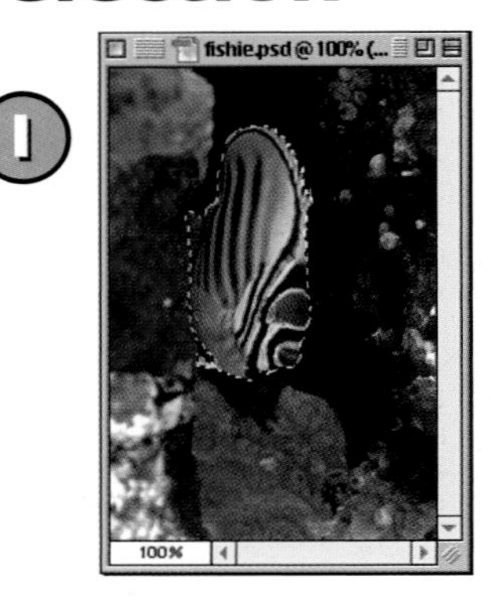

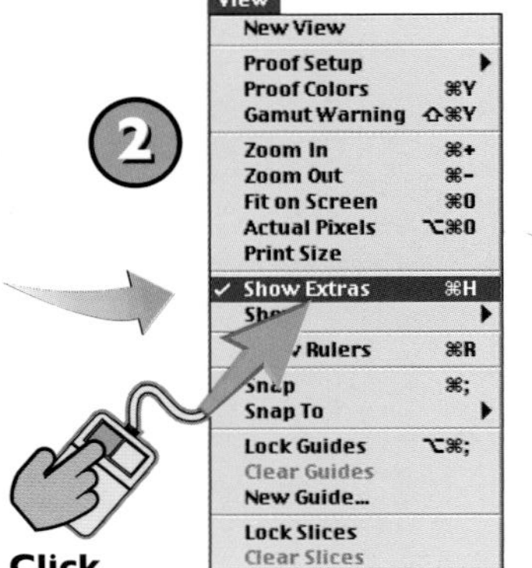

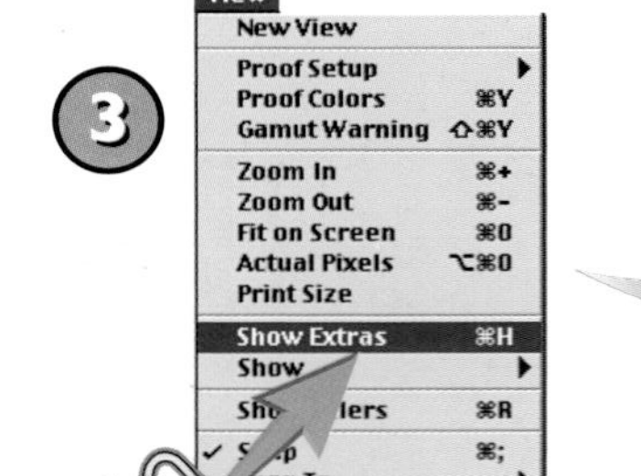

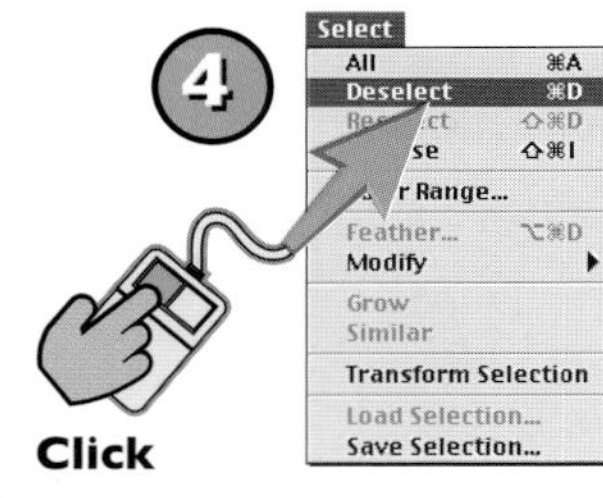

1 Make a selection by using any method.

2 To hide the marching ants, choose **View**, **Show Extras** or press **Cmd+H/Ctrl+H**.

3 To show the marching ants, choose **View**, **Show Extras** or press **Cmd+H/Ctrl+H** again.

4 To drop the selection, choose **Select**, **Deselect** or press **Cmd+D/Ctrl+D**.

To save a selection for future use before you drop it, see the next task, "Saving a Selection as a Channel."

Task 20: Saving a Selection as a Channel

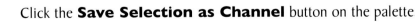

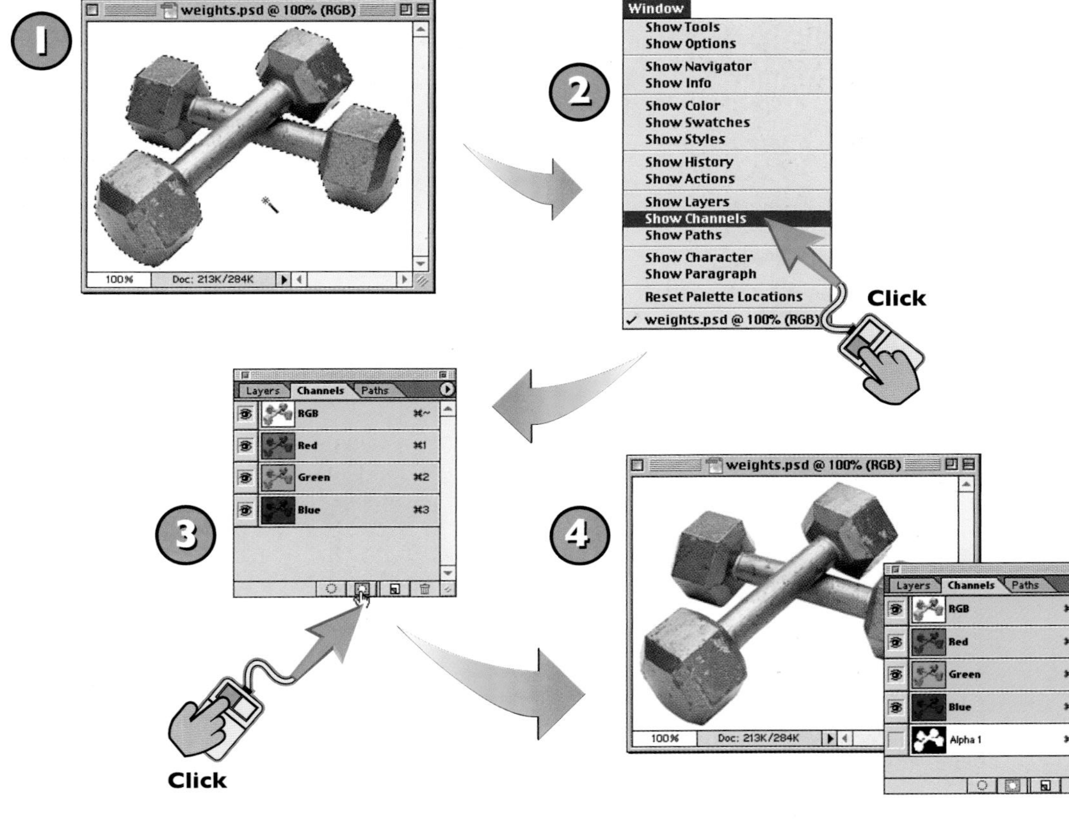

You can save selections as channels so that you can reactivate them if you later need to select the same area. Photoshop translates a selection into a grayscale image representing selected pixels with white, nonselected pixels with black, and partially selected pixels with gray.

1. Make a selection by using any method.
2. Choose **Window**, **Show Channels** to display the **Channels** palette.
3. Click the **Save Selection as Channel** button on the palette.
4. Press **Cmd+D/Ctrl+D** to drop the selection.

You can see the channel Photoshop created from your selection by clicking its name in the Channels palette—Alpha 1, if it's the first selection you've saved. To view the image again, click the top channel in the palette or press Cmd+~/Ctrl+~.

To reactivate the selection from the channel, see Task 24, "Creating a Selection from a Channel."

Task 21: Pasting into a Selection

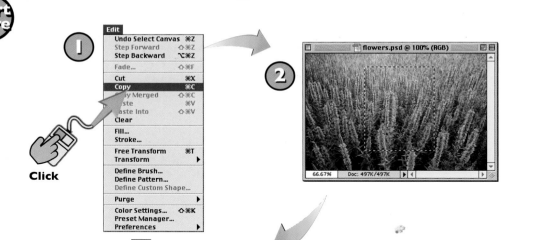

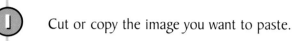

In addition to defining the area that will be affected by editing changes, selections can be used to define the area into which you can paste objects. This is actually a quick way to create a *layer mask*.

After you've created a layer mask, you can modify it to change its effect on the image. See Part 8, "Working with Layers."

Holding down Cmd/Ctrl temporarily turns whatever tool you're using into the Move tool, with which you can move the image on the current layer. Let go of the Cmd/Ctrl key to return to the original tool.

Start Here

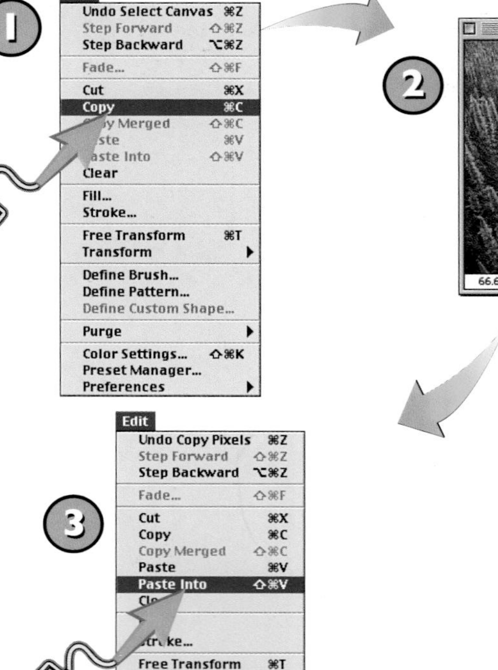

1. Cut or copy the image you want to paste.
2. Make a selection in the new image by using any method.
3. Choose **Edit**, **Paste Into** or press **Cmd+Shift+V/Ctrl+Shift+V**.
4. **Cmd+click/Ctrl+click** and drag to move the pasted image within the area defined by the selection.

End Task

Task 22: Removing "Fringes" from a Selection

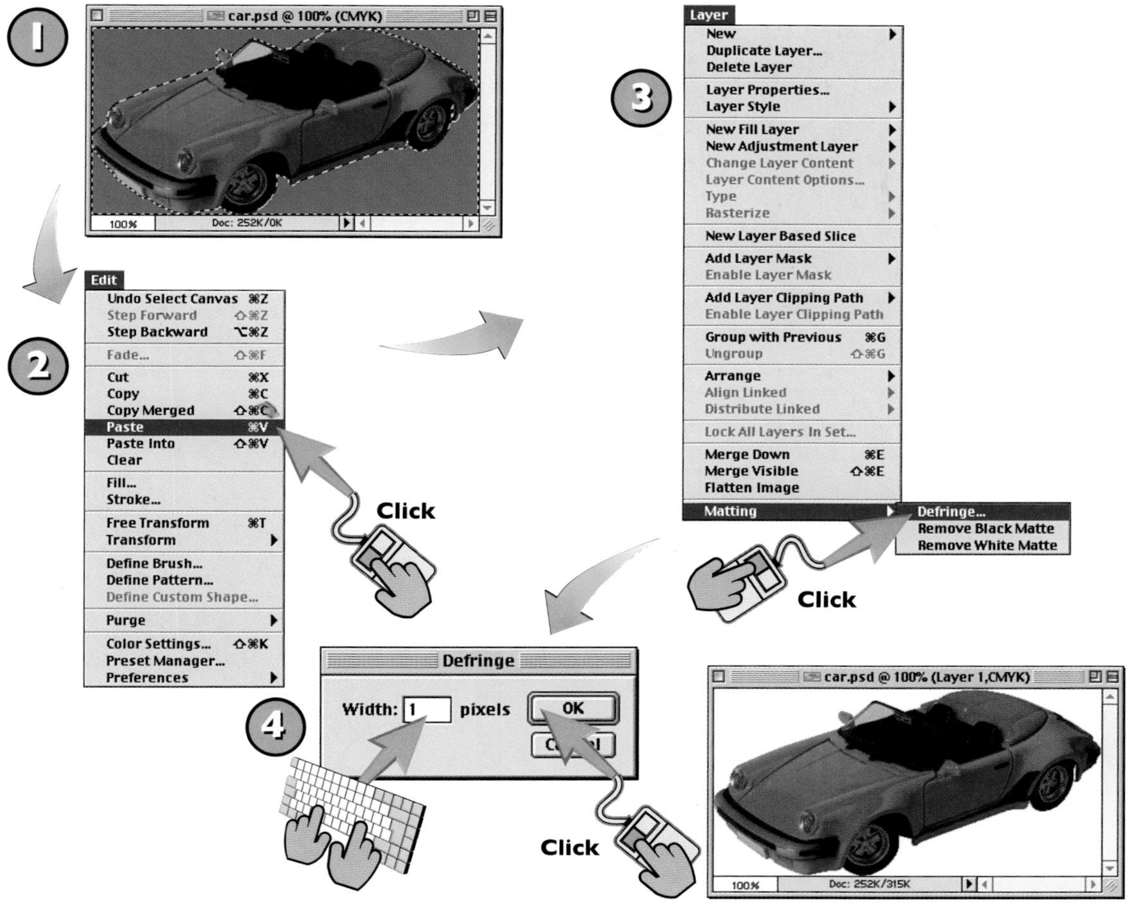

When you make a selection and then move or paste it, sometimes bits of the background colors come with it. Photoshop has a command designed specifically to remove those fringes from a pasted or moved selection.

1. Make a selection by using any method.
2. Copy the selection and then choose **Edit**, **Paste**.
3. Choose **Layer**, **Matting**, **Defringe**.
4. Enter the **Width** of the area to be affected (a value between 1 and 200 pixels), and click **OK**.

✓ Rather than clipping the edges of the pasted selection, Photoshop changes the pixels around the edge to colors that more closely match the colors of the selection.

✓ The **Remove Black Matte** and **Remove White Matte** commands work automatically on selections copied from black or white backgrounds.

Task 23: Using the Channels Palette

Photoshop's images are made up of channels—one for each color component of an image, and one for each selection you've saved for later use. Channels can also be used to indicate what areas of an image should be transparent when it's saved as a GIF file.

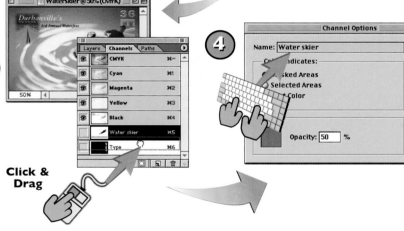

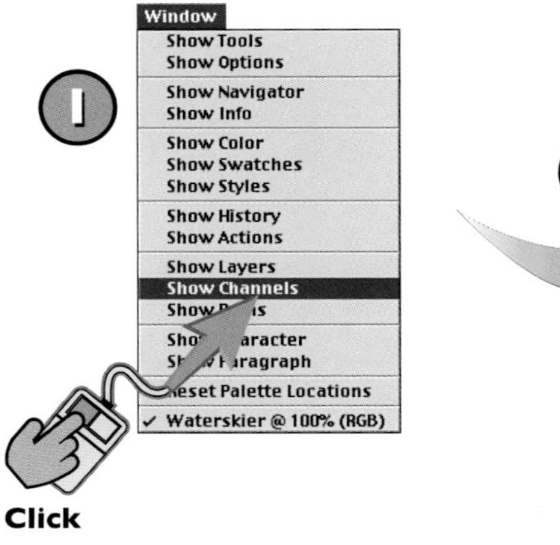

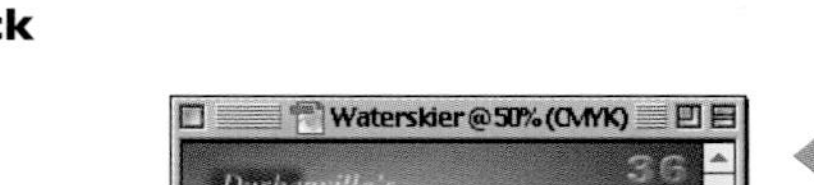

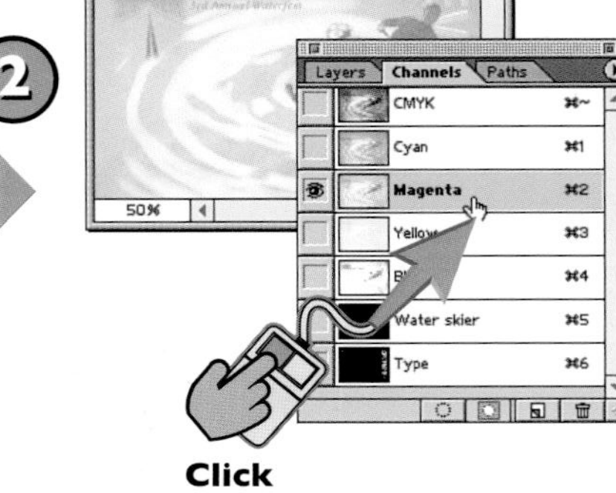

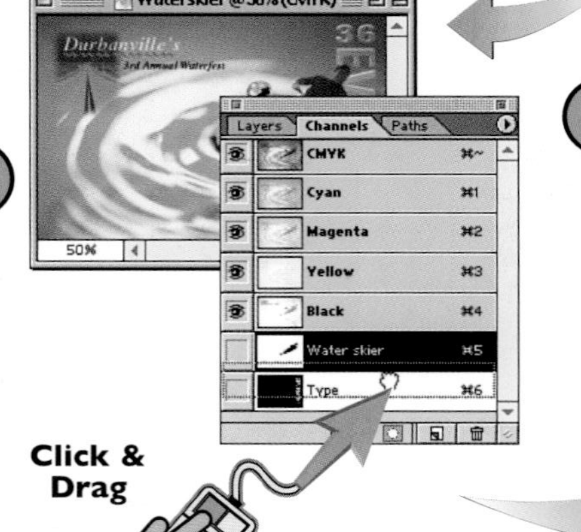

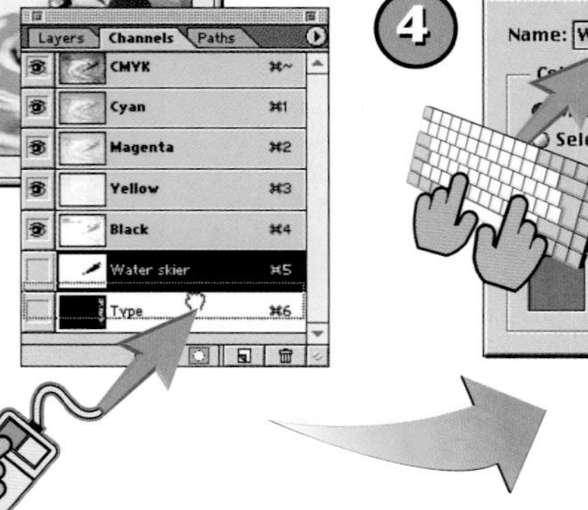

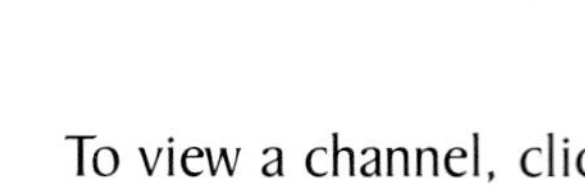

The Channels palette works like the Layers and Paths palettes, and by default it's grouped with them. You can view any of the three by clicking the appropriate tab at the top of the palette.

1. Choose **Window**, **Show Channels** to display the **Channels** palette.
2. To view a channel, click its name in the list.
3. To move a channel in the list, click and drag its name.
4. To change a channel's name, double-click it, enter a new name, and click **OK**.

Task 24: Creating a Selection from a Channel

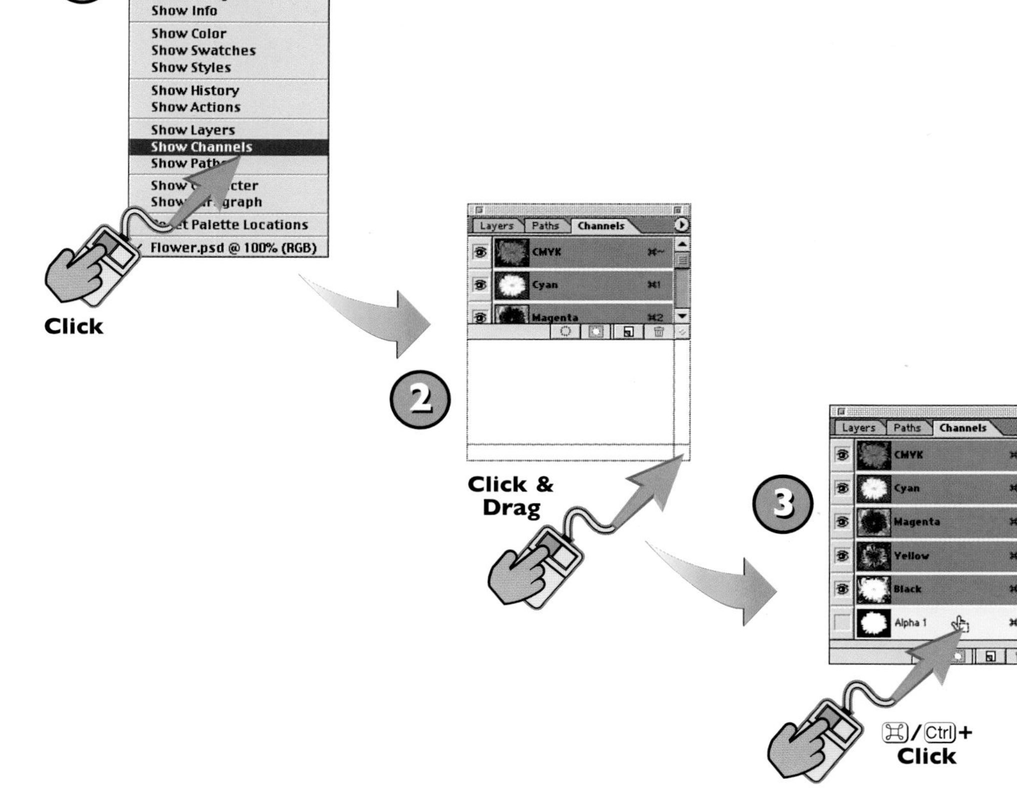

When you save a selection, Photoshop creates a grayscale representation of it and places that image in an *alpha channel*. These channels enable you to save selections for later use. You can re-create the original selection based on the channel.

1. Choose **Window**, **Show Channels** to display the **Channels** palette.
2. Resize the palette if necessary so you can see the name of the channel you want to use.
3. **Cmd+click/Ctrl+click** on the name of the alpha channel to load the selection.

This technique also works with the color channels, not just alpha channels. Depending on the image, this can be a good way to create a selection of the image's background or another part of the image.

An alternative method of loading a selection from a channel is to click the channel's name and click the **Load Channel as Selection** button at the bottom of the **Channels** palette. Then click the first channel in the list to view the entire image again.

Task 25: Creating a Selection from Multiple Channels

Start Here

Photoshop provides several ways to combine the selections stored in alpha channels. You can add and subtract channel selections from each other or from an earlier selection, and you can choose to select the places where two or more channel selections intersect.

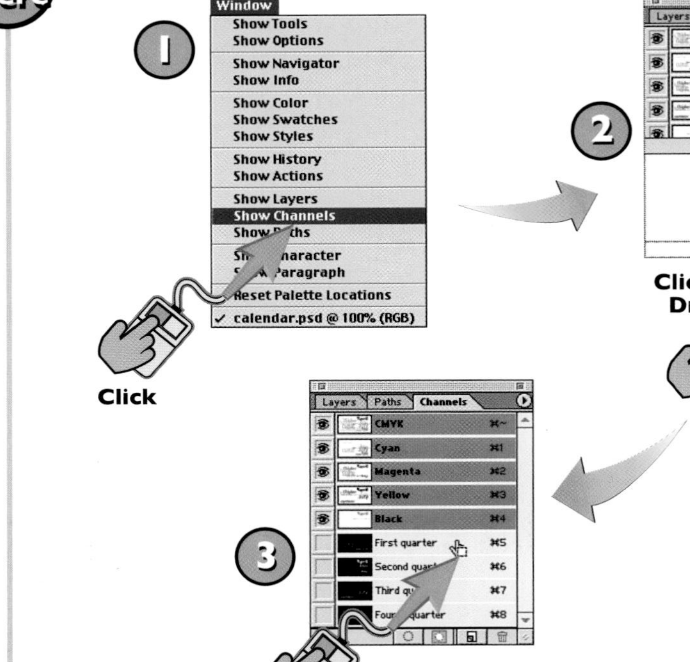

The procedure for adding and subtracting channel selections to and from the current selection is the same as that for adding and subtracting layer transparency selections (see Task 14, "Selecting the Non-Transparent Areas of a Layer").

1. Choose **Window**, **Show Channels** to display the **Channels** palette.
2. Resize the **Channels** palette so you can see all the alpha channels.

3. **Cmd+click/Ctrl+click** on a channel to load its selection.

Next Step

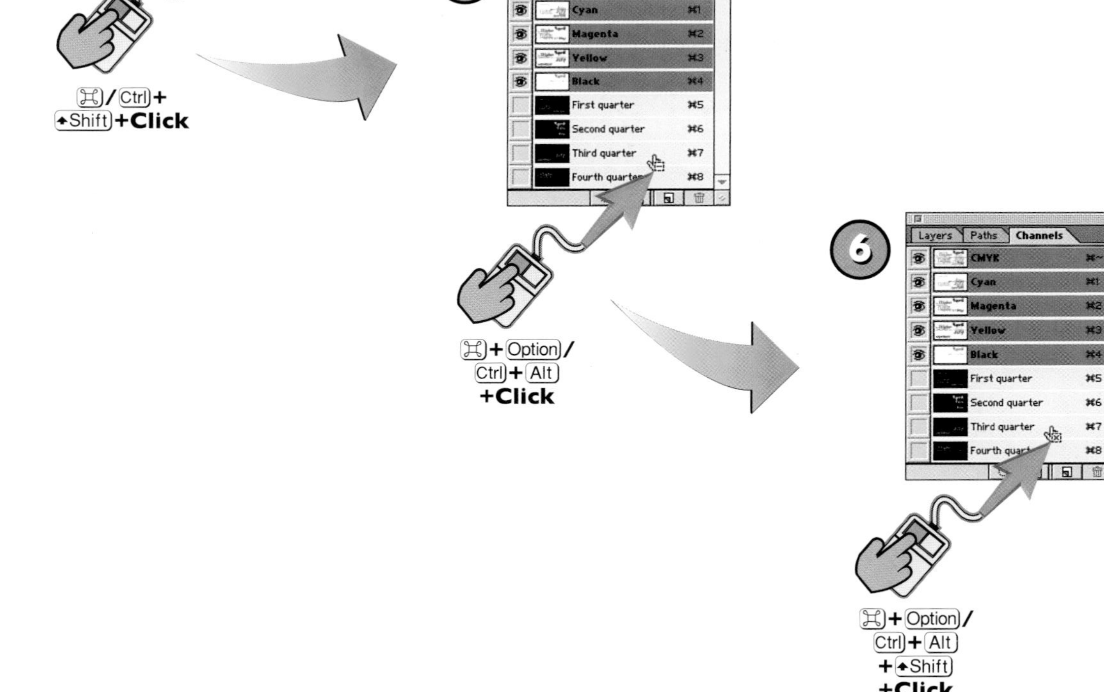

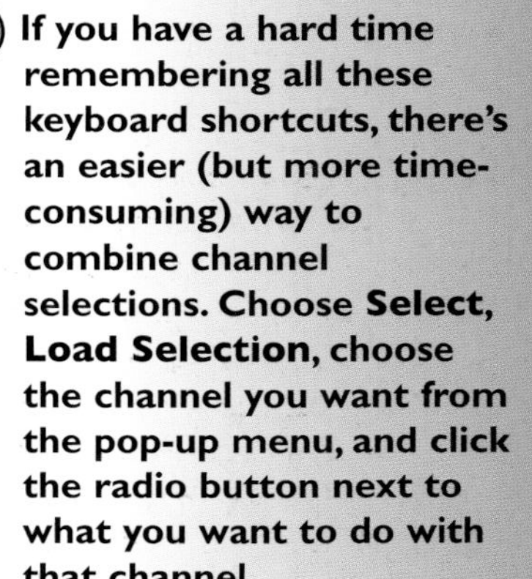

4 **Cmd+Shift+click/Ctrl+Shift+click** on the name of another channel to add that channel to the selection.

5 **Cmd+Option+click/Ctrl+Alt+click** the name of another channel to remove that channel's selection.

6 **Cmd+Option+Shift+click/Ctrl+Alt+Shift+click** a channel name to select the intersection of that channel and the active selection.

If you have a hard time remembering all these keyboard shortcuts, there's an easier (but more time-consuming) way to combine channel selections. Choose Select, Load Selection, choose the channel you want from the pop-up menu, and click the radio button next to what you want to do with that channel.

Task 26: Viewing Multiple Channels at the Same Time

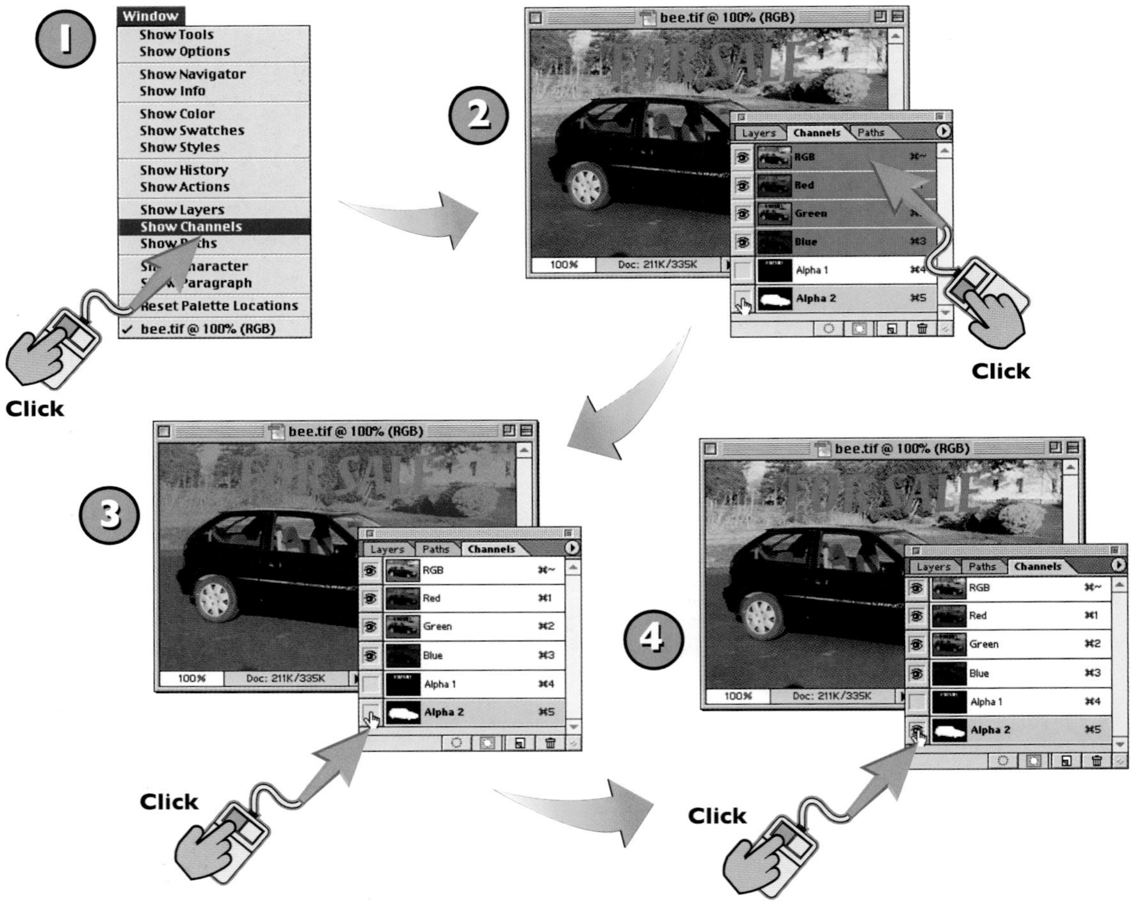

Ordinarily, when you work on an image in Photoshop, you're viewing just the image channels, not the alpha channels. But you can choose to overlay the alpha channels on the image, so you can see how they relate to it.

Start Here

Click

Click

Click

Click

1. Choose **Window**, **Show Channels**.
2. Click the first channel in the list to view the image alone.
3. Click in the blank square next to any alpha channel you want to view as an overlay.
4. Click the eye icons next to each channel to hide the overlaid channels.

✓ If viewing overlaid channels looks familiar, that's because they look like Quick Masks (see Task 6, "Creating a Selection by Painting"). In fact, Photoshop treats a Quick Mask as a temporary channel, and it's listed in the Channels palette while you're working on it.

Task 27: Viewing Channels in Color

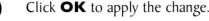

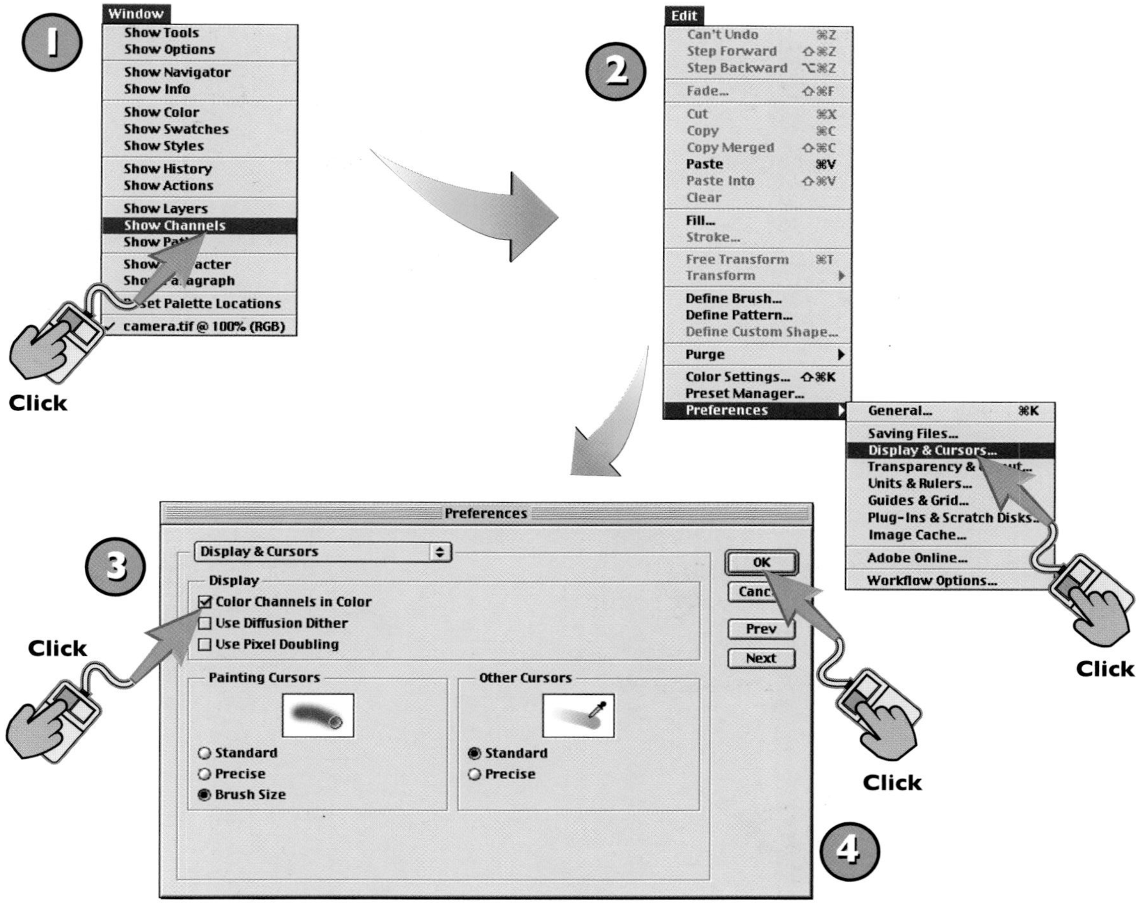

1. Choose **Window**, **Show Channels**.
2. Choose **Edit**, **Preferences**, **Display & Cursors**.
3. Click **Color Channels in Color**.
4. Click **OK** to apply the change.

By default, Photoshop displays the color channels in grayscale, so they look like film-based color separations. It's sometimes easier to understand just what each color channel is contributing to an image, though, if you view them in the colors that they represent.

Viewing color channels in color has no effect whatsoever on what the image itself looks like—it's just an easier way to comprehend the color information contained in each channel.

Because this setting is in the Preferences menu, it's global; that is, it applies to every image you open rather than just the current image.

Task 28: Using the Paths Palette

Another way to save and create selections in Photoshop involves the use of *Bézier paths*, like those used to draw objects in Adobe Illustrator. **Paths** are organized in a Paths palette that's grouped with the Channels and Layers palettes.

✓ When you create a path, it's saved temporarily in the **Paths** palette as **Work Path**. To keep this path, you must double-click its name in the palette and give it another name.

✓ The essential difference between using paths to define a selection and using channels to do the same thing is that, when you use paths, you draw them. When you use channels, you essentially paint them, so the difference is similar to the difference between drawing software such as Illustrator and painting software such as Photoshop.

Start Here

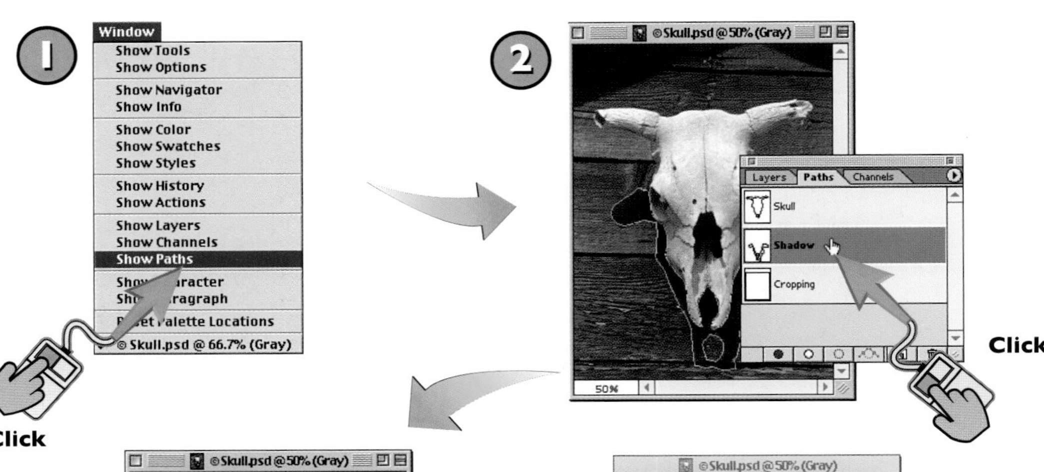

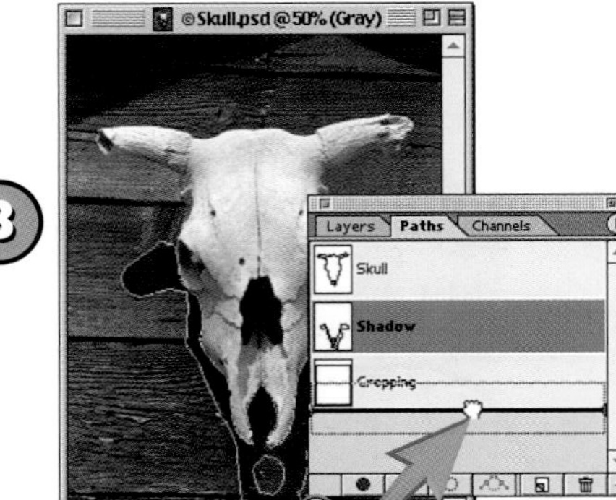

1. Choose **Window**, **Show Paths** to display the **Paths** palette.

2. To view a path, click its name in the list.

3. To move a path in the list, click and drag its name.

4. To change a path's name, double-click it, enter a new name, and click **OK**.

End Task

Task 29: Converting a Selection to a Path

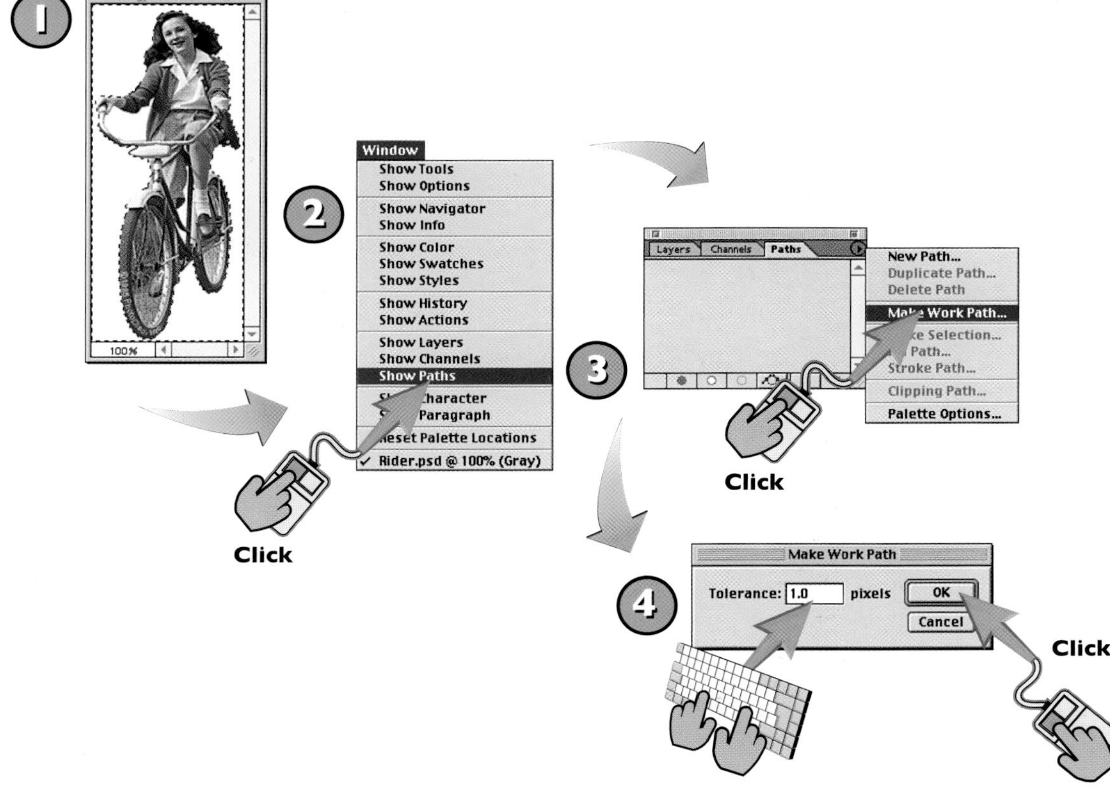

The most comprehensive way to alter a selection is to convert it to a path, edit the path, and then convert back to a selection. This gives you precise control over every angle and curve in the selection's shape. To convert paths to selections, see Task 31, "Converting a Path to a Selection."

1. Make a selection by using any method.
2. Choose **Window**, **Show Paths**.
3. Choose the **Paths** palette menu, and select **Make Work Path**.
4. Enter the desired **Tolerance** in pixels (between .5 and 10) and click **OK**.

✓ The **Tolerance** number in the **Make Work Path** dialog box indicates how precise you want Photoshop to be in creating the path. Lower numbers make more accurate—but more complex—paths.

Task 30: Drawing a Freehand Path

Drawing your own paths is the best way to create clean paths without the extra points you sometimes get by converting selections to paths. Getting the hang of working with the Pen tools Photoshop provides for creating and editing paths can be difficult, but practice makes perfect.

Start Here

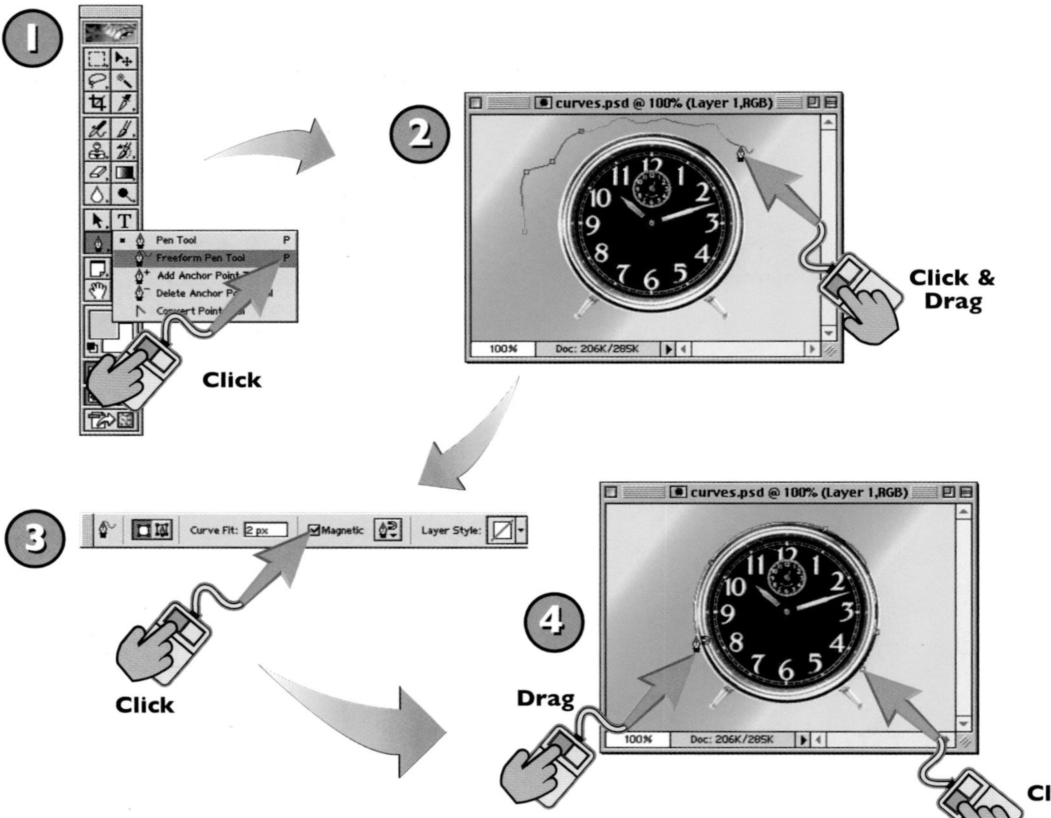

1. To draw a freeform path, click the **Pen** tool in the **Tool** palette and slide the mouse over to choose the **Freeform Pen** tool.
2. Click and drag to draw a path.
3. To draw a path around the edges of an object, select the **Freeform Pen** tool and click the **Magnetic** check box in the **Pen Options** bar.
4. Click where you want the path to start, and drag the cursor along the edge of the object to automatically create the path.

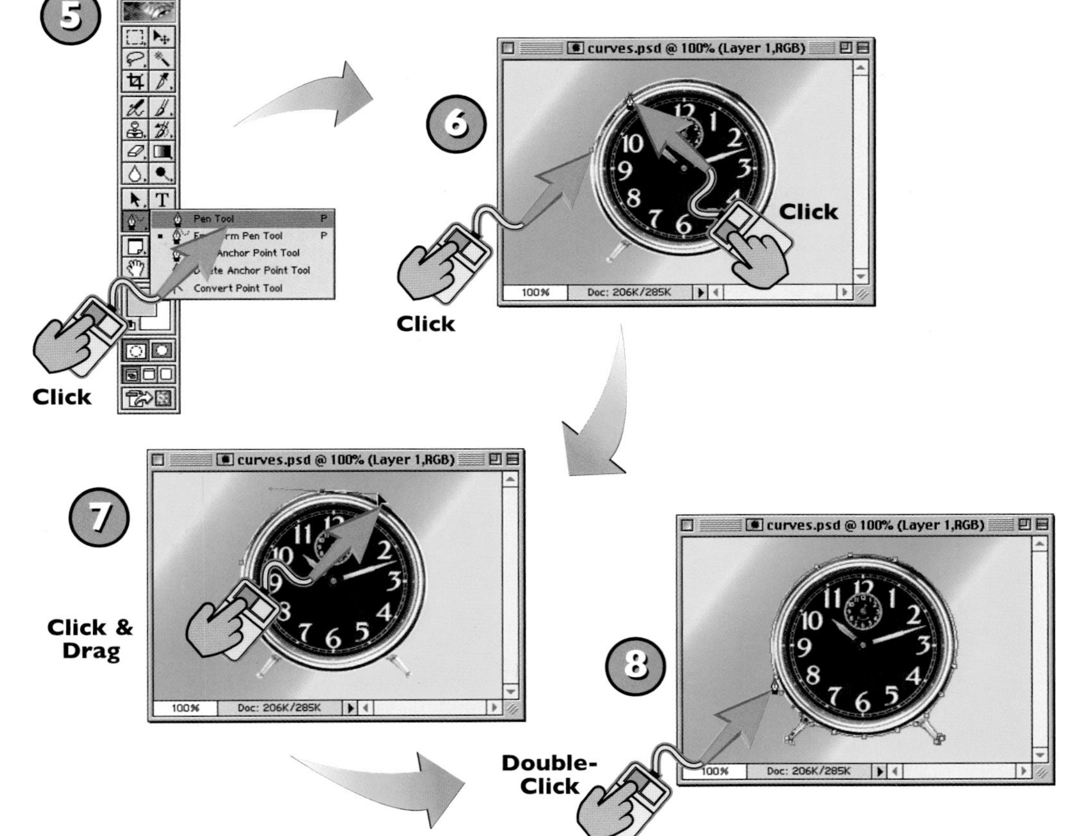

5 To draw a more structured path, choose the main **Pen** tool.

6 Click to start the path, and then click at the next place you want to add a point.

7 Click and drag while creating a point to change the angle of the path.

8 With any of the three tools, double-click to close the path, or click again on the starting point.

You can copy and paste paths just as you would in a drawing program, and a path can consist of more than one path element—in other words, you can create two or more closed paths within one Photoshop path.

When you click and drag while creating a new point, you're moving that point's curve handles to change the angle of the path. *Bézier paths* are defined mathematically by the positions of the points and each point's curve handles.

When you save images in EPS format, you can use a path to define the area of the image that should print; any pixels outside that *clipping path* don't show up when the image is imported into another application. Click a path name and choose the Paths palette menu, Clipping Path to choose a clipping path.

Task 31: Converting a Path to a Selection

Just as you can create a path from a selection, you can convert a path back into a selection. The selection will follow the path exactly, but the path might not have followed the original selection exactly because of a high tolerance setting.

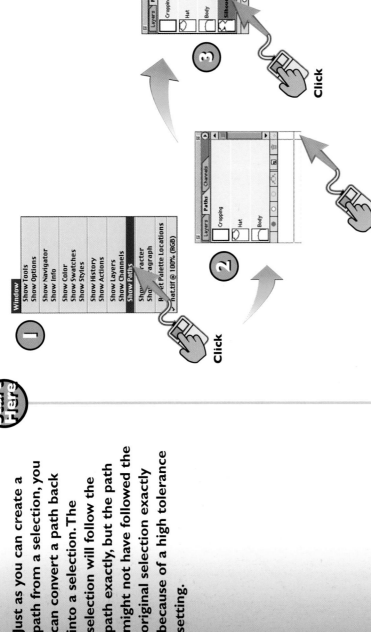

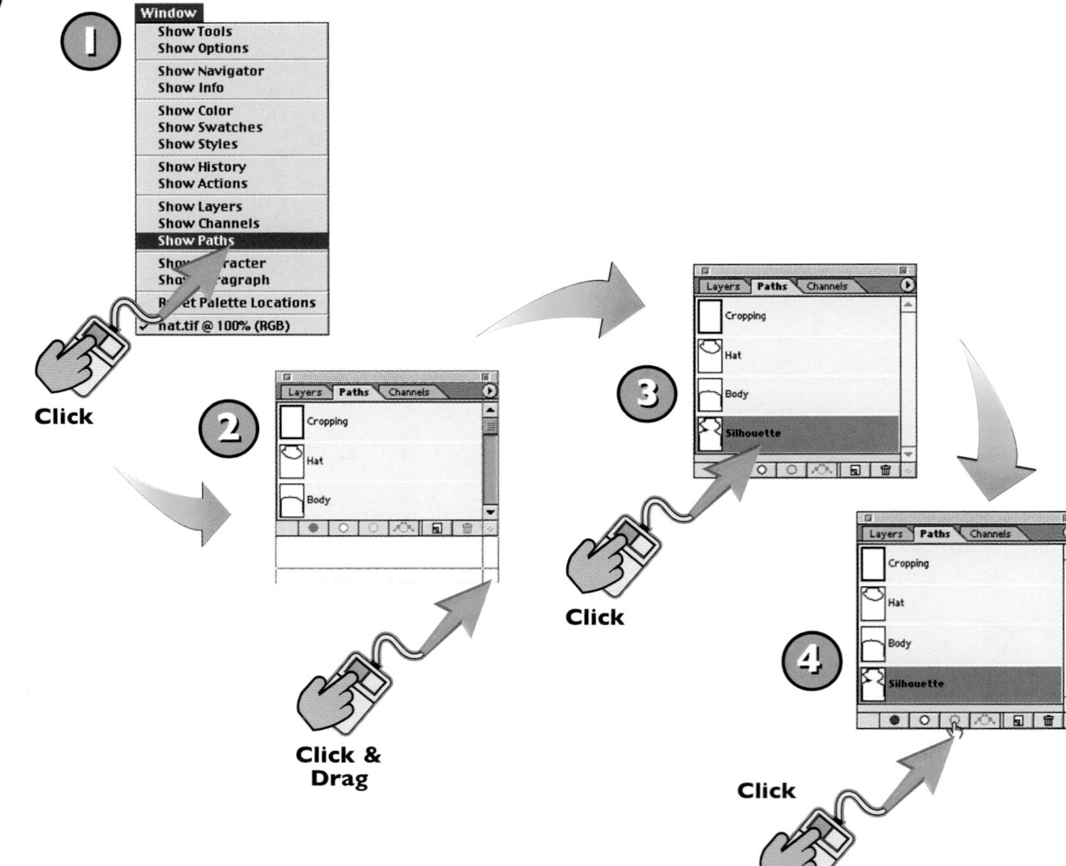

1. Choose **Window**, **Show Paths** to display the **Paths** palette.
2. Resize the palette if necessary so you can see the name of the path you want to use.
3. Click the name of the path.

4. Click the **Convert Path to Selection** button at the bottom of the palette.

✓ **Most paths created by using the Make Work Path command must be edited by adjusting the Bézier points before they're completely accurate.**

Task 32: Saving Paths in Adobe Illustrator Format

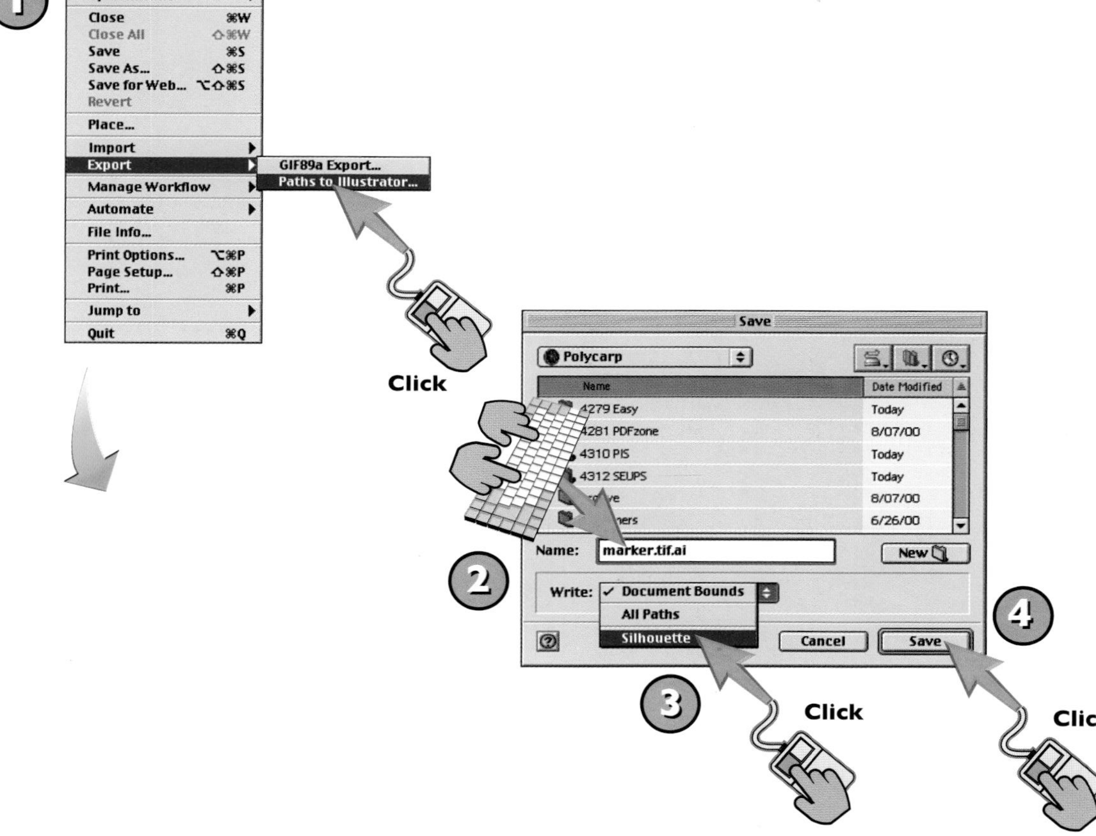

If you're used to working in Illustrator, you might want to export Photoshop paths to Illustrator format as the basis for a separate image in Illustrator. You can choose to export one path, all paths, or a rectangular path the same size as the document (Document Bounds).

1. Choose **File**, **Export**, **Paths to Illustrator**.
2. Enter a name for the file in the **Name** field.
3. Choose the path you want to export in the **Write** menu.
4. Click **Save** to save the Illustrator file.

✓ This procedure makes a new file; if you don't need a separate file, you can also copy and paste between Photoshop and Illustrator.

PART 4

Working with Colors and Patterns

Mixing colors in Photoshop is, for most people, "the fun part." With Photoshop's support for several different color modes, you can create and use any color you can think of. It's important to know ahead of time how an image will be used so you can mix colors in the right mode (CMYK for print projects, RGB for onscreen ones); some RGB colors can't be reproduced in print, and the same thing goes for some CMYK colors onscreen.

Part 4 shows you how to mix colors, use colors already present in an image, use spot colors that will print on a single printing plate, and swap one color in an image for another. In addition, this part explains how to create and use repeating patterns that will tile seamlessly for use as monitor wallpaper or Web page backgrounds.

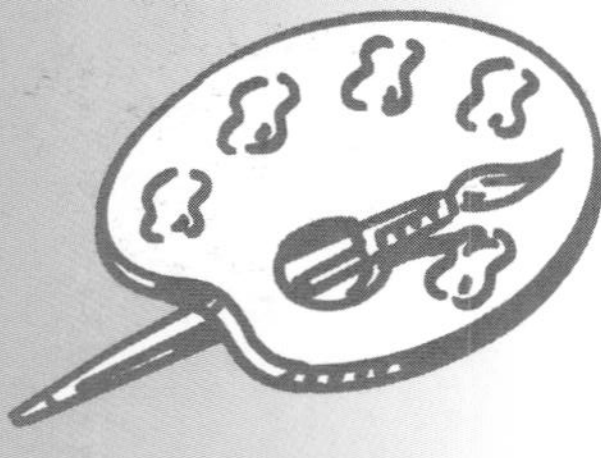

Tasks

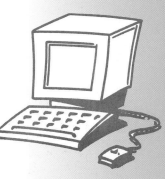

Task 1: Changing the Foreground and Background Colors

At all times, Photoshop has two active colors: the foreground color and the background color. You paint or draw with the foreground color, and if you erase pixels on the background layer, the space is filled with the background color.

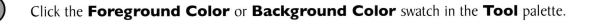

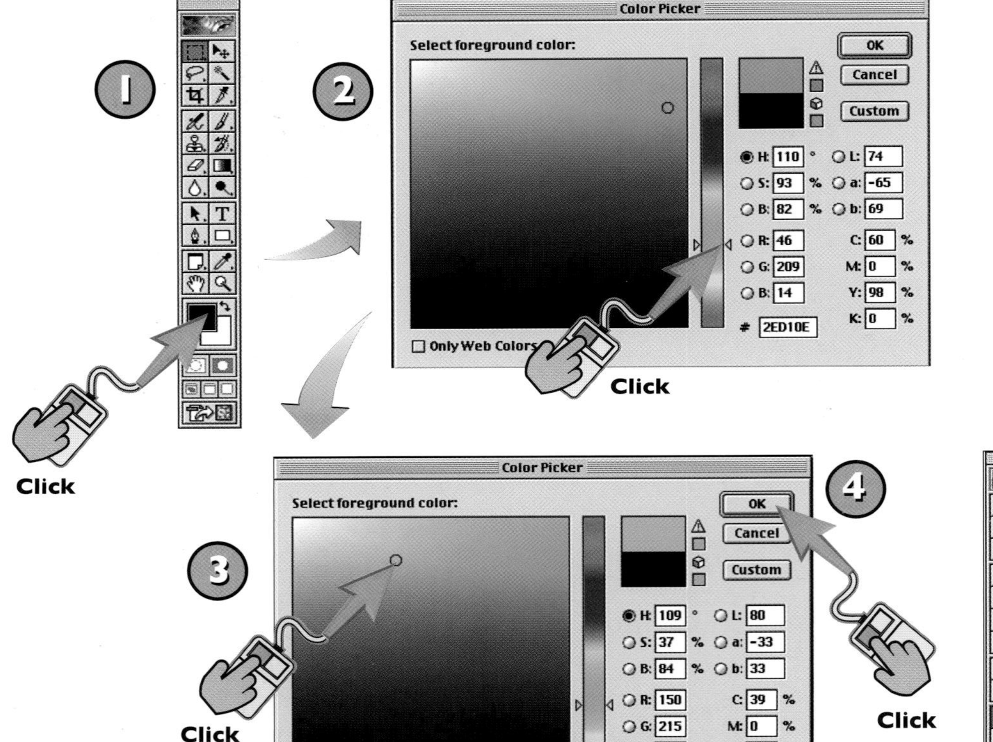

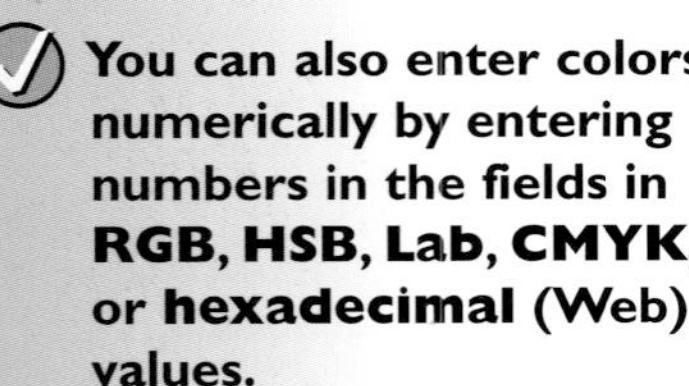

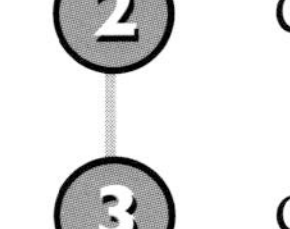

1. Click the **Foreground Color** or **Background Color** swatch in the **Tool** palette.
2. Click in the **color slider** to choose a general range of hues.
3. Click in the **color field** to choose lighter or darker versions of that hue.
4. Click **OK**.

✓ You can also enter colors numerically by entering numbers in the fields in **RGB**, **HSB**, **Lab**, **CMYK**, or **hexadecimal** (Web) values.

✓ You can switch quickly to black foreground, white background by pressing **D** for default colors. Press **X** to swap the foreground and background colors.

Task 2: Choosing a Color from an Image

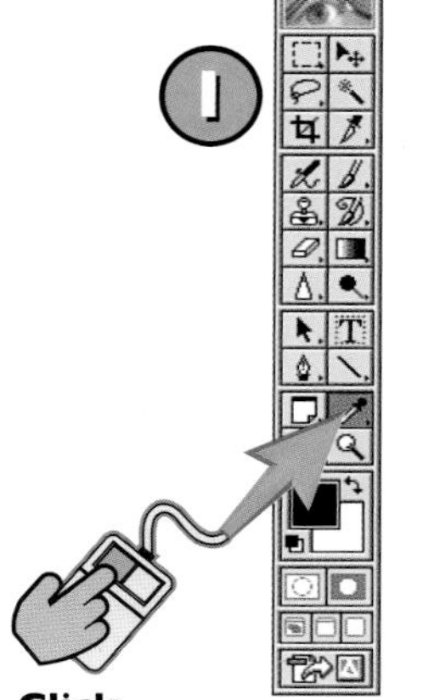

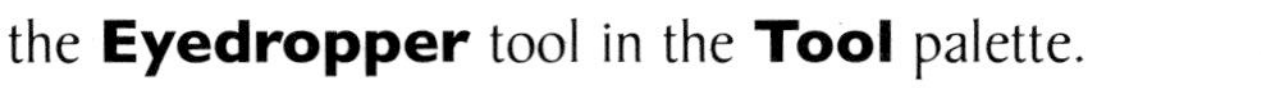

1. Click the **Eyedropper** tool in the **Tool** palette.
2. Click in the image to choose a foreground color.

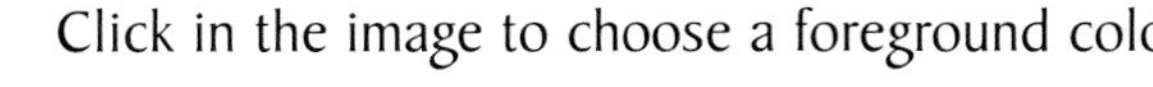

3. **Option+click/Alt+click** in the image to choose a background color.

The easiest way to mix a new color is not to mix it! You can choose a color from any pixel in an image by using the Eyedropper tool. This is a good technique for when you're "repairing" a scanned image, and it's a great way to choose harmonious colors for type.

✓ Sometimes you don't get the color you're expecting when you use the **Eyedropper** tool because many colors in an image are made up of different-colored pixels grouped together. Try clicking a few pixels over from the first place you clicked.

✓ You can access the Eyedropper any time you're using a painting tool, such as the Airbrush, Paintbrush, or Pencil, by **Option+clicking/ Alt+clicking** to choose a foreground color.

Task 3: Choosing a Spot Color

Photoshop enables you to use and print spot colors as well as process colors. Each spot color is made up of a single ink when printed, rather than a mix of process ink colors. To use spot colors, you must have printed swatchbooks showing how the colors look on paper.

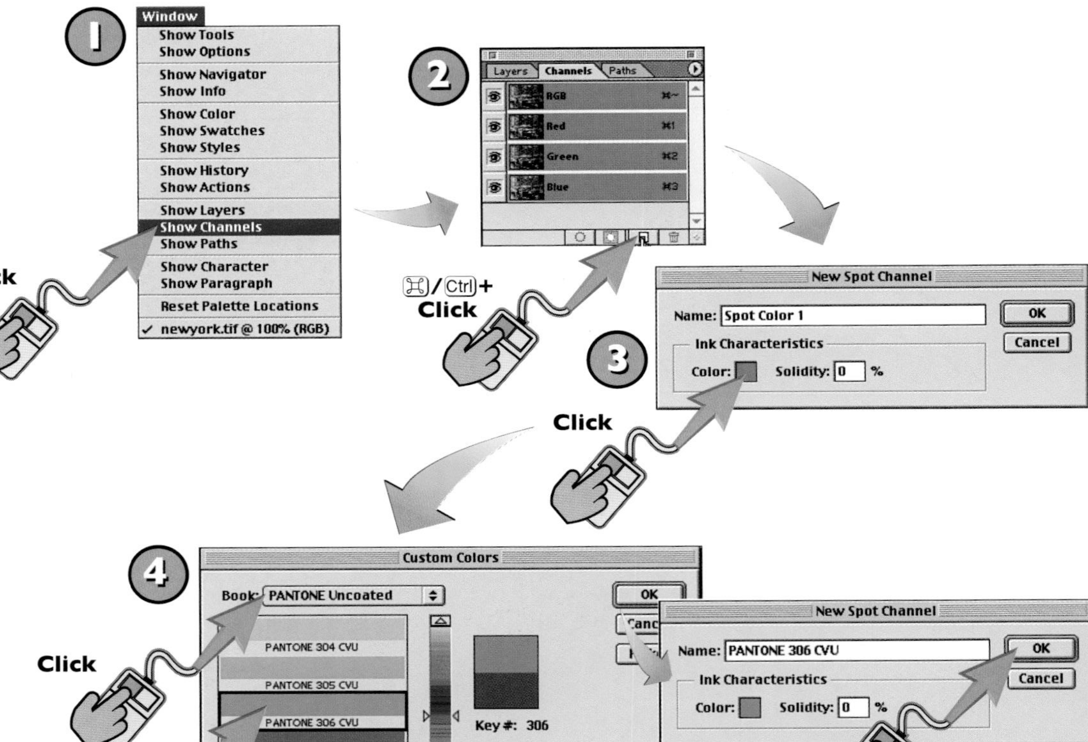

✓ You can convert an existing alpha channel to a spot channel by double-clicking its name in the **Channels** palette and clicking the **Spot Color** radio button. Then choose a spot color as in step 4.

✓ Images that contain spot color channels must be saved in DCS 2.0 format to retain the spot color data for color separations. See Part 2, "Opening and Saving Files," for more information on saving DCS files.

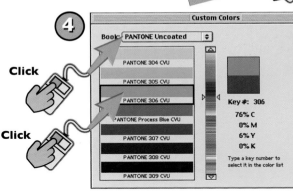

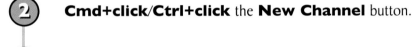

1. Choose **Window**, **Show Channels** to display the **Channels** palette.
2. **Cmd+click/Ctrl+click** the **New Channel** button.
3. Click the **Color** swatch to display the **Color Picker**, and then click **Custom**.
4. Choose a swatchbook. Click and drag in the **swatch list** to choose a color. Click **OK** in the Color Picker, and click **OK** in the **New Spot Channel** dialog box.

End Task

Task 4: Using the Color Palette

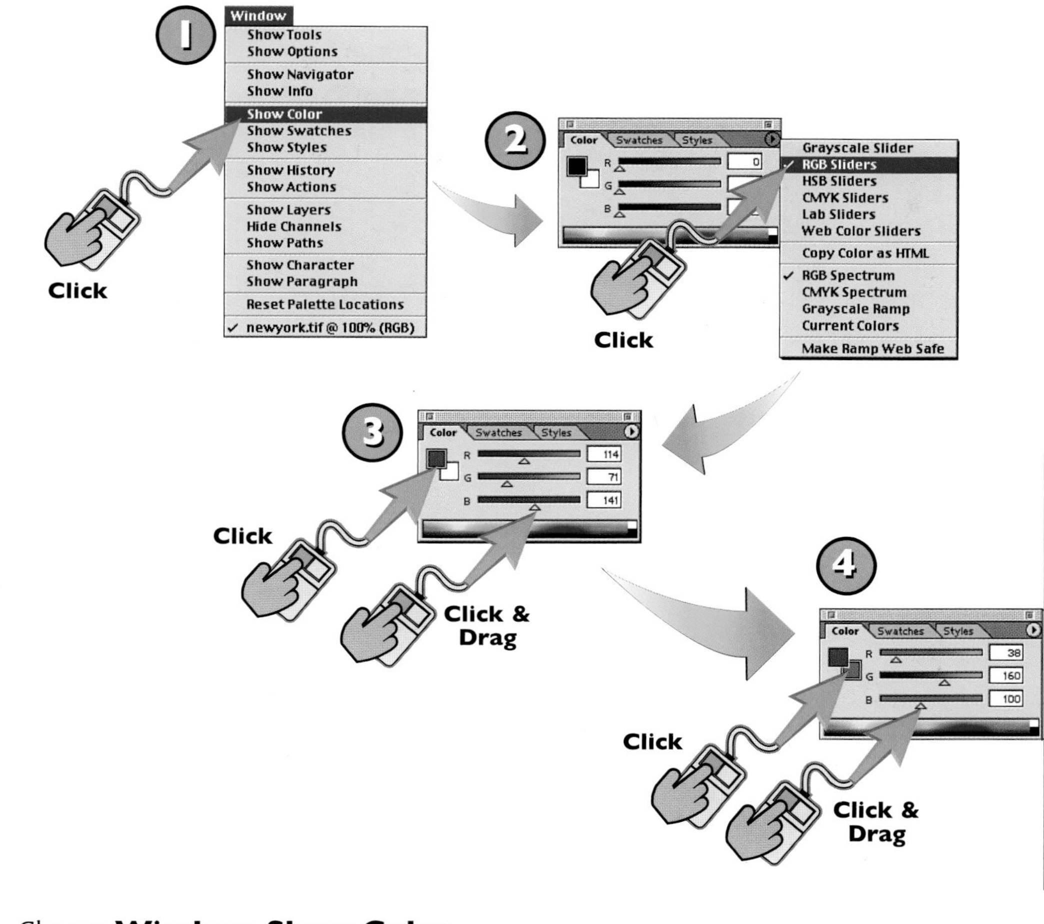

If you change colors frequently, it's faster to use the Color palette. It offers you access to the same color models that the Color Picker dialog box uses, and it can be left on the screen all the time for quick access.

1. Choose **Window**, **Show Color**.
2. Choose a color mode (such as **RGB Sliders**) from the **Color** palette menu.
3. If it's not highlighted, click the **foreground swatch** and mix a foreground color.
4. Click the **background swatch** and mix a background color.

If the file you're working in is in Grayscale mode, you won't be able to choose a color slider set from the **Color** palette menu in step 2. Choose **Image**, **Mode** and pick a color mode, and then go back to the **Color** palette menu to choose the sliders you want to use to mix colors.

The "highlighted" color swatch in the **Color** palette is the one with a box around it.

With each color model, you have the option of dragging the color sliders or entering numbers; if you prefer to enter numbers, press **Tab** to move to the next field, and press **Enter** when you're finished.

Task 5: Previewing CMYK Output Onscreen

Printed output uses cyan, magenta, yellow, and black inks on paper—a very different way of reproducing color from the red, green, and blue light that computer monitors use. When you're designing for printed output, one way to see how colors will look on paper is to use the CMYK preview option.

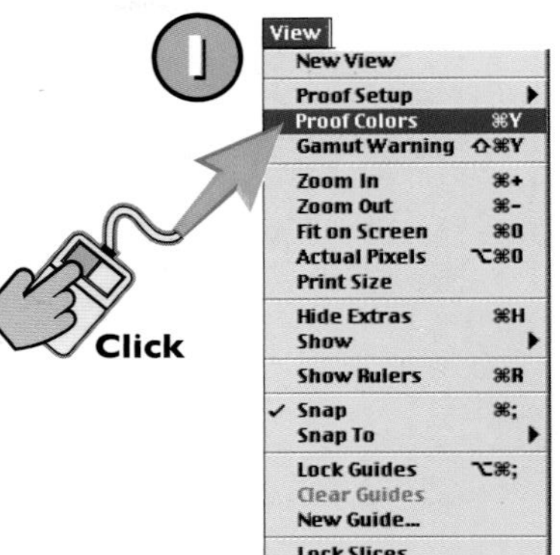

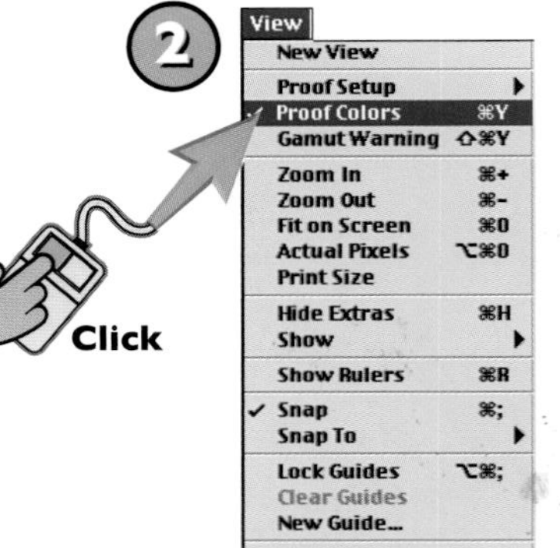

1. Choose **View**, **Proof Colors** or press **Cmd+Y/Ctrl+Y** to turn on the CMYK preview.
2. Choose **View**, **Proof Colors** again to turn off the CMYK preview.

CMYK preview mode gives you an idea of which colors will be affected by conversion to CMYK, but it doesn't necessarily show exactly how they'll look when printed.

Task 6: Replacing a Color with Another Color

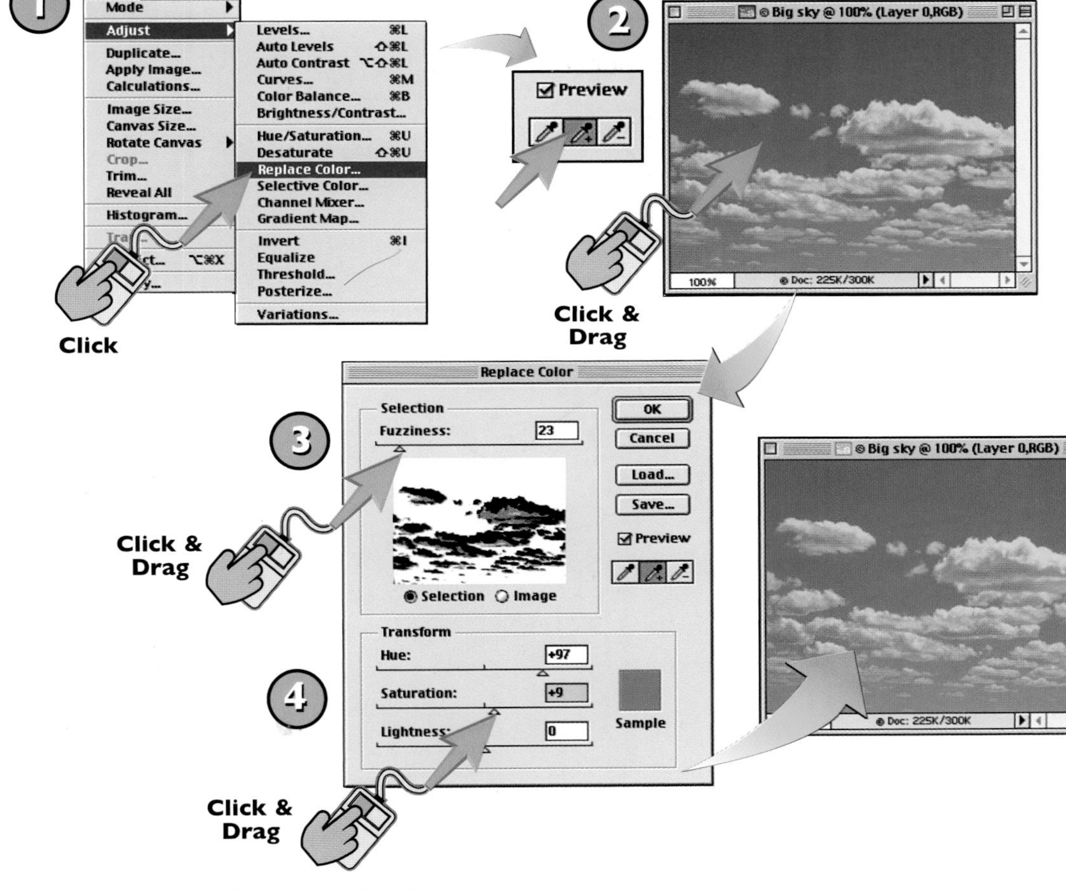

Here's a way to exercise some of that famous Photoshop magic. With the Replace Color command, you can turn a green sweater red or make a yellow flower blue. You use a thumbnail preview of the image to see which colors you're changing.

1. Choose **Image**, **Adjust**, **Replace Color**.
2. With the **plus eyedropper tool**, click and drag in the image to select the colors you want to change.
3. Drag the **Fuzziness** slider to adjust which colors are selected.
4. Drag the **Hue**, **Saturation**, and **Lightness** sliders to change the color, and then click **OK**.

It's okay if light areas of the image are partially selected (light gray) in the **Replace Color** dialog box's preview; that means that reflections of the color you're changing will change as well.

The **Replace Color** dialog box works much the same way as the **Color Range** dialog box does (see Part 3, Task 9, "Selecting Multiple Areas of the Same Color"). The key to good results in both techniques is lots of practice with the **Fuzziness** slider and the eyedropper tools.

Task 7: Creating a Seamless Pattern

Repeating patterns can be used for Web page backgrounds, computer desktop patterns, and many other design projects. This technique produces a pattern with no edges—the viewer can't tell where the pattern tile begins and ends. You must start with a squarish image that you want to turn into a repeating pattern.

It's a good idea to save each file you used to create a pattern. You can always redefine the pattern by opening the file and performing step 7.

For information on the Airbrush tool, see Part 5, Task 4, "Painting Soft-Edged Shapes." For information on the Rubber Stamp tool, see Part 5, Task 7, "Cloning Areas." For information on the Smudge tool, see Part 6, Task 8, "Smudging an Area."

Start Here

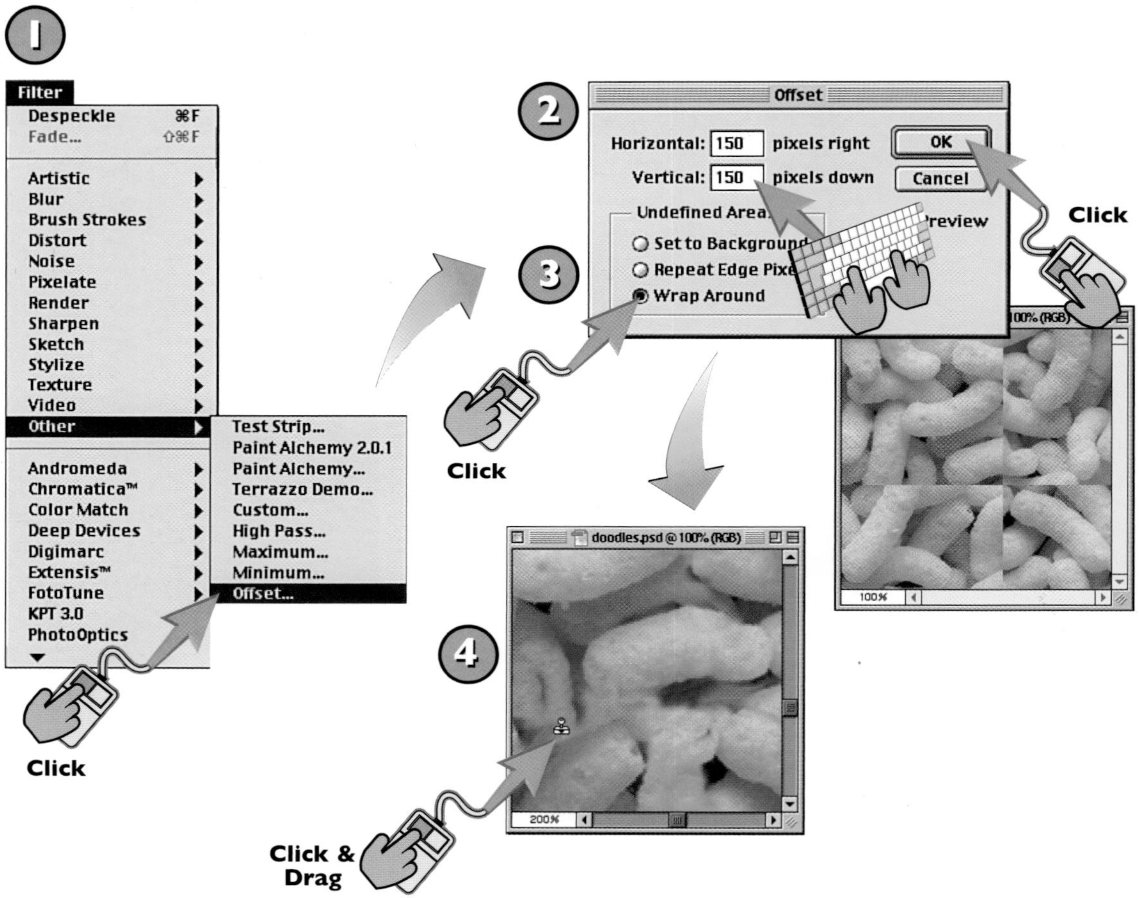

1. Choose **Filter**, **Other**, **Offset**.
2. Enter **Horizontal** and **Vertical** values that are about half the size of the image.
3. Click the **Wrap Around** radio button, and then click **OK**.
4. Edit out the hard edge lines with the **Smudge**, **Rubber Stamp**, and **Airbrush** tools.

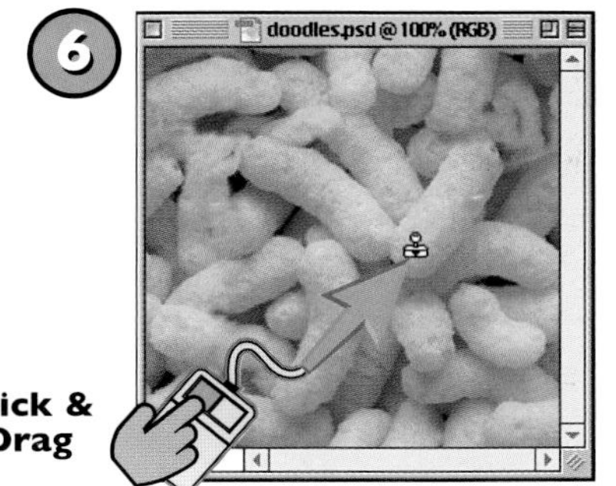

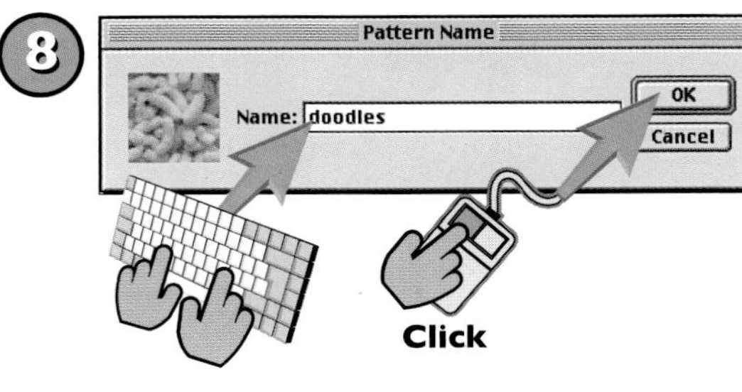
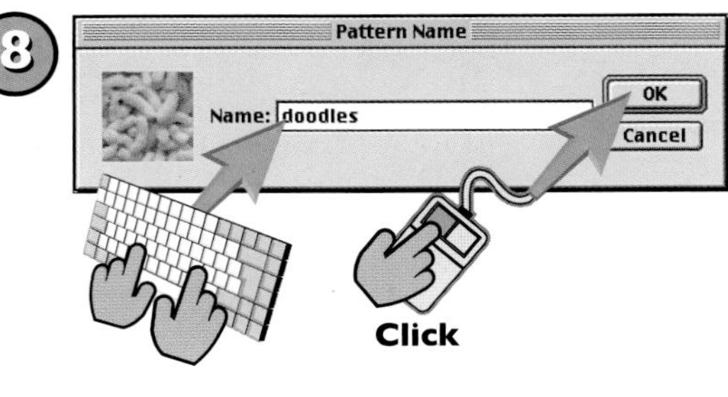

5 Choose **Select**, **All** or press **Cmd+A/Ctrl+A**. Press **Cmd+F/Ctrl+F** to reapply the **Offset** filter.

6 Clean up any remaining hard edges at the center of the image.

7 Select all (**Cmd+A/Ctrl+A**) and choose **Edit**, **Define Pattern**.

8 Give the pattern a name, and click **OK**.

When editing out edge seams, use a light touch and a medium-sized, soft-edged brush. Many short strokes usually look much more realistic than one long one.

You can define a pattern only when part of the image is selected, and the selection must be rectangular.

Task 8: Filling an Area with a Pattern

Filling an area with a pattern is much simpler than creating the pattern in the first place. The Fill command offers Pattern as an option, along with Foreground Color, History, Background Color, Black, 50% Gray, and White. Before filling with a pattern, you must define a pattern, as outlined in Task 7, "Creating a Seamless Pattern."

Start Here

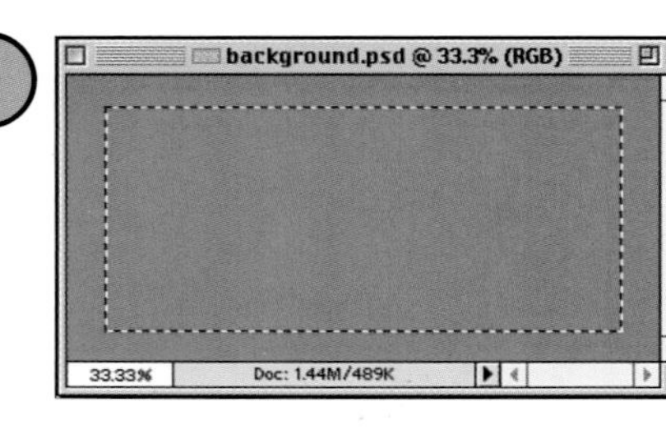

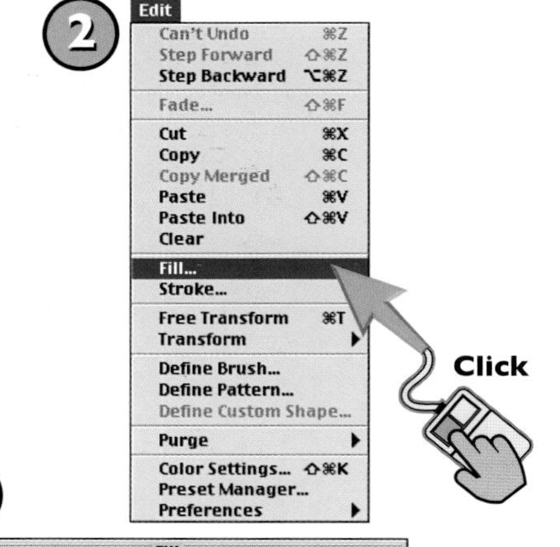

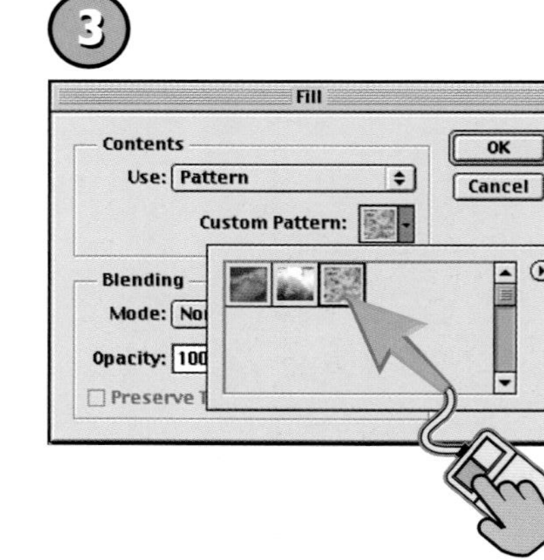

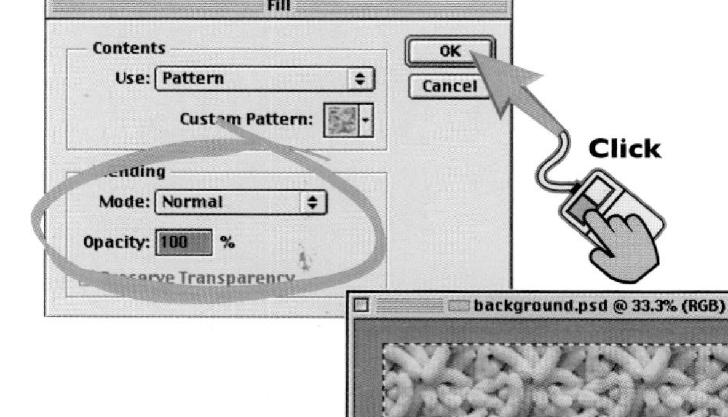

✓ The **Fill** dialog box's **Mode** menu refers to blending modes, different ways of blending new colors with the image's existing colors. Most of the time you will use **Normal**, but experimenting with the other modes will yield interesting results.

1. Select the area you want to fill.

2. Choose **Edit**, **Fill** or press **Shift+Delete/Shift+Backspace**.

3. Choose **Pattern** from the **Use** pop-up menu, and choose a pattern from the **Custom Pattern** menu.

4. Enter an **Opacity** percentage, choose a **Mode**, and click **OK**.

Task 9: Converting a Color Image to Grayscale

A lot of the color images in the world end up getting printed in grayscale rather than in color. If you're going to do this, you'll get better results by converting the image in Photoshop so you can make any needed adjustments to the image.

1

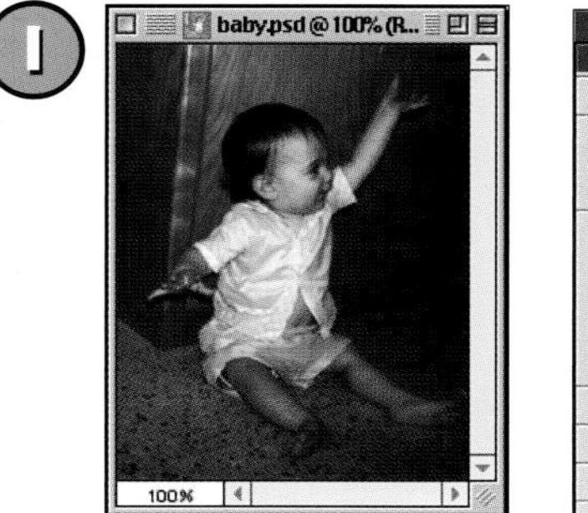

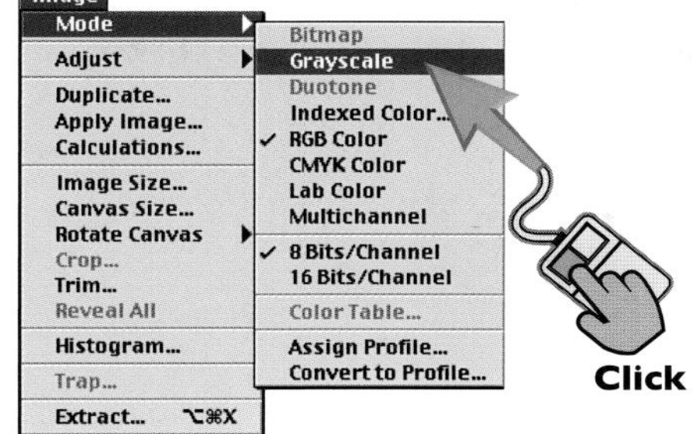

2

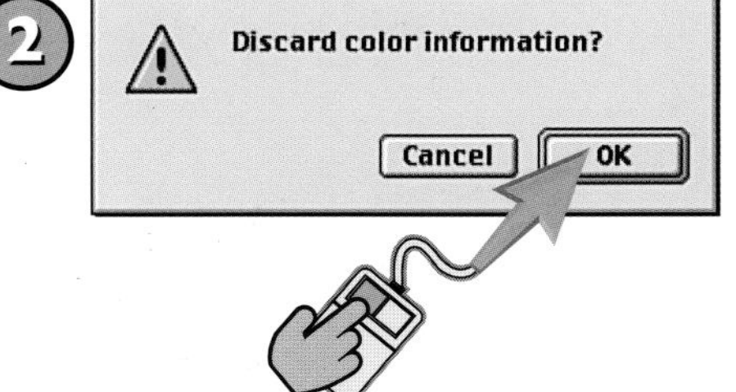

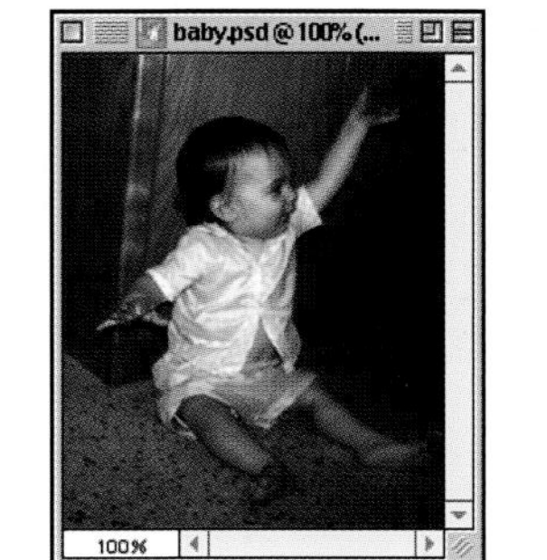

1. Choose **Image**, **Mode**, **Grayscale**.
2. Click **OK** in the alert box.

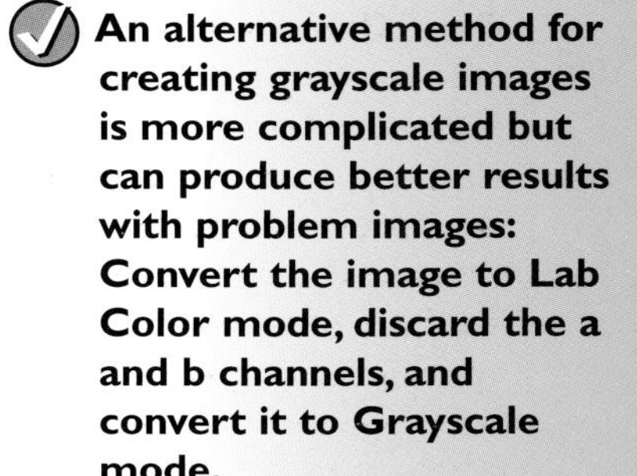

See Part 7, "Adjusting Colors and Tones," for ways to adjust an image for best reproduction.

An alternative method for creating grayscale images is more complicated but can produce better results with problem images: Convert the image to Lab Color mode, discard the a and b channels, and convert it to Grayscale mode.

Task 10: Creating a Duotone Image

Duotones use an extra ink color to add to an image's richness. They range from images that appear gray but with increased warmth and detail, to images with pronounced color. Variations on duotones include tritones and quadtones, using three or four inks.

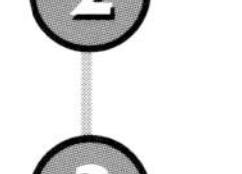

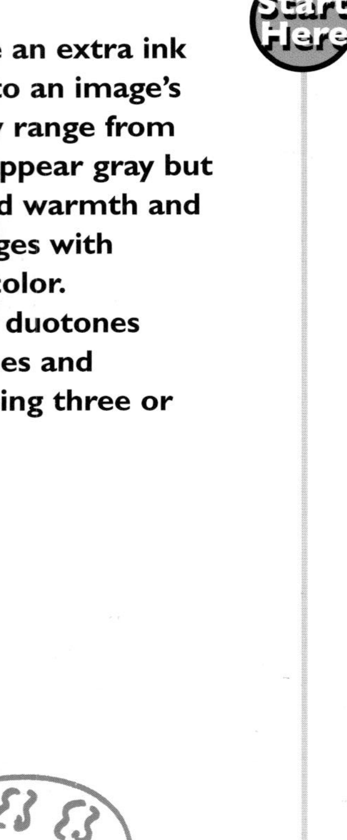

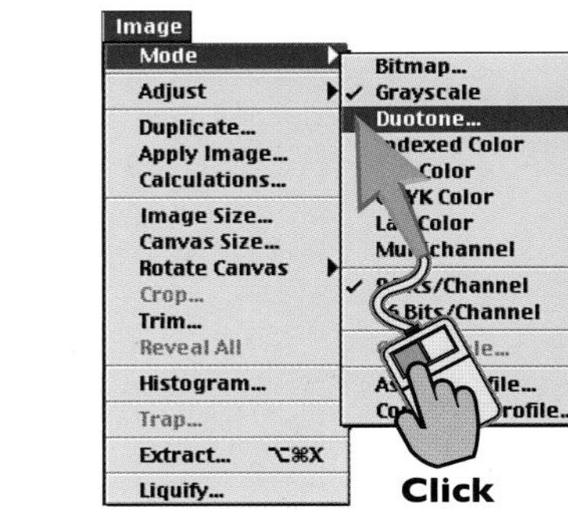

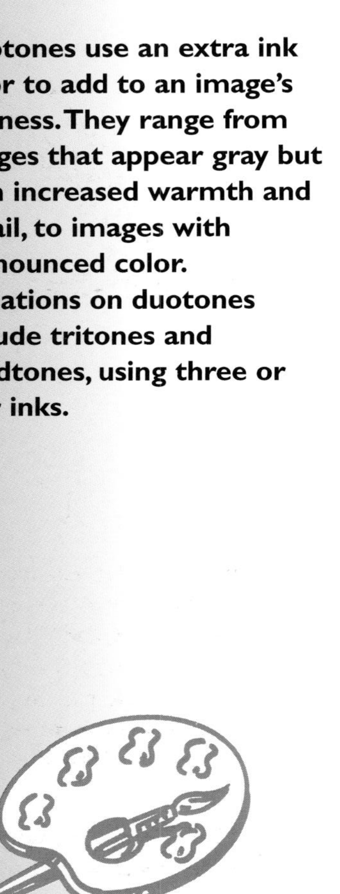

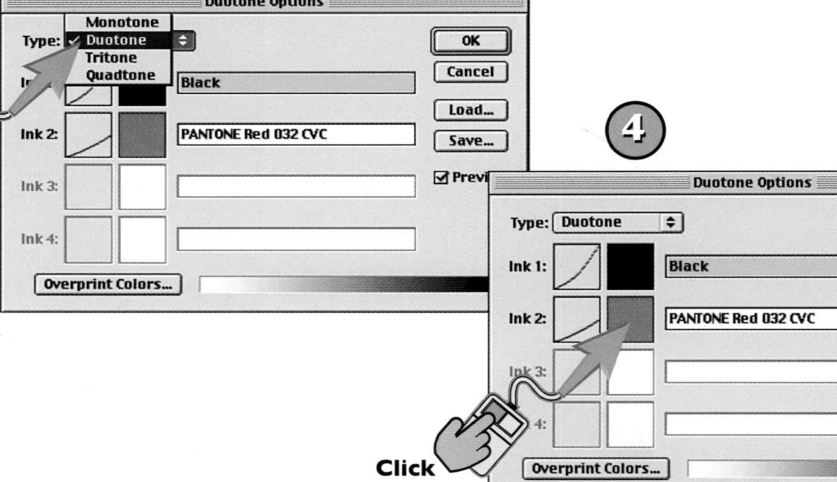

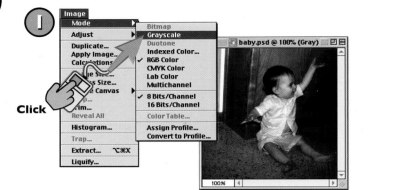

1. If the image is in color, choose **Image**, **Mode**, **Grayscale** and click **OK**.
2. Choose **Image**, **Mode**, **Duotone**.
3. Choose a **Type** from the pop-up menu.
4. For each ink color, click the **color swatch** to choose a color.

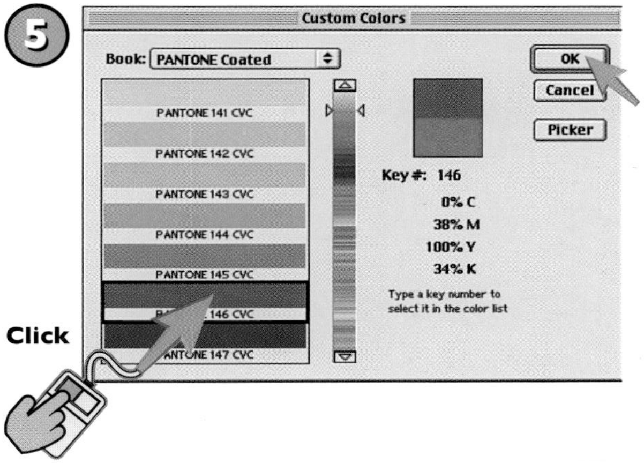

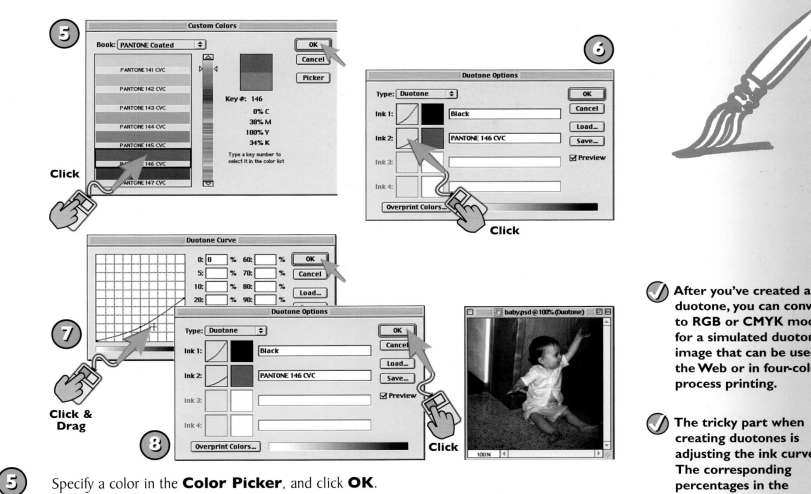

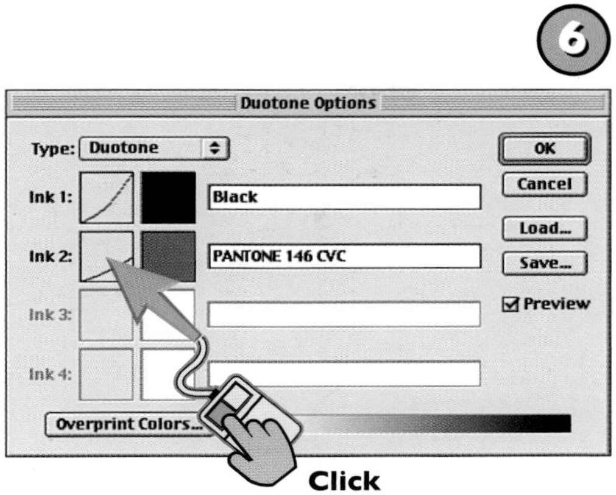

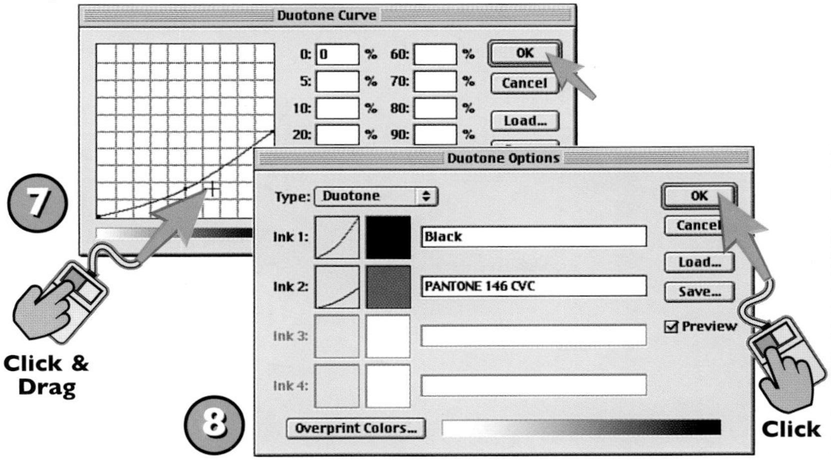

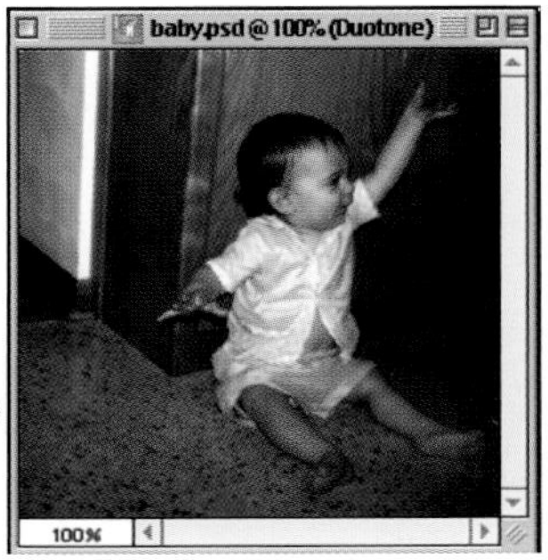

5 Specify a color in the **Color Picker**, and click **OK**.

6 For each ink color, click the **curve swatch** to adjust the ink coverage.

7 Drag the **curve**, watching the image window, to adjust the amount of color used for each brightness level, and then click **OK**.

8 Click **OK** in the **Duotone Options** dialog box to apply the duotone.

After you've created a duotone, you can convert it to RGB or CMYK mode for a simulated duotone image that can be used on the Web or in four-color process printing.

The tricky part when creating duotones is adjusting the ink curves. The corresponding percentages in the midtones should add up to about 50%; for example, at the 50% point, you might want 30% coverage of the spot color and 20% coverage of black.

PART 5

Painting Images

Photoshop's painting tools include paintbrushes, airbrushes, and pencils, along with special tools such as an eraser, a rubber stamp, and a line tool. With this tool set, you can create any image you can imagine, as well as retouch and add to existing images. Each painting tool has individual settings that you can change, such as the pressure with which the tool is applied, and each offers a selection of brush sizes and shapes from which to choose.

As with any operation in Photoshop, you can paint throughout an image or within a selection. Part 5 shows you how to use each painting tool, how to select and modify a brush, how to clone areas of an image with the Rubber Stamp tool, how to create gradients, and how to erase part of an image.

Tasks

Task 1: Filling a Selection with a Color

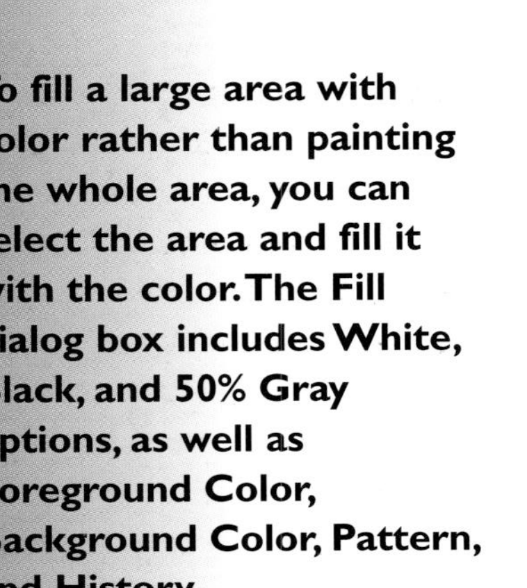

To fill a large area with color rather than painting the whole area, you can select the area and fill it with the color. The Fill dialog box includes White, Black, and 50% Gray options, as well as Foreground Color, Background Color, Pattern, and History.

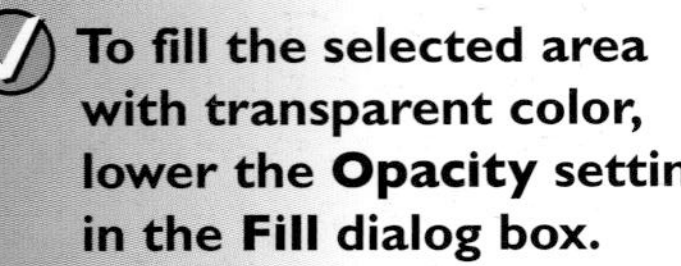

To fill the selected area with transparent color, lower the Opacity setting in the Fill dialog box.

To fill an area with a pattern, see Part 4, Task 8, "Filling an Area with a Pattern."

Start Here

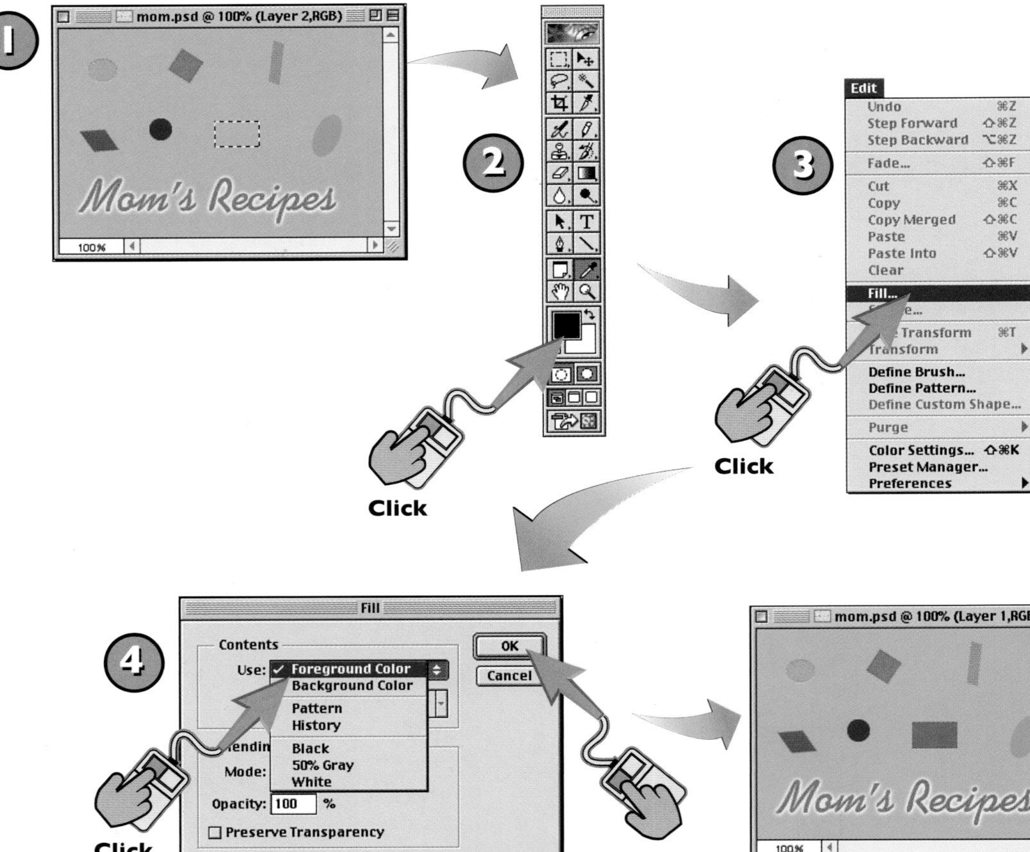

1. Make a selection by using any method.
2. Change the foreground color to the color you want to use.
3. Choose **Edit**, **Fill** or press **Shift+Delete/Shift+Backspace**.
4. Choose **Foreground Color** from the **Use** pop-up menu, and click **OK**.

End Task

Task 2: Choosing a Brush

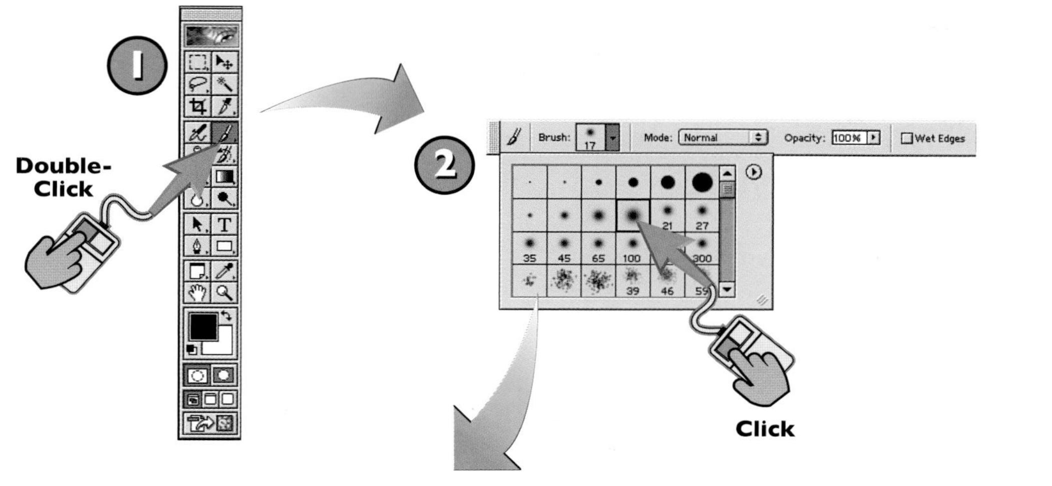

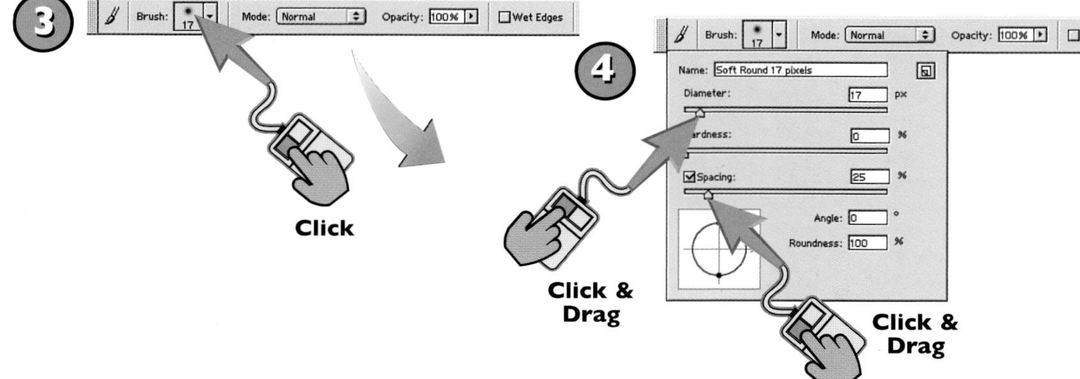

Each painting tool enables you to use different "brushes" that can vary in width and hardness. Soft-edged brushes make a fuzzy stroke; hard-edged brushes make a crisp stroke.

1 Double-click on a painting tool in the **Tool** palette to switch to that tool and display its **Options** bar.

2 Choose a brush from the **Brush** menu in the **Options** bar.

3 Click on the brush preview in the **Options** bar to display its attributes.

4 Adjust the brush's **Diameter**, **Hardness**, and **Spacing**, and then press **Enter**.

You can create a new brush by changing a brush's settings and then clicking the **New Brush** button at the upper-right corner of the Brush attributes panel. The **Diameter** setting determines the size, **Hardness** makes the brush soft or hard, and **Spacing** determines whether the brush "skips" as you paint with it. The **Angle** and **Roundness** fields let you make angled, flat brushes for calligraphic effects.

Task 3: Using Different Brush Cursors

By default, Photoshop's painting cursors are small pictures of the type of tool you're using. Two other types of cursor—Precise and Brush Size—enable you to paint with greater precision.

Start Here

Edit
Undo ⌘Z
Step Forward ⇧⌘Z
Step Backward ⌥⌘Z
Fade... ⇧⌘F
Cut ⌘X
Copy ⌘C
Copy Merged ⇧⌘C
Paste ⌘V
Paste Into ⇧⌘V
Clear
Fill...
Stroke...
Free Transform ⌘T
Transform
Define Brush...
Define Pattern...
Define Custom Shape...
Purge
Color Settings... ⇧⌘K
Preset Manager...
Preferences

General... ⌘K
Saving Files...
Display & Cursors...
Transparency & Gamut...
Units & Rulers...
Guides & Grid...
Plug-Ins & Scratch Disks...
Image Cache...
Adobe Online...
Workflow Options...

Click

Preferences
Display & Cursors
Display
☑ Color Channels in Color
☐ Use Diffusion Dither
☐ Use Pixel Doubling
Painting Cursors: Standard / Precise / Brush Size
Other Cursors: Standard / Precise
OK / Cancel / Prev / Next

Click

Click

Click

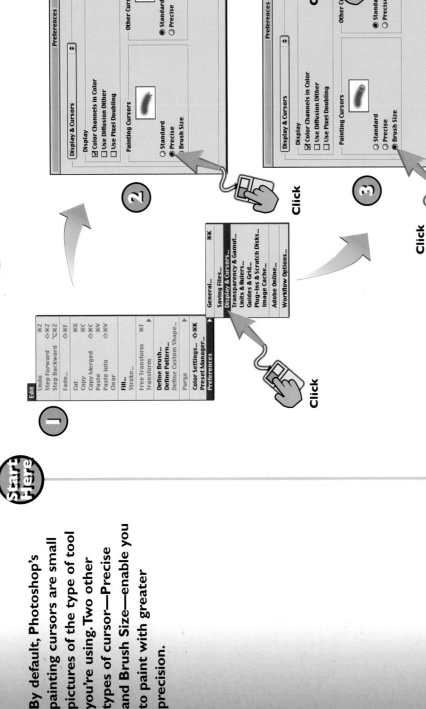

1. Choose **Edit**, **Preferences**, **Display & Cursors**.
2. In the **Painting Cursors** area, click **Precise** to use a crosshairs cursor.
3. Click **Brush Size** to use a circular cursor the same size as the brush in use.
4. Click **OK** to make the change.

You can use Precise cursors at any time by pressing Caps Lock. Turn Caps Lock off to return to Standard cursors.

The Other Cursors section enables you to specify Precise cursors for tools other than the painting tools.

Task 4: Painting Soft-Edged Shapes

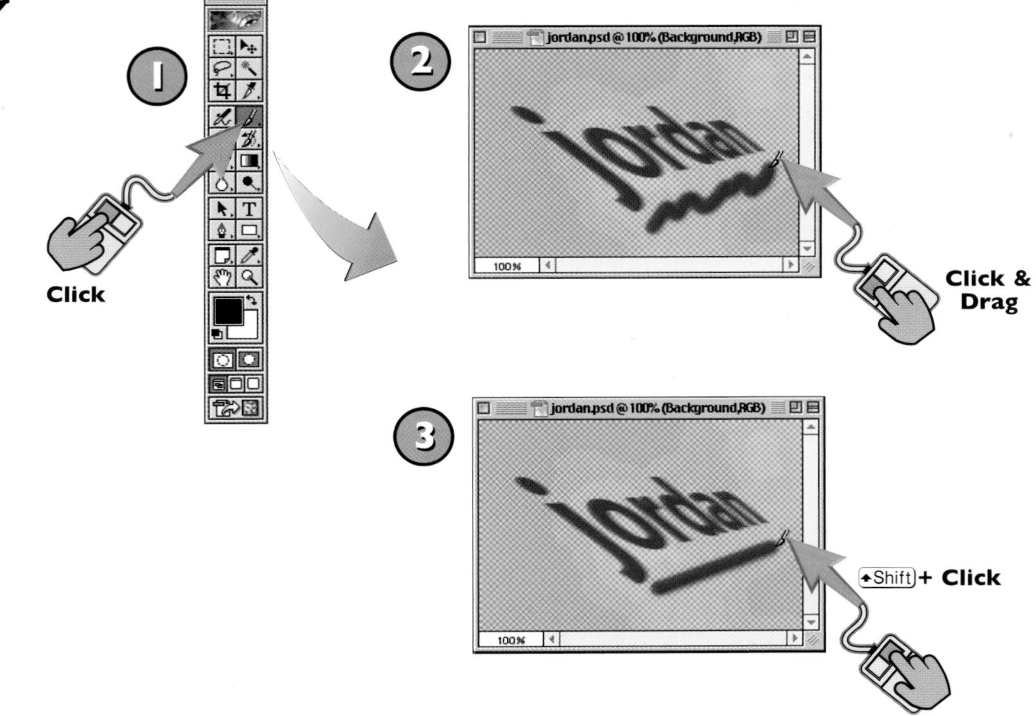

Two of Photoshop's painting tools create soft-edged lines: the Airbrush and the Paintbrush, which work like their real-life counterparts. Airbrush and Paintbrush strokes are *anti-aliased*, meaning the edge pixels are semi-transparent so they blend with the surrounding colors.

1. Click the **Paintbrush** or the **Airbrush** in the **Tool** palette.
2. Click and drag in the image to draw a line.
3. Click and **Shift+click** to draw a straight line between two points.

To change the size of the lines drawn by the Paintbrush and Airbrush, choose a different brush from the Brushes palette (see Task 2, "Choosing a Brush").

Task 5: Painting Hard-Edged Shapes

The Pencil tool is used for drawing clean, sharp lines in Photoshop. It's often most useful for filling in a pixel here and a pixel there in scanned images. Pencil strokes are not *anti-aliased*, so they don't blend in with the surrounding colors.

Start Here

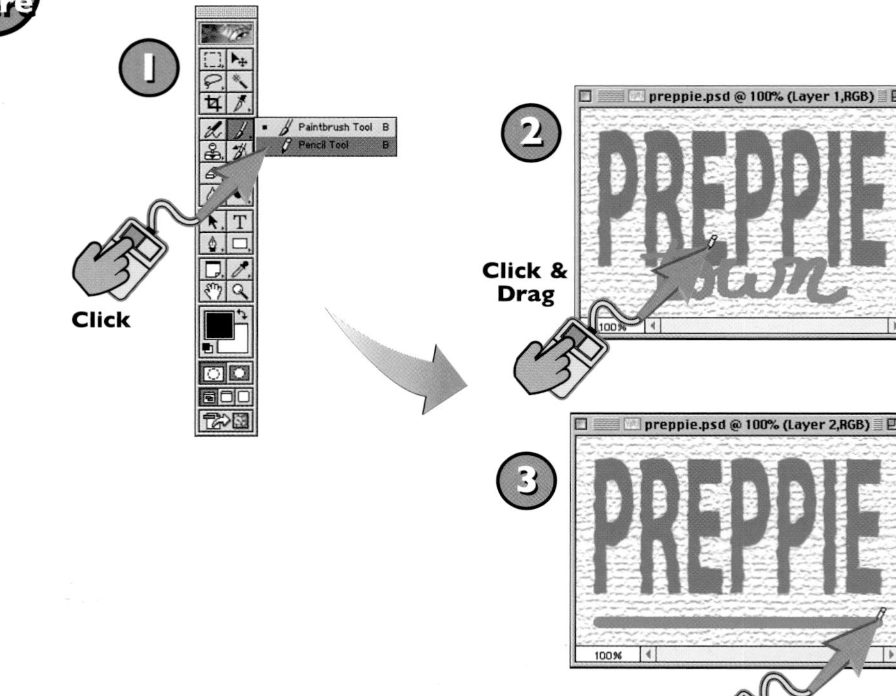

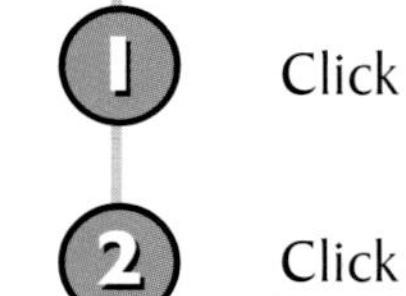

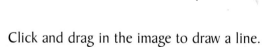

1. Click the **Pencil** in the **Tool** palette.
2. Click and drag in the image to draw a line.
3. Click and **Shift+click** to draw a straight line between two points.

To change the size of the lines drawn by the Pencil, choose a different brush from the Brushes palette (see Task 2).

You can restrict Pencil lines to 90- and 45-degree angles by holding down the Shift key as you draw.

End Task

Task 6: Drawing Lines

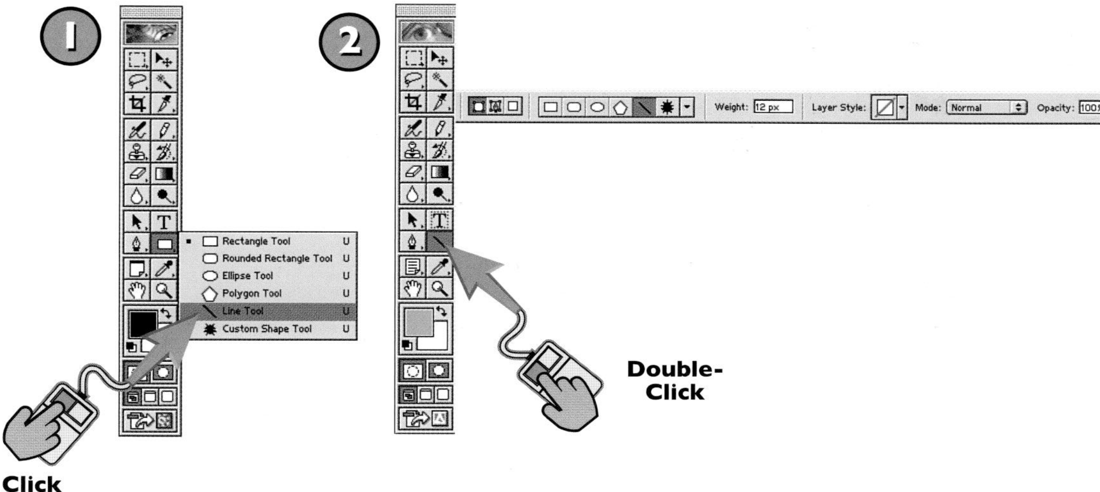

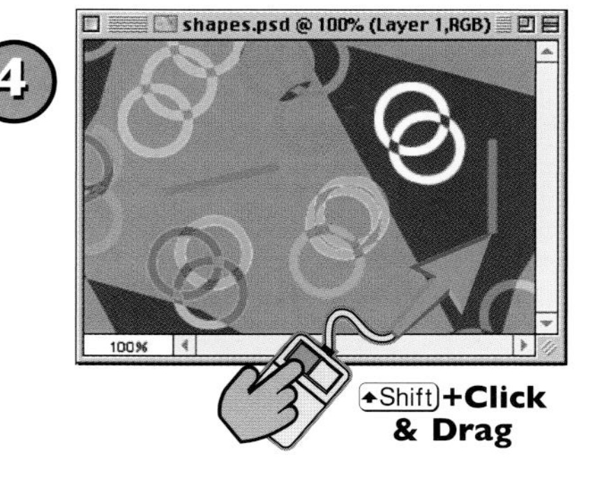

Photoshop's Line tool draws straight lines between two points. The lines can be anti-aliased or not, depending on your preference, and you can also restrict them to 45-degree increments if you choose.

1. Click the **Rectangle** tool and slide the cursor over to select the **Line** tool.
2. Double-click the **Line** tool to display the **Line Options** bar.
3. Enter a **Weight** for the line, and then click and drag to draw a line. Press **Enter** when you're finished.
4. Hold down **Shift** as you draw to restrict lines to 90- and 45-degree angles.

Before you can apply filters or adjust the colors of lines, you'll need to turn them from filled paths into pixels; do this by choosing Layer, Rasterize, Shape.

Task 7: Cloning Areas

To clone areas of an image, you use the Rubber Stamp tool. It enables you to reproduce elements by specifying an origin point and painting in a "clone" of the area around that point elsewhere in the image.

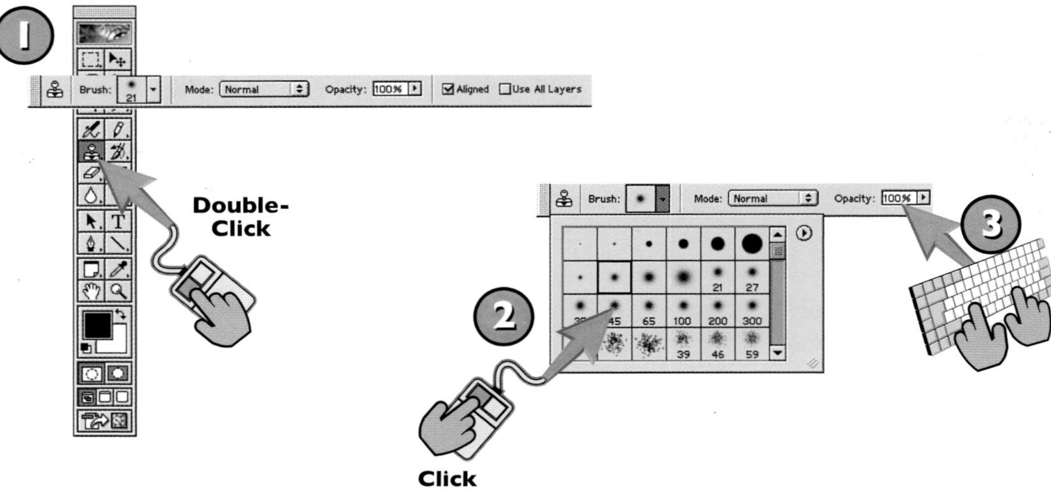

To clone from just the active layer, click off Use All Layers in the Rubber Stamp Options bar.

1. Double-click the **Rubber Stamp** tool in the **Tool** palette to select it and display the **Rubber Stamp Options** bar.
2. Choose a small or medium-sized brush with soft edges from the **Brush** menu in the **Rubber Stamp Options** bar.
3. Enter an **Opacity** percentage for the cloned pixels.

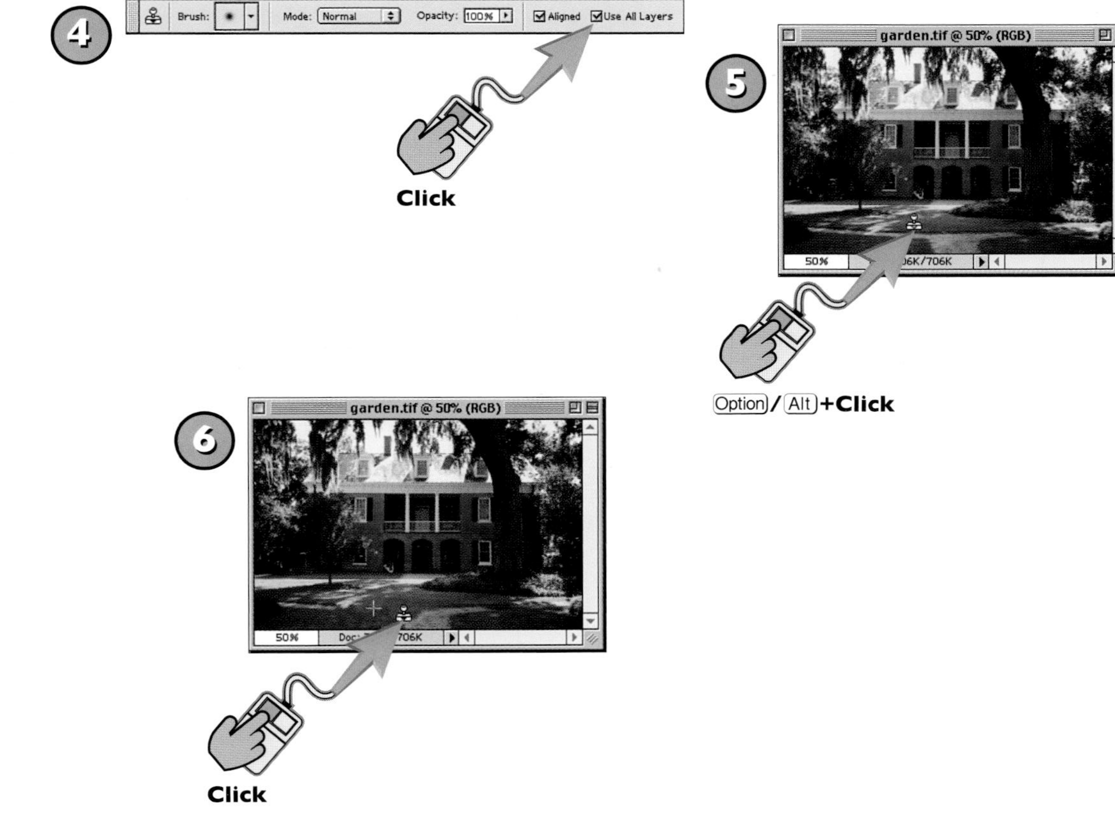

4. Click **Use All Layers** to clone from all the visible layers.
5. **Option+click/Alt+click** in the image to choose the point from which to copy.
6. Click anywhere else in the image to paint in a cloned image.

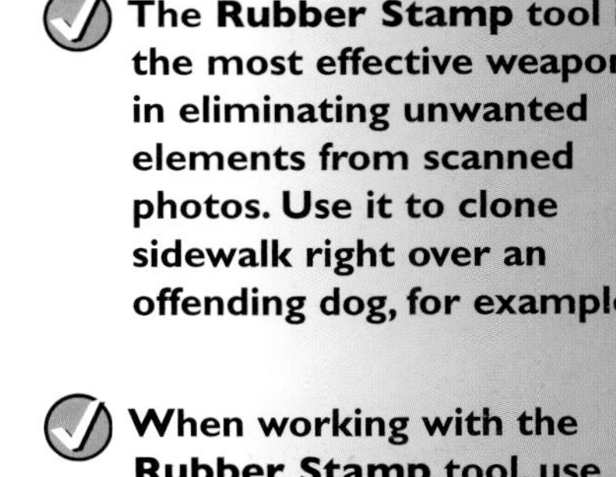

The **Rubber Stamp** tool is the most effective weapon in eliminating unwanted elements from scanned photos. Use it to clone sidewalk right over an offending dog, for example.

When working with the **Rubber Stamp** tool, use several small strokes instead of one large one for more realistic results.

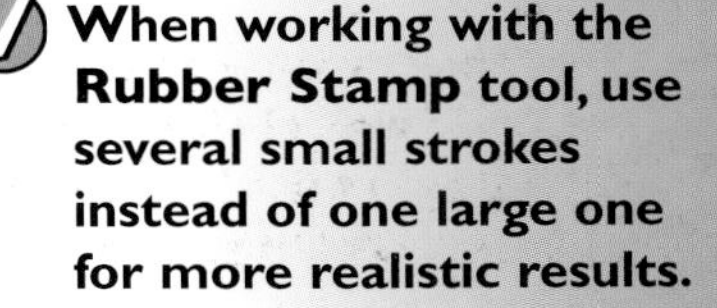

Gradients, in which one color fades into another, are among the most impressive, yet easiest, effects Photoshop offers. The Gradient tools enable you to choose from dozens of prebuilt gradients and five shape variations.

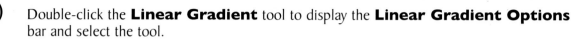

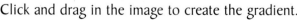

By default, Photoshop uses the foreground color for the beginning of the gradient, where you first click and hold, and the background color for the end, where you let go.

To use a different gradient shape, click a gradient button on the **Options** bar to choose the **Radial**, **Angle**, **Reflected**, or **Diamond Gradient** tool. They all work the same, just with different shapes.

Task 8: Applying a Gradient to an Image

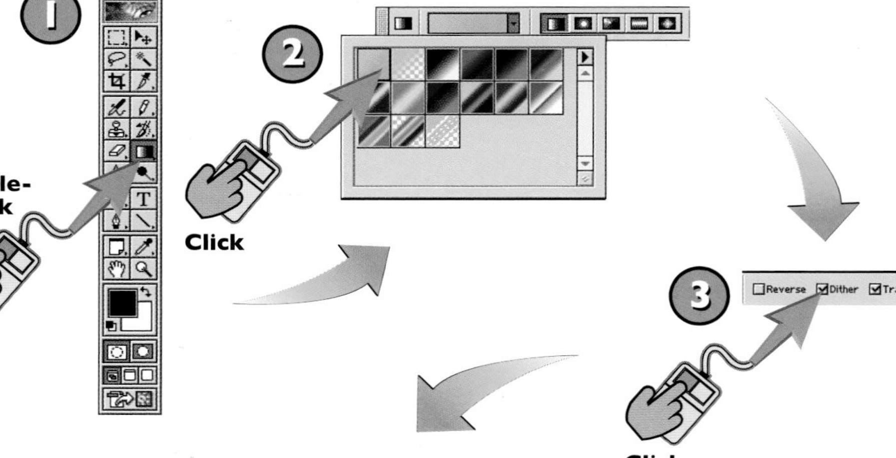

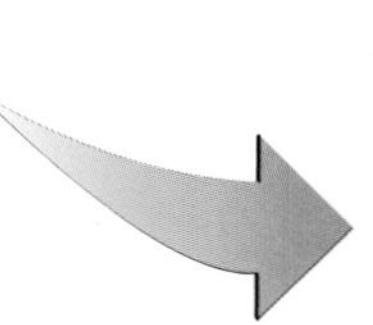

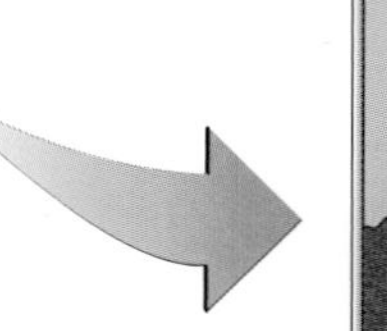

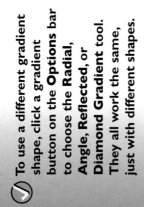

 Double-click the **Linear Gradient** tool to display the **Linear Gradient Options** bar and select the tool.

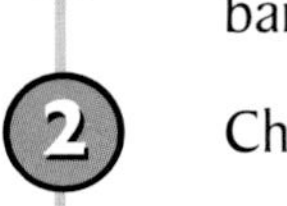 Choose a **Gradient** type from the pop-up menu.

 Click **Dither** to create a smooth blend without banding.

 Click and drag in the image to create the gradient.

Task 9: Creating a New Gradient Type

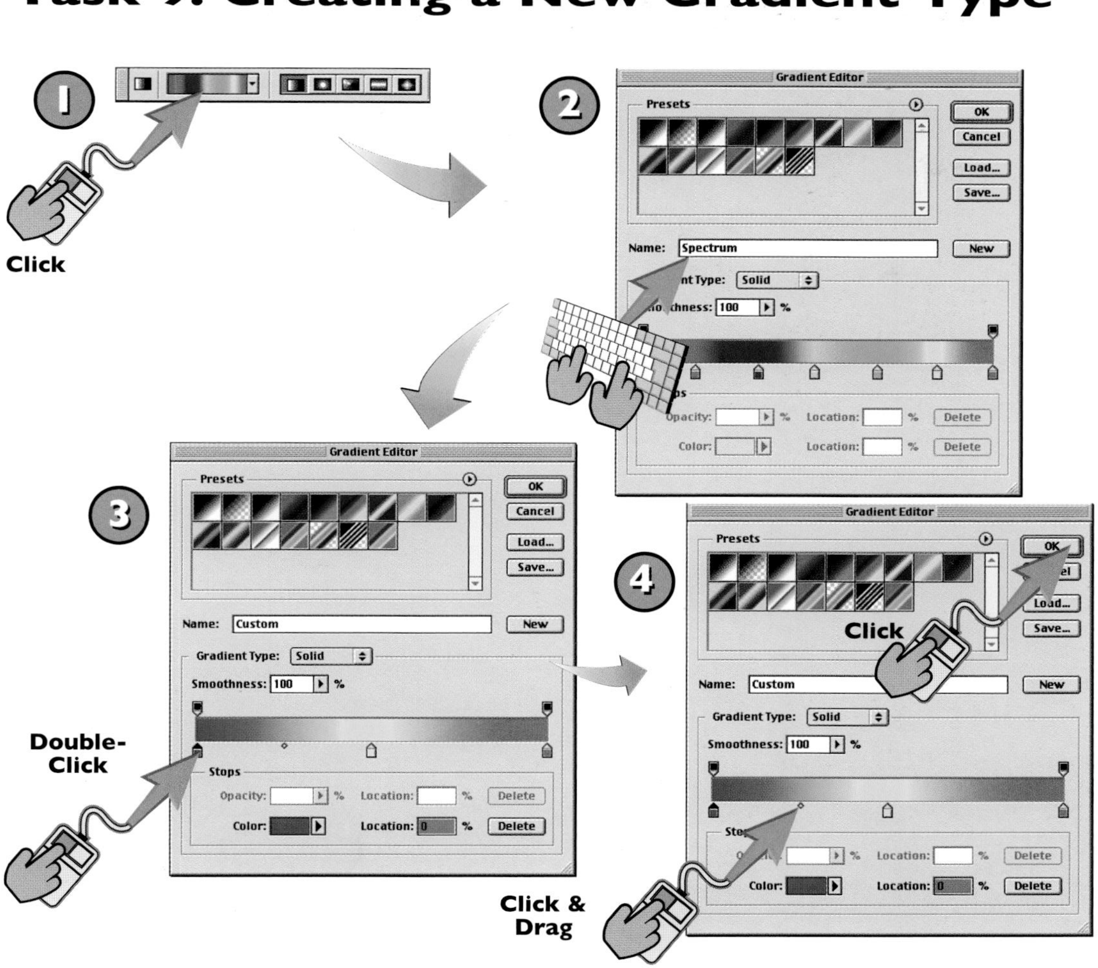

In addition to the built-in gradients, you can create your own, specifying the colors and intensity you want to use at each point in the gradient.

Click

Click

Double-Click

Click & Drag

1. Click the gradient thumbnail in the **Gradient Options** bar, and then click **New** in the **Gradient Editor** dialog box.
2. Give the gradient a name.
3. Double-click the "houses" below the gradient slider to change their color; click once below the line to add a new "house."
4. Drag the diamonds below the gradient to change the position at which the color changes, and then click **OK**.

In addition to creating your own gradients, you can edit the ones that are already there (the ugly Red, Green one is a good candidate for this). You can always get the originals back by choosing **Reset Tool** from the **Gradient** palette menu.

Rather than trying to paint perfect circles and rectangles, you can stroke a circular or rectangular selection to create hollow shapes. Photoshop can place the stroke inside, outside, or centered on the selection marquee.

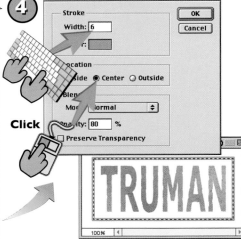

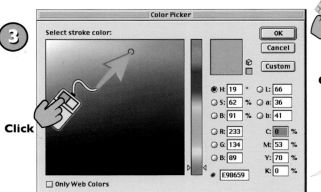

Task 10: Adding a Stroke Around a Selection

Start Here

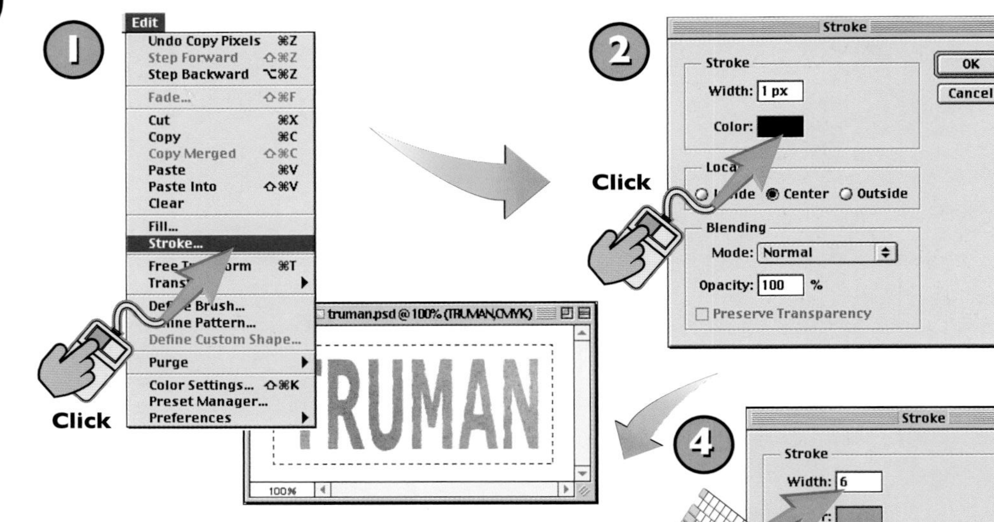

1. With a selection active, choose **Edit**, **Stroke**.
2. Click the **color swatch** to choose a color to use for the stroke.
3. In the Color Picker, select a color and click **OK**.
4. Enter a **Width** for the stroke and click in the **Location** area to determine its location.

The **Mode** menu enables you to apply a stroke by using different blending modes to combine the stroke color with the image's existing colors; experiment with different modes for different effects.

End Task

Task 11: Erasing Part of an Image

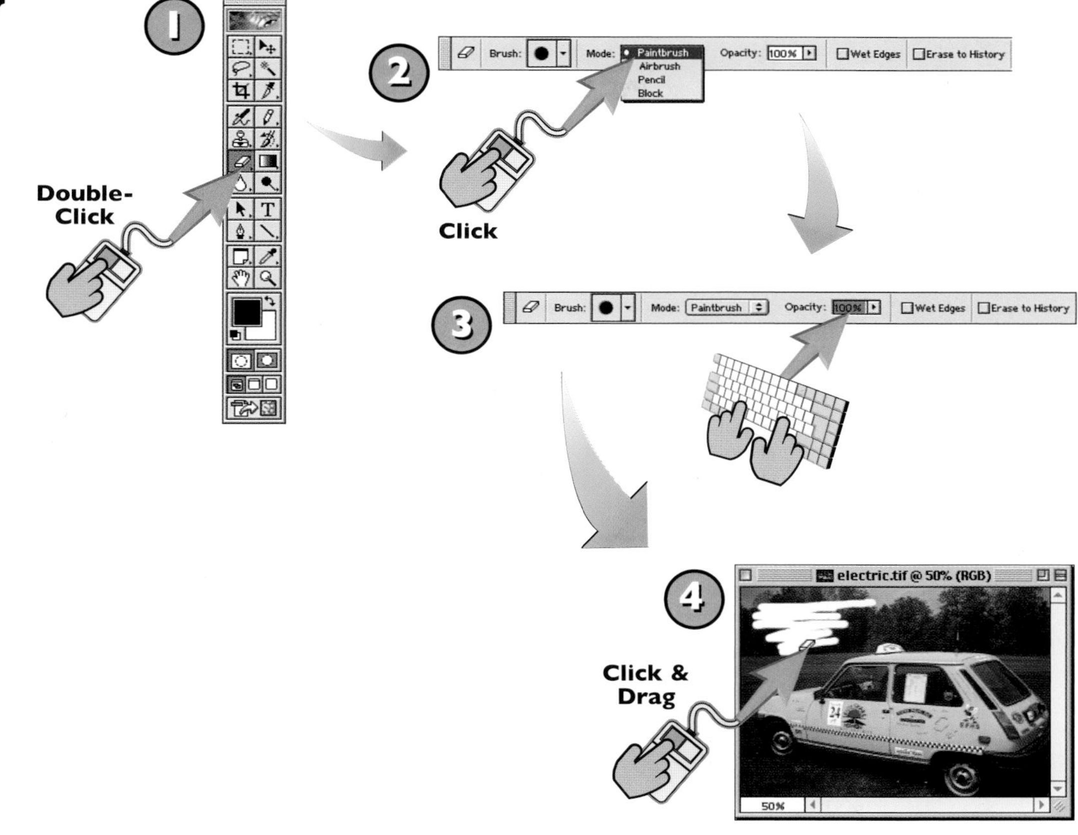

The Eraser tool does just what it sounds like: It erases pixels. It can work like a square block eraser—the kind used in older programs such as MacPaint—or it can operate like a paintbrush, airbrush, or pencil for more specialized erasing tasks.

1. Double-click the **Eraser** tool to select the tool and display the **Eraser Options** bar.
2. Choose an eraser **Mode** from the pop-up menu.
3. Enter an **Opacity** percentage other than 100 to partially erase pixels.
4. Click and drag in the image to erase.

The block eraser always erases the same amount of space on your screen, so it erases bigger areas of the image the more you zoom out and smaller areas the more you zoom in.

Task 12: Changing Painting Tool Settings

Each tool, including the painting tools, has special settings accessible in the Options bar. The bar changes its name and controls depending on which tool is selected, and the Options bar for each tool can be displayed by double-clicking that tool.

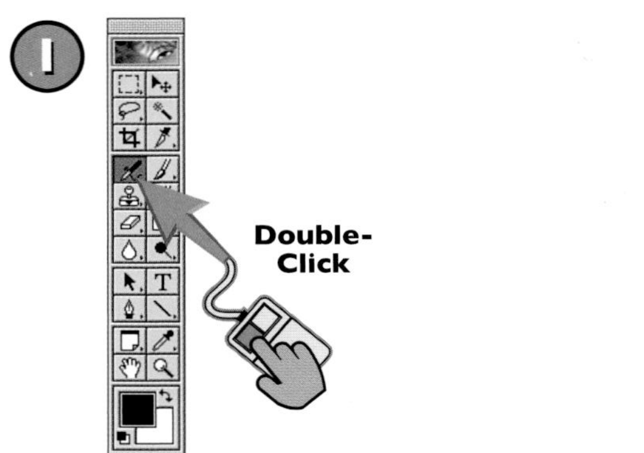

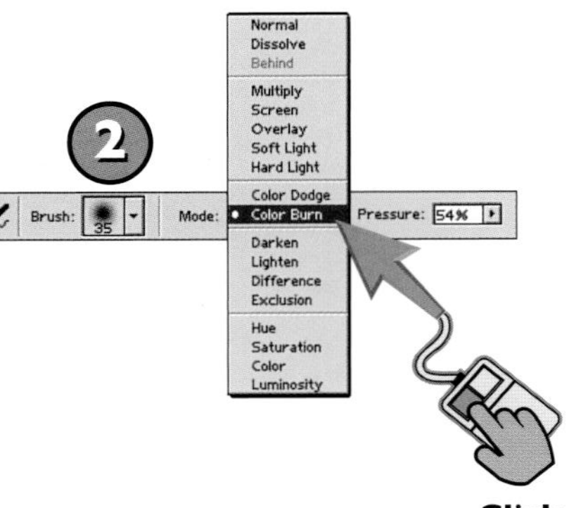

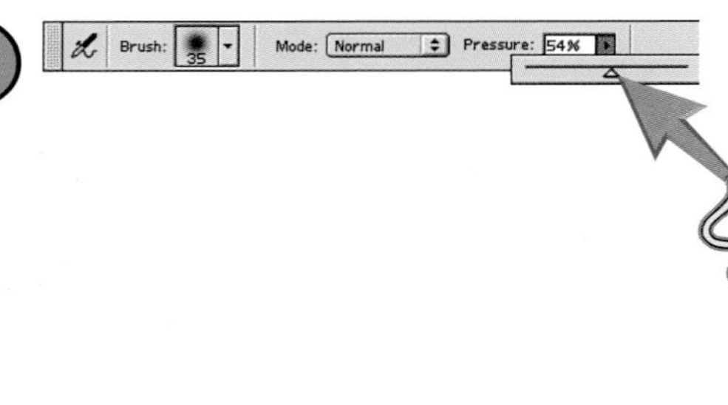

1. Double-click the tool whose settings you want to change to display the **Options** bar.
2. When using the **Paintbrush**, **Airbrush**, **History Brush**, or **Pencil**, choose a blending mode.
3. When using the **Airbrush**, choose a **Pressure** percentage.

✓ *Blending modes* affect the way the colors you apply mix with existing colors in the image. Experiment with different modes for different effects.

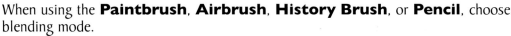

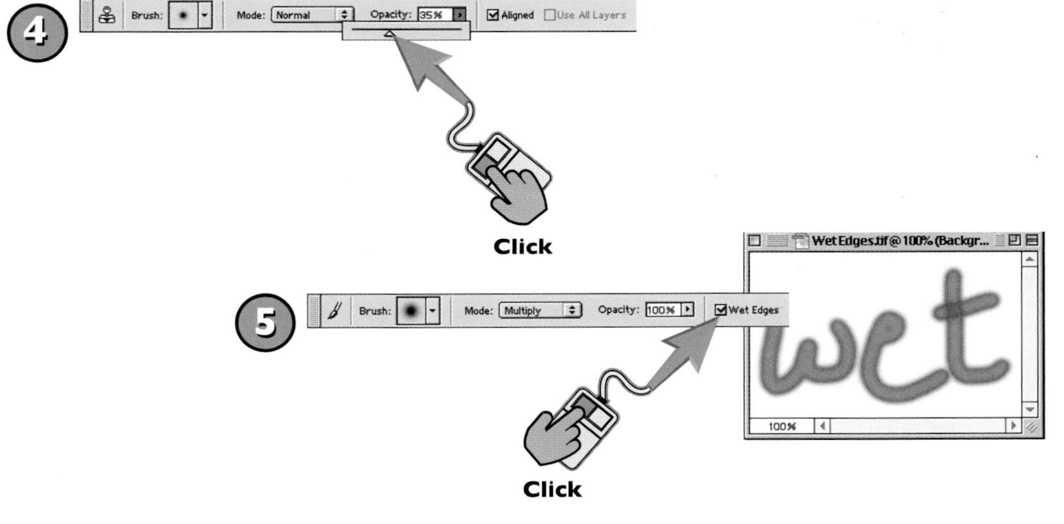

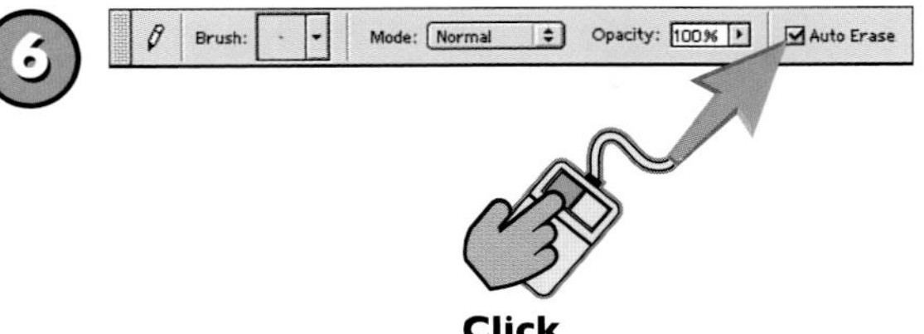

4 When using the **Paintbrush**, **History Brush**, or **Rubber Stamp**, choose an **Opacity** percentage.

5 When using the **Paintbrush** or the **Eraser** in Paintbrush mode, click **Wet Edges** to simulate watercolor painting.

6 When using the **Pencil**, click **Auto Erase** to draw the background color when clicking pixels of the foreground color, and vice versa.

Photoshop's Art History brush enables you to manipulate the pixels in an existing image to look as though they're a painting with real brush strokes rather than a photo. It's not perfect, but it's a nice effect that you can apply at varying levels to produce "paintings" that are quite close to the original images—or ones that are quite a different image indeed.

Task 13: Turning an Image into a Painting

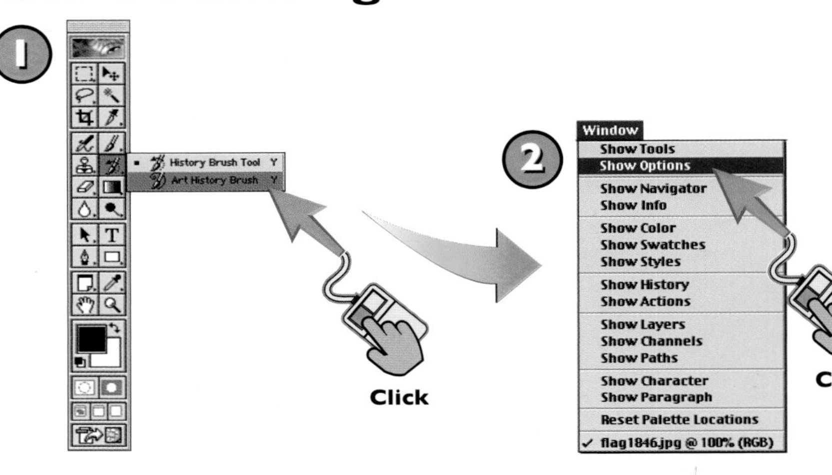

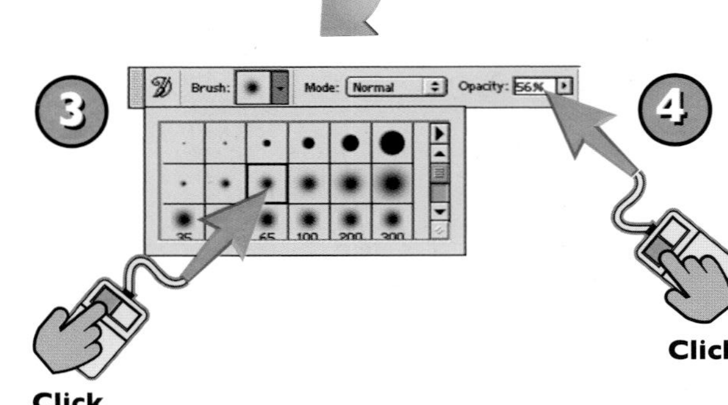

1. Click on the **History Brush** in the **Tool** palette and slide the cursor over to select the **Art History Brush**.

2. Choose **Windows**, **Show Options** to make sure that the **Art History Brush Options** bar is displayed.

3. Choose a brush from the **Brush** menu in the **Art History Brush Options** bar.

4. Enter an **Opacity** percentage; percentages lower than 100% allow more of the original image to show through your brushstrokes.

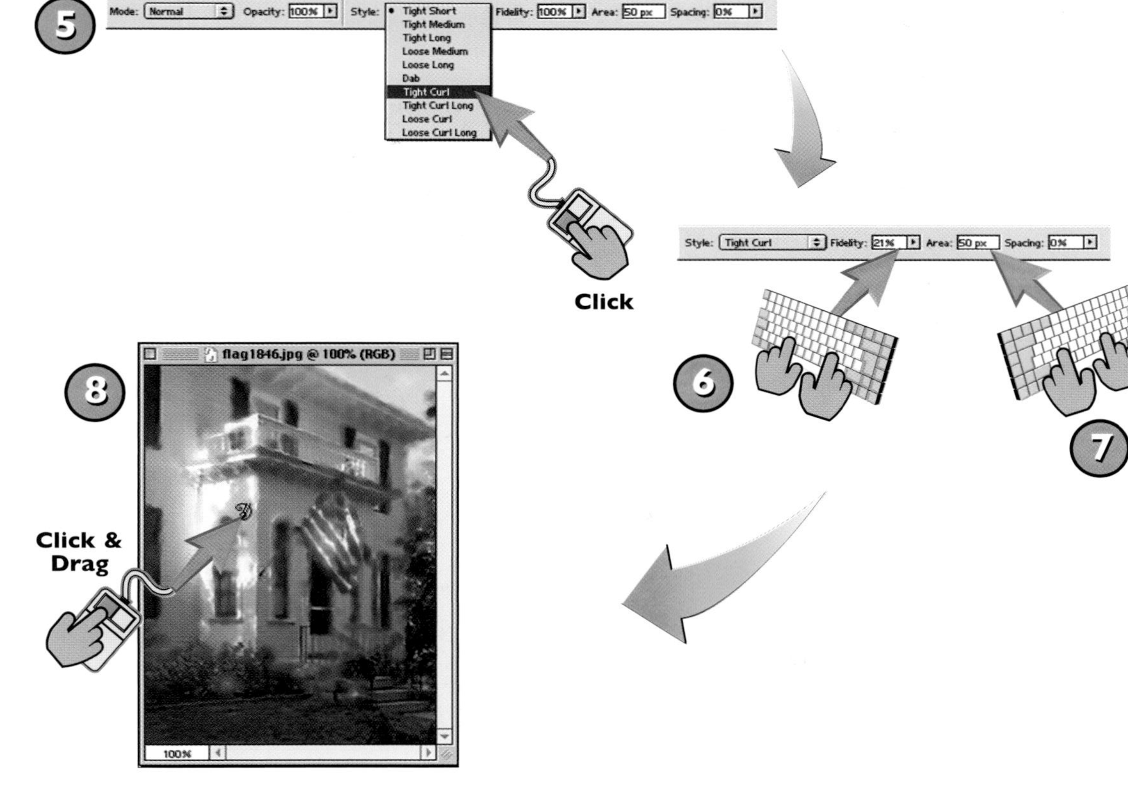

5 Choose a brushstroke **Style**—really a shape.

6 Enter a **Fidelity** percentage to determine how close the new brush strokes stay to the image's original colors.

7 Enter an **Area** value between 0 and 500 pixels to determine how far from the cursor the artistic effect extends.

8 Click and drag in the image to apply the "artistic" brush strokes.

Try using the Art History brush in a blank or abstract image to create pastel brushstrokes that are an attractive background. Just click in the image and keep dragging the brush slightly until you get an arrangement of brushstrokes that looks good—like turning a kaleidoscope.

The Dab Style option produces pointillist-style brushstrokes, small and round.

PART 6

Editing Images

With the "digital darkroom" represented by the powerful capabilities of Photoshop, it's easy to make any existing image look just the way you want. You can quickly remove, add, or modify details of an image with Photoshop's painting and editing tools. Transformation commands enable you to rotate, skew, scale, and apply perspective to an object or entire image. Each command explained in this part can be applied to the entire image or just to a selected area.

Part 6 shows you how to transform an image in several ways, sharpen and blur details, darken or lighten areas, duplicate an image, and remove the moiré pattern that sometimes shows up in scanned images.

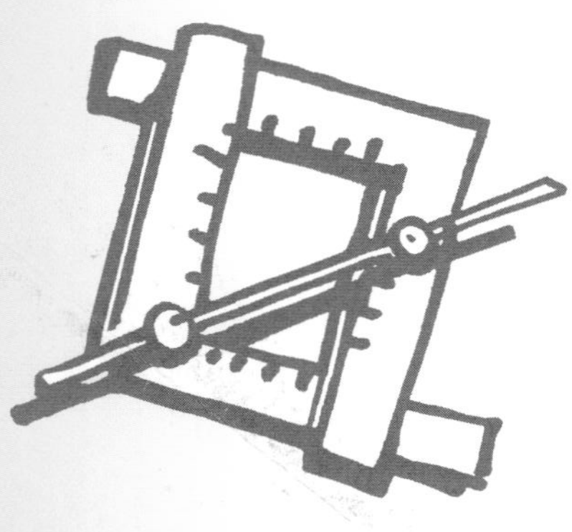

Tasks

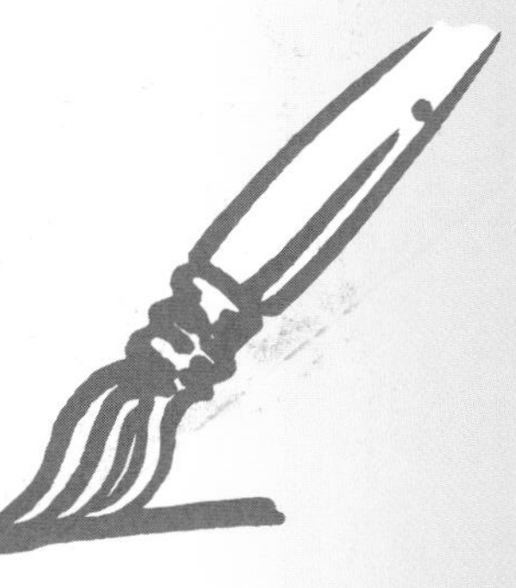

Task 1: Moving an Object a Specified Distance

Start Here

The Move tool is designed to move pixels from one point in an image to another. But if you want to move pixels a specific distance from their starting point, Photoshop's Offset filter is just what you need. Because it moves an entire layer at a time, you must put the pixels you'll be moving onto their own layer first.

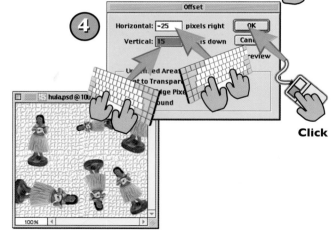

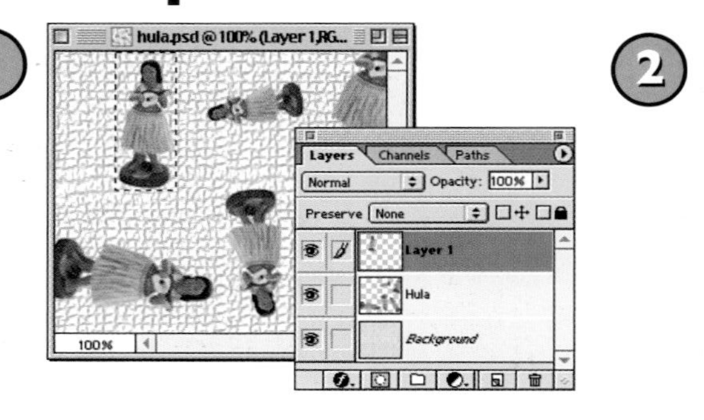

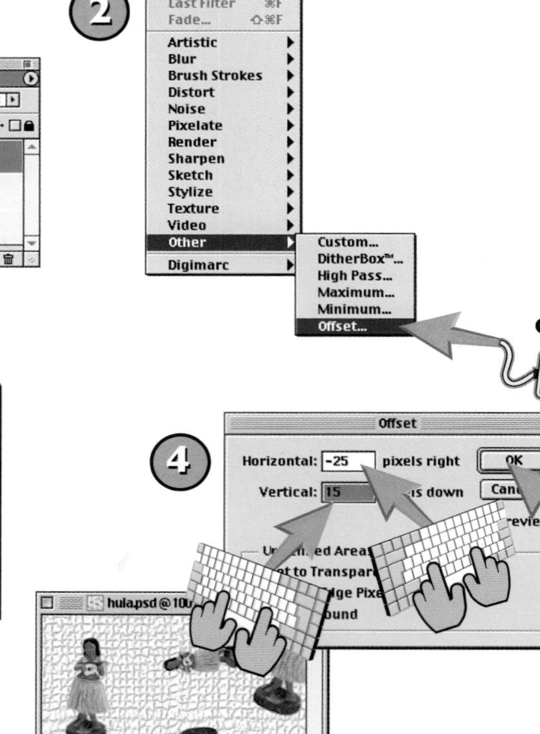

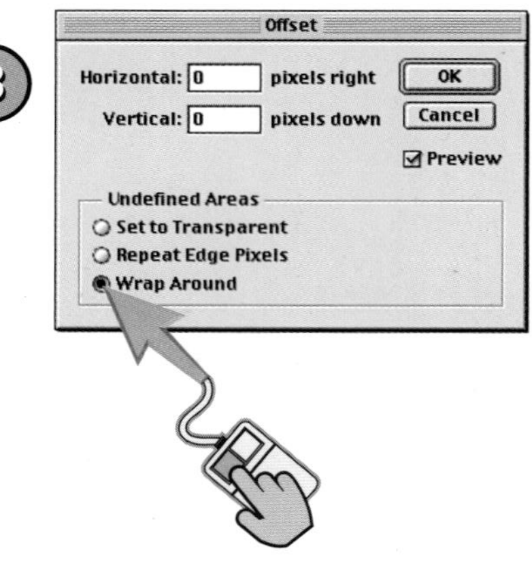

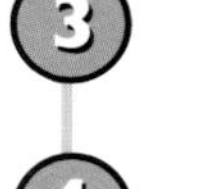

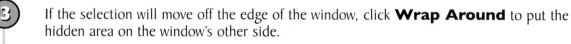

If you use the Offset filter on a layer that's entirely filled with pixels, use the Repeat Edge Pixels option instead of placing a specific object on a new transparent layer as in step 1. Select it to extend the edge pixels of the object from its previous position to its new one.

1. Select the area you want to move and press **Cmd+Shift+J/Ctrl+Shift+J** to shift the selected area to a new layer.
2. Choose **Filter**, **Other**, **Offset**.
3. If the selection will move off the edge of the window, click **Wrap Around** to put the hidden area on the window's other side.
4. Enter **Horizontal** and **Vertical** distances in pixels and click **OK**.

End Task

Task 2: Aligning Objects with One Another

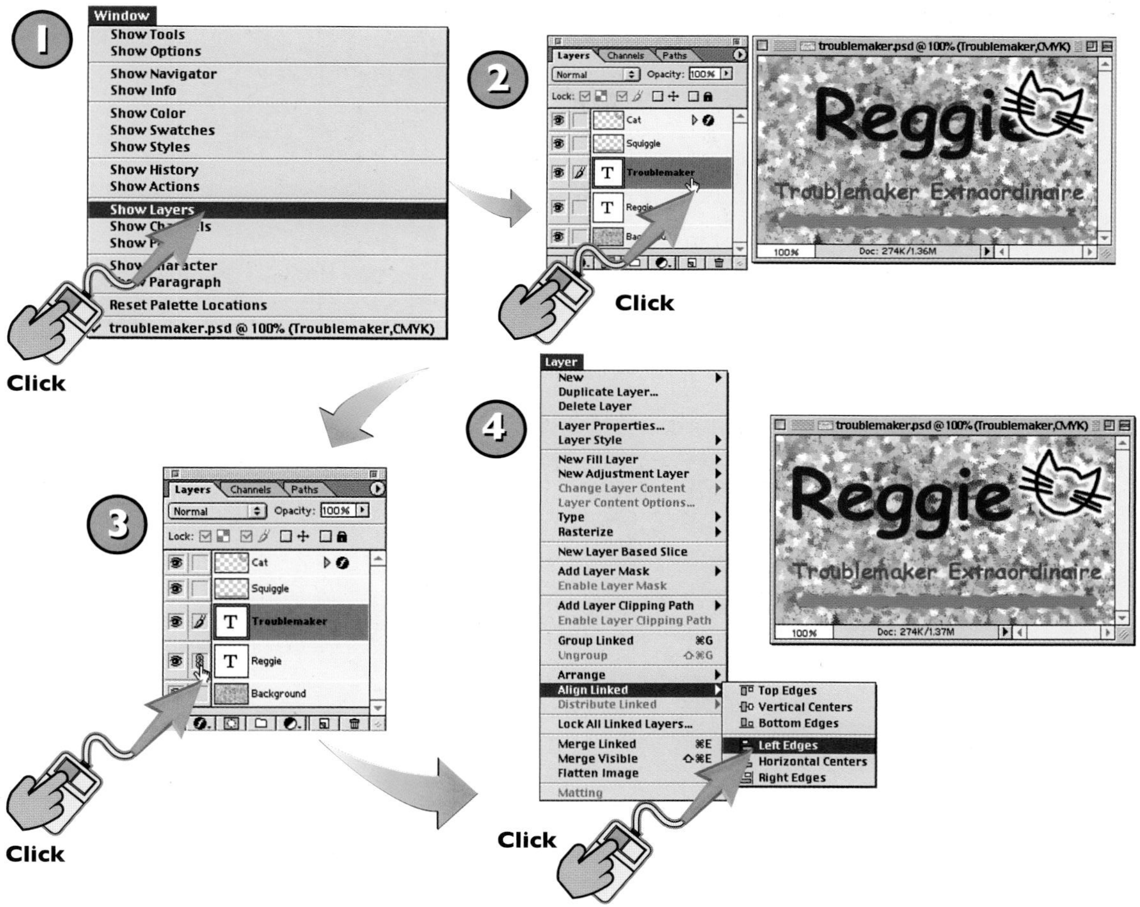

Click

Click

Click

Click

Photoshop can align objects on different layers. It looks for nontransparent pixels to tell it where the edges of objects are, so the Align commands really work only when each object is on its own layer and surrounded by transparent pixels.

1. Choose **Window**, **Show Layers**.
2. Click the name of the layer to which you want to align objects.
3. Click in the blank box to the left of each layer you want to align to the active layer.
4. Choose **Layer**, **Align Linked** and choose an option from the submenu.

Make sure you press Cmd+D/Ctrl+D to drop any active selection before aligning layers; when a selection is active, Photoshop aligns layers with respect to the selection.

Task 3: Rotating an Object

Transformations are actions that change the shape of a selected area. One of the most useful transformations is rotation. Photoshop enables you to rotate selected areas in either direction, as far as you want to.

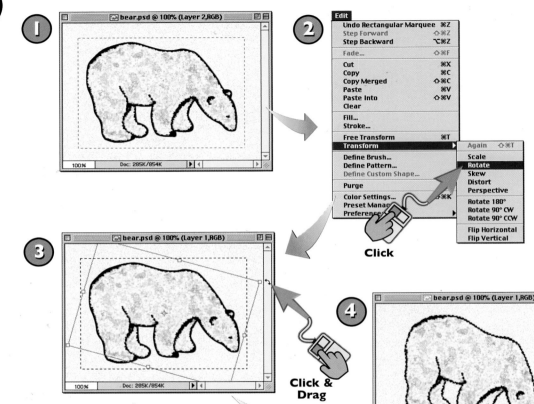

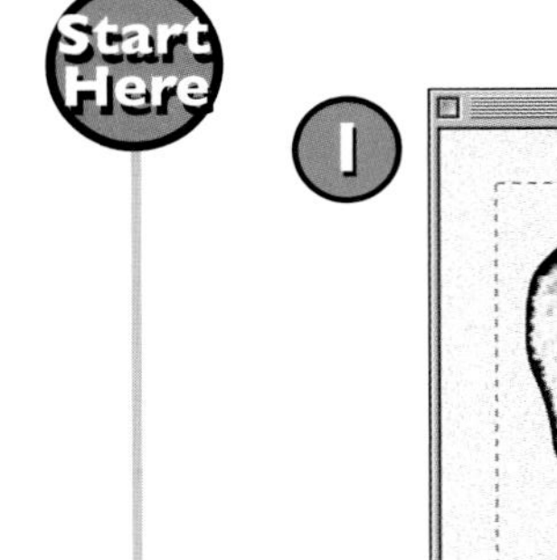

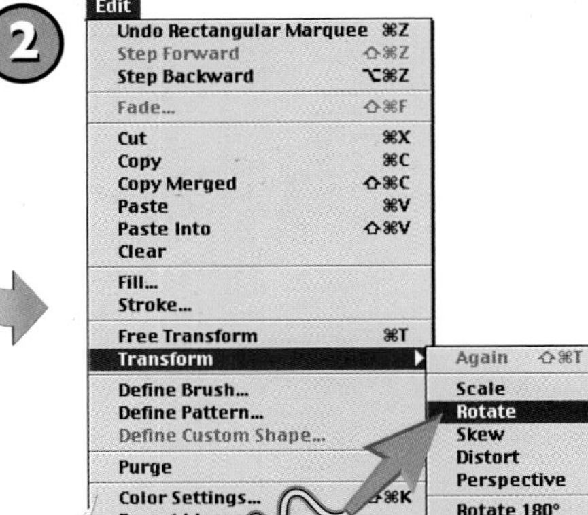

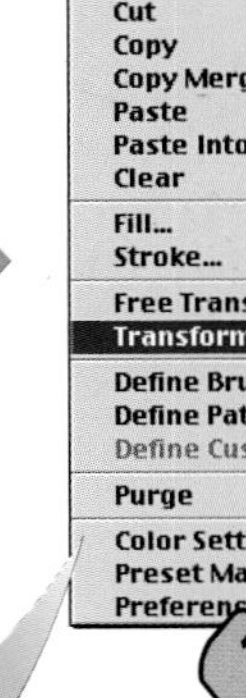

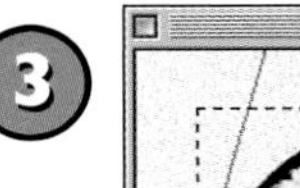

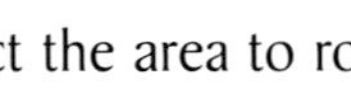

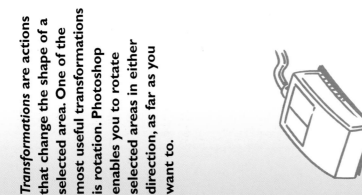

1. Select the area to rotate.
2. Choose **Edit**, **Transform**, **Rotate**.
3. Click outside the transformation box and drag to rotate.
4. Press **Enter** to apply the rotation or **Esc** to cancel it.

If the **Transform** command isn't available, check to make sure the image is in Grayscale or a color mode. Transformations don't work in Bitmap mode.

End Task

Task 4: Skewing an Object

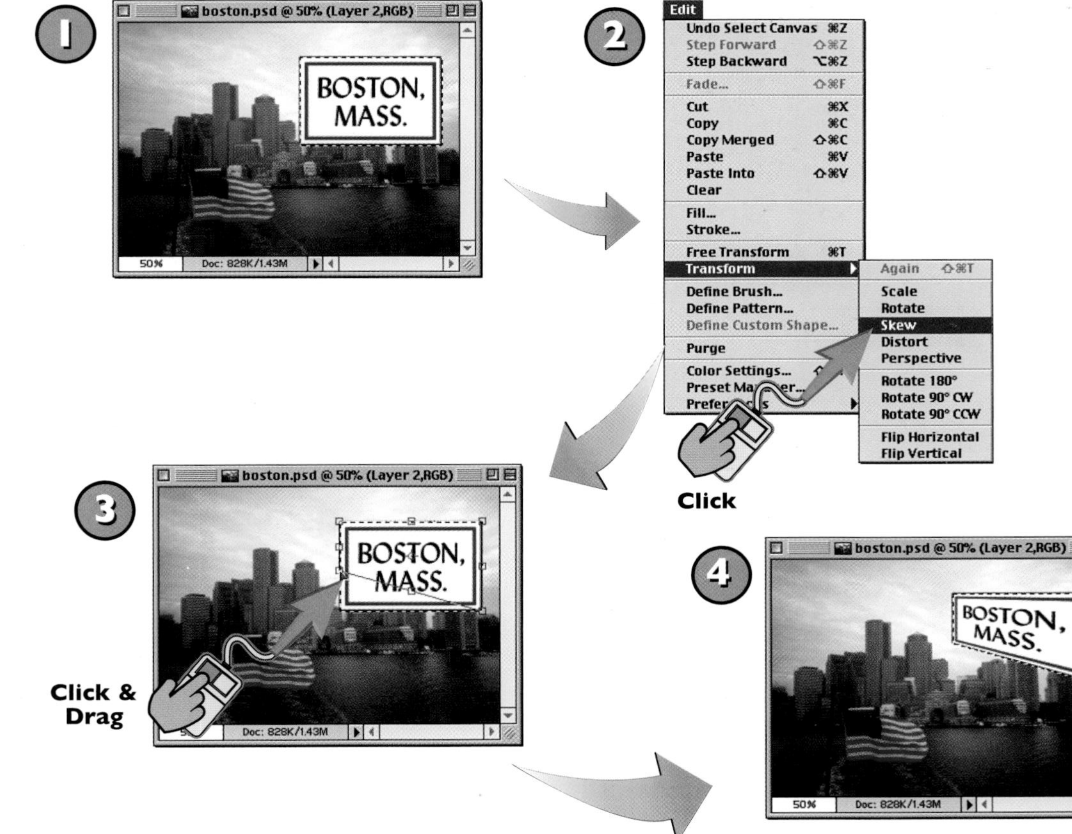

Skewing an object ordinarily involves tilting it to one side while keeping its top and bottom level. In Photoshop, you can apply skew in any direction by dragging transformation handles, and you can skew a selection in more than one direction with one operation.

1. Select the area to skew.
2. Choose **Edit**, **Transform**, **Skew**.
3. Drag any handle of the transformation box to skew the selected area.
4. Press **Enter** to apply the skew or **Esc** to cancel it.

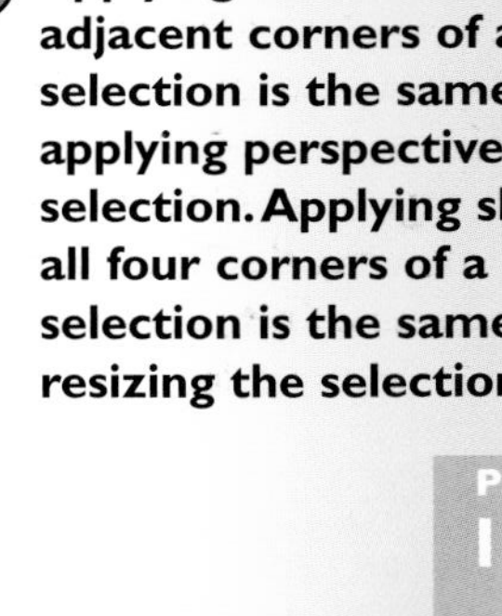

Applying skew to two adjacent corners of a selection is the same as applying perspective to the selection. Applying skew to all four corners of a selection is the same as resizing the selection.

Task 5: Scaling an Object

Whereas the Image Size command enables you to change the size of an entire image, the Scale command resizes only the selected area. You can resize proportionally or nonproportionally, as required.

Start Here

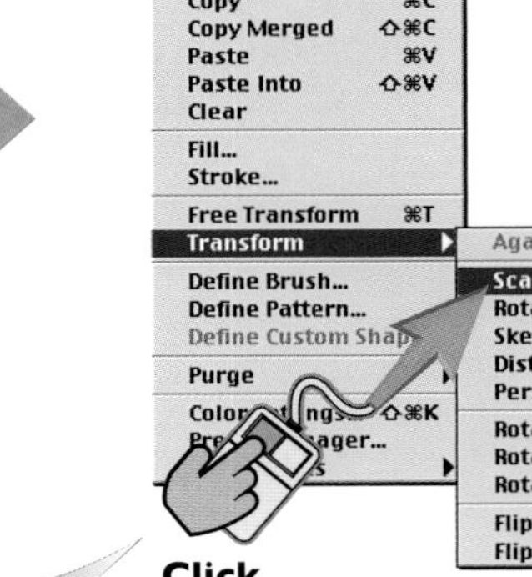
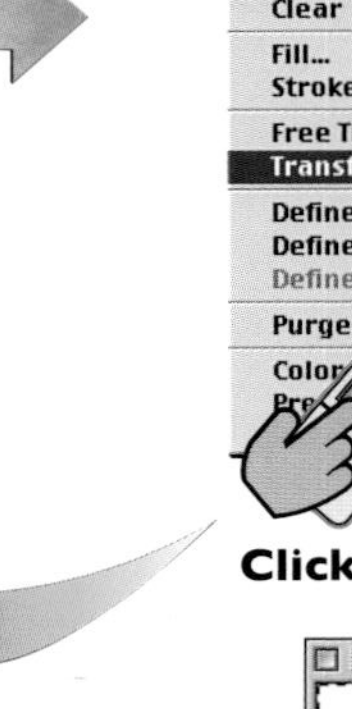

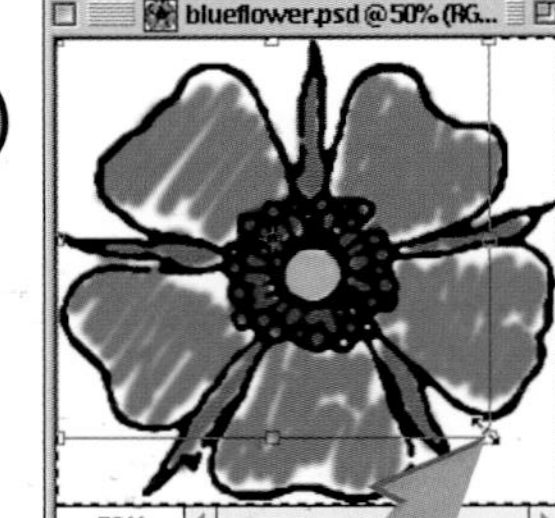

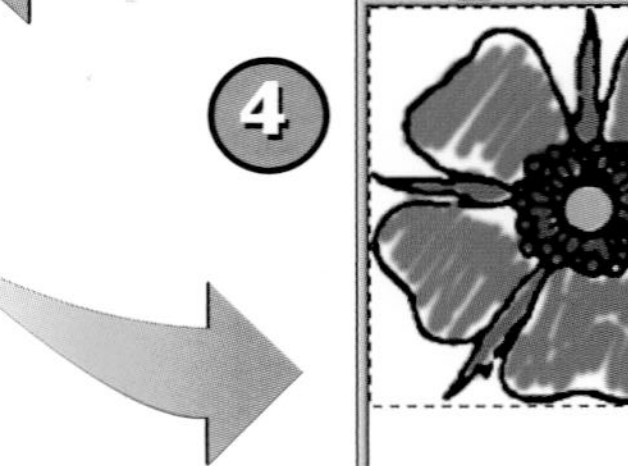

- To make sure that you're resizing the selected area proportionally, hold down **Shift** as you drag the transformation handle.
- Until you press **Enter** to apply the transformation, you can choose **Edit**, **Undo** or press **Cmd+Z/Ctrl+Z** to undo the latest change made to the transformation box. Undo works with any transformation, not just Scale.

1. Select the area to resize.
2. Choose **Edit**, **Transform**, **Scale**.
3. Drag any handle of the transformation box to resize the selected area.
4. Press **Enter** to apply the change in size or **Esc** to cancel it.

End Task

Task 6: Rotating an Image

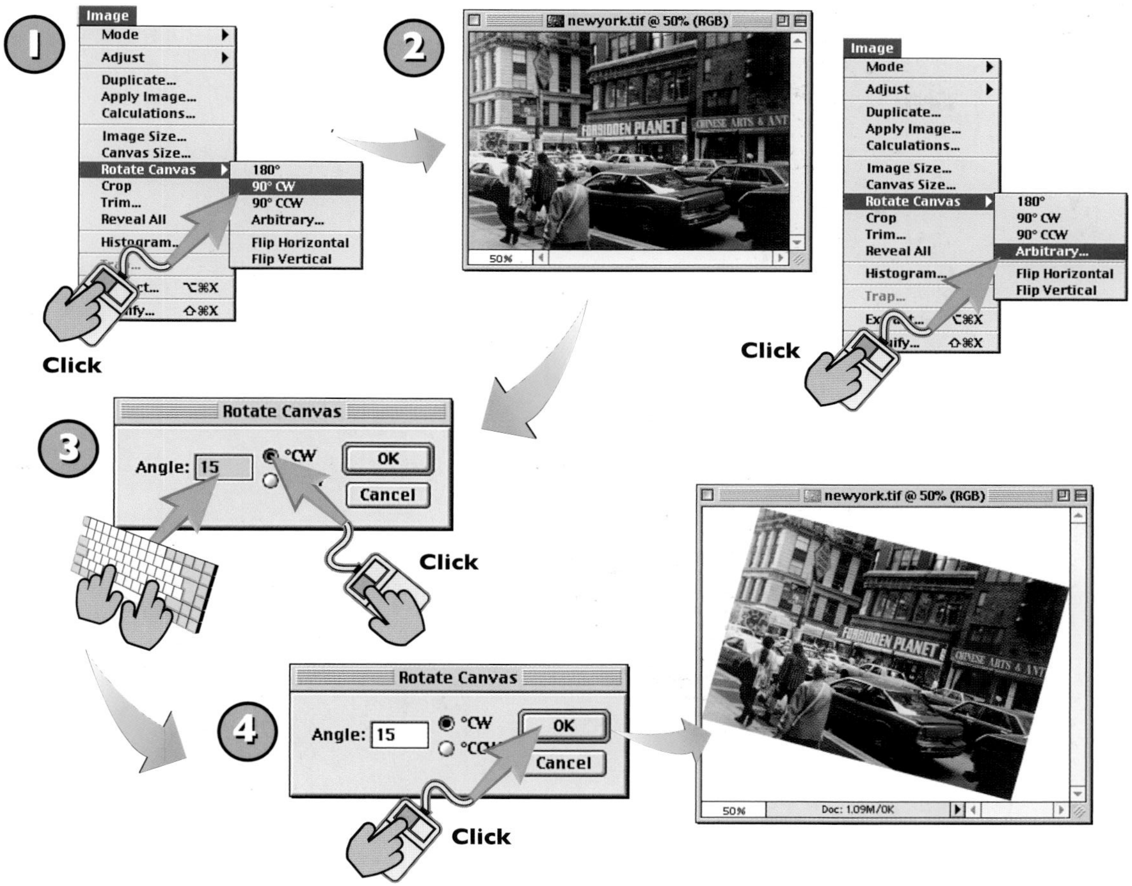

Use the **Rotate Canvas** command when you need to rotate an entire image. You can choose three built-in options—useful if you've scanned an image sideways and just need to rotate it 90 degrees—or you can specify an arbitrary number of degrees clockwise or counterclockwise.

Photoshop automatically adjusts the canvas size to fit the entire rotated image; that's why the command is called **Rotate Canvas** instead of **Rotate Image**.

The **Flip Horizontal** and **Flip Vertical** commands in the **Rotate** submenu do just what you'd think they would do—flip (or "flop," in prepress-speak) the image from side to side or top to bottom.

1. To rotate the image by 90 or 180 degrees, choose **Image**, **Rotate Canvas** and choose from the submenu.
2. To rotate the image an arbitrary number of degrees, choose **Image**, **Rotate Canvas**, **Arbitrary**.
3. Enter a number of degrees in the **Angle** field and click **CW** (clockwise) or **CCW** (counterclockwise).
4. Click **OK** to rotate the image.

Quick artistic perspective effects are within your grasp with Photoshop's Perspective transformation. Applying perspective is like skewing two corners of a selected area by exactly the same amount.

Start Here

Task 7: Applying Perspective to an Object

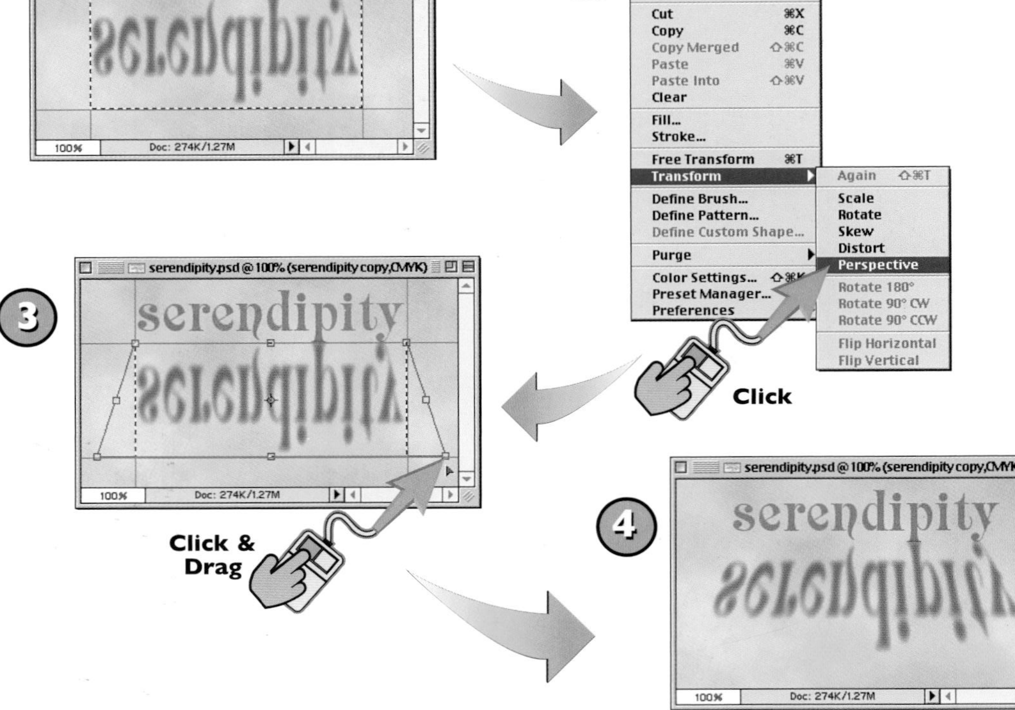

1. Select the area to which perspective will be applied.
2. Choose **Edit**, **Transform**, **Perspective**.
3. Drag any handle of the transformation box to create the perspective effect.
4. Press **Enter** to apply the perspective or **Esc** to cancel it.

✓ **By using perspective, you can blend added elements into an image, such as a sign or book that must be at an angle to the viewer.**

Task 8: Smudging an Area

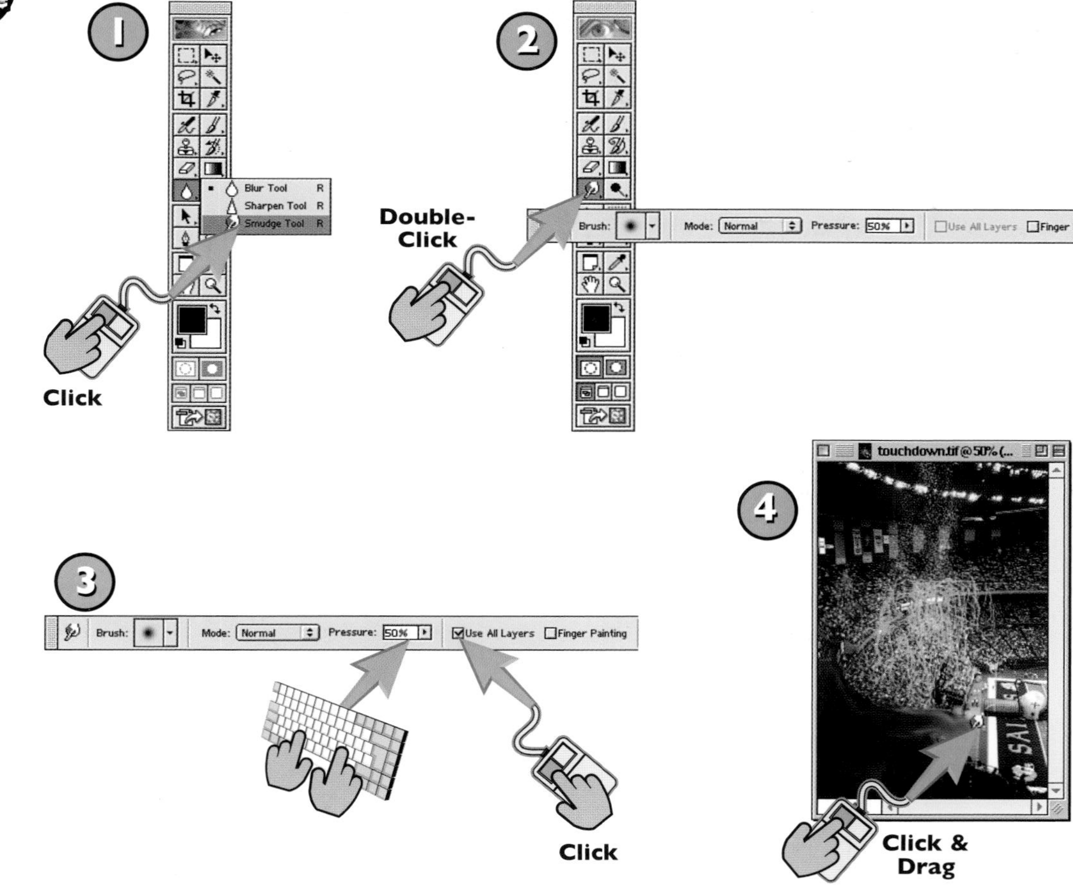

To help you get rid of unwanted details in an image, Photoshop provides a Smudge tool that looks and works just like a finger through wet paint. It can be used to touch up images, to eliminate scratches and dust, or to create special effects that focus attention on the unsmudged areas of an image.

1. Click the **Blur** tool and slide over to select **Smudge Tool**.
2. Double-click the **Smudge** tool to show the **Smudge Options** bar.
3. Enter a **Pressure** percentage, and then click **Use All Layers** if you want to smudge more than one layer at a time.
4. Click and drag in the image to smudge.

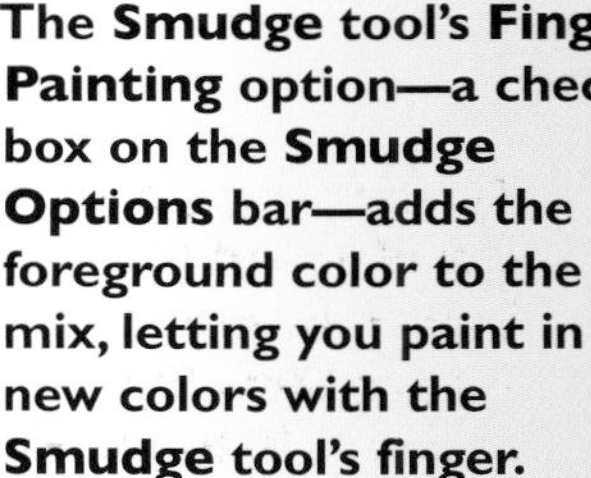

The Smudge tool's Finger Painting option—a check box on the Smudge Options bar—adds the foreground color to the mix, letting you paint in new colors with the Smudge tool's finger.

Task 9: Sharpening or Blurring Details

Photoshop's Sharpen filters enable you to sharpen entire images or selected areas. When you need to sharpen a few details here and there, such as the sparkle of an eye or the reflection in a mirror, you can use the Sharpen tool to apply the effect right where you want it.

Start Here

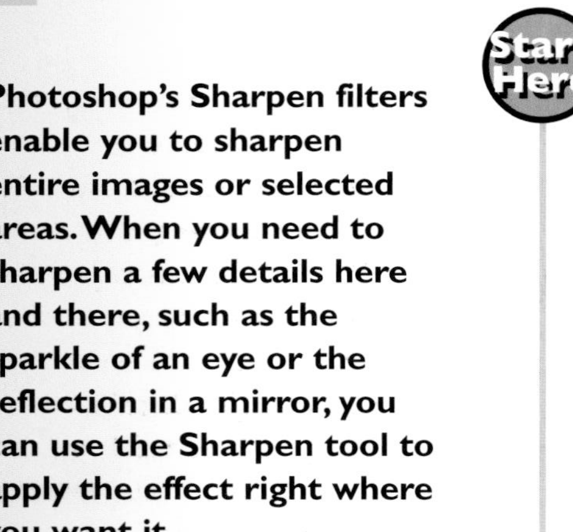

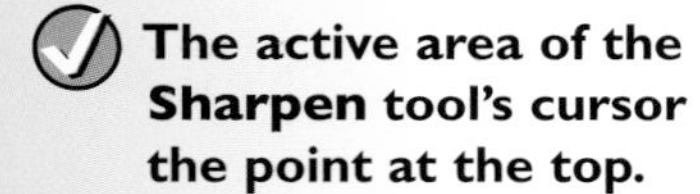

- The active area of the **Sharpen** tool's cursor is the point at the top.
- The **Sharpen** tool really is intended for close-up detail work, not for sharpening entire images. If you find yourself using it in more than two or three places in an image, consider using a **Sharpen** filter.
- The **Blur** tool works just like the **Sharpen** tool, except that it blurs the area of the image on which you use it rather than sharpens details.

1. Click the **Blur** tool and slide over to select the **Sharpen** tool.
2. Double-click the **Sharpen** tool to show the **Sharpen Options** bar.
3. Enter a **Pressure** percentage; higher pressure produces more sharpening.
4. Click and drag in the image to sharpen.

Task 10: Intensifying or Toning Down an Area

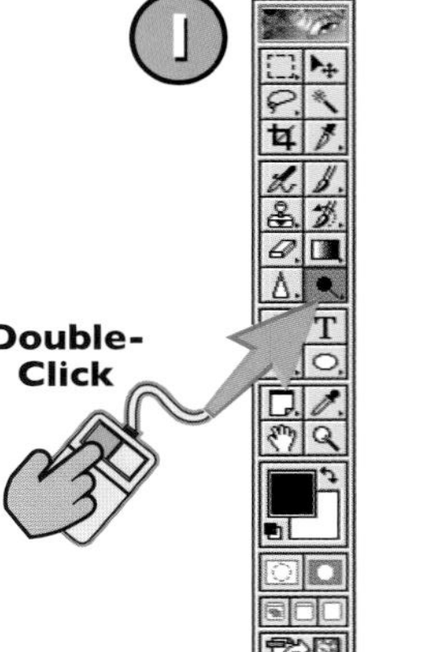

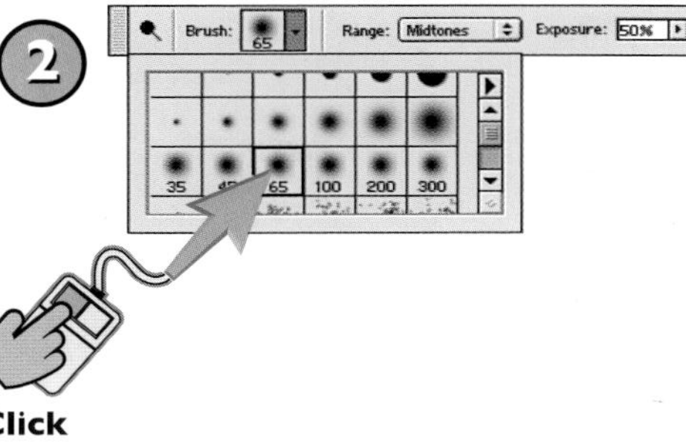

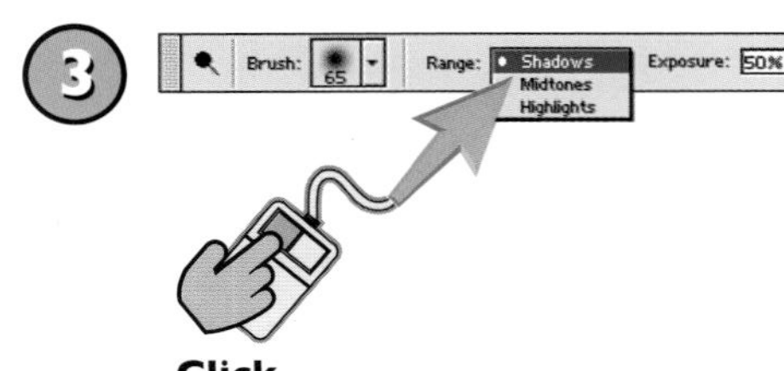

Two darkroom techniques can emphasize or de-emphasize areas of an image: *burning* and *dodging*. Photoshop has equivalent tools with the same names. The Burn tool enables you to intensify details of an image, whereas the Dodge tool fades areas you want to tone down.

1. Double-click the **Dodge** or **Burn** tool to display the **Dodge** or **Burn Options** bar.
2. Choose a brush from the **Brushes** menu of the **Options** bar.
3. Choose **Shadows**, **Midtones**, or **Highlights** from the pop-up menu on the **Options** bar.
4. Click and drag in the image to dodge or burn.

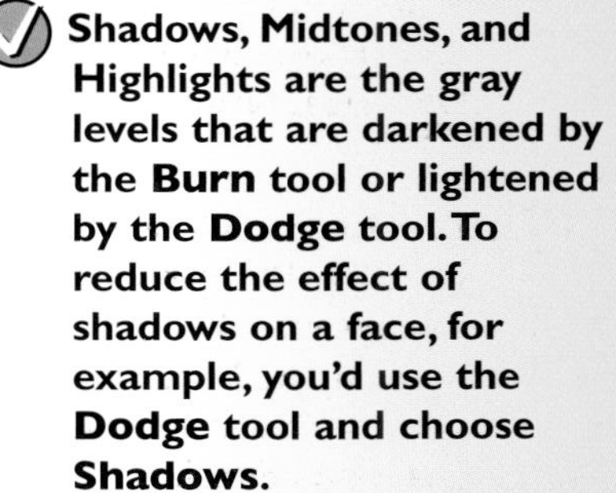

Shadows, Midtones, and Highlights are the gray levels that are darkened by the **Burn** tool or lightened by the **Dodge** tool. To reduce the effect of shadows on a face, for example, you'd use the **Dodge** tool and choose **Shadows**.

Task 11: Duplicating an Image

Photoshop can create a new file that duplicates an existing open file. Use the Duplicate command if you need two versions of a file, or to create a testing ground for new effects. You can compare multiple versions side-by-side by using duplicate files.

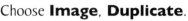

Start Here

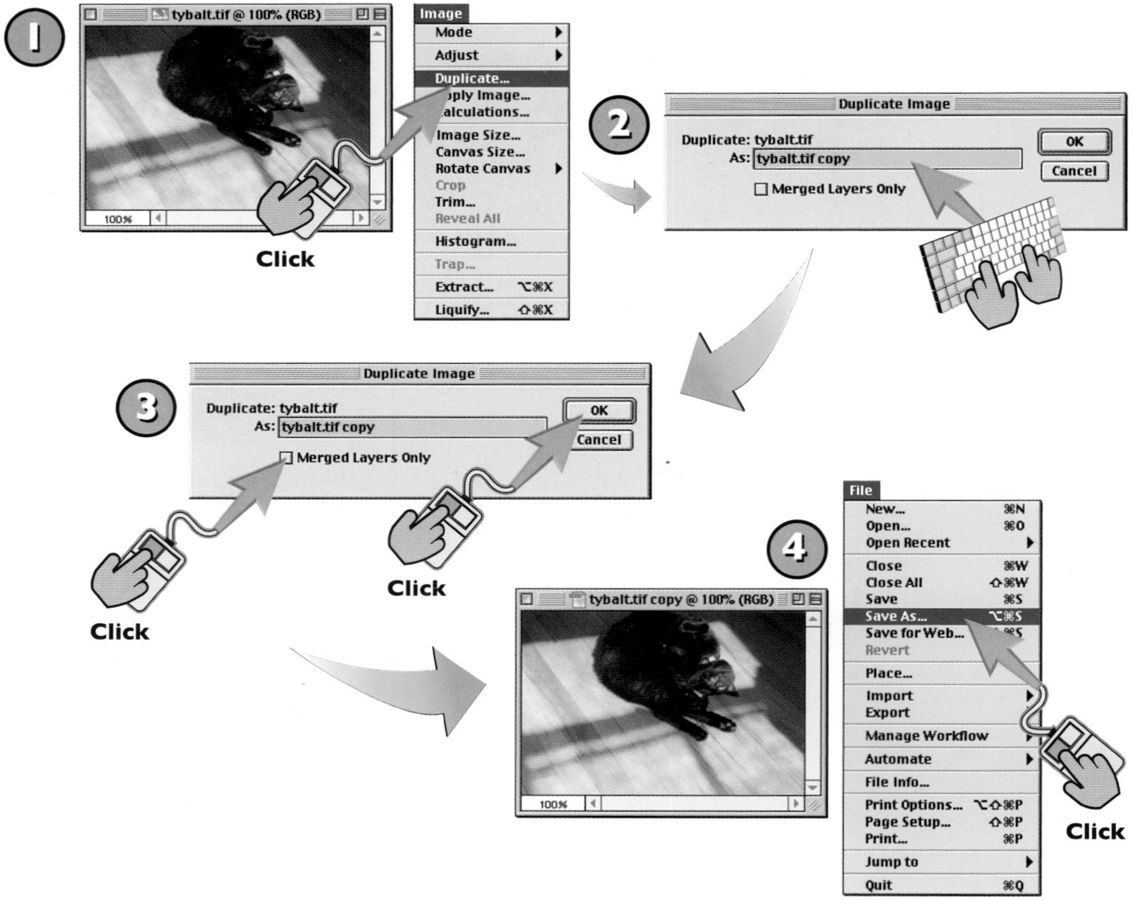

1. Choose **Image**, **Duplicate**.
2. Enter a name for the new file.
3. Click **Merged Layers Only** to duplicate all visible layers as one layer, and then click **OK**.
4. Choose **File**, **Save As** to save the file.

Leave Merged Layers Only unchecked to duplicate the individual layers rather than merging them into one layer in the new file.

Task 12: Saving a Snapshot of an Image for Later Use

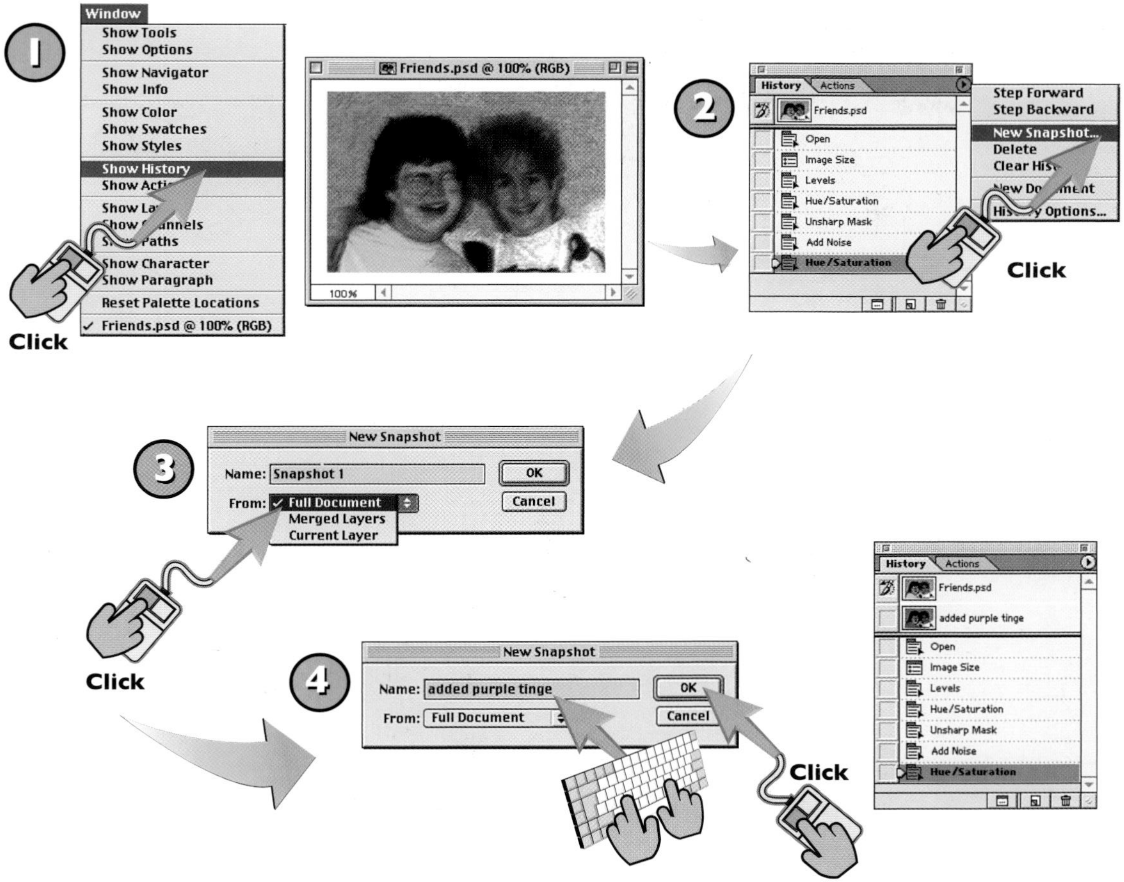

When you need to return to a specific point in the history of an image, the History palette can be a little confusing. Snapshots, the alternative, are just what they sound like: previous versions of an image. You can assign names to snapshots and return the image to each snapshot state at any time.

1. Choose **Window**, **Show History** to display the **History** palette.
2. Choose **New Snapshot** from the **History** palette menu.
3. Choose **Full Document**, **Merged Layers** (to merge all layers in the snapshot), or **Current Layer** (to include only the active layer).
4. Enter a name for the snapshot and click **OK**.

✓ Use snapshots for before-and-after comparisons when you're trying new techniques or creating new actions. To view a snapshot, click on its name at the top of the History palette.

✓ Snapshots go away when you close a file, so if you need to save versions of an image for another session, use the **Save a Copy** option in the **Save As** dialog box.

Combining two images is much easier in Photoshop than in the darkroom—no double exposures required. Blending modes enable you to jazz up a double image quickly, and you can size each image as required for the effect you seek.

Linking the two layers keeps them in the same relative positions, even if you move one of them later.

Before you link the layers, press Cmd+T/Ctrl+T to resize or reshape them, if required. Hold down the Shift key and drag any corner to resize proportionally.

Task 13: Laying an Image Over Another Image

Start Here

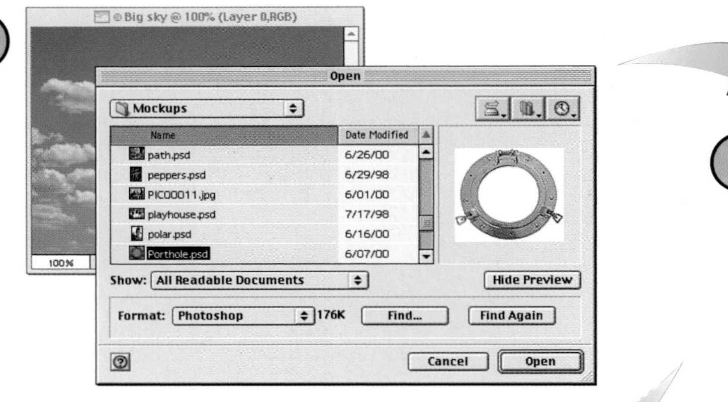

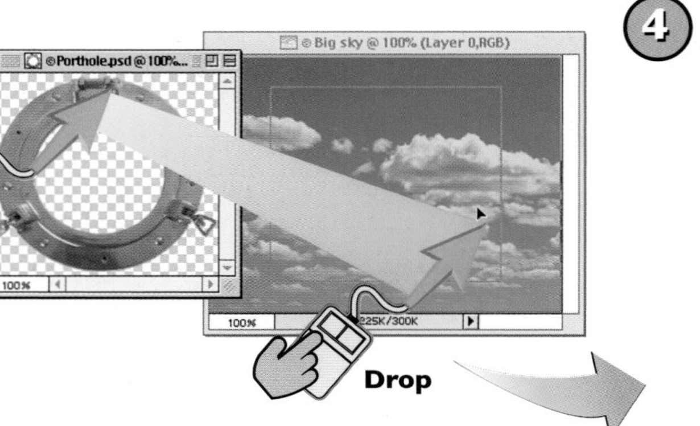

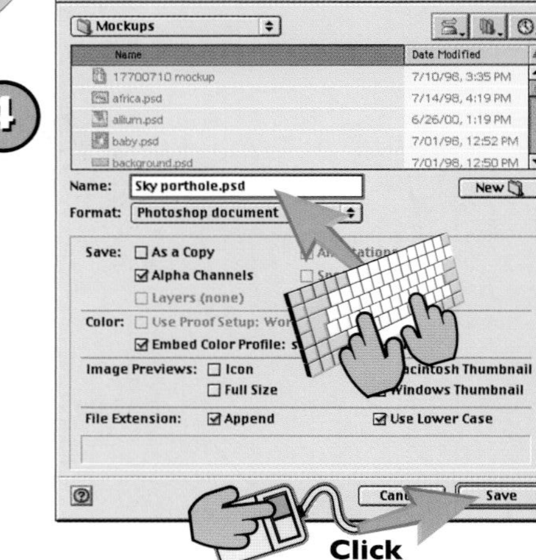

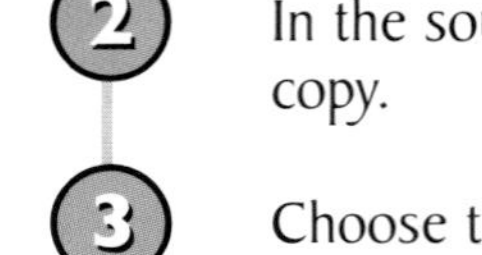

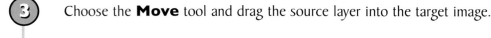

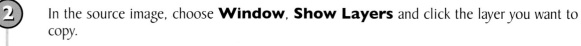

1 Open a source image to copy from and a target image to copy into.

2 In the source image, choose **Window**, **Show Layers** and click the layer you want to copy.

3 Choose the **Move** tool and drag the source layer into the target image.

4 Choose **File**, **Save As** to save the combined image with a new name, and click **Save**.

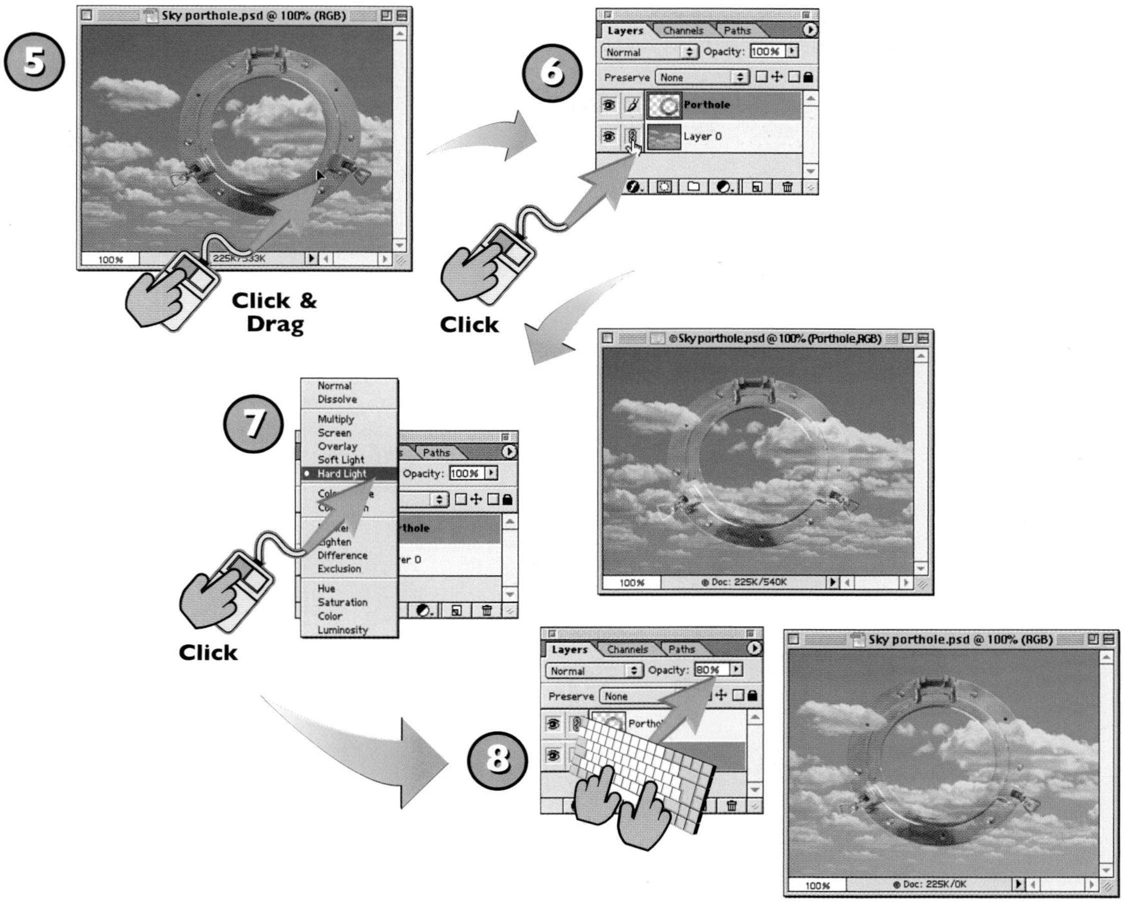

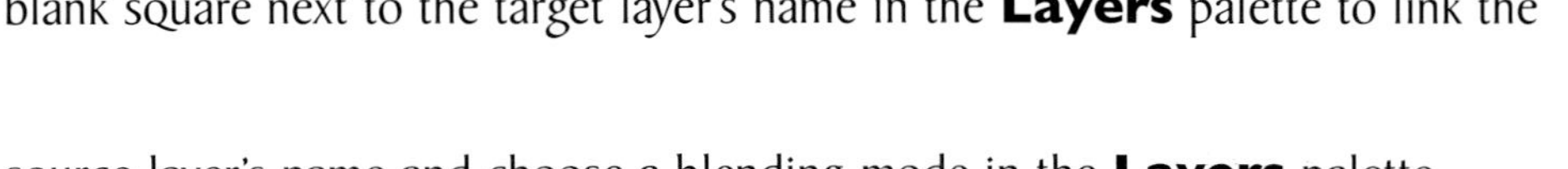

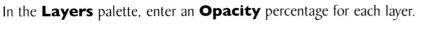

5. Use the **Move** tool to position the new layer as you want it.

6. Click the blank square next to the target layer's name in the **Layers** palette to link the layers.

7. Click the source layer's name and choose a blending mode in the **Layers** palette.

8. In the **Layers** palette, enter an **Opacity** percentage for each layer.

Blending modes determine how the colors in the two layers combine. Experiment with different modes for different effects—the most useful ones in this context are Normal (with a lowered opacity), Hard Light, Diffuse, and Difference.

Task 14: Removing a Moiré Pattern from a Scan

A moiré pattern is a checkerboard pattern that occurs when a pattern in the image isn't correctly reproduced by the scanner. The most common cause of moiré patterns is scanning printed images that contain halftone patterns, but they also show up in scans of objects such as cloth, house siding, and shingled roofs.

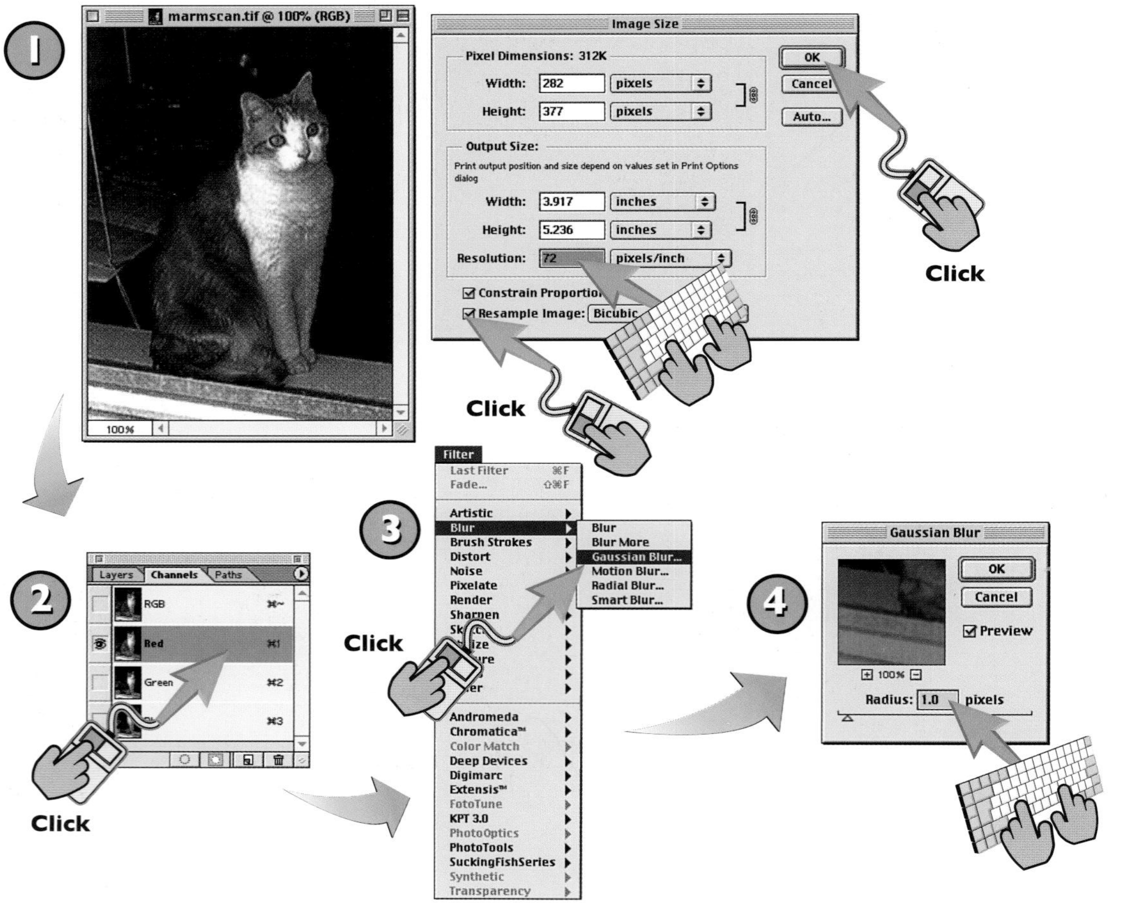

1. Choose **Image**, **Image Size**; enter the desired resolution, click **Resample Image**, and click **OK**.
2. Choose **Window**, **Show Channels**, and click the first color channel in the palette.
3. Choose **Filter**, **Blur**, **Gaussian Blur**.
4. Enter a **Radius** of 1–2 pixels and click **OK**.

For best results, scan the image as straight as possible and at the highest possible resolution. Then adjust the resolution before trying to remove the moiré.

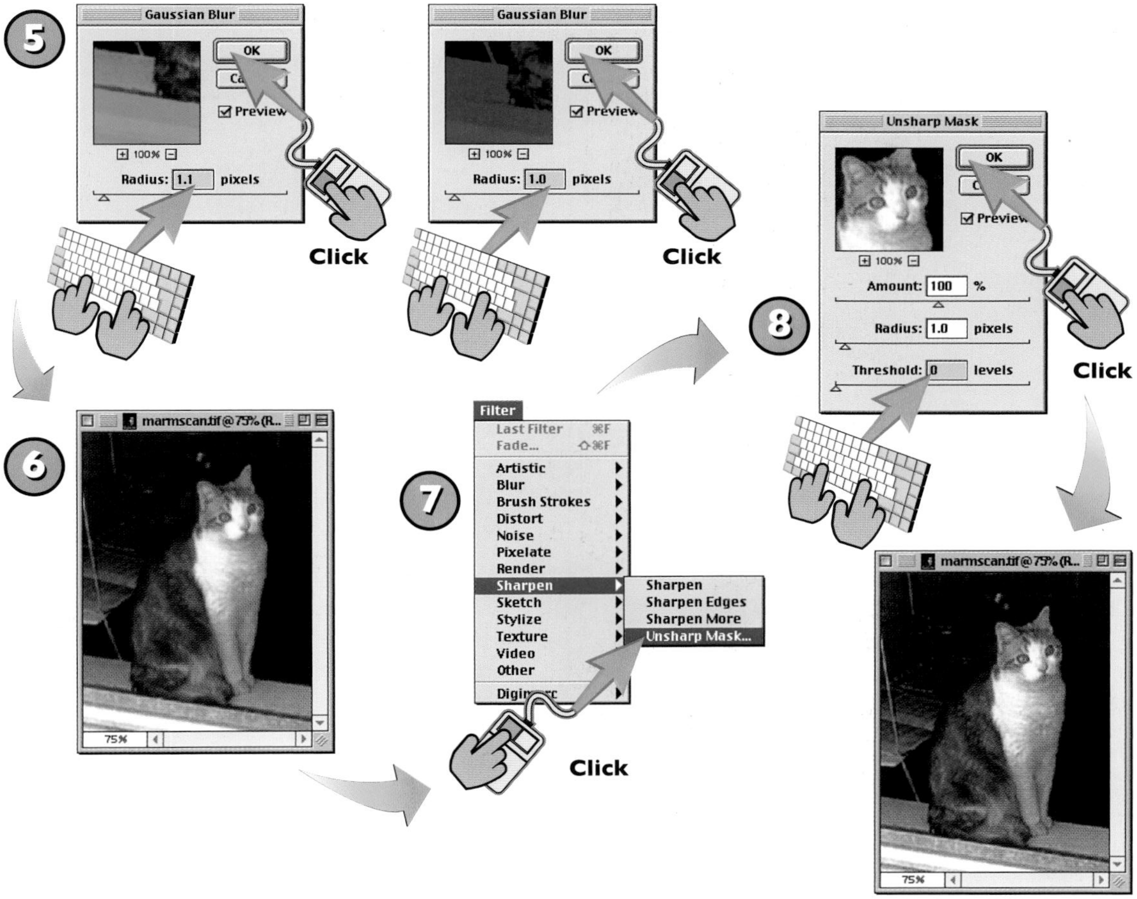

5 Repeat steps 3 and 4 for each color channel.

6 Press **Cmd+~/Ctrl+~** to display the composite image—all the color channels at once.

7 Choose **Filter**, **Sharpen**, **Unsharp Mask**.

8 Enter an **Amount** of **100%**, **Radius** of **1-2**, and **Threshold** of **0**, and then click **OK**.

When applying the Gaussian Blur filter, check Preview and watch the image as you adjust the Radius value. Use the lowest value that removes the moiré.

Use approximately the same Radius value with the Unsharp Mask filter as you did with the Gaussian Blur filter.

Task 15: Restoring Part of the Image to an Earlier Stage

Both snapshots and the History palette enable you to return to an earlier stage in an image's creation. The History Brush does the same thing, but it operates on only part of the image at a time, leaving the rest at its current appearance.

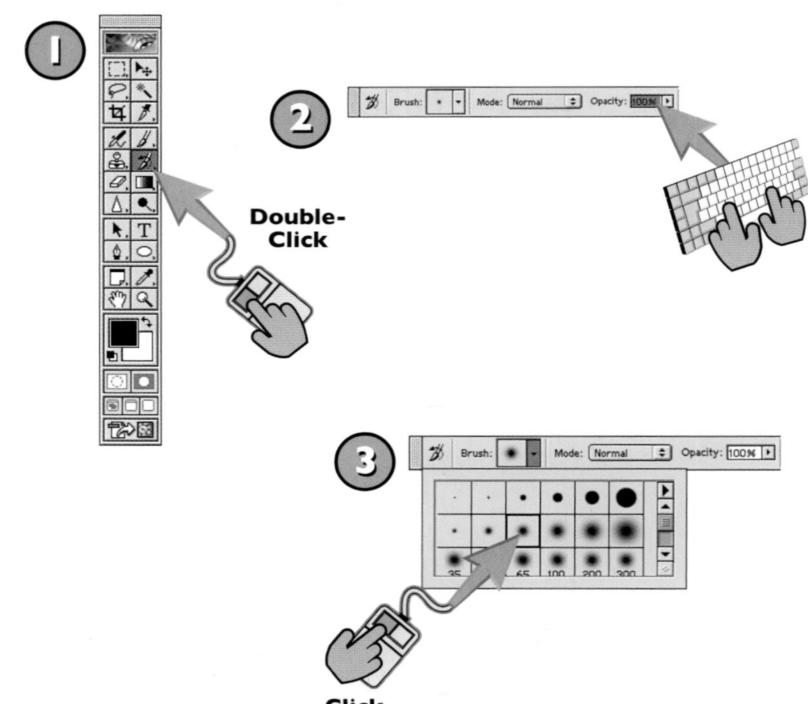

1. Double-click the **History Brush** to display the **History Brush Options** bar.
2. Enter an **Opacity** percentage.
3. Choose a brush from the **Brushes** menu in the **Options** bar.

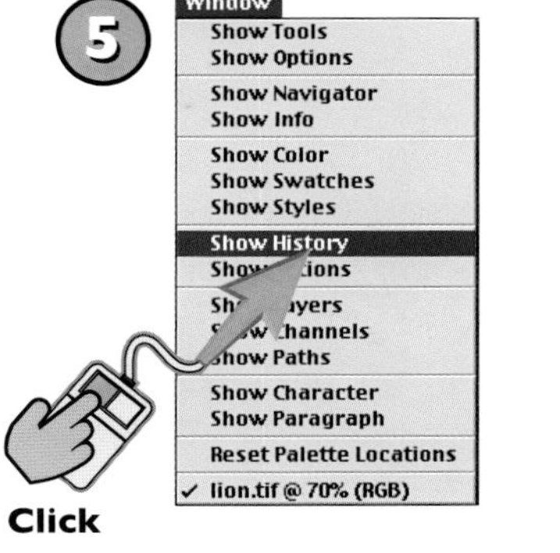

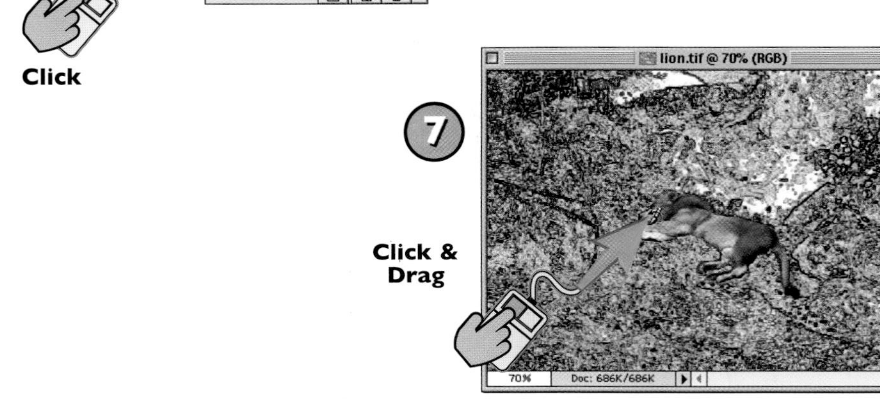

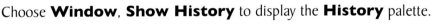

4. Choose **Window**, **Show History** to display the **History** palette.
5. Click in the blank square to the left of the history state you want to restore.
6. Click in the image and drag to restore.

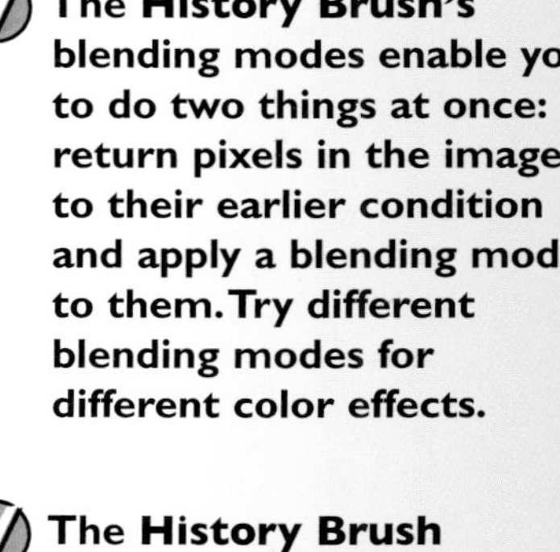

The **History Brush's** blending modes enable you to do two things at once: return pixels in the image to their earlier condition and apply a blending mode to them. Try different blending modes for different color effects.

The **History Brush** doesn't work on images you've just opened because they don't have a history.

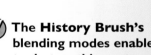

Task 16: Erasing an Image's Background

Silhouetting an image to remove a busy background—or one that's just the wrong color—is one of the most useful Photoshop tasks. The Extract command makes this procedure about as simple as it can be. Just outline what you want to keep, and Photoshop takes everything else away.

Start Here

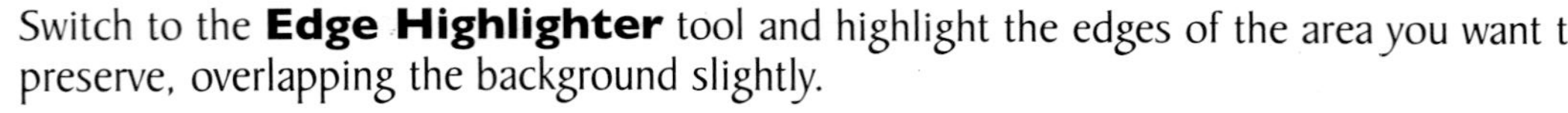

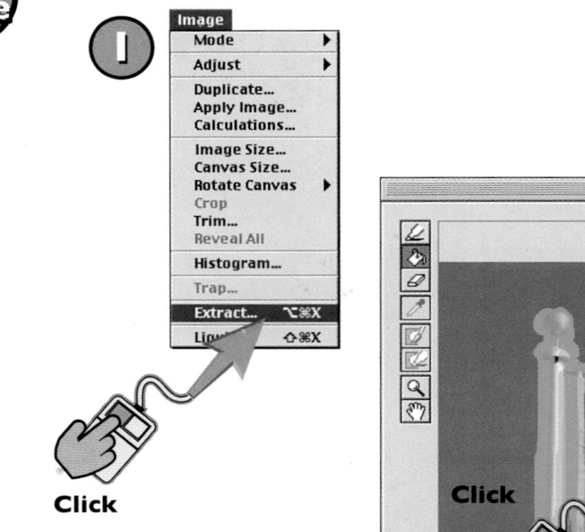

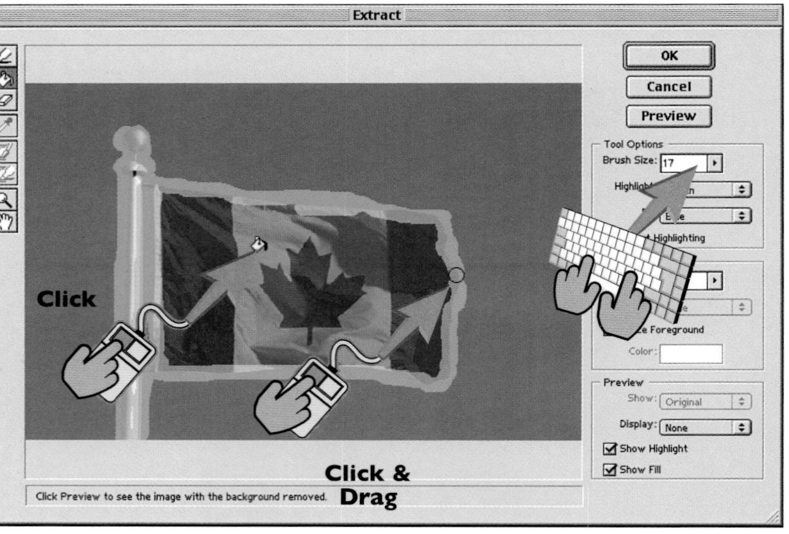

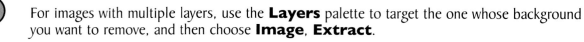

1. For images with multiple layers, use the **Layers** palette to target the one whose background you want to remove, and then choose **Image**, **Extract**.
2. Choose a **Brush Size** by entering a pixel value or by using the pop-up slider.
3. Switch to the **Edge Highlighter** tool and highlight the edges of the area you want to preserve, overlapping the background slightly.
4. Switch to the **Fill** tool and click inside the highlighted edges to fill in the area you want to preserve.

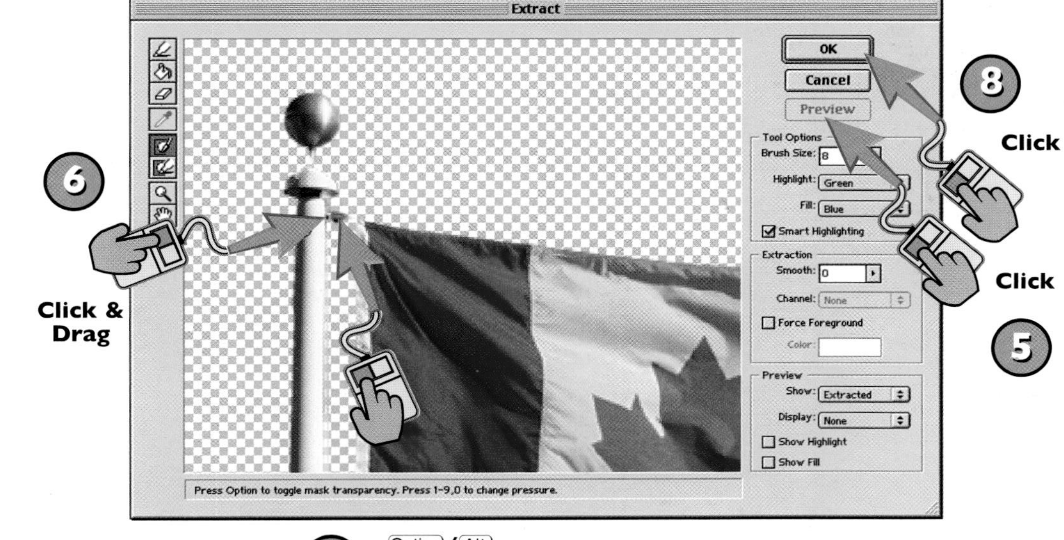

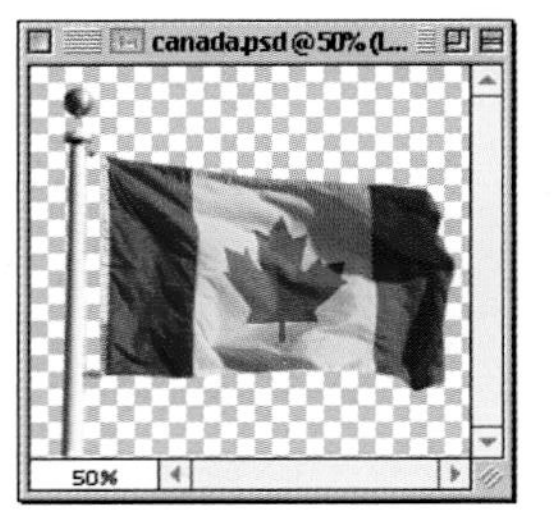

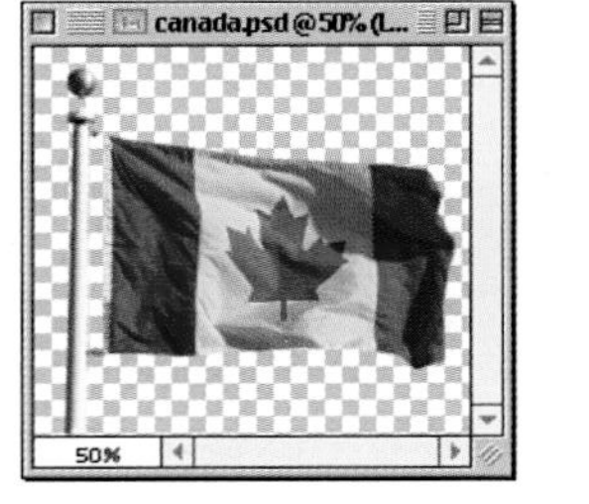

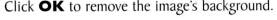

5 Click **Preview** to see the results of your current highlighted selection.

6 To remove more pixels, choose the **Cleanup** tool, and then click and drag in the image to make more areas transparent.

7 To restore pixels that have been deleted, hold down **Option/Alt** while using the **Cleanup** tool.

8 Click **OK** to remove the image's background.

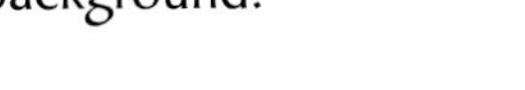

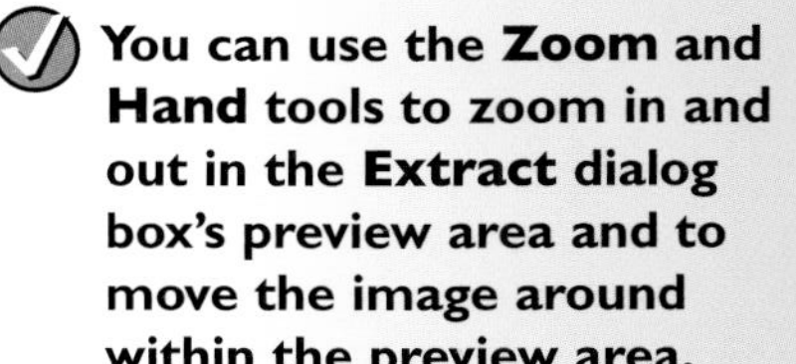

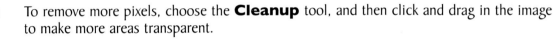

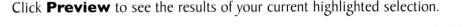

If you're highlighting a sharply defined edge, you can click Smart Highlighting to have Photoshop help you stick to the edge—it's similar to the way the Magnetic Lasso and Magnetic Pen tools work. Just make sure that your first click is right on the edge of the object you're outlining.

You can use the Zoom and Hand tools to zoom in and out in the Extract dialog box's preview area and to move the image around within the preview area.

Task 17: Making Notes Within an Image

Just as a photographer might add notes to the back of a print or a proof sheet, you can leave yourself or others messages within your Photoshop files. Annotations can contain information about an image's contents (such as identifying people or places) or information about what changes you've made to an image (such as which filters you ran or what Unsharp Mask settings you used).

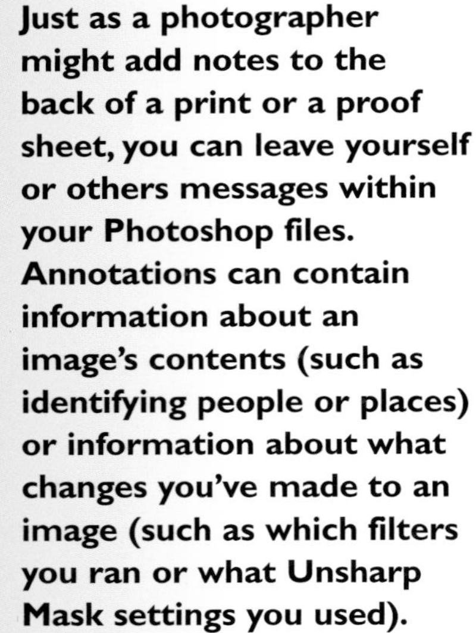

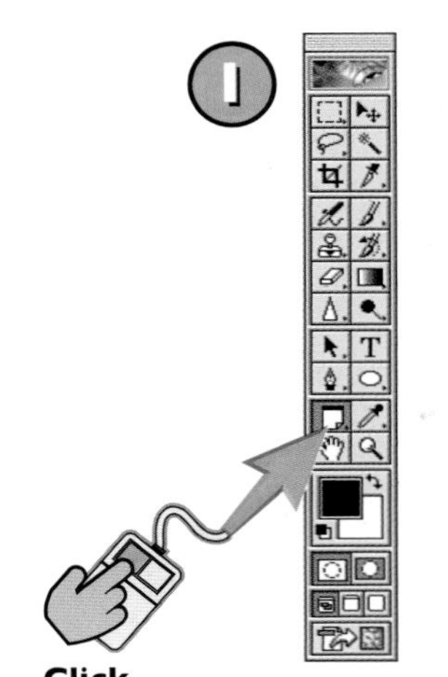

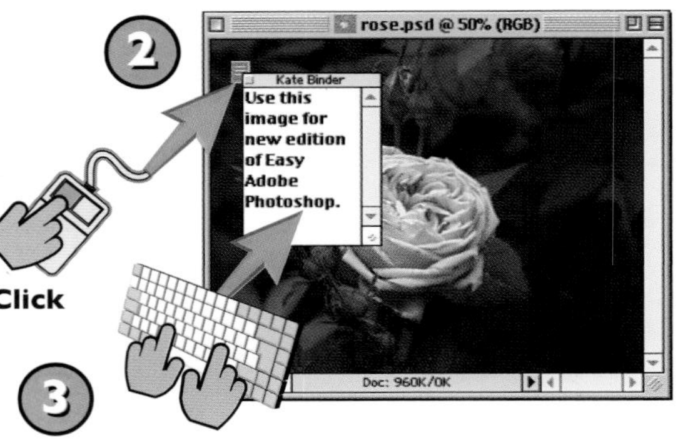

✓ You can change the font, text size, and icon color of text annotations using the pop-up menus in the **Notes Options** bar; double-click the **Notes** tool or choose **Window**, **Show Options** to display the **Options** bar. For audio annotations, the **Options** bar only enables you to change the icon color.

1. To insert a text note, choose the **Notes** tool from the **Tool** palette.
2. Click in the image to create a note.
3. Enter the note text and click the close box to minimize the note to an icon.
4. To view a text note, double-click its icon.

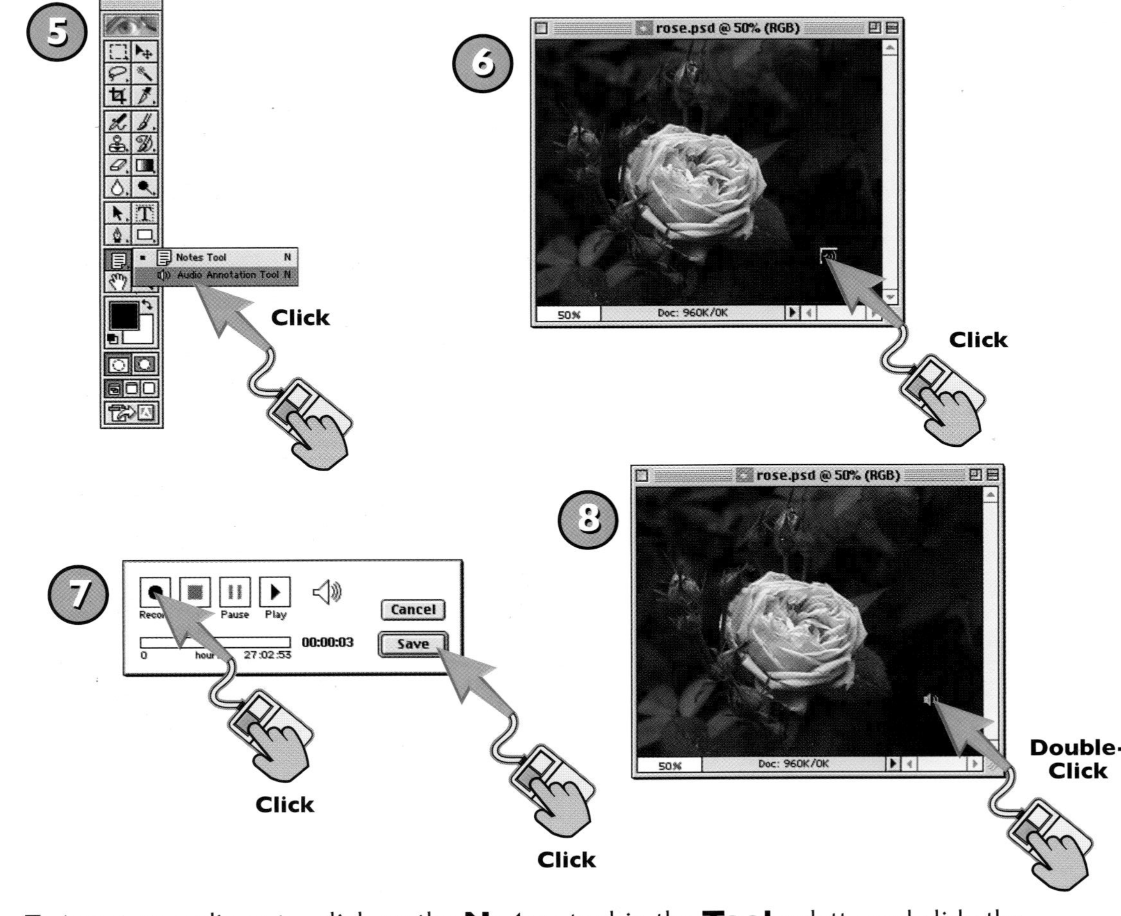

5 To insert an audio note, click on the **Notes** tool in the **Tool** palette and slide the cursor over to select **Audio Annotation Tool**.

6 Click in the image to create an audio note.

7 Click **Record** and speak into your computer's microphone. Click **Save** when you're finished.

8 To play an audio annotation, double-click its icon.

To delete a text note or audio annotation, click on its icon and press Delete, and then click OK in the resulting dialog box. You can also click on an icon and drag it to a new position in the image.

If you don't have a microphone for your computer, you won't be able to create audio annotations.

End Task

PART 7

Adjusting Colors and Tones

As an image editor, perhaps Photoshop's most commonly used function is to improve the color, contrast, and sharpness of existing images, such as scanned photographs. Several tools provide ways to make these adjustments with varying levels of complexity. Like any effect, these changes can be applied to the entire image or just to selected areas; for example, you can remove shadows that fall on a person's face or tone down a background to focus attention on a figure in the foreground.

Part 7 shows you how to adjust an image's bright, dark, and medium areas; correct colors for printing; change a file's color mode for use with a different medium; and make multiple adjustments at one time based on changes previewed in small thumbnail images.

Tasks

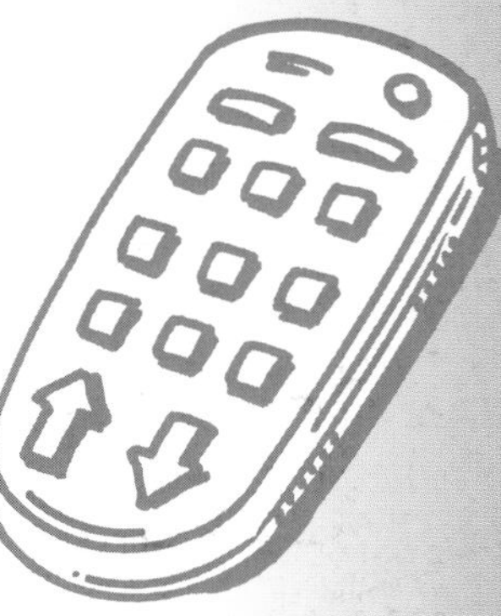

Although Photoshop includes tools for adjusting each individual gray or color level in an image, sometimes all you need is a quick tweak. In this case, you can turn to the **Brightness/Contrast** command—just don't overdo it.

Start Here

Task 1: Brightening or Darkening an Image

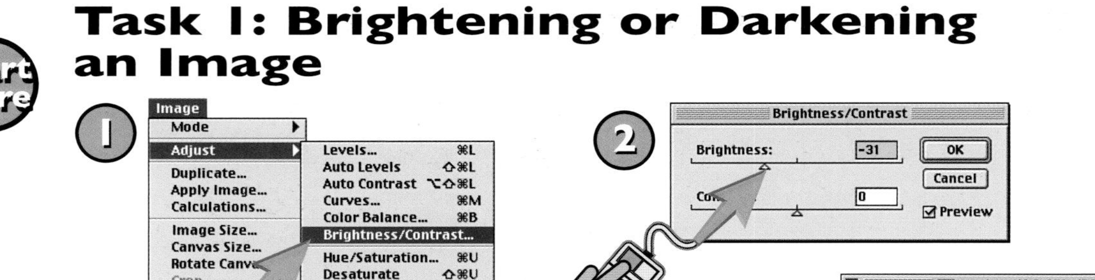

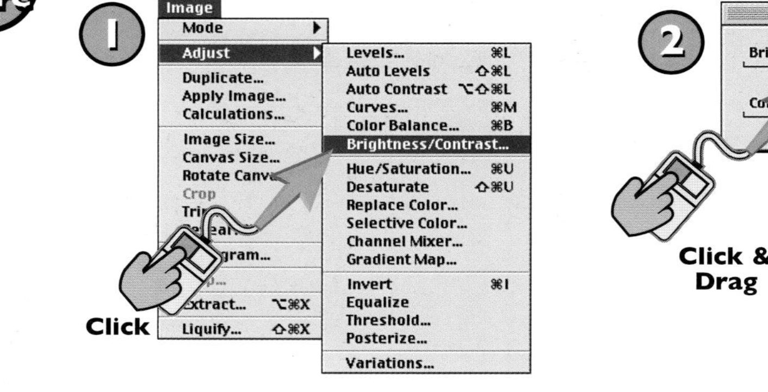

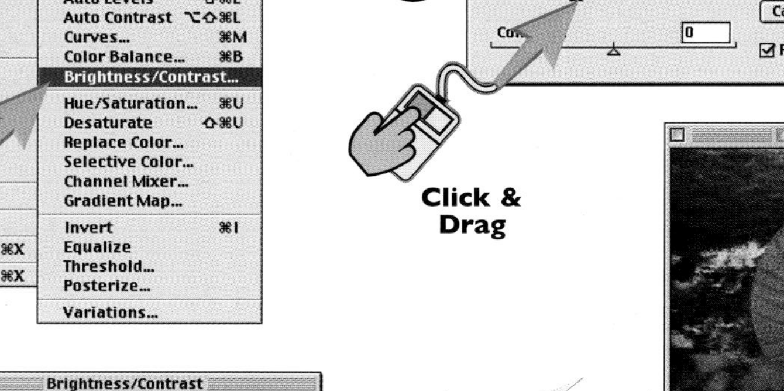

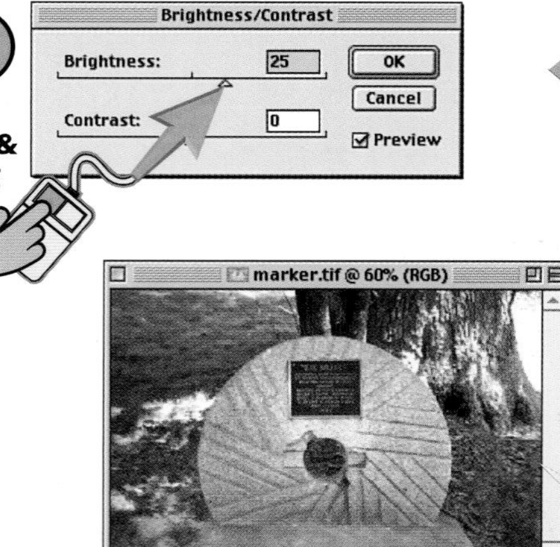

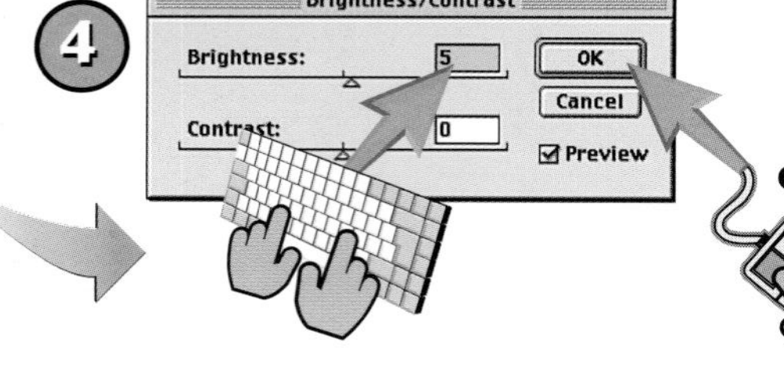

1. Choose **Image**, **Adjust**, **Brightness/Contrast**.
2. Drag the **Brightness** slider left to darken the image.
3. Drag the **Brightness** slider right to lighten the image.
4. Enter a positive or negative numeric value to lighten or darken the image, and then click **OK**.

✓ If you want to adjust a group of images exactly the same way, use the slider to adjust the first image, and then enter the resulting number in the dialog box for each of the other images.

Task 2: Increasing Contrast

Click

Click & Drag

Click & Drag

Click

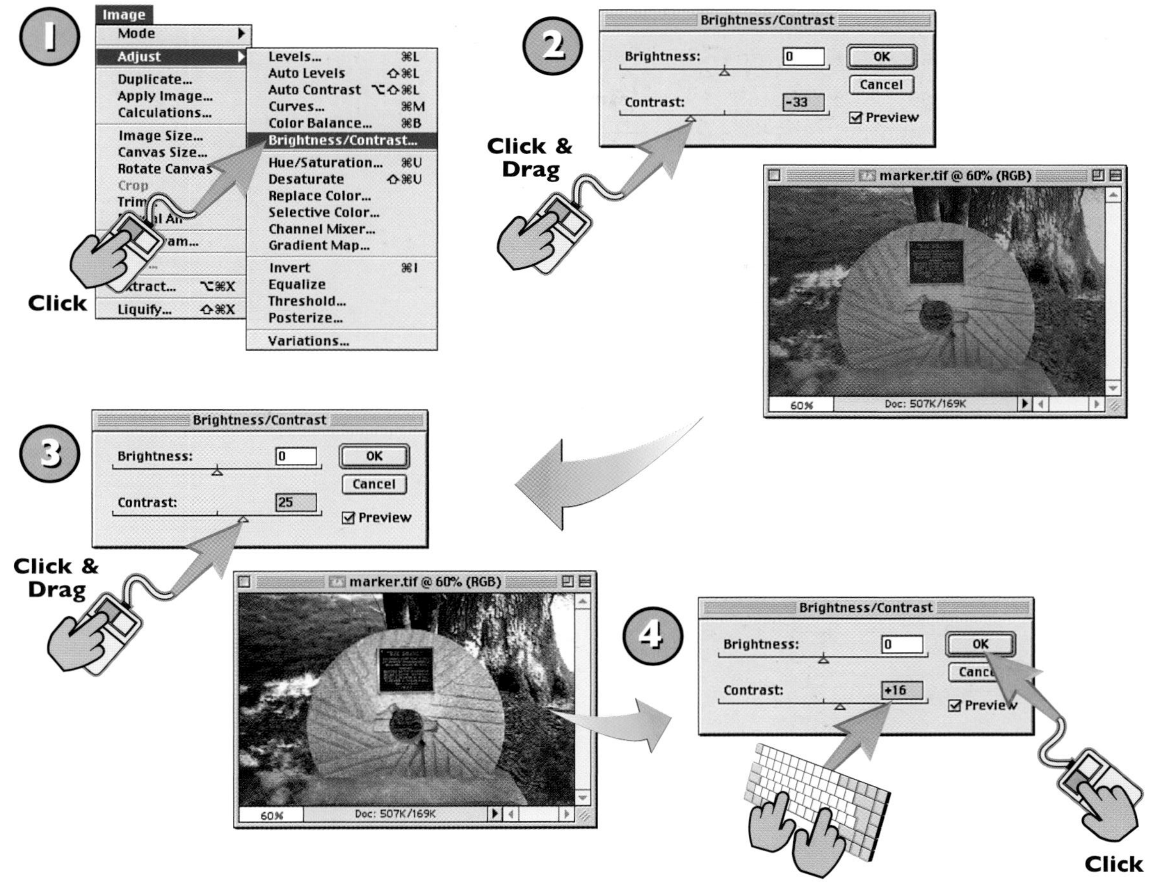

Photoshop's Brightness/ Contrast dialog box enables you to bump up the contrast in an image with a simple slider. Watch out, though; it's easy to turn a lovely photograph into a cartoon with a contrast adjustment.

1. Choose **Image**, **Adjust**, **Brightness/Contrast**.
2. Drag the **Contrast** slider left to reduce contrast.
3. Drag the **Contrast** slider right to increase contrast.
4. Enter a positive or negative numeric value to increase or reduce contrast, respectively, and click **OK**.

Try adjusting the contrast all the way up or most of the way down for some cool special effects. These are things you wouldn't normally do to an image, but they have their uses.

PART

Task 3: Adjusting an Image's Overall Tones

Start Here

Photoshop's Levels dialog box is the professional's favorite way to quickly adjust all the tones within an image, whether it's color or grayscale. With Levels, you can show Photoshop the lightest and darkest areas in an image and force the software to remap areas in between for a smooth range of brightness throughout the image.

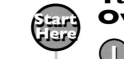

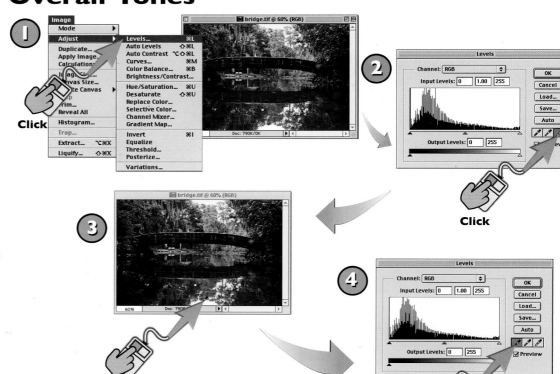

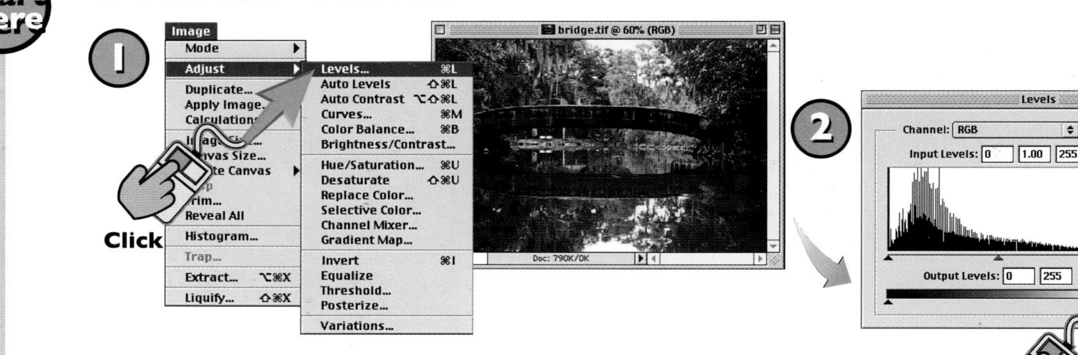
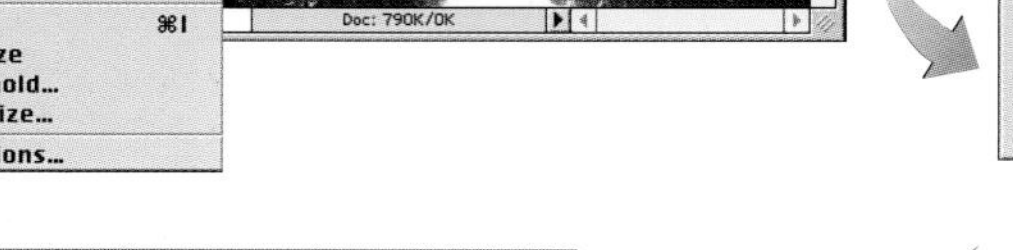

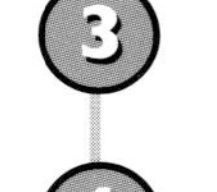

1. Choose **Image**, **Adjust**, **Levels**, or press **Cmd+L/Ctrl+L**.
2. Click the **white eyedropper** tool.
3. Click in the lightest area of the image.
4. Click the **black eyedropper** tool.

The **Levels** dialog box is one place where it's crucial to click on **Preview** so you can see your changes as you work.

Next Step

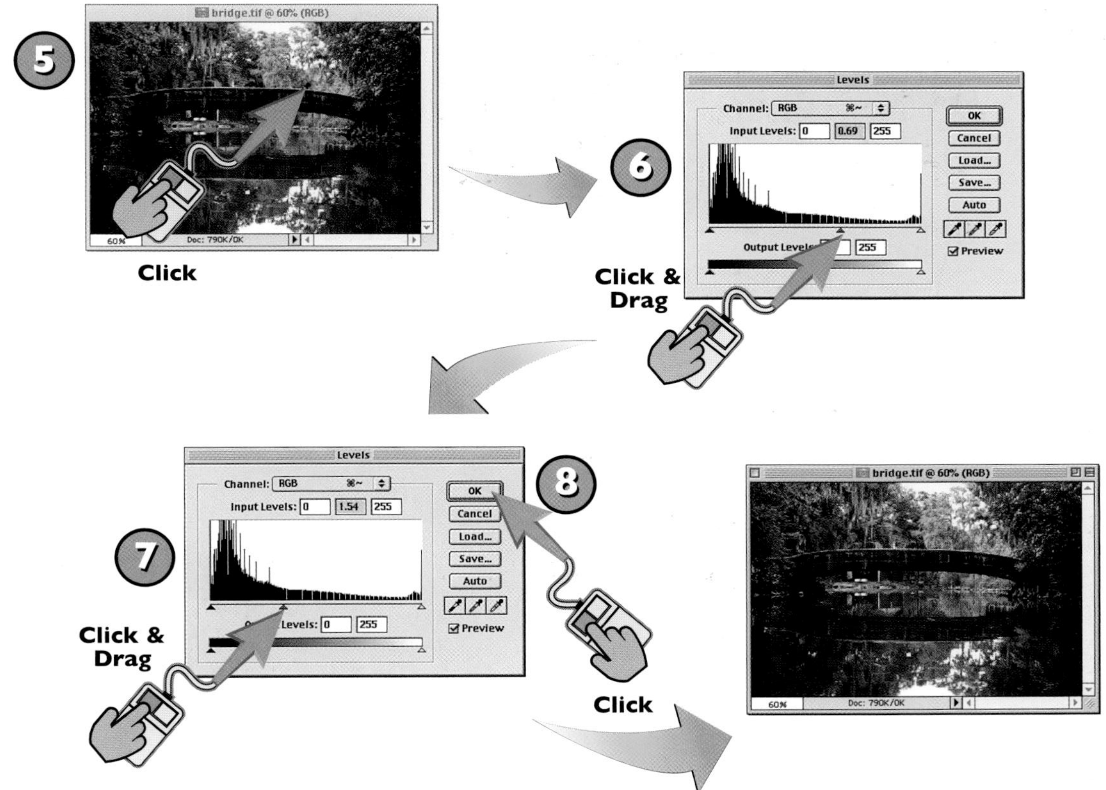

5 Click in the darkest area of the image.

6 Drag the middle slider to the right to darken the image.

7 Drag the middle slider to the left to lighten the image.

8 Click **OK** to apply the changes.

Press Cmd+Shift+L/ Ctrl+Shift+L to automatically adjust an image's levels without opening the Levels dialog box.

To apply the same adjustments to multiple images, click Save in the Levels dialog box to save a file containing the settings you've just made. Click Load to load those settings back into the dialog box at any time.

Task 4: Equalizing an Image's Bright and Dark Areas

Start Here

Equalizing distributes an image's brightness values evenly so that there are as many white pixels as black and gray. It's an occasional fix for an image that's too light or dark, but it will do bad things to an image that's supposed to be high-contrast.

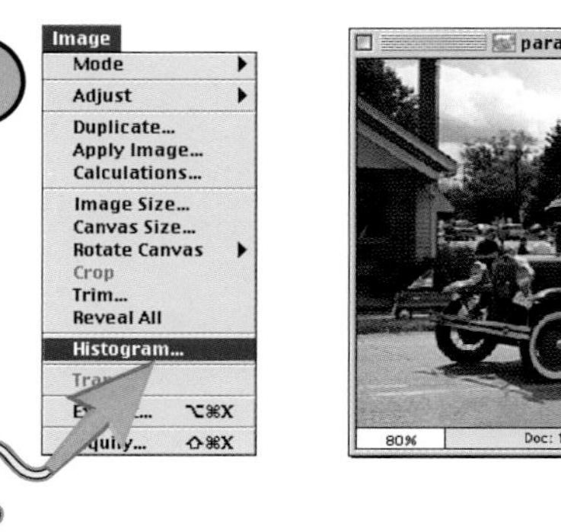

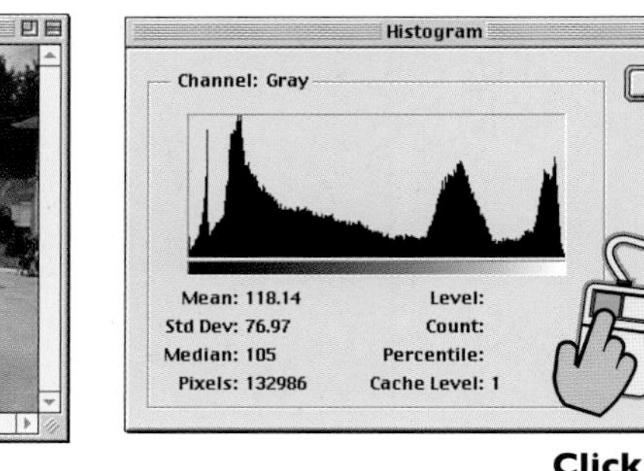
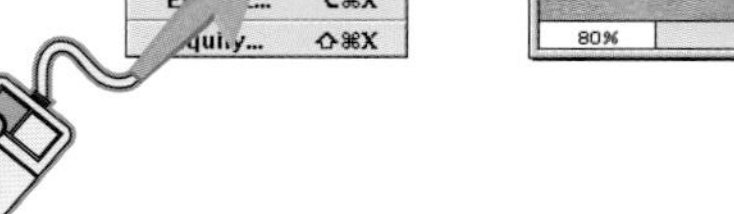

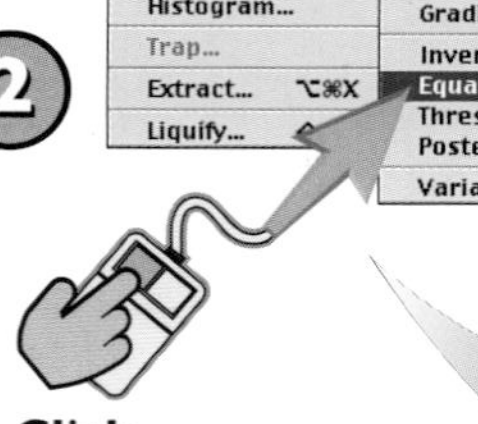

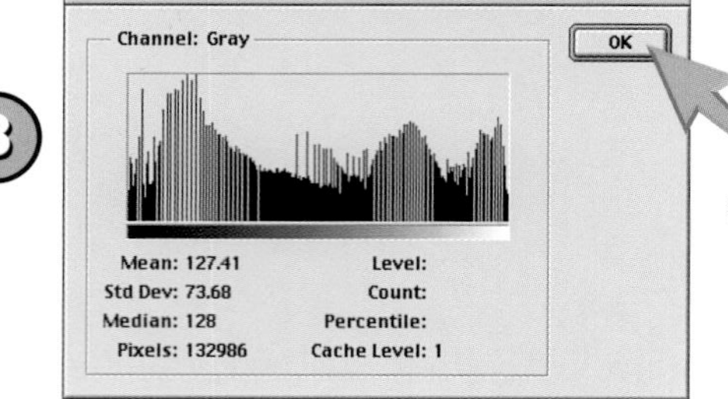

✓ The **Histogram** command isn't required when you're equalizing an image—it's just a good way to get an idea of what the **Equalize** command is doing.

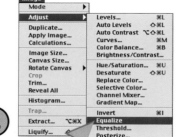

1. Choose **Image**, **Histogram** to see a graph of the image's brightness values, and then click **OK** in the **Histogram** dialog box.

2. Choose **Image**, **Adjust**, **Equalize**.

3. Choose **Image**, **Histogram** to view the adjusted histogram, and then click **OK** in the **Histogram** dialog box.

End Task

Task 5: Inverting an Image

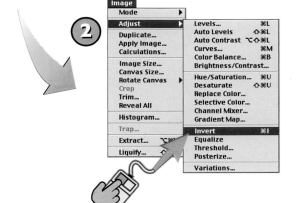

Most often useful for special effects, the **Invert** command creates a negative image—or turns a negative into a positive. A common artistic technique is to invert half of an image, leaving the other half as a positive.

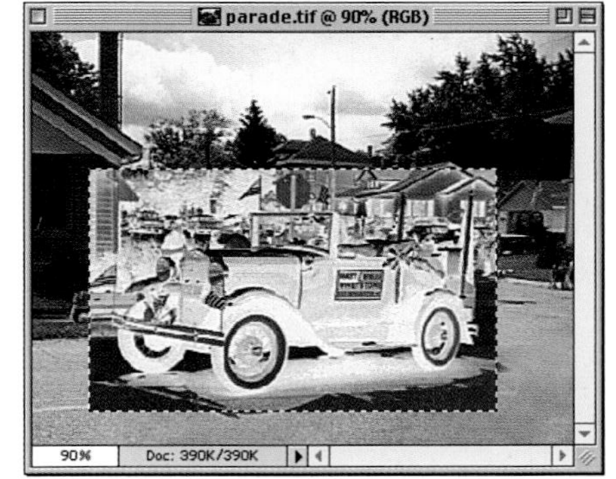

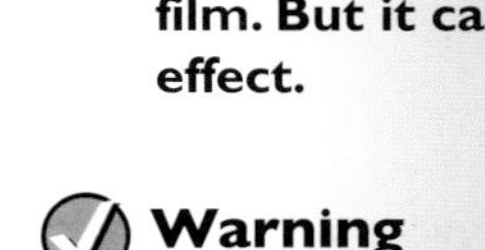

This negative image is not truly like a film negative because of the compensation in film for the orange-colored base of film. But it can be a neat effect.

Warning
The **Invert** command is often confused with the **Inverse** command (**Cmd+Shift+I/Ctrl+Shift+I**), which reverses a selection.

1. To invert part of an image, select that part; if there is no active selection, the whole image will be inverted.

2. Choose **Image**, **Adjust**, **Invert** or press **Cmd+I/Ctrl+I**.

Task 6: Creating a High-Contrast Black-and-White Image

For some designs, a black-and-white image is more desirable than a color one. The Threshold command turns images into areas of solid black and white with no grays. It's useful for creating images that will photocopy well or even for designing screen printing images.

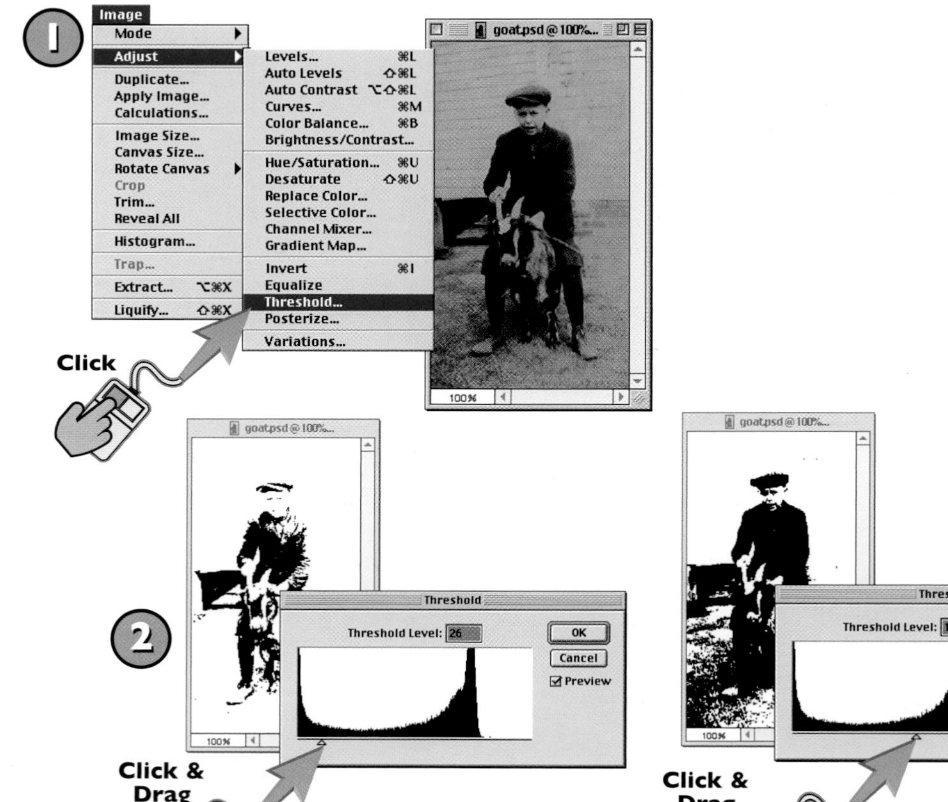

When using the **Threshold** dialog box, it's important to click **Preview** so you can see the effects of your changes as you make them.

You can apply the **Threshold** command to just part of the image by selecting that part before choosing **Image, Adjust, Threshold.**

1. Choose **Image**, **Adjust**, **Threshold**.
2. Drag the slider to the left to increase the amount of white in the image.
3. Drag the slider to the right to increase the amount of black in the image.
4. Click **OK**.

Task 7: Locating and Correcting Colors that Won't Print Correctly

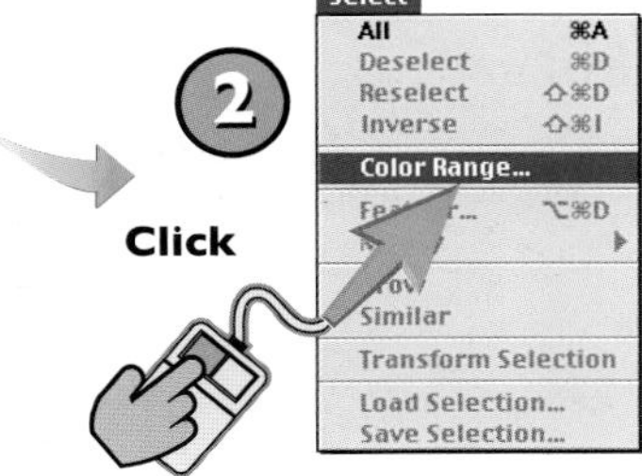

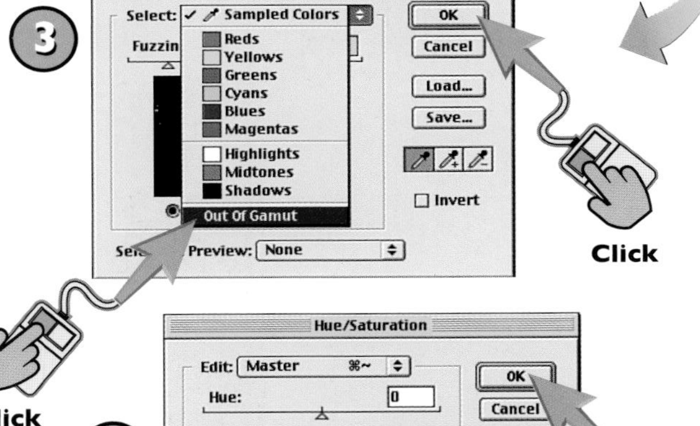

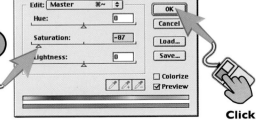

1 Press **Cmd+Shift+Y/Ctrl+Shift+Y** to show out-of-gamut colors.

2 Choose **Select**, **Color Range**.

3 Select **Out of Gamut** from the pop-up menu and click **OK**.

4 Press **Cmd+U/Ctrl+U**, drag the **Saturation** slider left to get rid of the gamut alarm color, and click **OK**.

One of the biggest problems in working with color images is trying to make color prints match what you see on your monitor. Colors that won't print correctly are called out-of-gamut colors, and Photoshop can help you identify and fix them.

Press Cmd+D/Ctrl+D to drop the selection.

It's easier to see the gamut alarm color while you're working in the Hue/Saturation dialog box if you press Cmd+H/Ctrl+H to hide the selection first.

The gamut alarm color is gray by default, but it's easier to see if you change it to a bright color that doesn't appear in your image. Choose Edit, Preferences, Transparency and Gamut, and click the color swatch to choose a new color.

Task 8: Desaturating an Area

Converting an entire image to grayscale involves changing its color mode (see Task 10), but you can choose to "drain" the color from just part of an image with the Desaturate command.

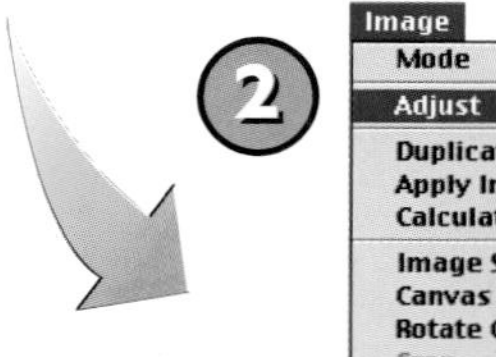

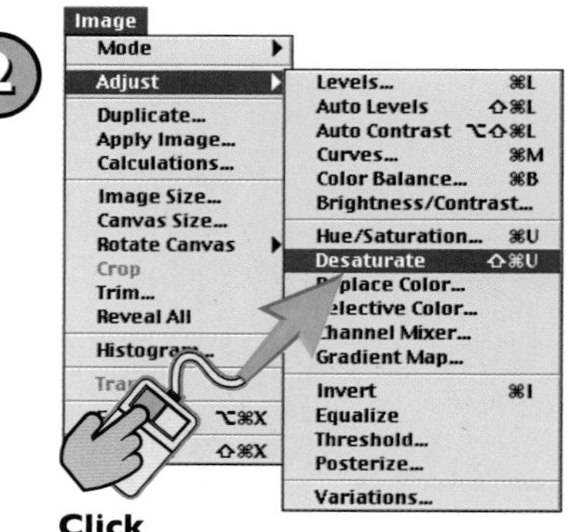

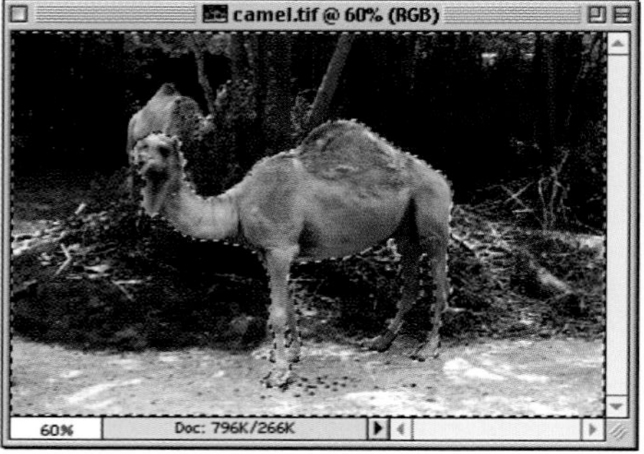

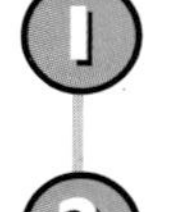

1. Select the area you want to desaturate.
2. Choose **Image**, **Adjust**, **Desaturate**.

If you decide to put some of the color back into the desaturated area, choose **Edit, Fade Desaturate** and drag the slider left; then click **OK**.

To make an image more colorful, use the **Hue/Saturation** command (see the next task).

End Task

Task 9: Increasing the Color Saturation of an Area

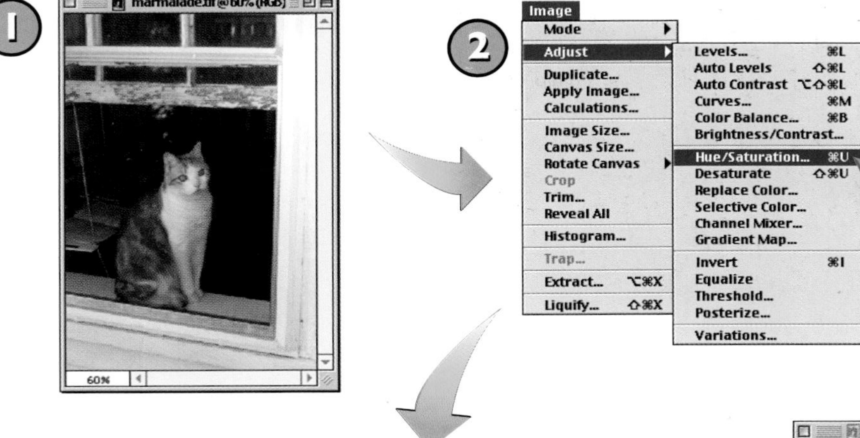

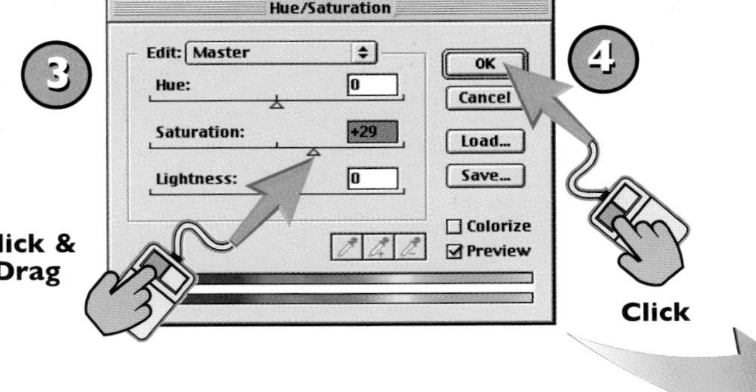

Color intensity is referred to as *saturation* in Photoshop—the more intense a color is, the more saturated it is. An image with no saturation at all is a grayscale image with no color. Highly saturated images look like cartoons.

1. Select the portion of the image to adjust.
2. Choose **Image**, **Adjust**, **Hue/Saturation**.
3. Drag the **Saturation** slider right to increase the saturation or left to decrease it.
4. Click **OK** to apply the change.

✓ To adjust the saturation of an entire image, don't make a selection before choosing **Image, Adjust, Hue/Saturation.**

✓ Avoid increasing the saturation too much in images that will be printed—most color printers can't reproduce highly saturated images anyway.

Photoshop's color modes enable you to define color in different ways. Different image formats also require specific color modes, and even Bitmap and Grayscale are considered color modes. Changing color mode has a permanent effect on an image, so always save a copy first. The options covered here are the most common color modes.

Task 10: Changing a File's Color Mode

1

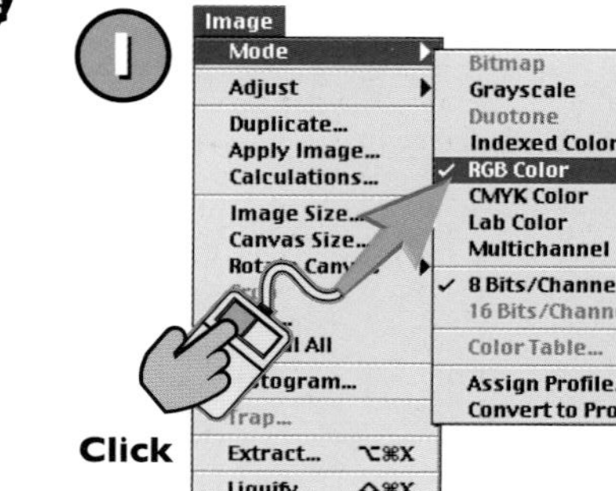

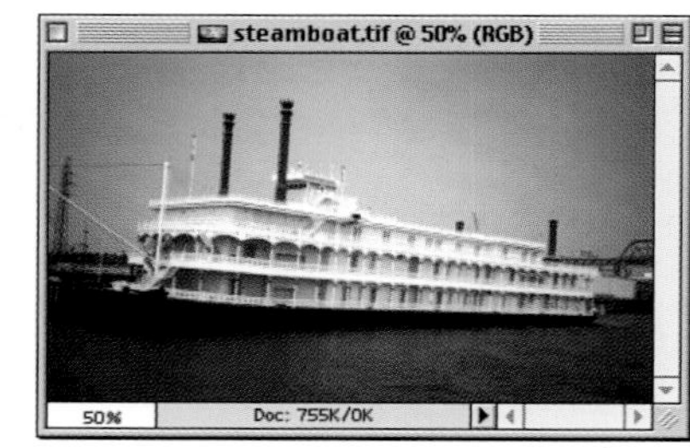

2

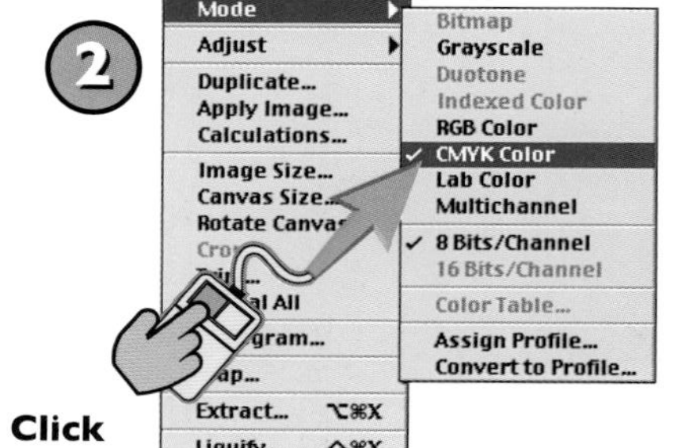

3

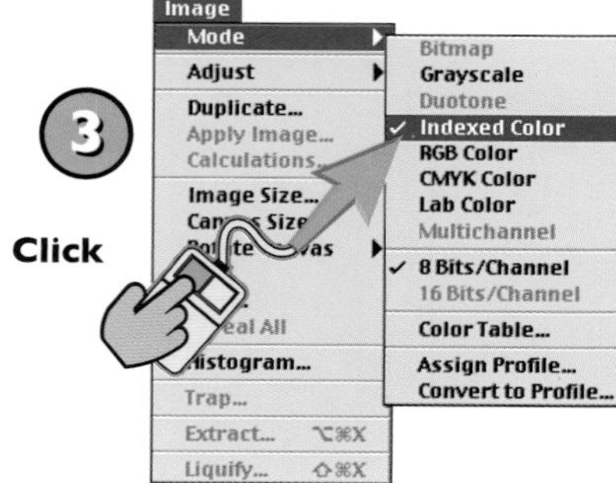

1. Choose **Image**, **Mode**, **RGB Color** to create images for onscreen display.
2. Choose **Image**, **Mode**, **CMYK Color** to create images for printing.
3. Choose **Image**, **Mode**, **Indexed Color** to convert images for display on the Web.

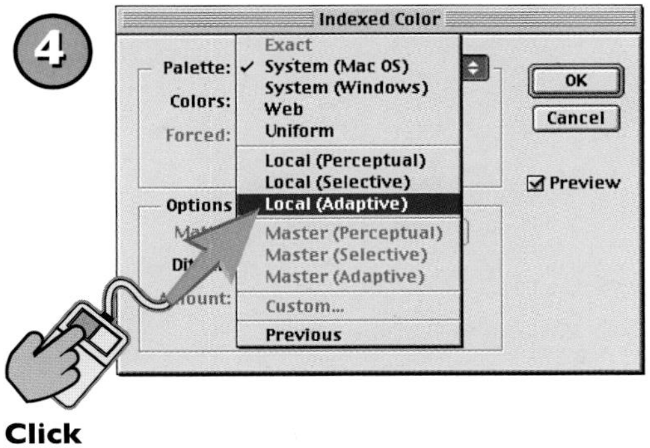

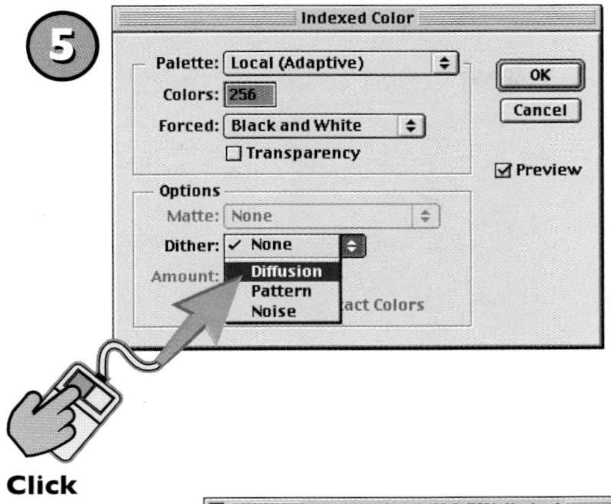

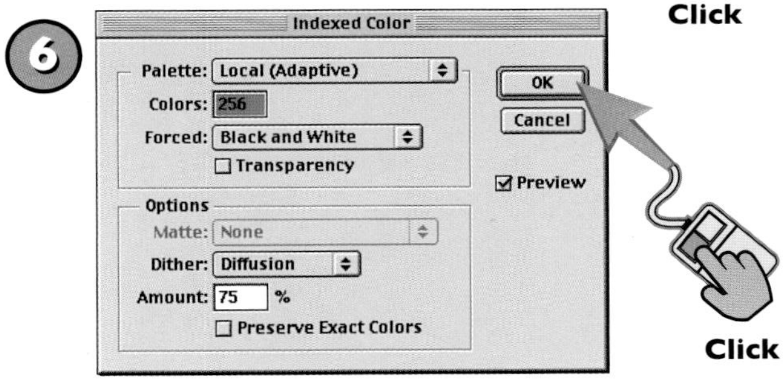

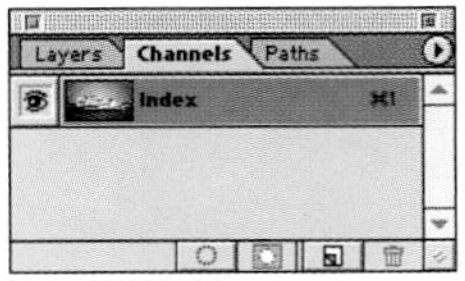

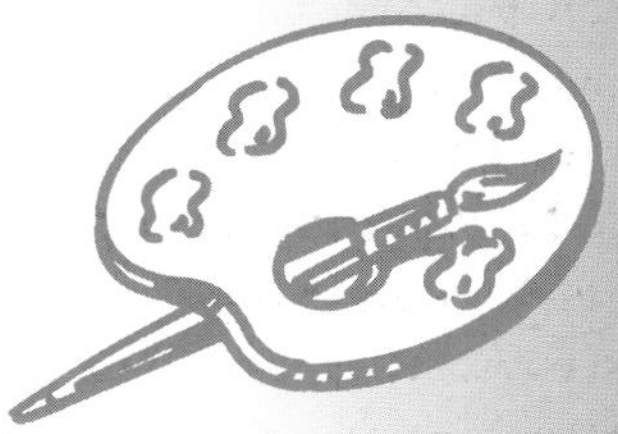

5 Choose **Local (Adaptive)** from the **Palette** pop-up menu.

6 Choose **Diffusion** from the **Dither** pop-up menu.

7 Click **OK** to convert the image.

To convert an image to grayscale mode, see Part 4, Task 9, "Converting a Color Image to Grayscale." To convert an image to a duotone, see Part 4, Task 10, "Creating a Duotone Image."

Task 11: Adjusting an Image's Color Balance

Often image colors tend toward one extreme, such as being too magenta or too yellow. The Color Balance command enables you to adjust distorted colors—called *color casts*—by moving the colors in the image more toward the opposite side of the color spectrum.

Start Here

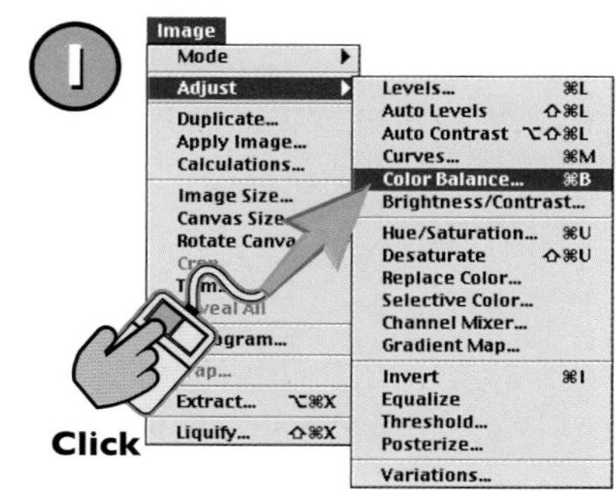

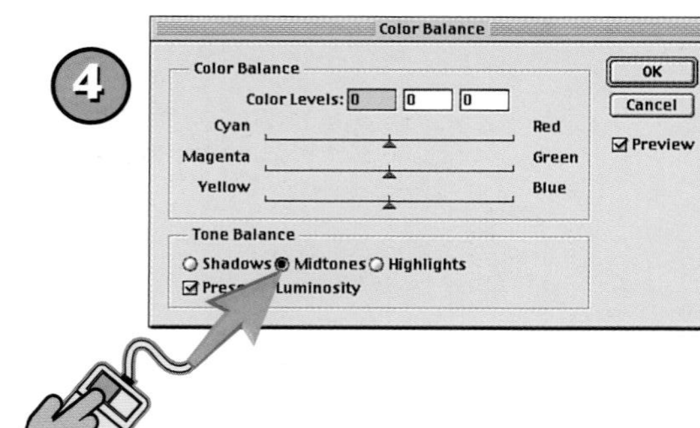

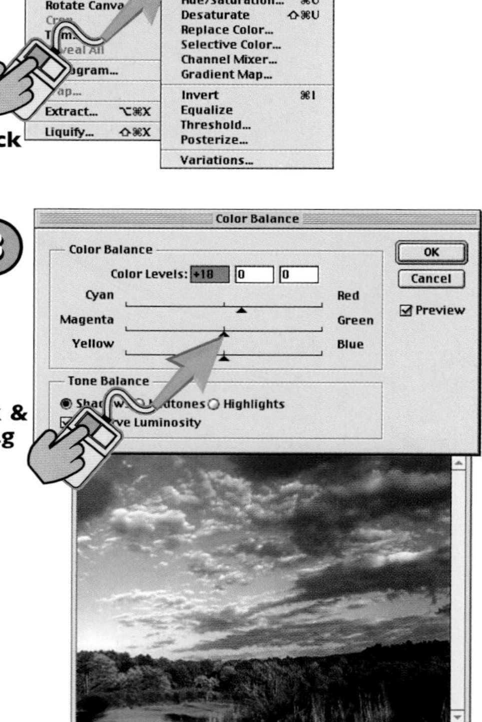

1. Choose **Image**, **Adjust**, **Color Balance** or press **Cmd+B/Ctrl+B**.
2. Click **Shadows** to adjust the image's dark colors.
3. Adjust the **Cyan**, **Magenta**, and **Yellow** tones in dark areas by dragging the sliders.
4. Click **Midtones** to adjust the image's medium colors.

To make sure the overall lightness or darkness of the image isn't affected, click Preserve Luminosity.

Not every image will need adjustments in all three tonal areas: highlights, midtones, and shadows. Before using Color Balance, determine what areas contain color casts.

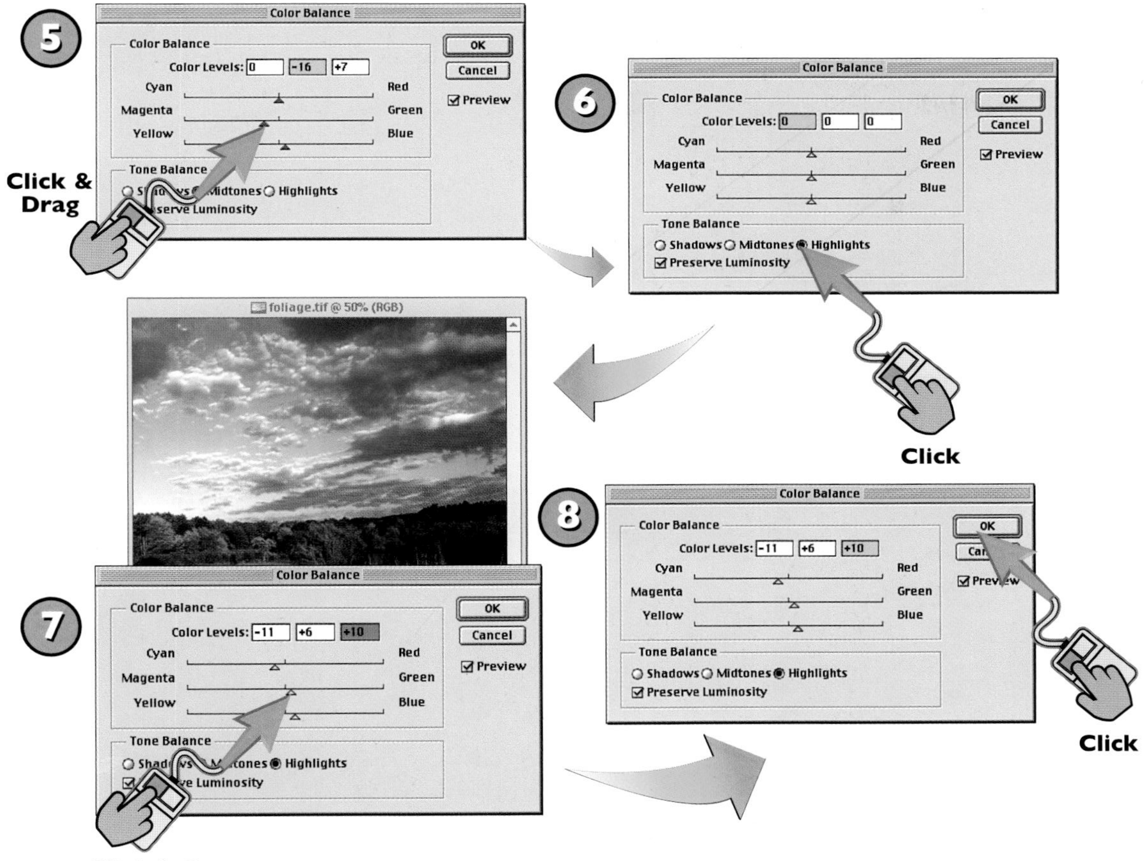

5 Click & Drag

6 Click

7 Click & Drag

8 Click

5 Adjust the **Cyan**, **Magenta**, and **Yellow** tones in medium areas by dragging the sliders.

6 Click **Highlights** to adjust the image's light colors.

7 Adjust the **Cyan**, **Magenta**, and **Yellow** tones in light areas by dragging the sliders.

8 Click **OK** to apply the changes.

The colors at opposite ends of the Color Balance sliders are complementary colors—opposites, in other words. Adding more cyan to an image gets rid of a red cast, and so on, with magenta complementing green and yellow complementing blue.

When you're working with color images, a big step in the adjustment process is the Hue/Saturation dialog box. It also controls the brightness of the image.

Start Here

Task 12: Changing an Image's Hue and Saturation

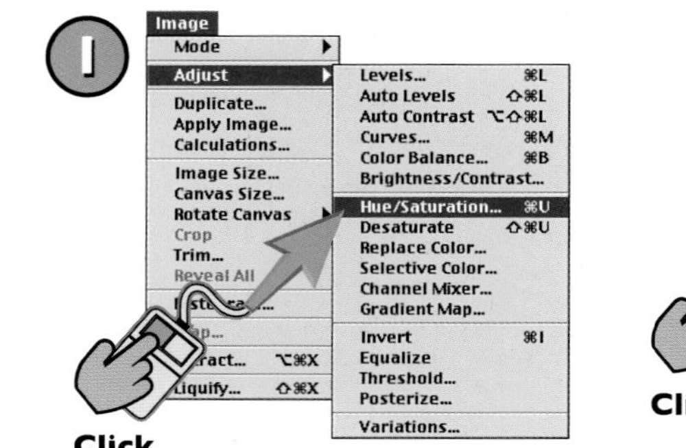

Click

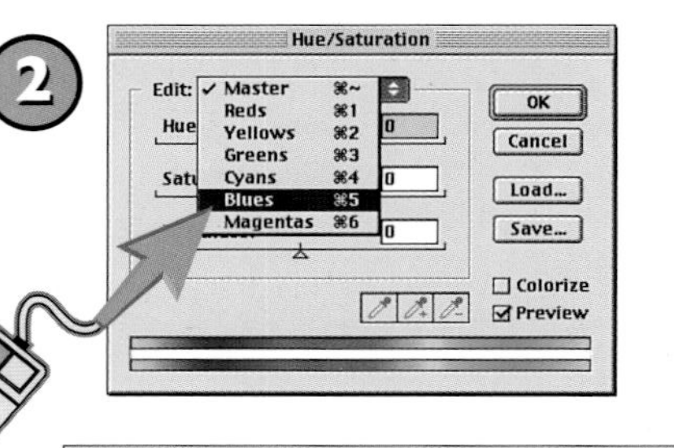

Click

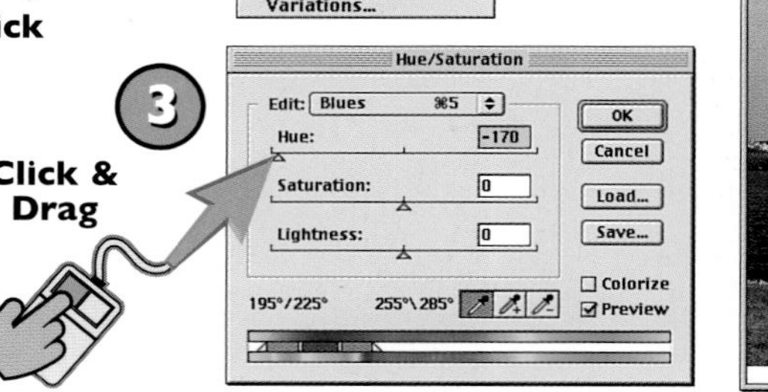

Click & Drag

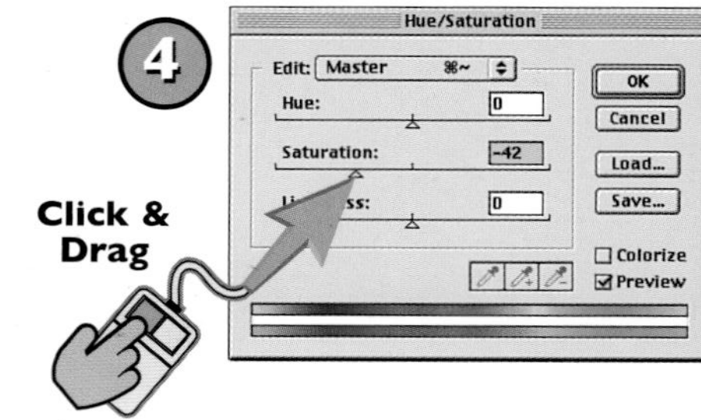

Click & Drag

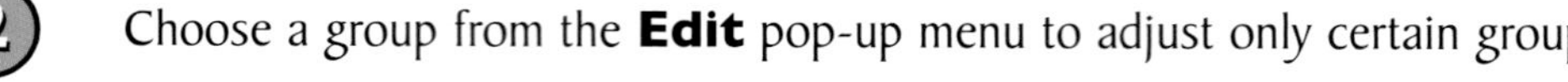

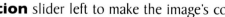

1. Choose **Image**, **Adjust**, **Hue/Saturation**, or press **Cmd+U/Ctrl+U**.

2. Choose a group from the **Edit** pop-up menu to adjust only certain groups of colors.

3. Drag the **Hue** slider to change the image's hue.

4. Drag the **Saturation** slider left to make the image's colors less intense.

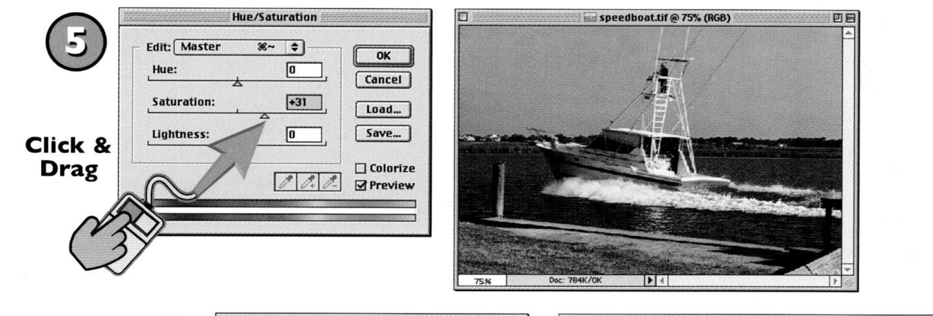

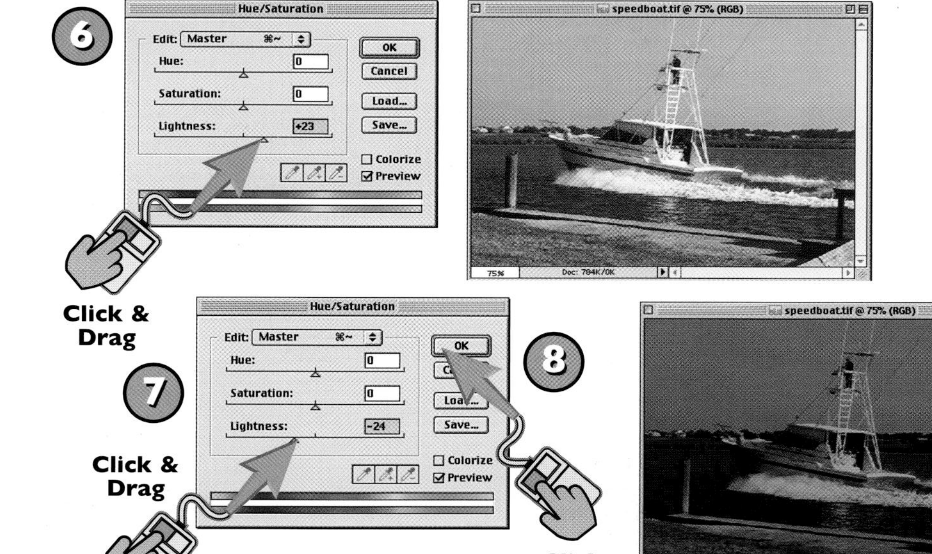

5 To make the image's colors more intense, drag the **Saturation** slider right.

6 Drag the **Lightness** slider right to lighten the image.

7 Drag the **Lightness** slider left to darken the image.

8 Click **OK** to apply the changes.

Hue/Saturation operates on all the colors in an image, light and dark—if you need to adjust just one color, use Selective Color (see Task 13). If you need to adjust only light colors, for example, use Levels (see Task 3).

Click the Colorize check box to change all the colors in the image to the color indicated by the Hue slider.

If you don't know which group in the Edit menu contains the colors you want to change, choose any group. Then click the eyedropper tool and click the color in the image to specify the correct group.

Task 13: Changing Individual Colors

Photoshop enables you to change colors in an image, either all at once or one at a time. The latter situation is where Selective Color comes in—choose this command to change just the reds or just the blues in an image.

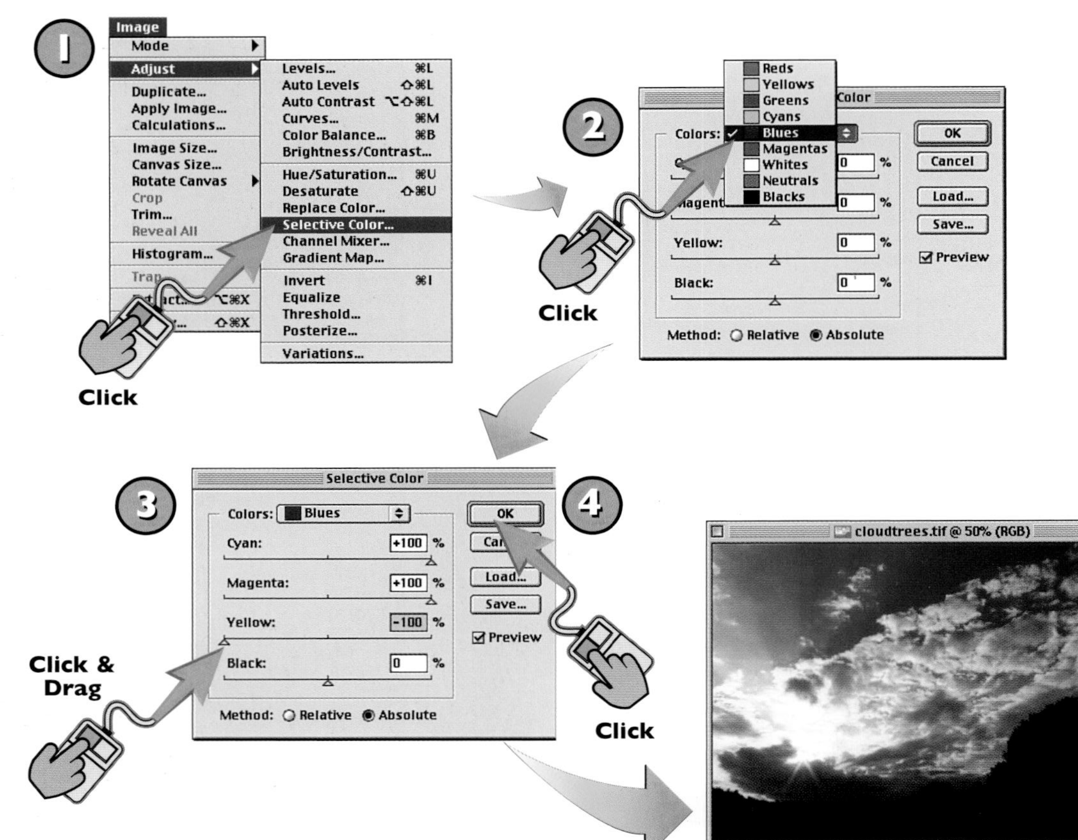

1. Choose **Image**, **Adjust**, **Selective Color**.
2. Choose the colors to adjust from the **Colors** pop-up menu.
3. Drag the four sliders to adjust the colors.
4. Click **OK** to apply the changes.

Click Relative to change colors proportionally with respect to how much of the target color they contain, or click Absolute to change colors by adding the specified percentage of color to all the colors in the target group.

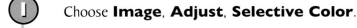

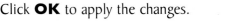

Task 14: Reducing the Number of Colors in an Image

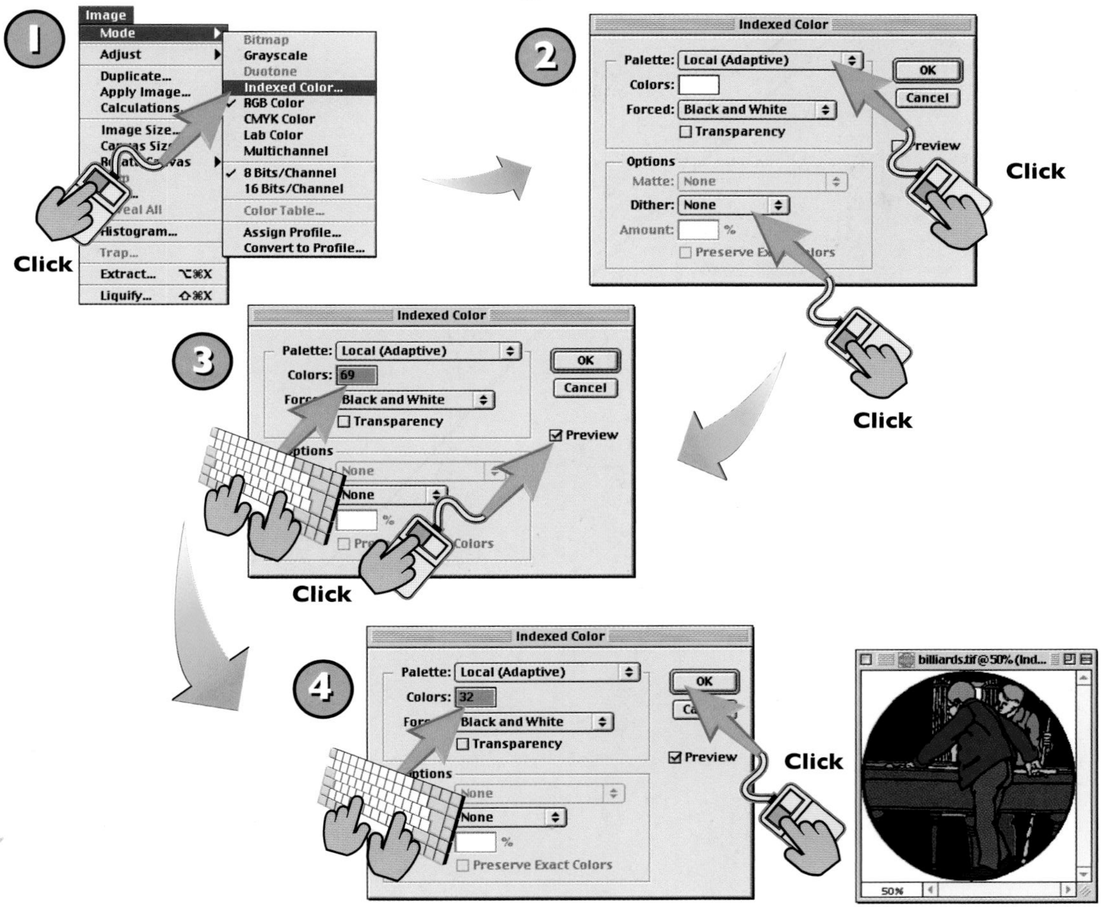

1 Choose **Image**, **Mode**, **Indexed Color**.

2 Choose **Local (Adaptive)** from the **Palette** pop-up menu and **None** from the **Dither** pop-up menu.

3 Click **Preview** and enter a number of colors.

4 Adjust the number of colors if necessary, and click **OK** to apply the change.

When you're creating images for use on the World Wide Web, you must use as few colors as possible so that the image files will be as small as possible. Converting images to Indexed Color mode enables you to specify how many colors are used in an image.

The number of colors you use in an image depends on how important it is that the image look exactly like the original. Photos generally need more colors; logos and other "flat" artwork can do with fewer colors.

Click Preview off and on to compare the original with your changed version.

Mixing channels is a fascinating way to make color adjustments. Getting used to the Channel Mixer command takes a little experimentation, but it can produce great special effects and make lovely hand-tinted effects.

Start Here

Task 15: Adjusting Colors by Mixing Channels

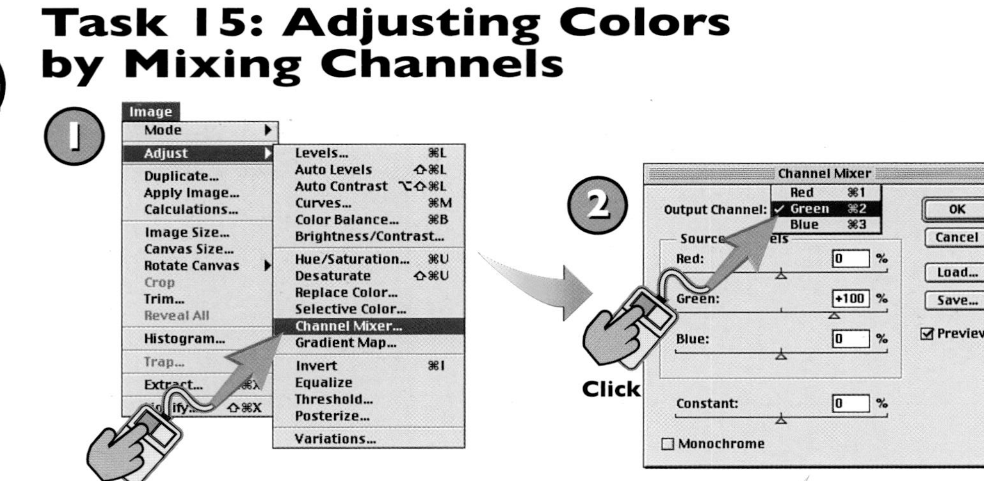

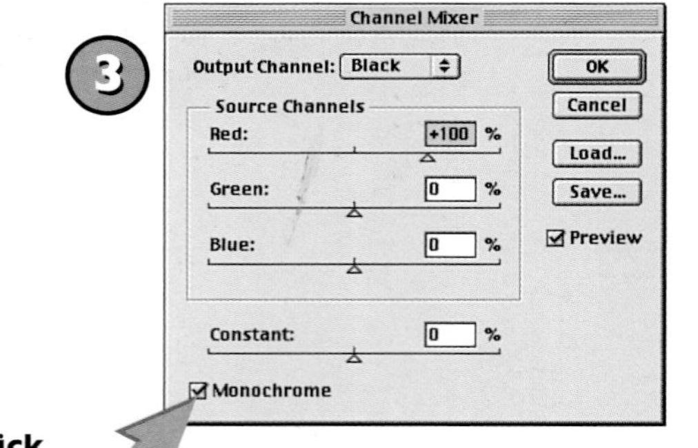

3

Click

✓ What's really happening when you use the Channel Mixer? Photoshop changes the grayscale image contained in one of your image's color channels by overlaying the images from the other color channels in the percentages you specify.

1 Choose **Image**, **Adjust**, **Channel Mixer**.

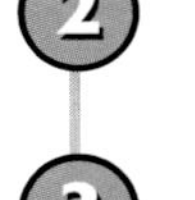

2 Choose the channel to "mix" in from the **Output Channel** pop-up menu.

3 Click **Monochrome** to make a grayscale image.

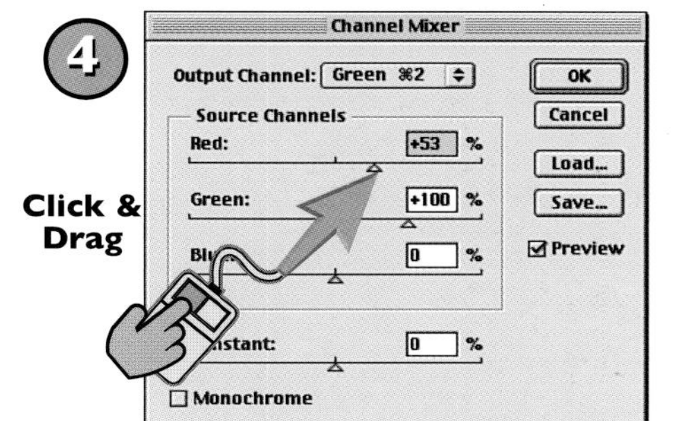

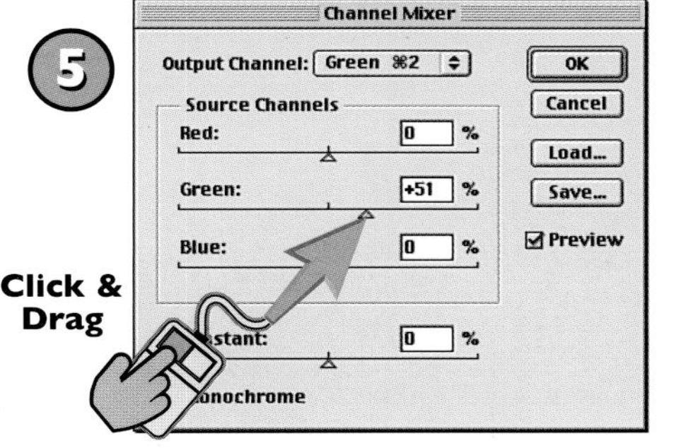

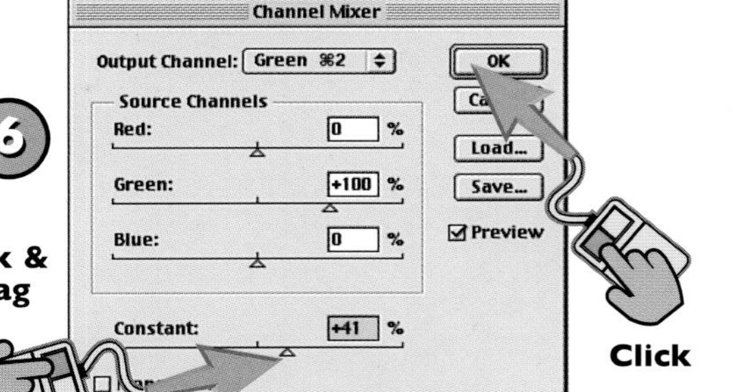

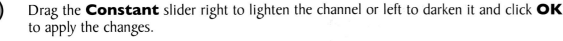

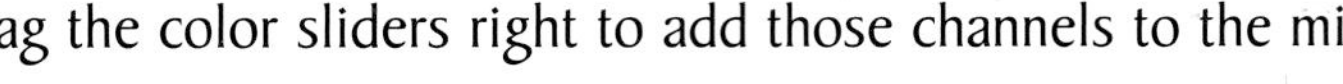
4 Drag the color sliders right to add those channels to the mix.

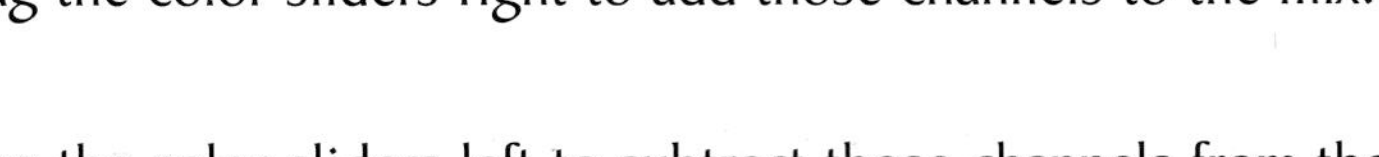
5 Drag the color sliders left to subtract those channels from the mix.

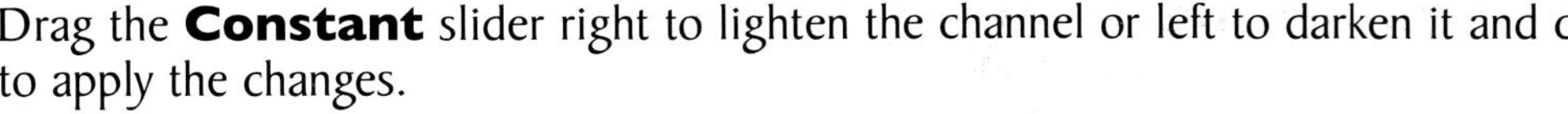
6 Drag the **Constant** slider right to lighten the channel or left to darken it and click **OK** to apply the changes.

Click Monochrome to make hand-tinted images, and then click it off and adjust the color channels. What you've done is create a three- or four-channel grayscale image with intensified or toned-down individual color channels to add color tints.

Photoshop contains a lot of very technical tools, and it's not always possible to predict in advance what their effects will be. The **Variations** command enables you to adjust images based on tiny thumbnails that show you exactly what effect your changes will have.

Task 16: Adjusting an Image Based on Thumbnail Images

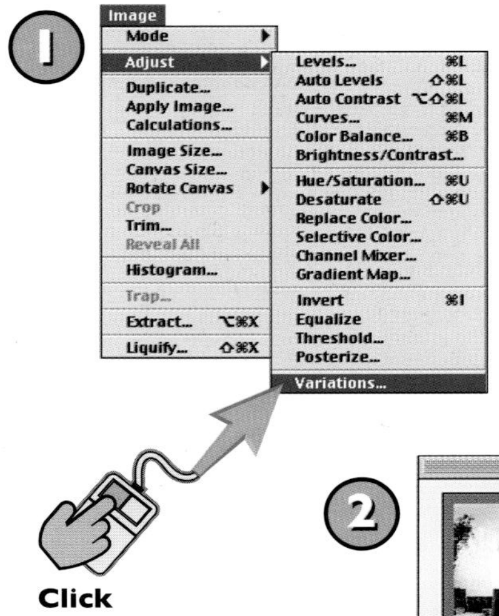

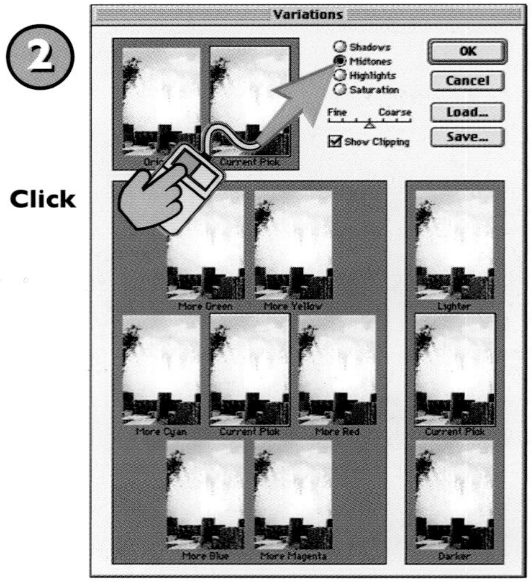

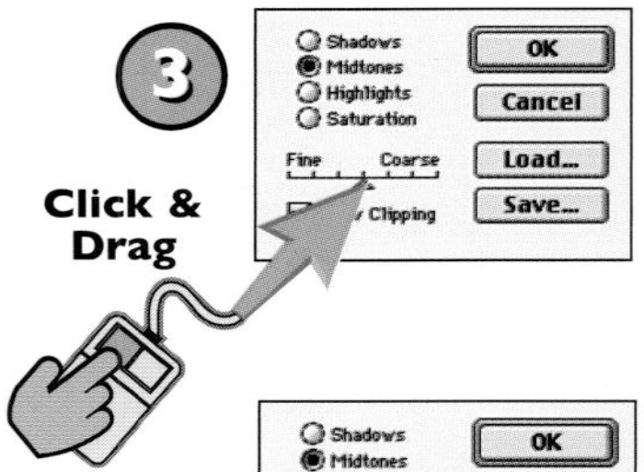

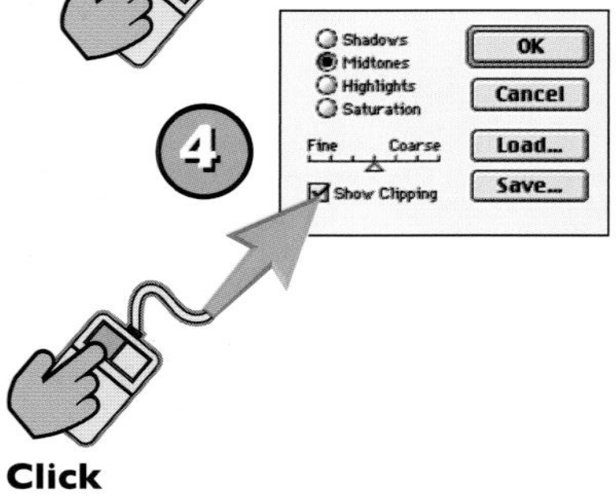

1. Choose **Image**, **Adjust**, **Variations**.
2. Click **Shadows**, **Midtones**, or **Highlights** to adjust dark, medium, or light colors.
3. Drag the slider to change the amount each click changes the image.
4. Click **Show Clipping** to see colors that will change to black or white.

✓ If you're working on a grayscale image, the **Variations** dialog box looks different; your only choices are to make highlights, midtones, and shadows darker or lighter, and there's no saturation control (because a grayscale image doesn't contain any color).

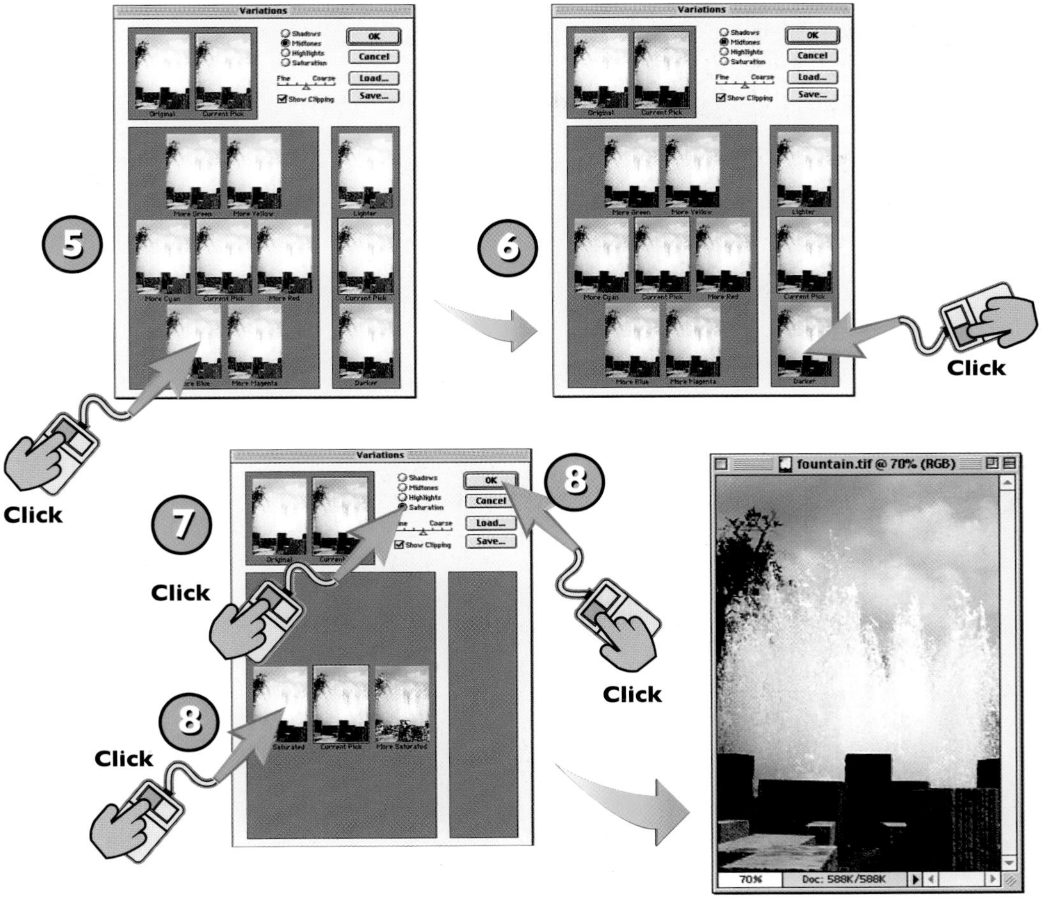

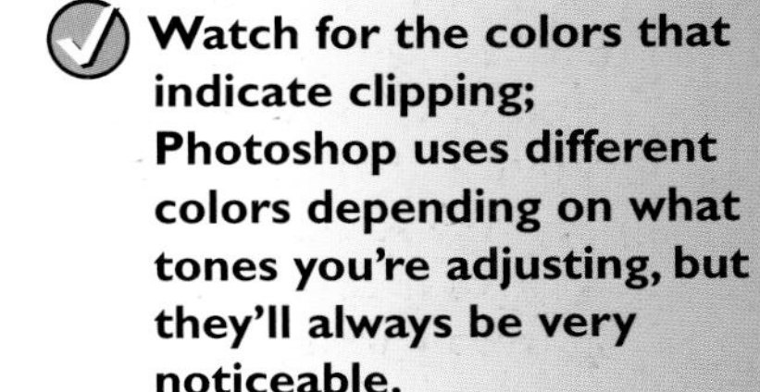

5 Click the thumbnails on the left to change the image's hues.

6 Click the thumbnails on the right to change the image's brightness.

7 Click **Saturation** to adjust the image's color intensity.

8 Click the left thumbnail to reduce saturation or the right one to increase it, and then click **OK**.

Watch for the colors that indicate clipping; Photoshop uses different colors depending on what tones you're adjusting, but they'll always be very noticeable.

PART

Working with Layers

Layers enable you to keep different elements within an image organized so you can move, hide, duplicate, and edit them without affecting the rest of the image. Photoshop's Layers palette is the control center for layers, enabling you to reorder layers, hide them, and create new ones. Special ***adjustment layers*** can contain effects that exist independent of image elements, which enables you to revise the effects throughout the image creation process.

Part 8 shows you how to view the Layers palette, create and name layers, mask layers, create layer sets, and make selections based on the contents of one or more layers. Other tasks in this part explain how to apply ***layer styles***: embossing, beveling, shadows, and glows that can be quickly created for any layer.

Tasks

Task 1: Using the Layers Palette

Whether you're building complex composite images or just editing scans, layers are the basis for almost all work in Photoshop. You can paint to your heart's content on a layer without affecting the pixels on any other layer, so it's easy to change your mind. The Layers palette is the key to manipulating the layers in an image.

Start Here

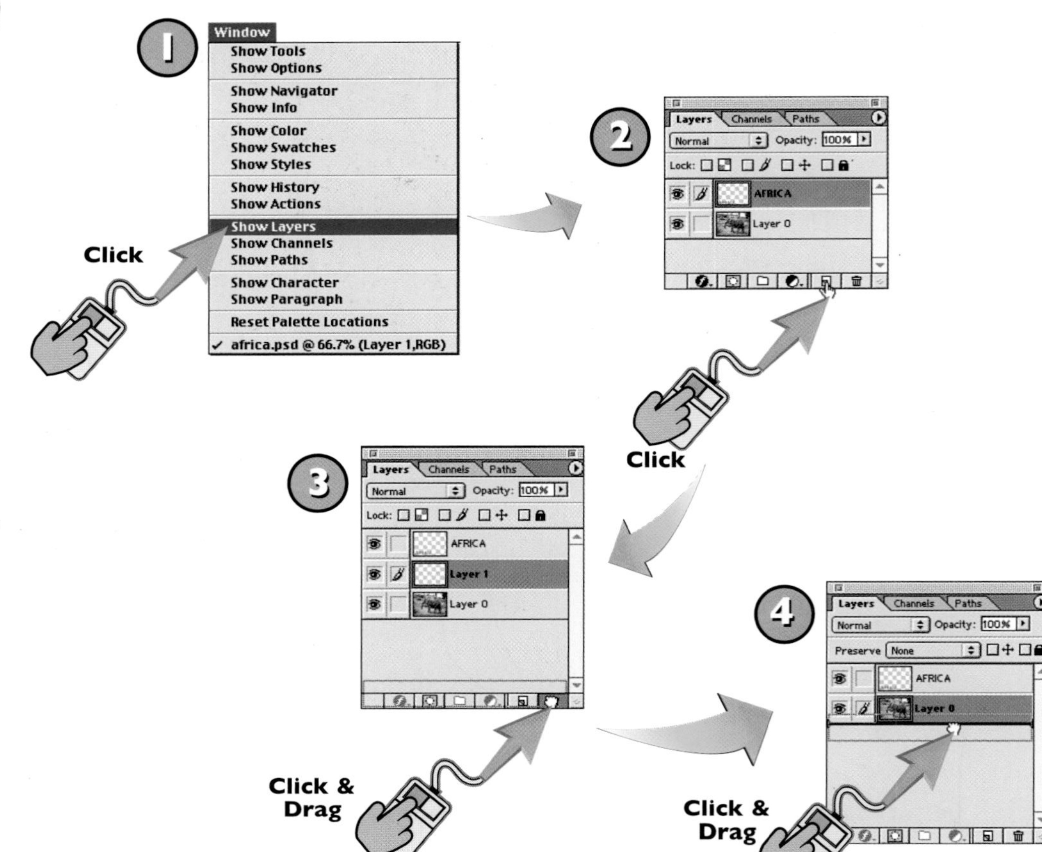

1. Choose **Window**, **Show Layers** to display the **Layers** palette.
2. To add a layer, click the **Add Layer** button.
3. To delete a layer, drag it to the trash icon.
4. To change a layer's stacking order, drag it up or down in the palette.

In the Layers palette, top equates with front and bottom equates with back. In other words, the top layer in the palette is in front of all the layers shown under it.

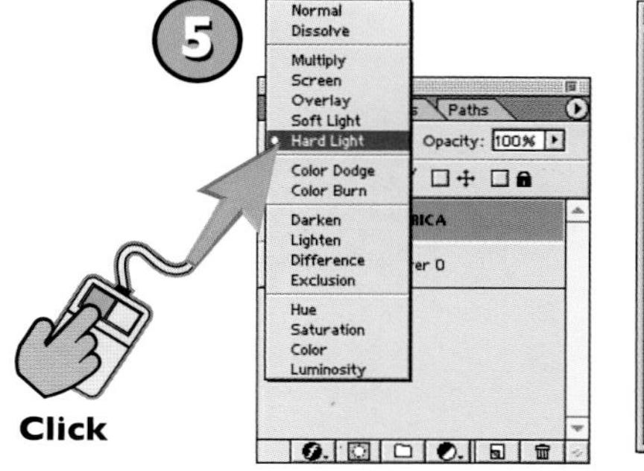

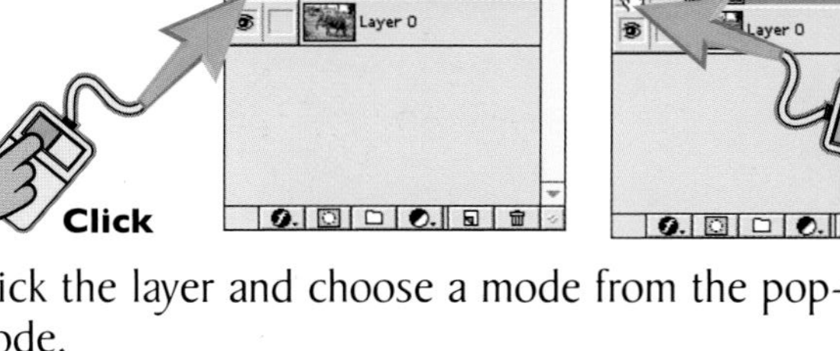

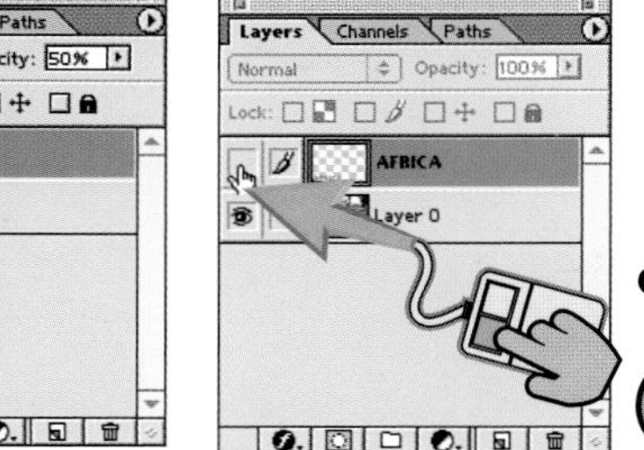

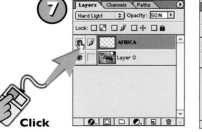

5. Click the layer and choose a mode from the pop-up menu to change a layer's blending mode.

6. Click the layer and enter a new percentage in the **Opacity** field to change a layer's opacity.

7. Click the eye icon next to a layer's name to hide it.

8. Click in the left-hand blank space next to a layer's name to show a hidden layer.

Blending modes control how the colors in a layer affect the colors in other layers; experiment with different blending modes for different effects.

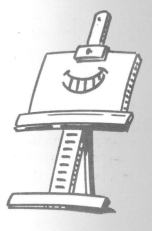

Task 2: Renaming a Layer

Photoshop assigns names to new layers that you create, whether by adding type, pasting, or clicking the New Layer button. But it's usually easier to keep track of the different layers in an image if you assign them your own names.

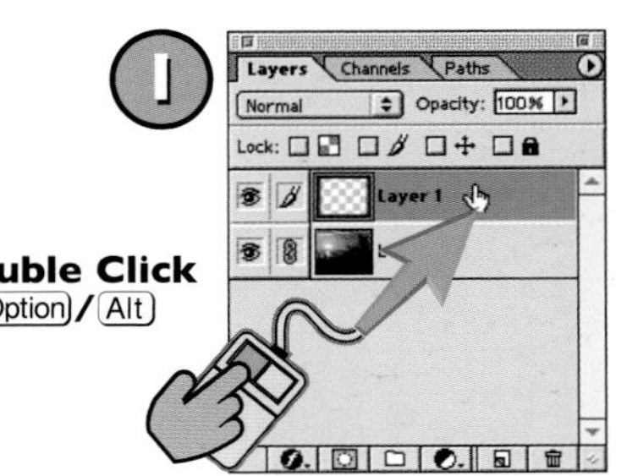

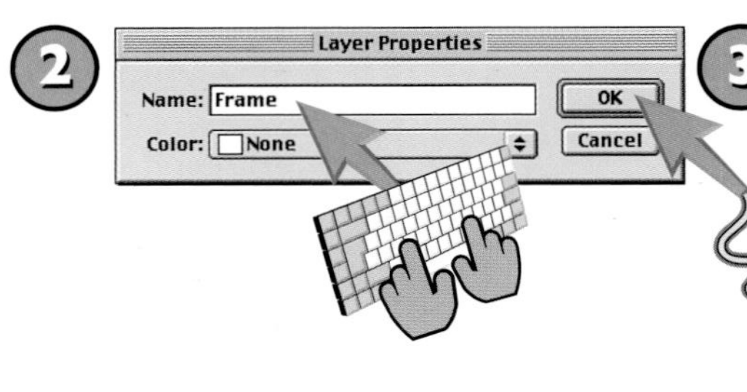

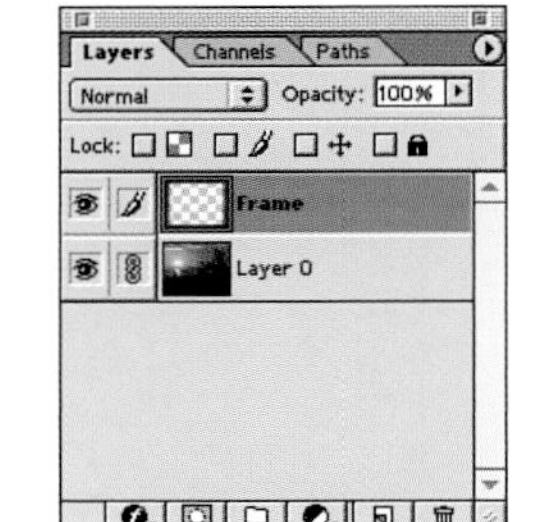

Layer names can be up to 250 characters, and you can widen the **Layers** palette to show the entire name if you've used a long one. If the entire name doesn't show in the **Layers** palette, hold the cursor over the part of the name that does show and, after a second, Photoshop displays the whole name.

1. **Option/Alt+double-click** the name of the layer you want to rename.
2. Enter a new name in the **Name** field.
3. Click **OK** to apply the change.

Task 3: Filling an Entire Layer

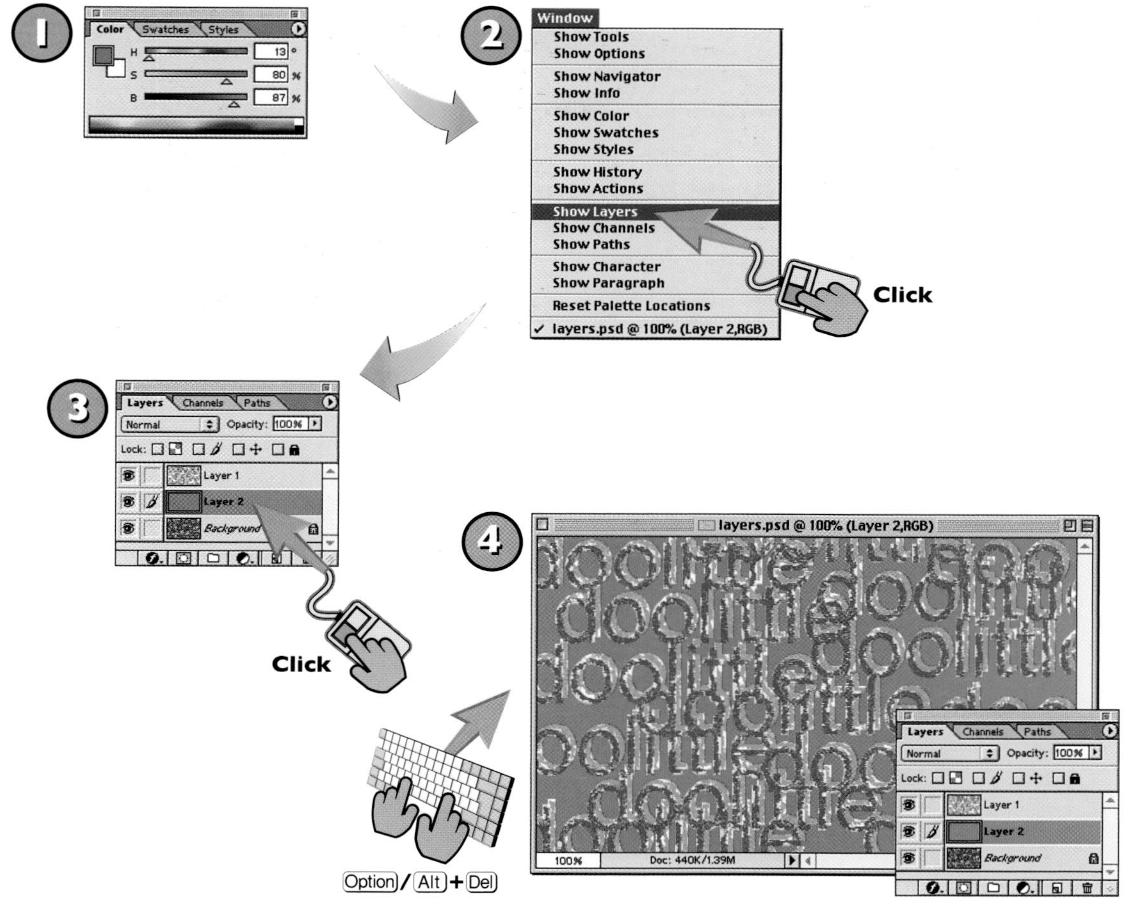

Some Photoshop filters need colored pixels on which to operate—they won't work if you invoke them while a completely transparent layer is active. For this and other situations, you must know how to fill an entire layer with a color.

1. Choose the foreground color you want to use.
2. Choose **Window**, **Show Layers**.
3. Click the layer to fill.
4. Press **Option+Delete/Alt+Delete**.

If you want more control over the fill operation—such as filling with the background color, with white or black, or with a reduced opacity, press **Shift+Delete/Alt+Delete** or choose **Edit**, **Fill** to bring up the **Fill** dialog box.

Task 4: Organizing Layers with Sets

Layer sets offer a handy way to reorder, show, and hide more than one layer at a time. They're especially useful if you're creating multiple versions of an image within one file—you can duplicate a set of layers all at once and make changes to them to create a new version of the image without affecting the original.

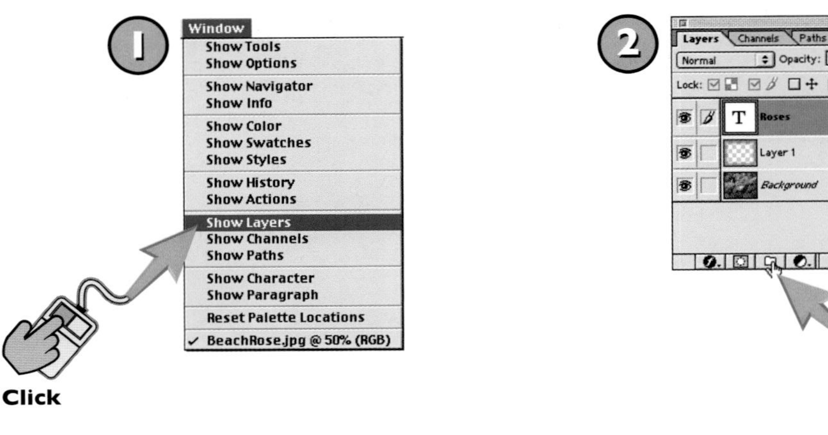

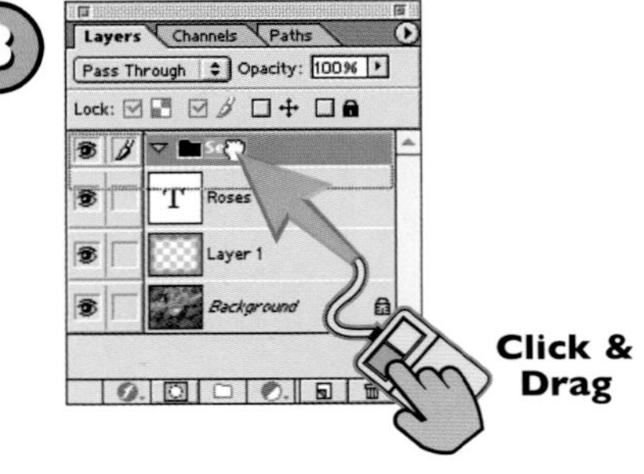

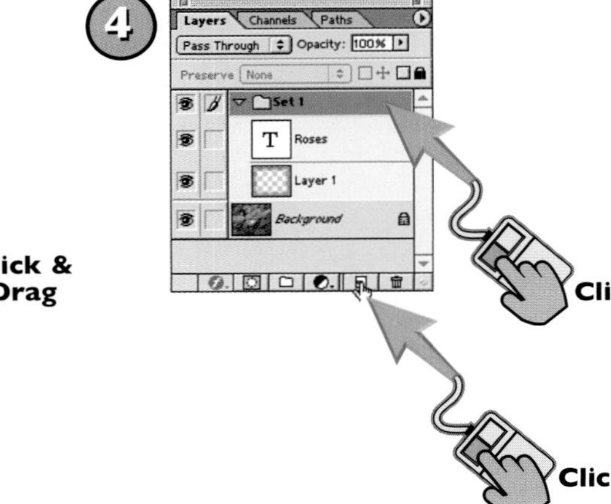

1 Choose **Window**, **Show Layers** to bring up the **Layers** palette.

2 To create a new layer set, click the **New Set** button.

3 To move an existing layer into that set, drag it on top of the set in the **Layers** palette.

4 To create a new layer in the set, click on the set, and then click the **New Layer** button.

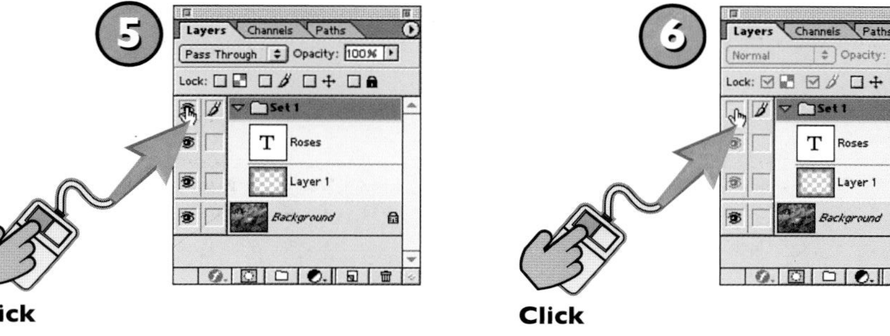

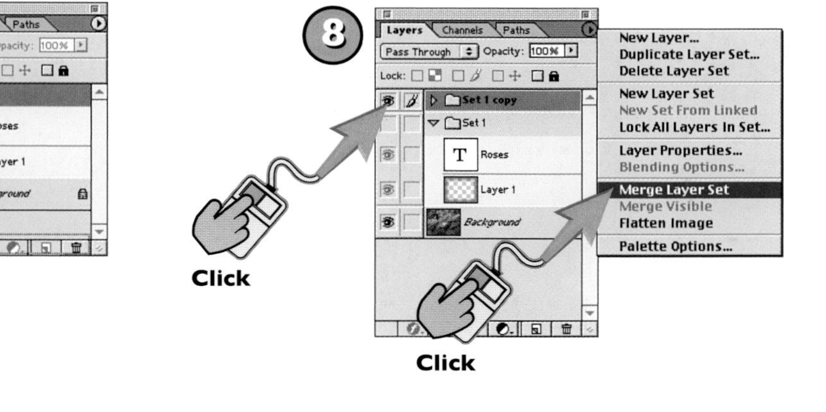

5 To hide a set, click the eye icon next to its name.

6 To show a hidden set, click the blank space to restore the eye icon.

7 To duplicate a set, drag the set onto the **New Set** button.

8 To merge all the layers in a set into one layer, click on the set and choose **Merge Layer Set** from the **Layers** palette menu.

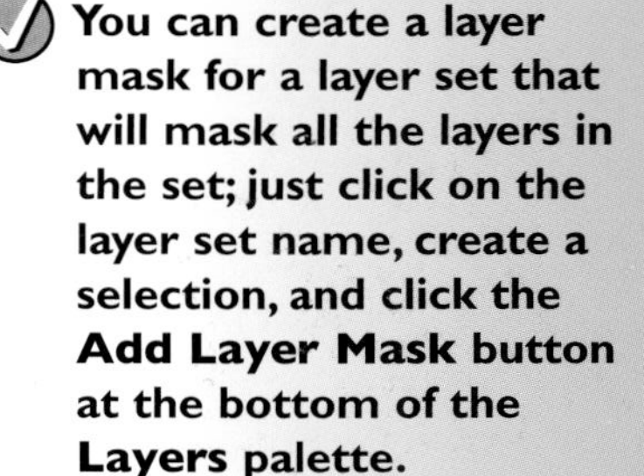

You can create a layer mask for a layer set that will mask all the layers in the set; just click on the layer set name, create a selection, and click the Add Layer Mask button at the bottom of the Layers palette.

You can't merge a layer set that contains a type layer; you must rasterize the type layer first (see Part 9, Task 3, "Rendering Type into Pixels").

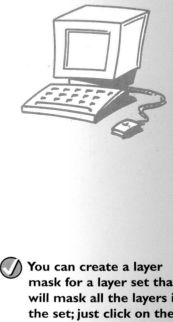

Photoshop's adjustment layers enable you to make image adjustments with tools such as Levels, Hue/Saturation, and the Channel Mixer. Unlike the normal way of using these tools, though, adjustment layers enable you to go back and change settings at any time.

Task 5: Creating a New Adjustment Layer

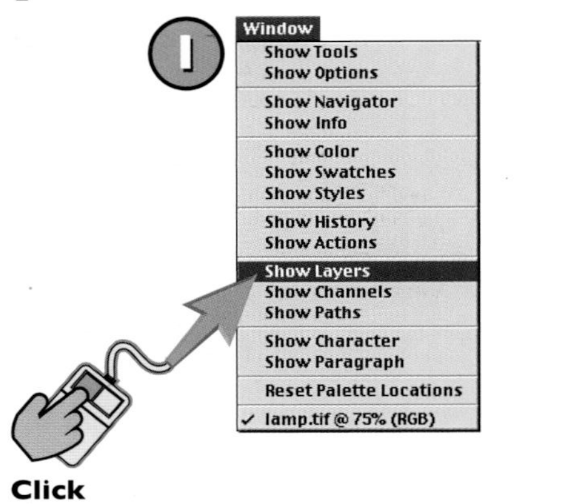

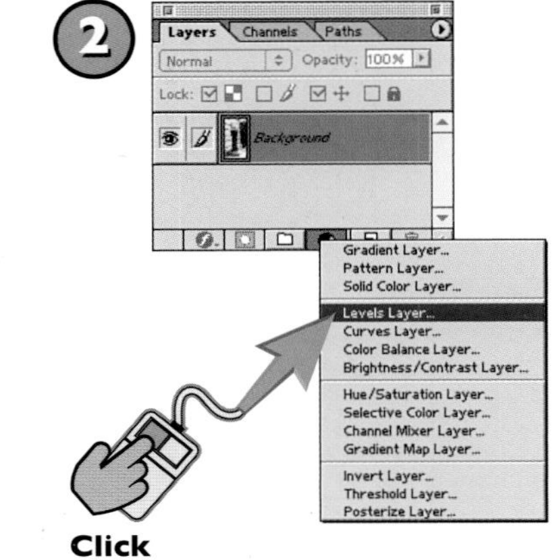

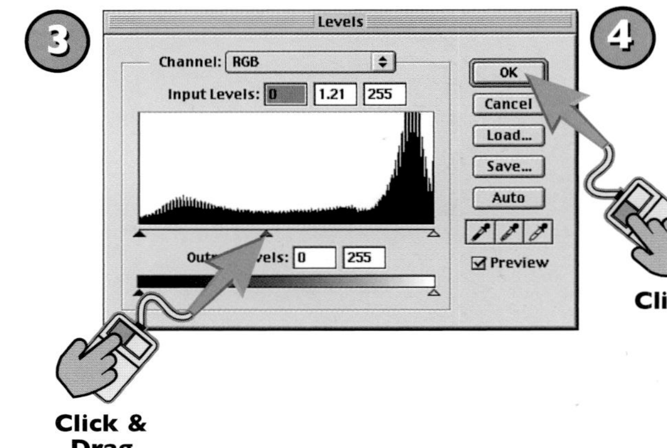

1 Choose **Window**, **Show Layers**.

2 Click the **Adjustment Layer** button on the **Layers** palette to display a pop-up menu, and choose what kind of layer you want to create.

3 In the resulting adjustment dialog box, make the settings you want to apply to the image.

4 Click **OK** to create the layer.

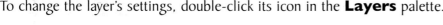

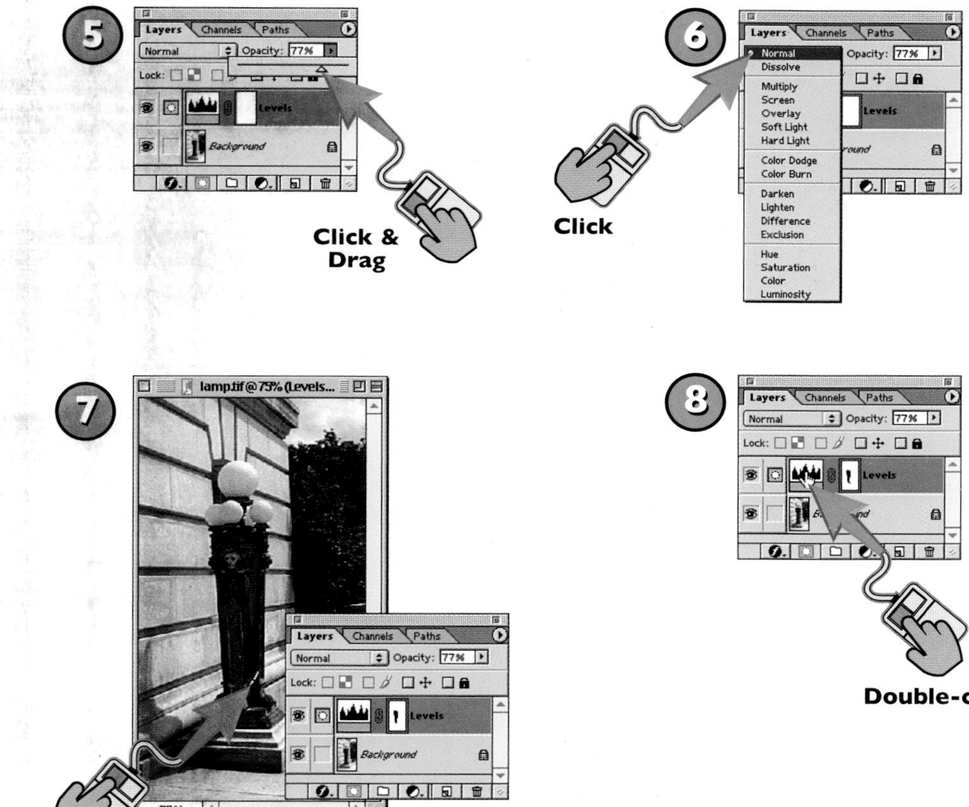

5 Set the **Opacity** for the new dynamic fill layer.

6 Choose a blending mode—usually **Normal**.

7 To apply the adjustment to just part of the image, make black the foreground color and paint over the parts you don't want to include.

8 To change the layer's settings, double-click its icon in the **Layers** palette.

Many of the tools that you can use with dynamic fill layers are covered in Part 7. To use levels to adjust an image's brightness and contrast, see Task 3, "Adjusting an Image's Overall Tones." To change an image's hue and saturation, see Task 12, "Changing an Image's Hue and Saturation." And to use the Channel Mixer, see Task 15, "Adjusting Colors by Mixing Channels."

To change the name of a dynamic fill layer, choose Layer Properties from the Layers palette menu.

When you paint on a dynamic fill layer to mask its effects as in step 7, you're creating a layer mask. To learn more about layer masks, see the next task, "Creating and Editing a Layer Mask."

Task 6: Creating and Editing a Layer Mask

A layer mask, as its name indicates, masks off portions of a layer that are then hidden from view but not deleted. Using layer masks is a great way to create composite images while preserving each component image in its entirety.

Start Here

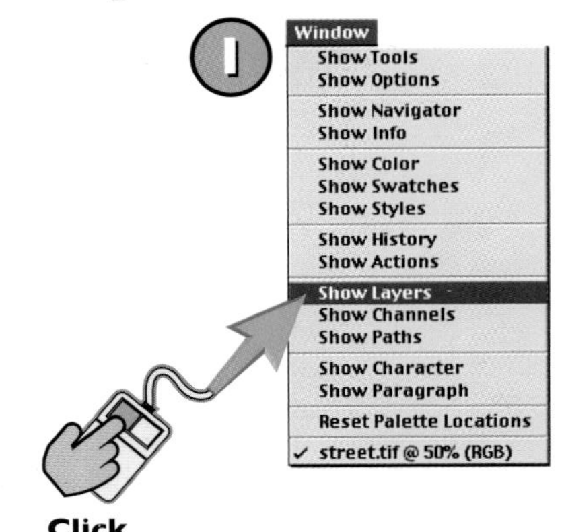

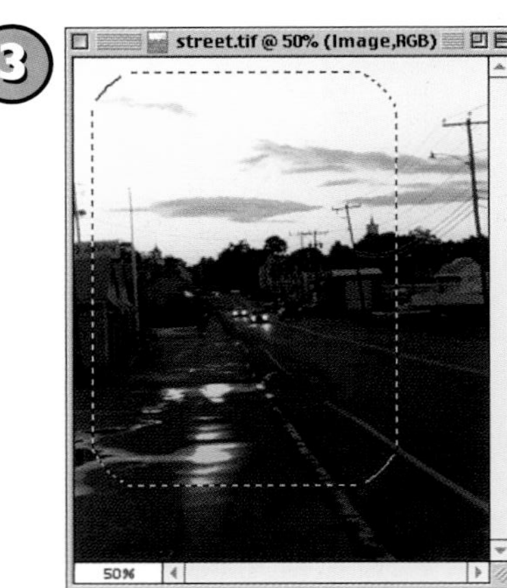

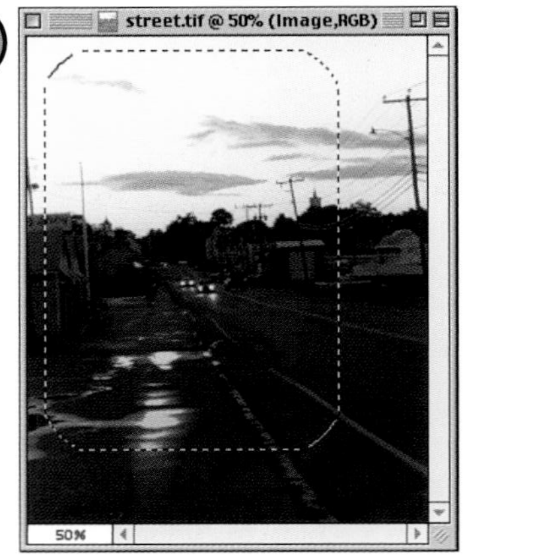

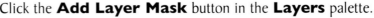

1. Choose **Window**, **Show Layers**.
2. Click the layer that you want to mask.
3. Make a selection in the image to define the area that will show through the mask.
4. Click the **Add Layer Mask** button in the **Layers** palette.

You can't create a layer mask for the Background layer.

Gray areas of the mask only mask partially, black areas mask the image completely, and white areas allow the image to show through completely.

Next Step

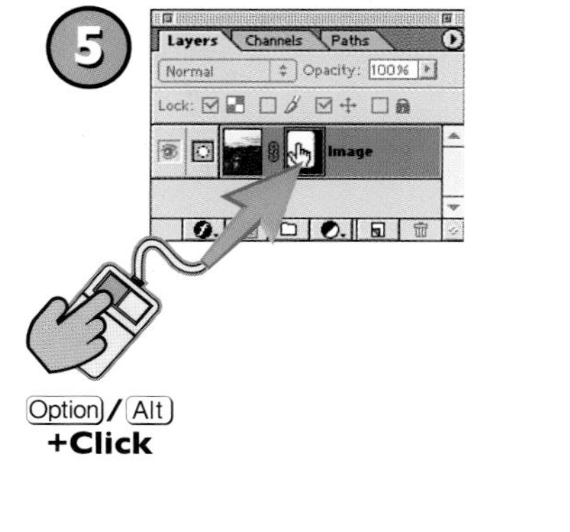

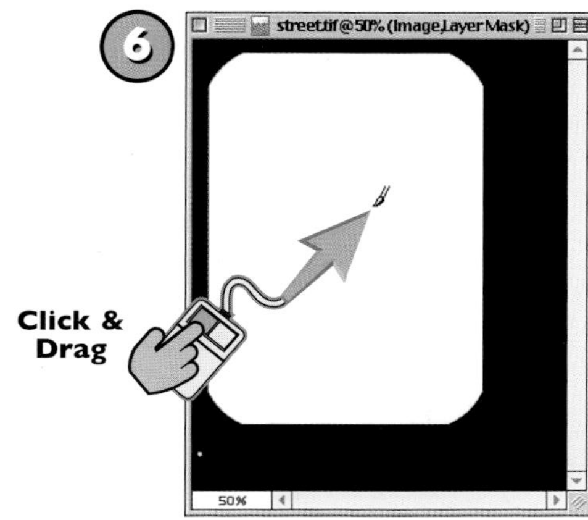
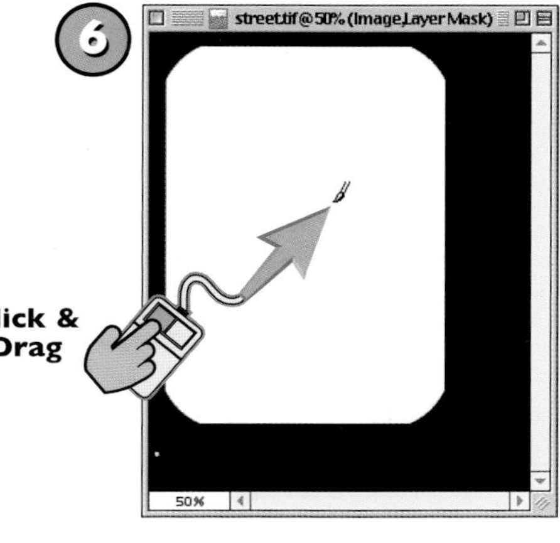

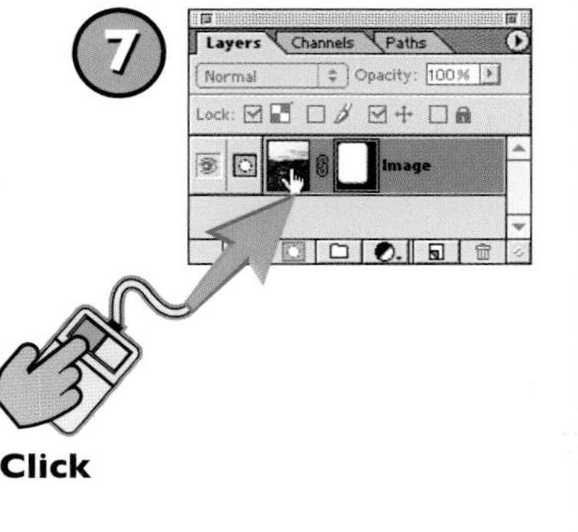

5 **Option+click/Alt+click** the layer mask thumbnail to view the layer mask.

6 Paint on the layer mask with black, white, or gray to edit it.

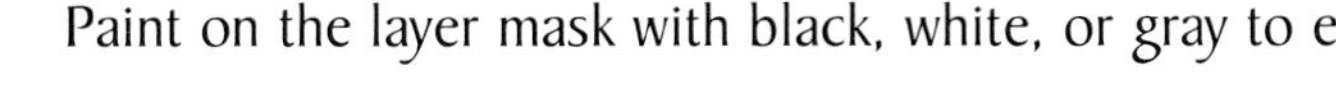

7 Click the layer image thumbnail to return to viewing the layer.

To delete a layer mask, drag its thumbnail to the trash icon on the Layers palette; in the dialog box, choose to discard its effects or apply them by deleting the portions of the layer that were masked.

Task 7: Masking a Layer with the Contents of Another Layer

Start Here

In addition to layer masks, Photoshop enables you to use one layer to mask another. This is useful for special effects. For example, you could use a seashell image to mask an image of a beach; the shell wouldn't show at all, and the beach image would only show inside the shape of the shell.

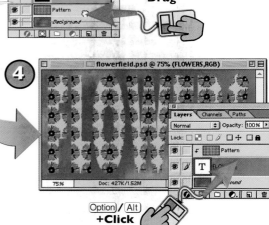

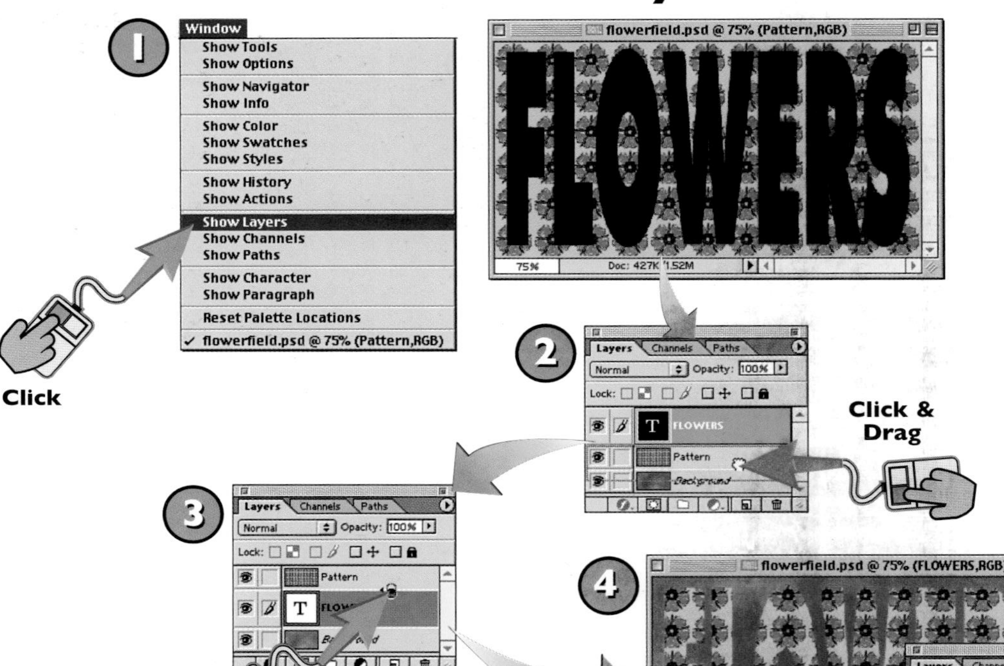

✓ Photoshop calls this technique "grouping" layers and refers to the grouped layers as a "clipping group." To ungroup a layer, **Option+click/Alt+click** again on the border between the two layers in the **Layers** palette.

✓ You can group as many layers as you want—there's no limit.

1. Choose **Window**, **Show Layers**.
2. Drag the masking layer so that it's below any layers you want to mask.
3. **Option+click/Alt+click** the line separating the masking layer from the next layer.
4. **Option+click/Alt+click** the lines between any other layers to be masked, and the mask is activated.

Task 8: Converting a Layer Style to Individual Layers

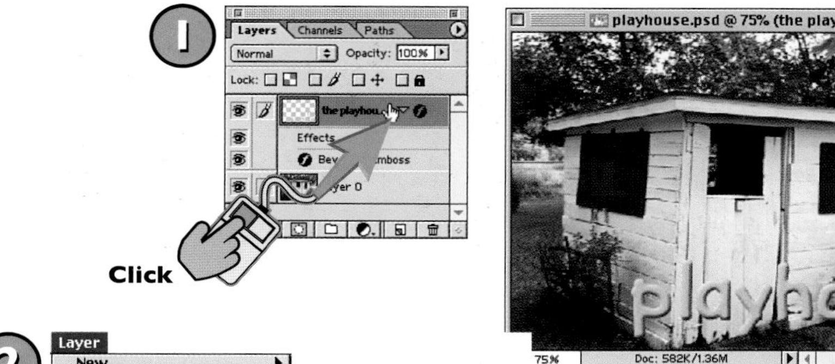

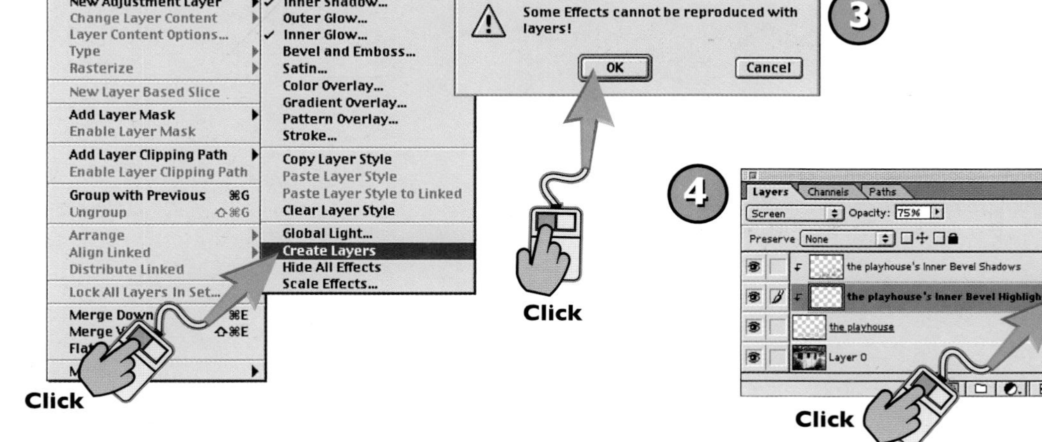

Layer styles can't be edited except using the dialog box. However, if you need to change a layer style in some way—such as to cut out a piece of shadow so it won't overlap another element—you can convert a layer style to its constituent pieces, each on a layer of its own.

1. Make sure the layer with the style you want to convert is active.
2. Choose **Layer**, **Layer Style**, **Create Layers**.
3. Click **OK** in the warning dialog box if you see one.
4. To edit a style layer, click it in the **Layers** palette, as you would any layer.

When you turn a layer style into individual layers, you'll end up with a different number of layers depending on the style. Each layer will be labeled to let you know which component of the layer it contains; for example, "Layer 1's Outer Glow."

Bevel and Emboss layer effects result in two layers above the original layer, whereas Glow and Shadow layer effects result in one layer below the original layer.

Task 9: Adding a Shadow to a Layer

Photoshop's layer styles enable you to add one or more special effects to a layer with (almost) just one click. The Drop Shadow layer style creates a drop shadow behind an object on a transparent layer.

Start Here

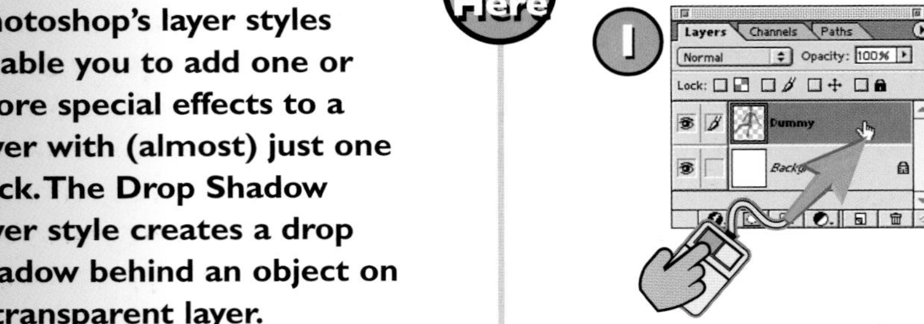

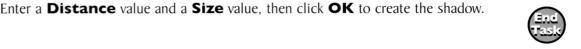

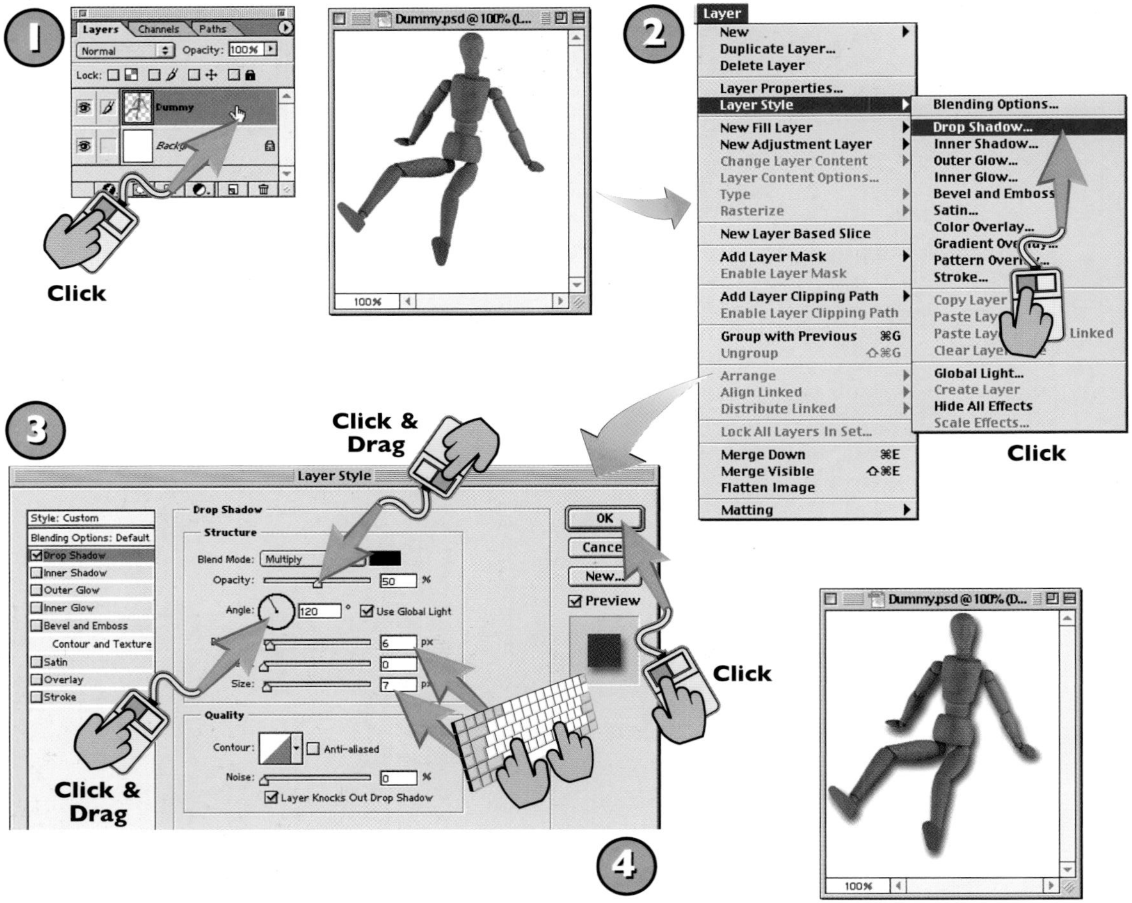

1. Make sure the desired layer is active.
2. Choose **Layer**, **Layer Style**, **Drop Shadow**.
3. Select an **Opacity** and an **Angle** for the shadow.
4. Enter a **Distance** value and a **Size** value, then click **OK** to create the shadow.

The Distance value determines the amount of the shadow that sticks out from behind the object casting the shadow, and the Blur value determines how fuzzy the shadow is.

Task 10: Adding a Glow to a Layer

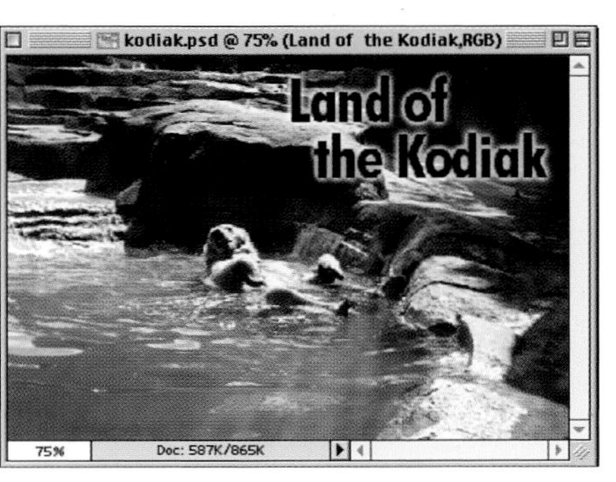

The Inner Glow and Outer Glow layer styles work the same way; both add a colored glow to an object on an otherwise transparent layer. They work with both images and type, and unlike filters they can be applied to type without rendering the type into pixels.

1. Make sure the desired layer is active.
2. Choose **Layer**, **Layer Style**, **Outer Glow** or **Inner Glow**.
3. Enter an **Opacity** for the glow.
4. Enter a **Size** value and click **OK** to create the glow.

You can change the color of the glow by clicking the color swatch in the **Layer Style** dialog box and choosing a different color in the **Color Picker**.

Try choosing different blending modes from the **Mode** pop-up menu for different effects; **Exclusion** makes a particularly neat-looking glow.

Task 11: Beveling a Layer

Creating a bevel used to require a lot of work with selections, channels, and the Levels controls. These days, beveling an object or type is much easier. Like all layer styles, this technique is designed to work with an image or type on an otherwise transparent layer.

Start Here

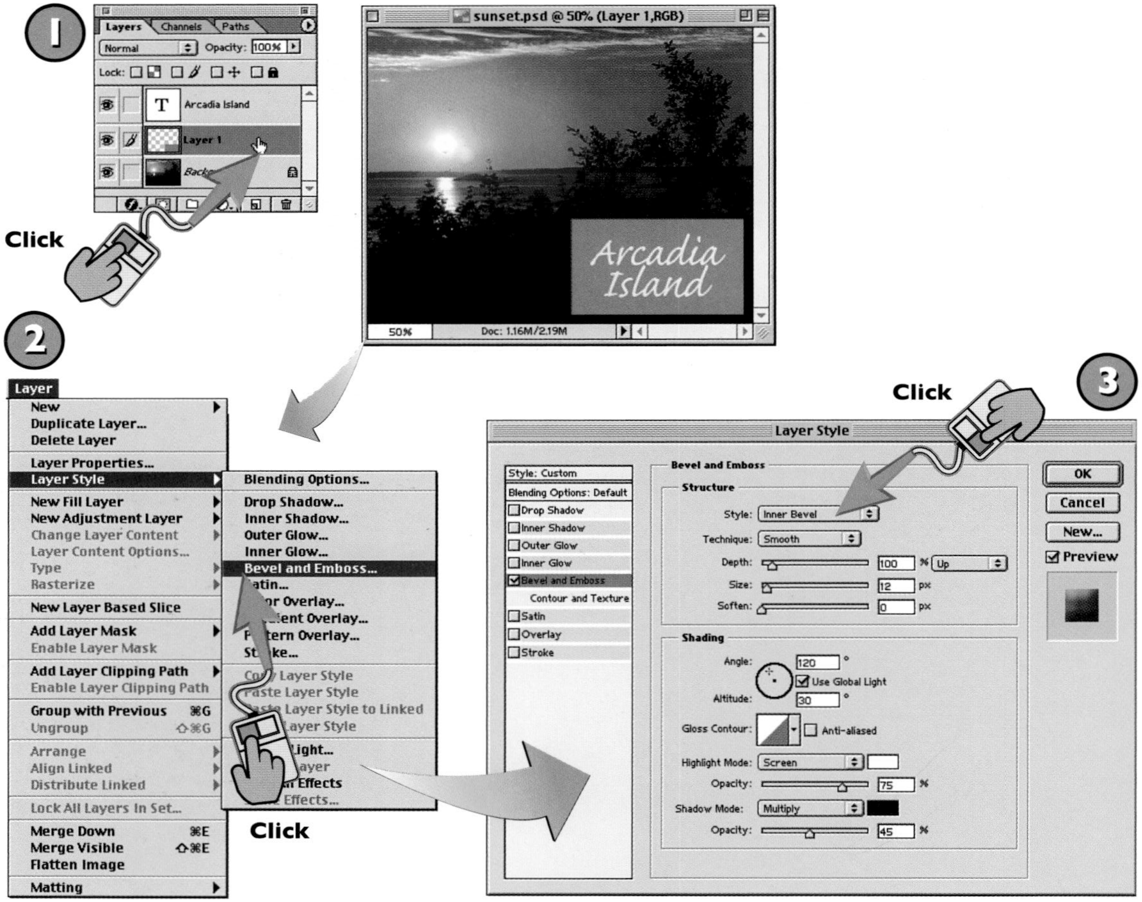

1. Make sure the desired layer is active.

2. Choose **Layer**, **Layer Style**, **Bevel and Emboss**.

3. Choose a bevel style from the **Style** menu.

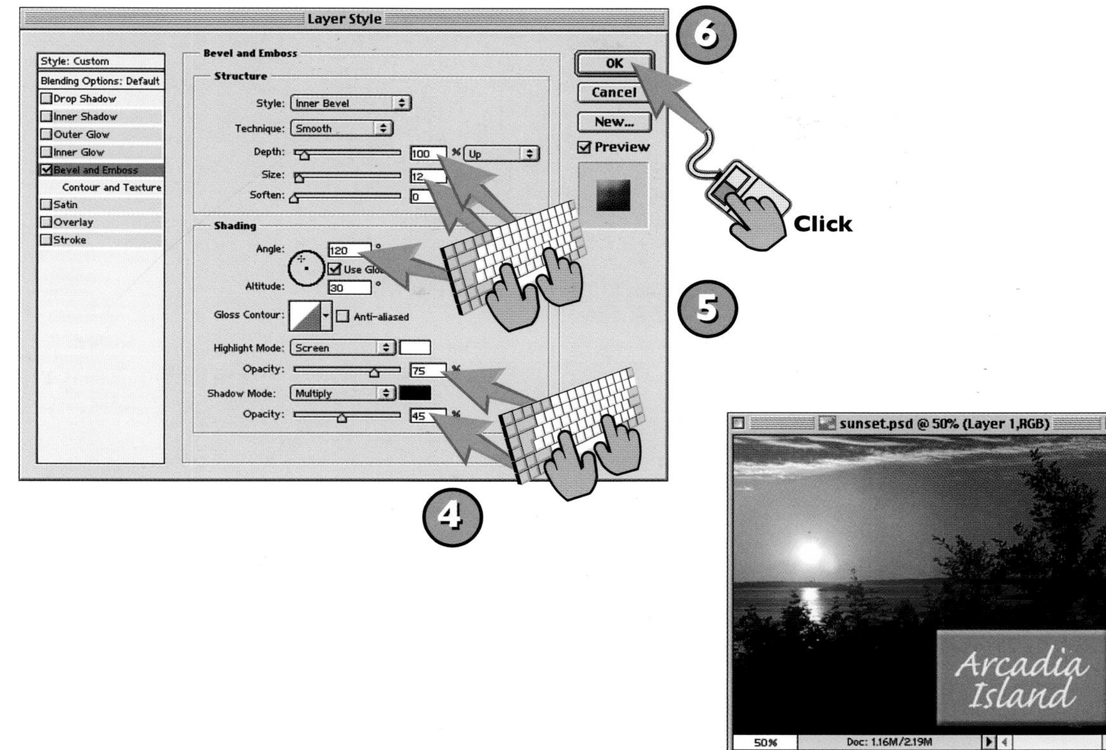

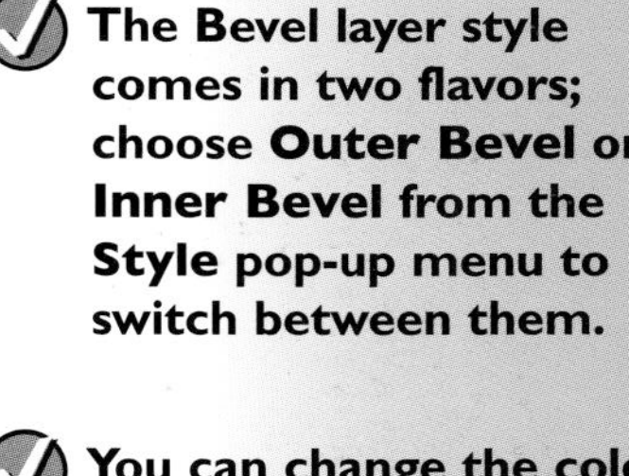

4 Enter **Opacity** values under **Highlight Mode** and **Shadow Mode**.

5 Enter values for the **Angle**, **Depth**, and **Size**.

6 Click **OK** to create the bevel.

The Bevel layer style comes in two flavors; choose Outer Bevel or Inner Bevel from the Style pop-up menu to switch between them.

You can change the color of the "light" that creates the bevel effect by clicking the white and black color swatches in the Shading area and choosing new colors in the Color Picker.

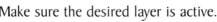

Task 12: Embossing a Layer

Photoshop's built-in Emboss filter doesn't produce very attractive results. Fortunately, the Emboss layer style is much more useful. It creates a three-dimensional embossing effect that can be any height you desire, or even a reverse emboss (sometimes called debossing).

Start Here

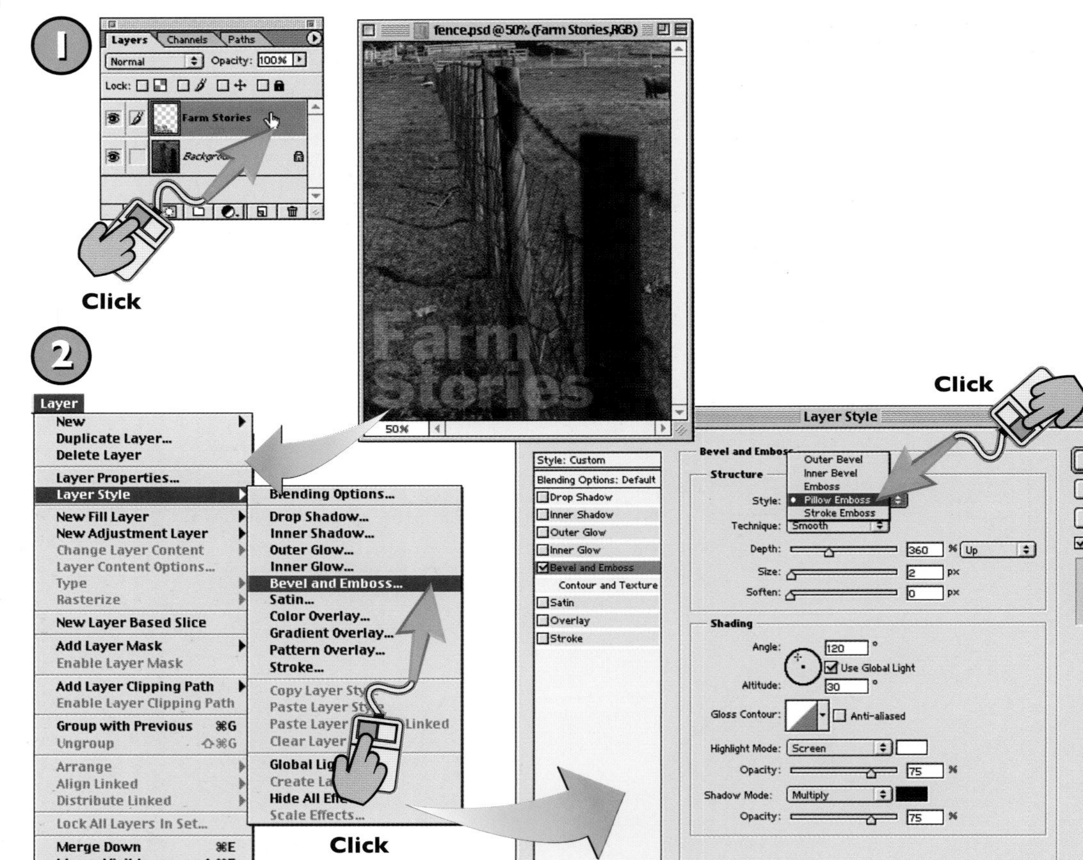

1. Make sure the desired layer is active.
2. Choose **Layer**, **Layer Style**, **Bevel and Emboss**.
3. Choose an embossing style from the **Style** menu.

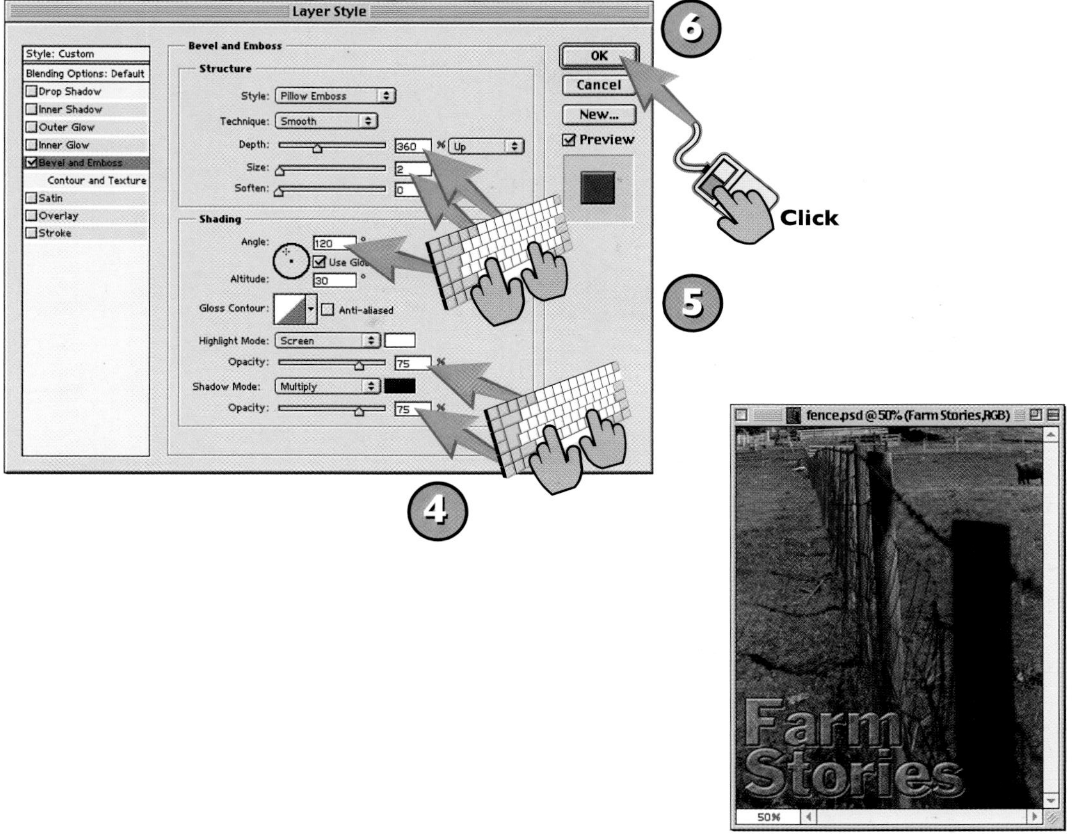

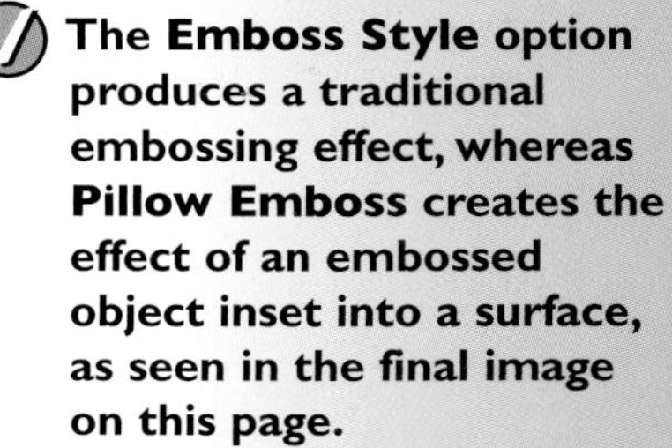

4 Enter **Opacity** values under **Highlight Mode** and **Shadow Mode**.

5 Enter values for **Angle**, **Depth**, and **Size**.

6 Click **OK** to create the embossing.

The **Emboss Style** option produces a traditional embossing effect, whereas **Pillow Emboss** creates the effect of an embossed object inset into a surface, as seen in the final image on this page.

Photoshop's Copy command works only on the active layer; to copy from more than one layer at a time, you must use the Copy Merged command. Copy Merged copies non-transparent pixels from all visible layers at one time.

Task 13: Copying an Area from More than One Layer

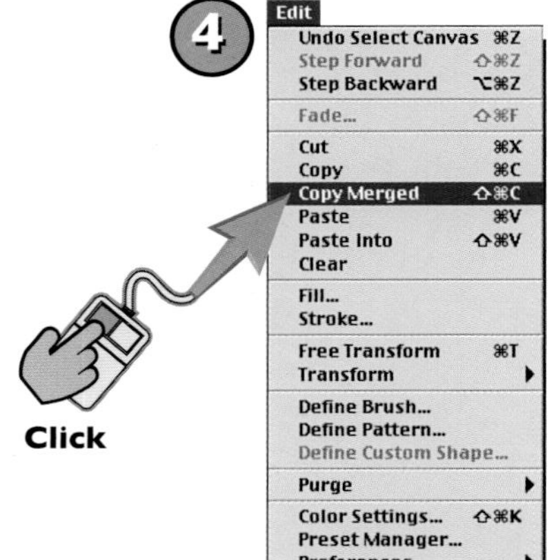

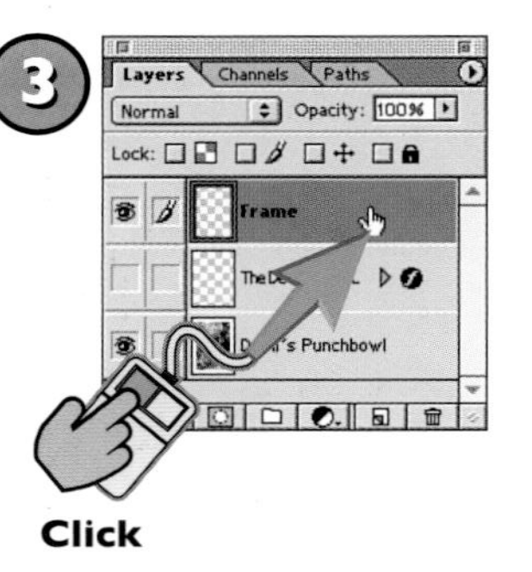

Edit
Undo Select Canvas ⌘Z
Step Forward ⇧⌘Z
Step Backward ⌥⌘Z
Fade... ⇧⌘F
Cut ⌘X
Copy ⌘C
Copy Merged ⇧⌘C
Paste ⌘V
Paste Into ⇧⌘V
Clear
Fill...
Stroke...
Free Transform ⌘T
Transform
Define Brush...
Define Pattern...
Define Custom Shape...
Purge
Color Settings... ⇧⌘K
Preset Manager...
Preferences

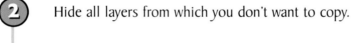

Click

1. Select the area to copy.
2. Hide all layers from which you don't want to copy.
3. Make active one of the layers you're copying.
4. Choose **Edit**, **Copy Merged**.

When only transparent pixels are selected, neither the **Copy** nor the **Copy Merged** command is available. They're also unavailable if the active layer is hidden.

End Task

Task 14: Merging Layers

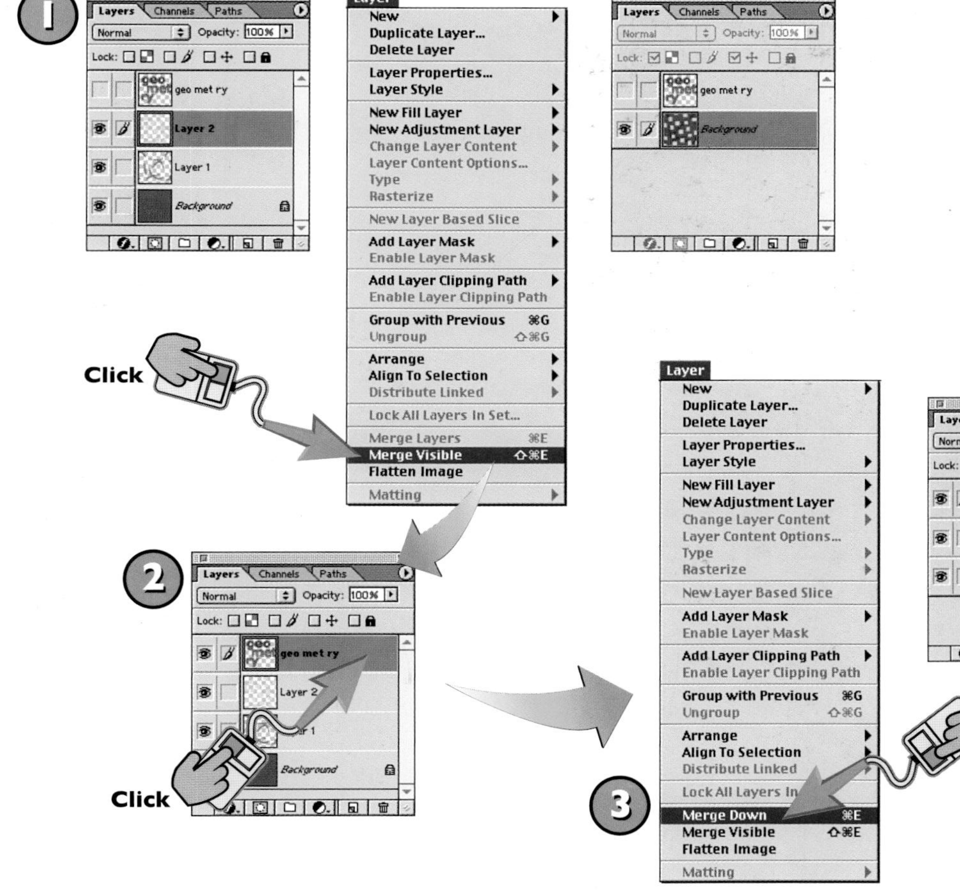

Layers are convenient, but the number of them can get out of hand. When you're sure that you won't need objects to exist on separate layers any more, you can combine the layers to simplify your life. You have a choice of merging layers two at a time or all visible layers at once.

1. To merge all visible layers, choose **Layer**, **Merge Visible**.
2. To merge two layers, make the upper (frontmost) of the two layers active.
3. Choose **Layer**, **Merge Down**.

To merge all an image's layers at once, choose Layer, Flatten Image. You'll need to do this to save images using any format other than Photoshop.

PART 9

Creating and Editing Type

Even in Photoshop, the king of image editors, there's a place for type. Photoshop's type tools enable you to create editable type that can be formatted character by character and edited as many times as you wish. Photoshop enables you to use any font installed on your computer system; it offers the usual text-formatting options such as bold and italic, along with more sophisticated controls such as kerning and tracking.

After you have the words you want just the way you want them, you convert them to pixels—at that point you can apply filters and other effects to them just like any other part of the image. This part shows you how to create and edit type, how to render it into pixels, and how to create a couple of fun special effects with type, such as flaming type.

Tasks

Task 1: Creating Type

Even in Photoshop, the king of image editors, type has a place. The type controls in Photoshop are greatly improved over earlier versions—you can edit type after it's created, and you can apply different formatting to individual words and characters. Type is always added to an image on a new layer.

Start Here

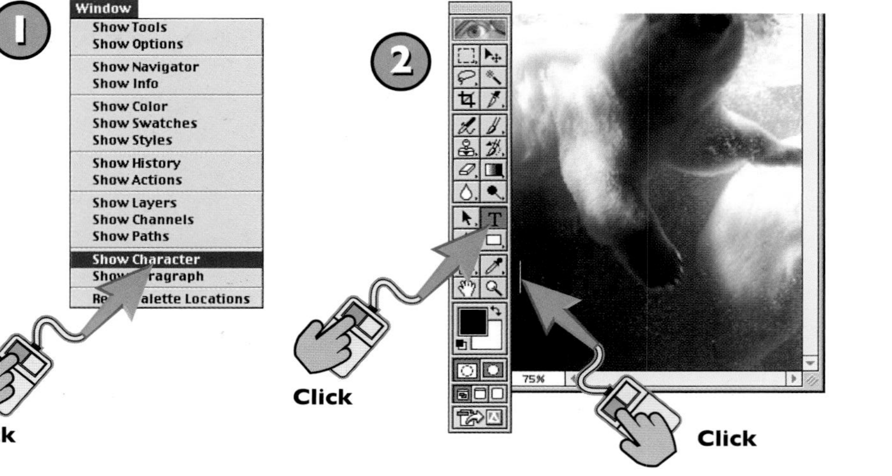

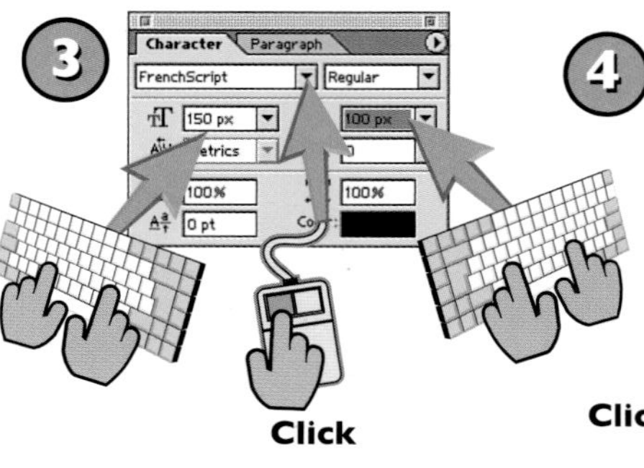

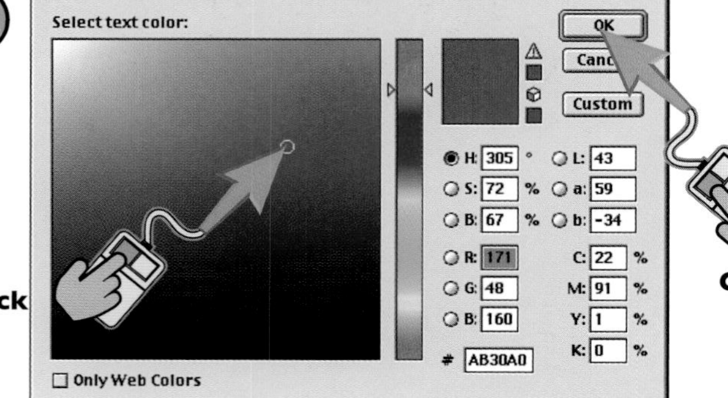

1. Choose **Window**, **Show Character** to bring up the **Character** palette.
2. Click the **Type** tool in the **Tool** palette, and click in the image where you want the type to be.
3. Choose a font, size, and leading.
4. Choose a color by clicking the color swatch. Click **OK**.

✓ By default, the current foreground color appears in the **Character** palette's color swatch, so the fastest way to choose a type color is to change the foreground color before using the **Type** tool. For type over photographs, use the **Eyedropper** tool to choose a color from the image—this guarantees that the color will complement the image.

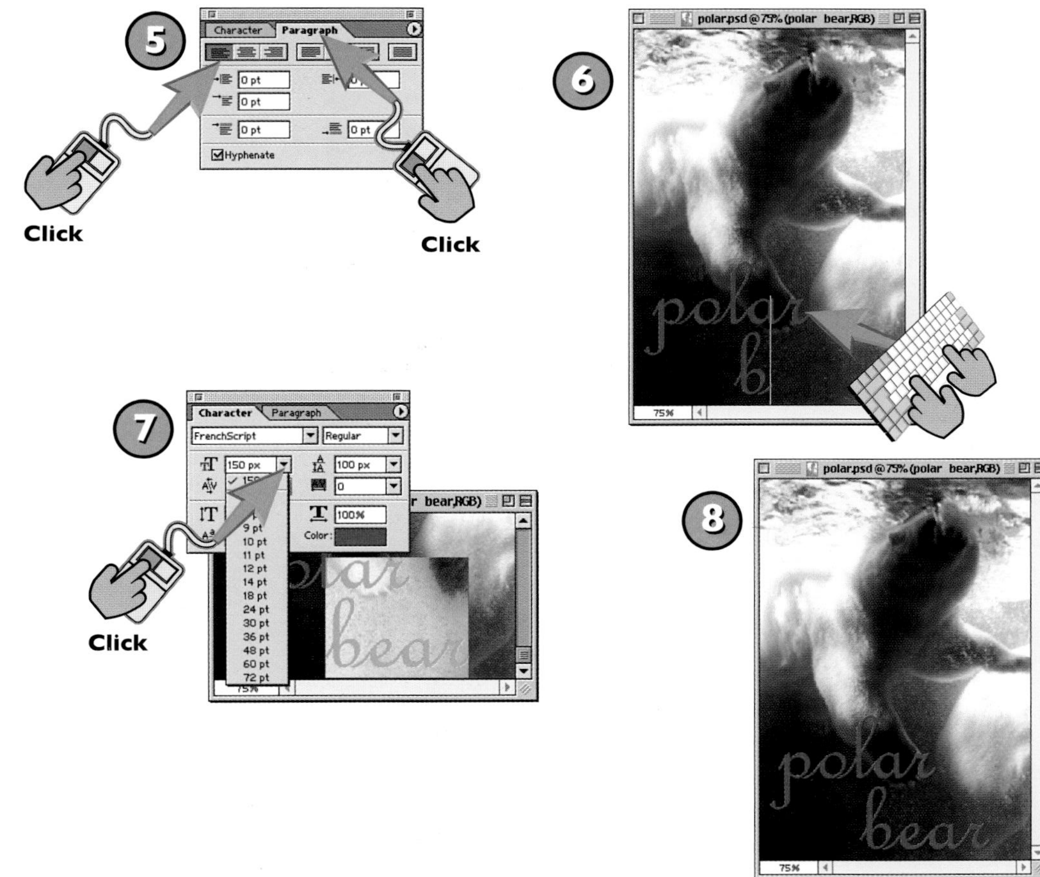

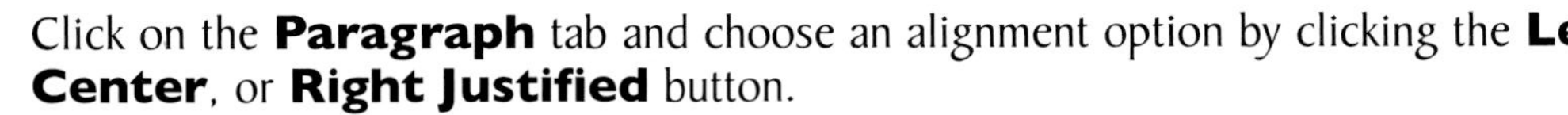

5 Click on the **Paragraph** tab and choose an alignment option by clicking the **Left**, **Center**, or **Right Justified** button.

6 Enter the text in the image window.

7 To reformat some of the type, select that portion and change its settings.

8 Press **Enter** to create the type.

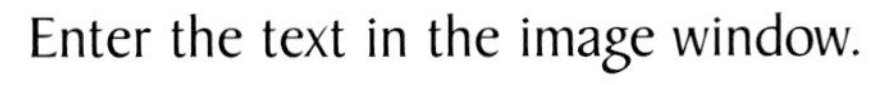

Tracking refers to spacing between a selected range of characters, and kerning refers to spacing between two specific characters.

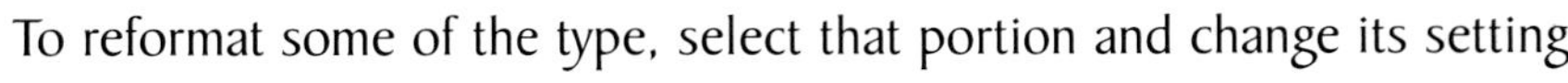

Choose Metrics from the Kerning menu to have Photoshop adjust the spacing between letters for the most even visual effect.

End Task

Task 2: Editing Type

Photoshop 6's new type features are a big improvement over those in earlier versions. The biggest advance is the fact that you can create and edit type right in the image window—no special dialog box required. All Photoshop's type controls are now accessible in the Character and Paragraph palettes, as well as on the Type Options bar.

Start Here

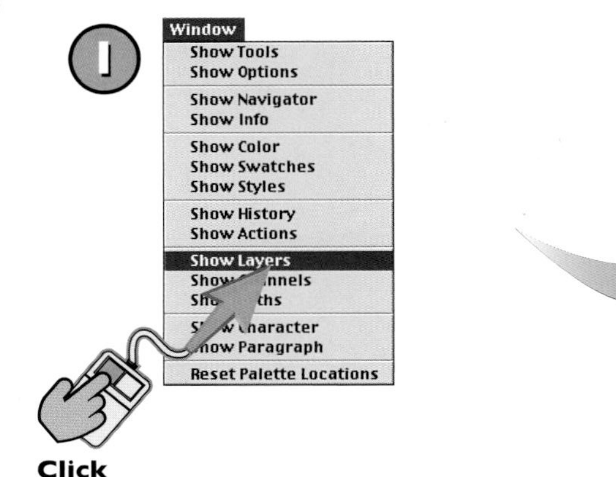

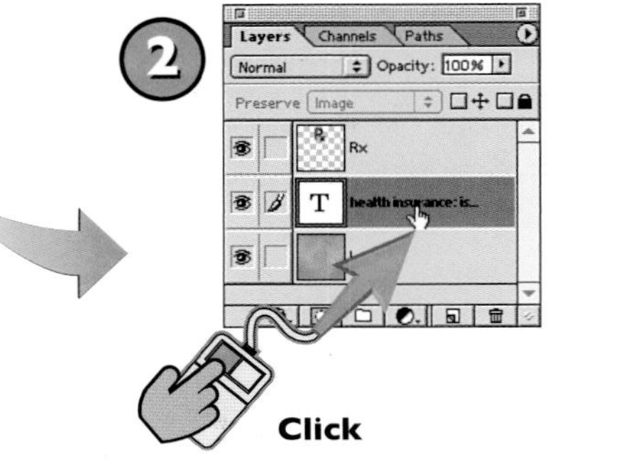

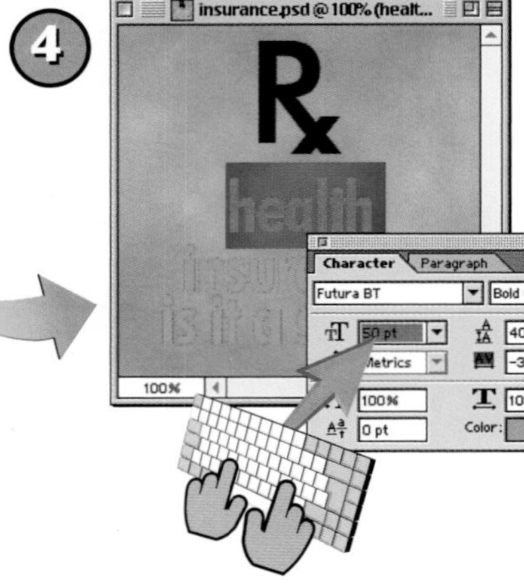

1. Choose **Window**, **Show Layers**.
2. Click on the type layer you want to edit.
3. To edit the text, select it as you would in a word processor and make the changes.
4. To change formatting, select all or some of the text, change the settings in the **Character** or **Paragraph** palette, and then press **Enter**.

You can tell which type layers haven't yet been rendered into pixels because of the distinctive "T" symbol in their icons in the Layers palette.

End Task

Task 3: Rendering Type into Pixels

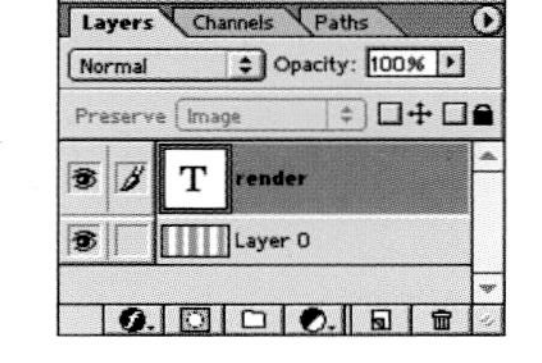

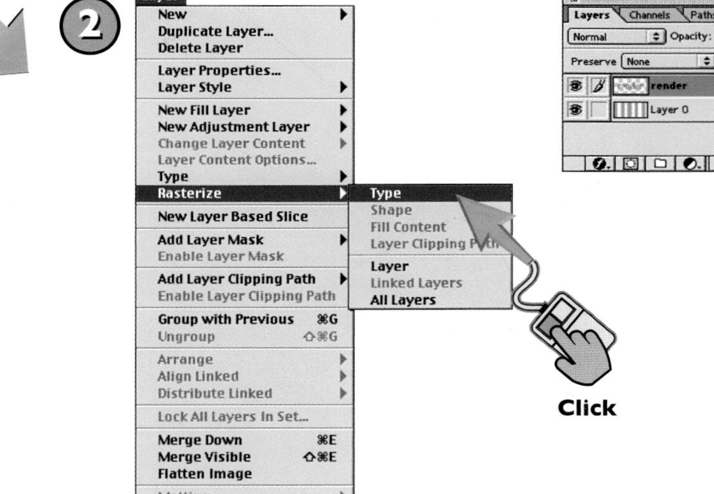

To make sure you can edit type after it's created, Photoshop doesn't *render* the type into pixels until you tell it to. You can't run filters on type until you render it, because filters operate on the individual pixels of the object to which they're applied.

Although you can't run filters on unrendered type, you can fill it with a color, and you can apply layer effects to create glows, shadows, and beveling or embossing effects.

Before you render a type layer, create a copy of it, and then make it invisible. Later, if you realize you need to edit the type, you can make it visible and don't have to start from scratch.

1. Create the type.
2. Choose **Layer**, **Rasterize**, **Type**.

Type doesn't have to be clean, clear, and boring. Photoshop's fun filters can be applied to type as well as to images, and an unlimited number of effects can be achieved by combining two or more filters. Distressed type looks as though it's really been through the wringer.

Task 4: Creating Distressed Type

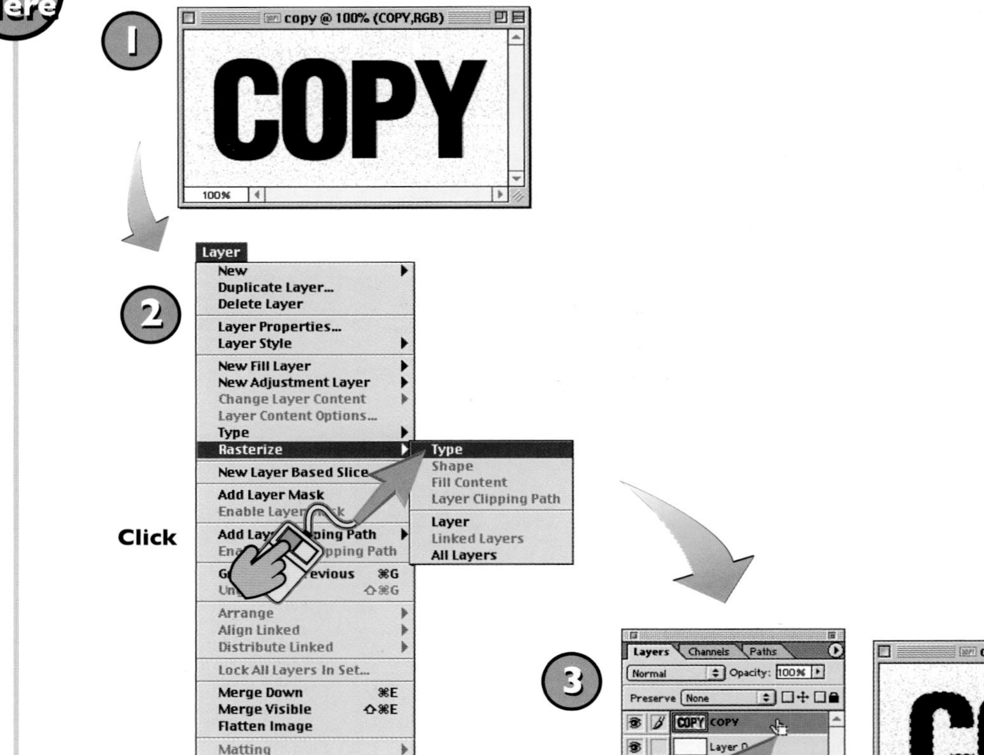

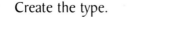

1. Create the type.
2. Choose **Layer**, **Rasterize**, **Type** to turn the type into pixels.
3. **Cmd+click/Ctrl+click** the type layer to select the type.

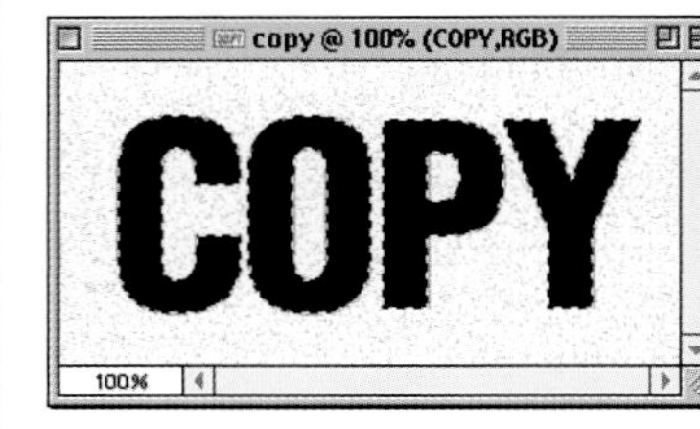

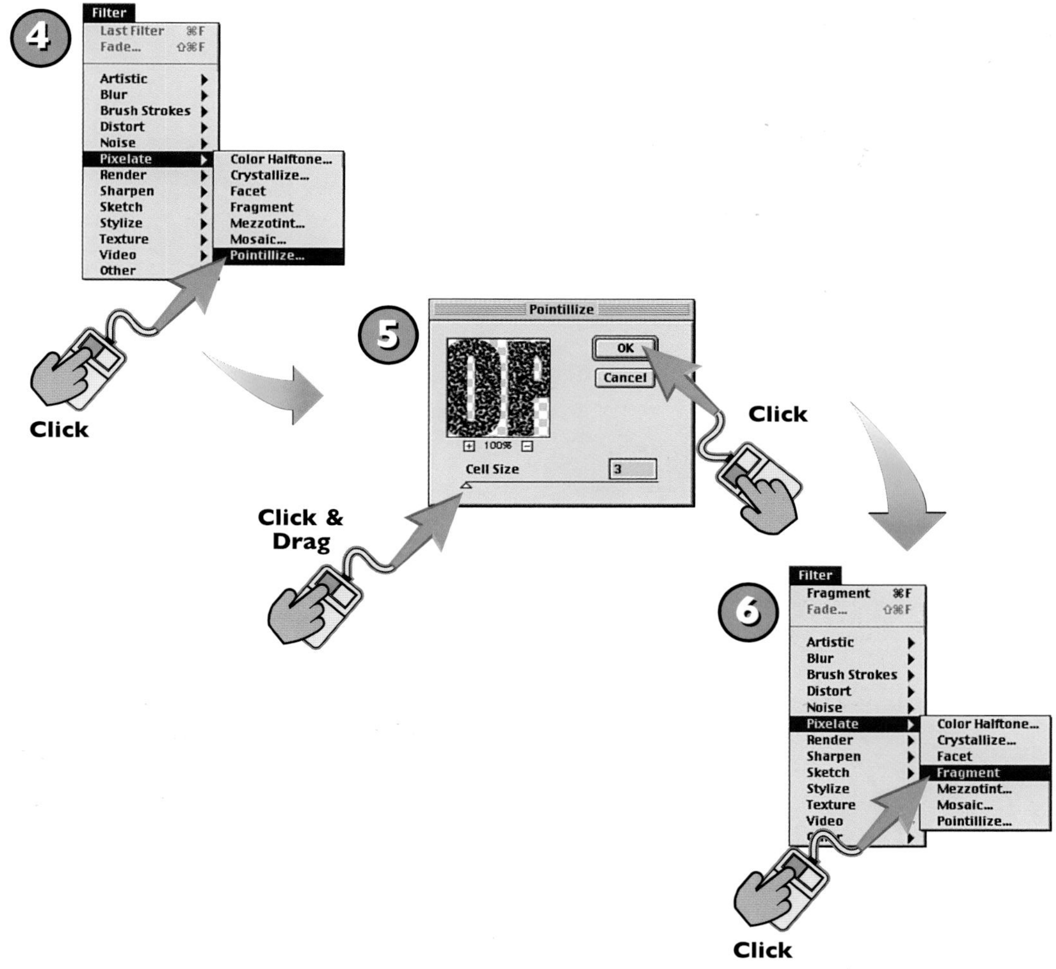

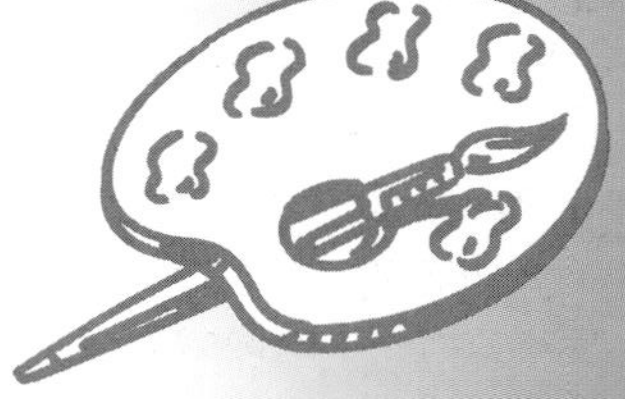

4. Choose **Filter**, **Pixelate**, **Pointillize**.

5. Enter the lowest setting and click **OK**.

6. Choose **Filter**, **Pixelate**, **Fragment**.

If you're working in a color image, your type will turn out rainbow-colored. To change its color, choose **Image**, **Adjust**, **Hue/Saturation**, click **Colorize**, drag the **Hue** slider until you like the color, and then click **OK**.

Creating Distressed Type Continued

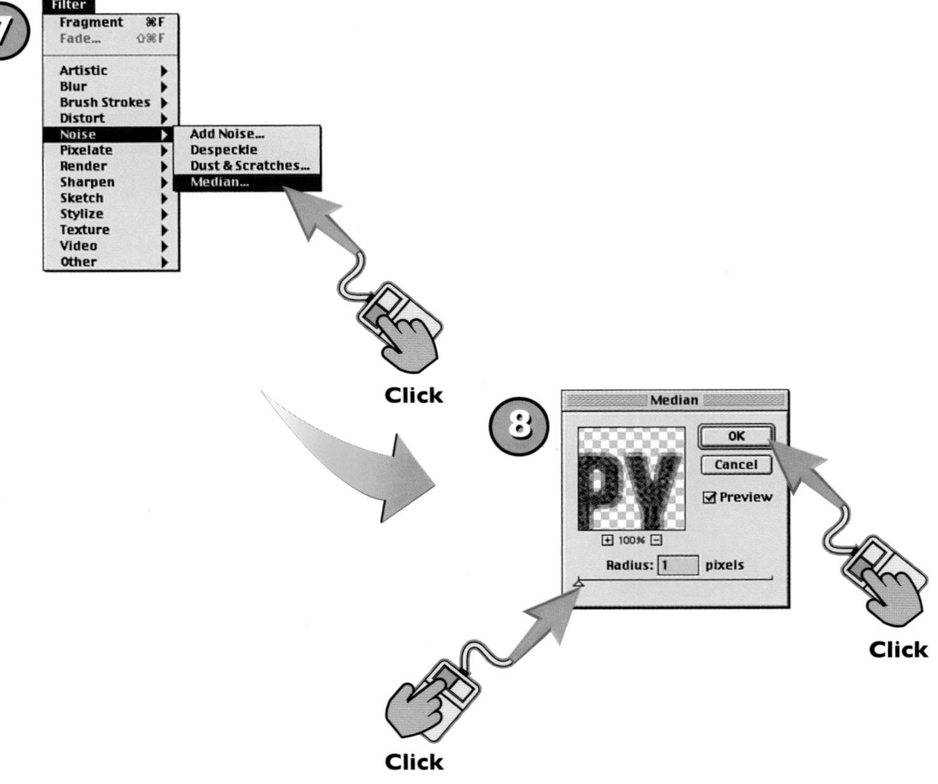

 Deselect and choose **Filter**, **Noise**, **Median**.

 Use a very low setting and click **OK**.

Next Step

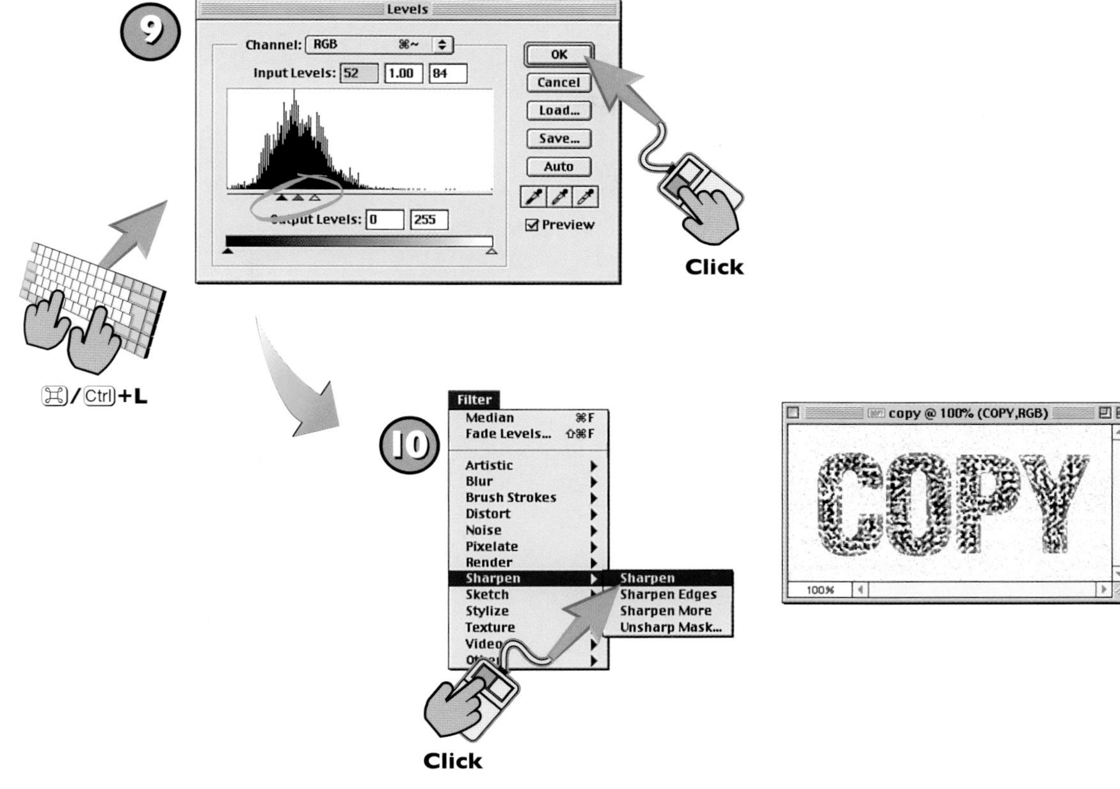

9 Press **Cmd+L/Ctrl+L**, cluster the three sliders close together under the black "hill," and then click **OK**.

10 Choose **Filter**, **Sharpen**, **Sharpen**.

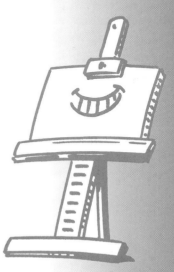

Flaming type is one of the coolest type effects Photoshop has to offer, yet it's very easy to accomplish—for the most part. You just run several filters with their default settings. You must start with an empty image in Grayscale mode.

Task 5: Creating Flaming Type

Start Here

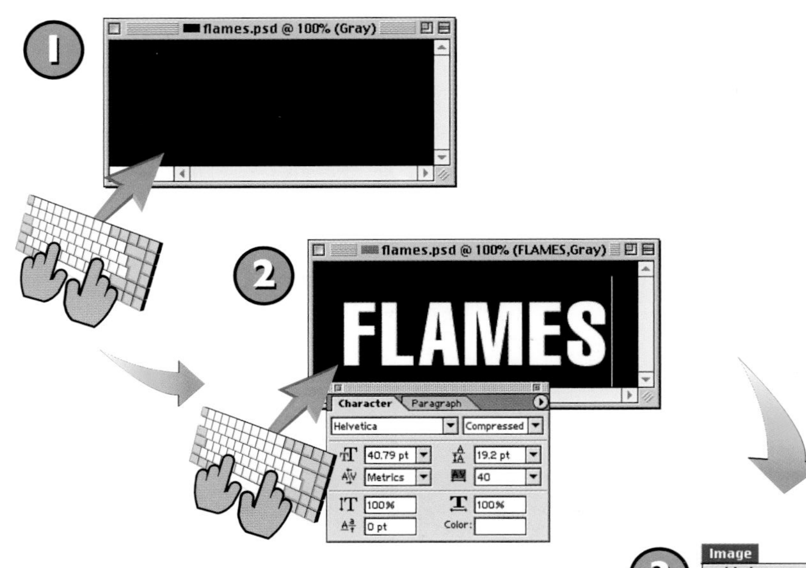

1. Press **D**, and then press **Option+Delete/Alt+Backspace** to fill the image with black.
2. Create the type you want to flame; use a thick font and make it white.
3. Press **Cmd+E/Ctrl+E**, and then choose **Image**, **Rotate Canvas**, **90° CCW**.

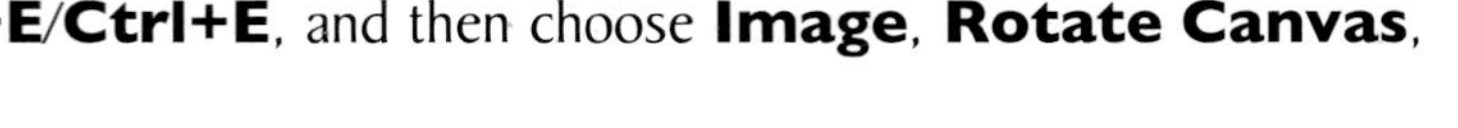

Next Step

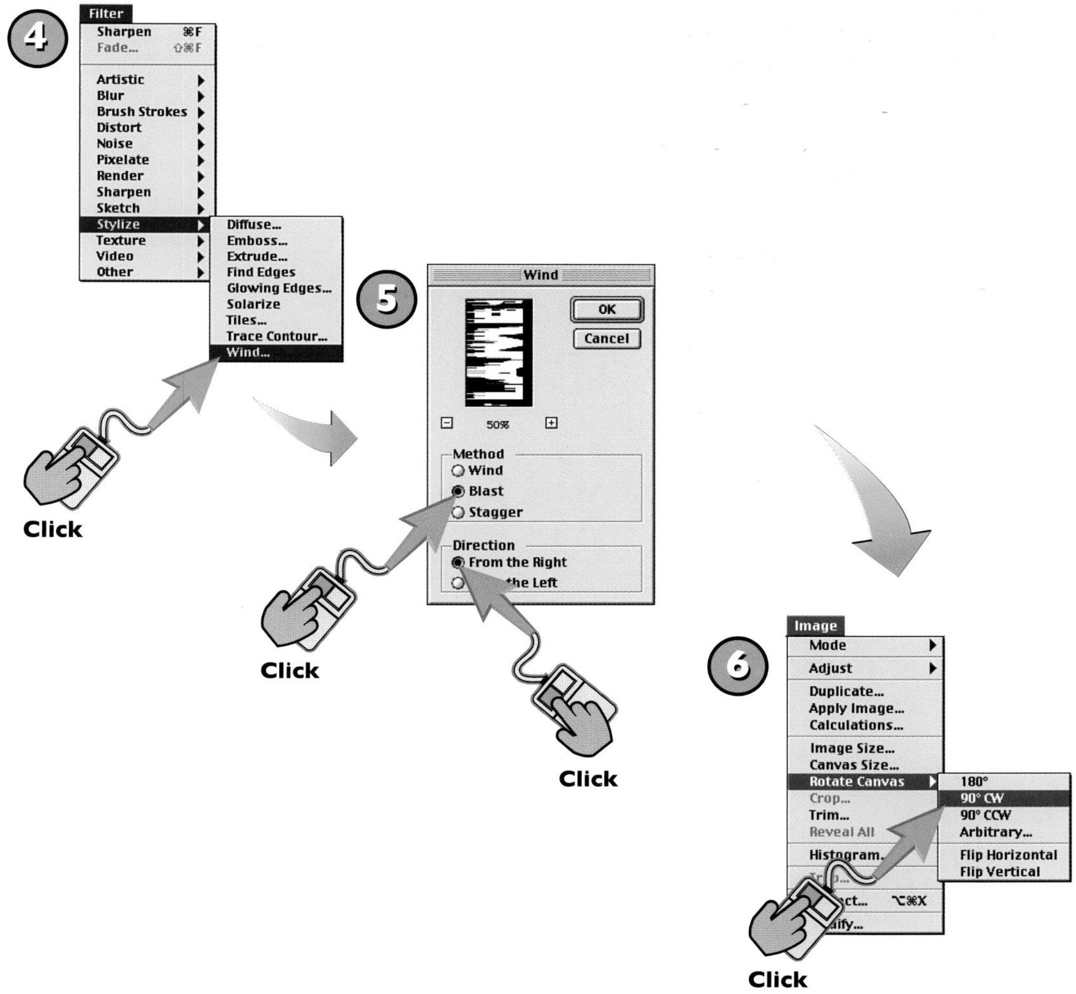

4 Choose **Filter**, **Stylize**, **Wind**.

5 Select the **Blast** and **From the Right** settings and click **OK**.

6 Choose **Image**, **Rotate Canvas**, **90°CW**.

The settings you use in step 5 determine the overall texture of the flames. Any settings will work, but you can experiment with different settings for a different feel.

Creating Flaming Type Continued

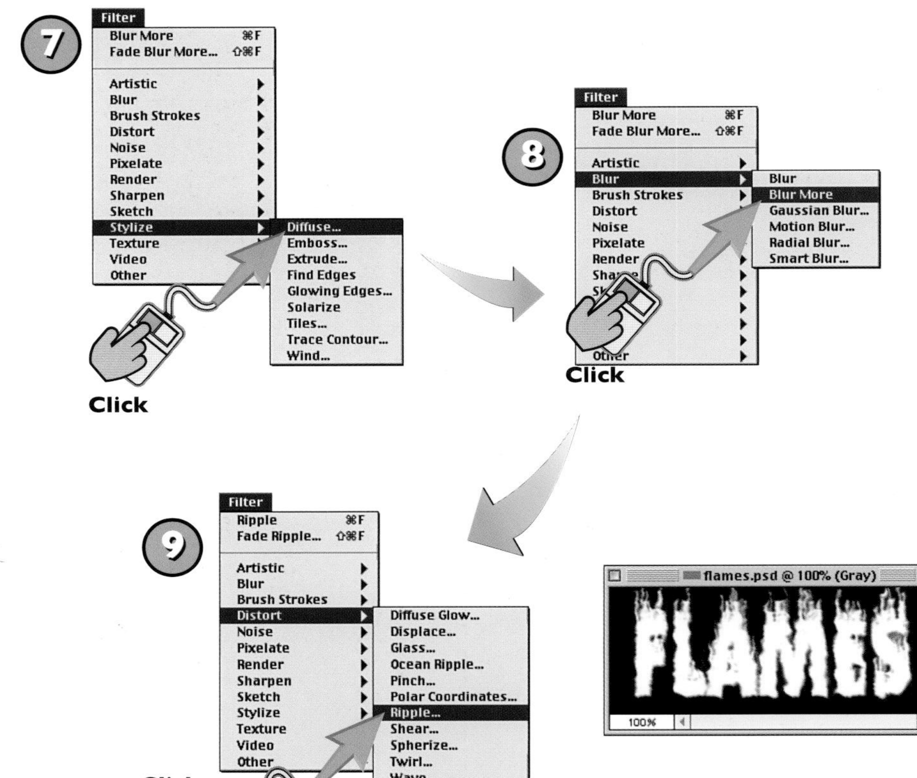

- You can make black type with flaming edges with a bit more work. After step 3, select the transparency mask of the type layer and save the selection. After step 6, load the selection, contract it a bit and feather it a bit, and fill it with black. Then go on to steps 7 and 8.

- For more information on selecting transparency masks, see Part 3, Task 14, "Selecting the Non-Transparent Areas of a Layer." To feather selections, see Part 3, Task 18, "Feathering the Edges of a Selection." To contract selections, see Part 3, Task 13, "Making a Selection Smaller or Larger."

7. Choose **Filter**, **Stylize**, **Diffuse**.
8. Choose **Filter**, **Blur**, **Blur More**.
9. Choose **Filter**, **Distort**, **Ripple**.

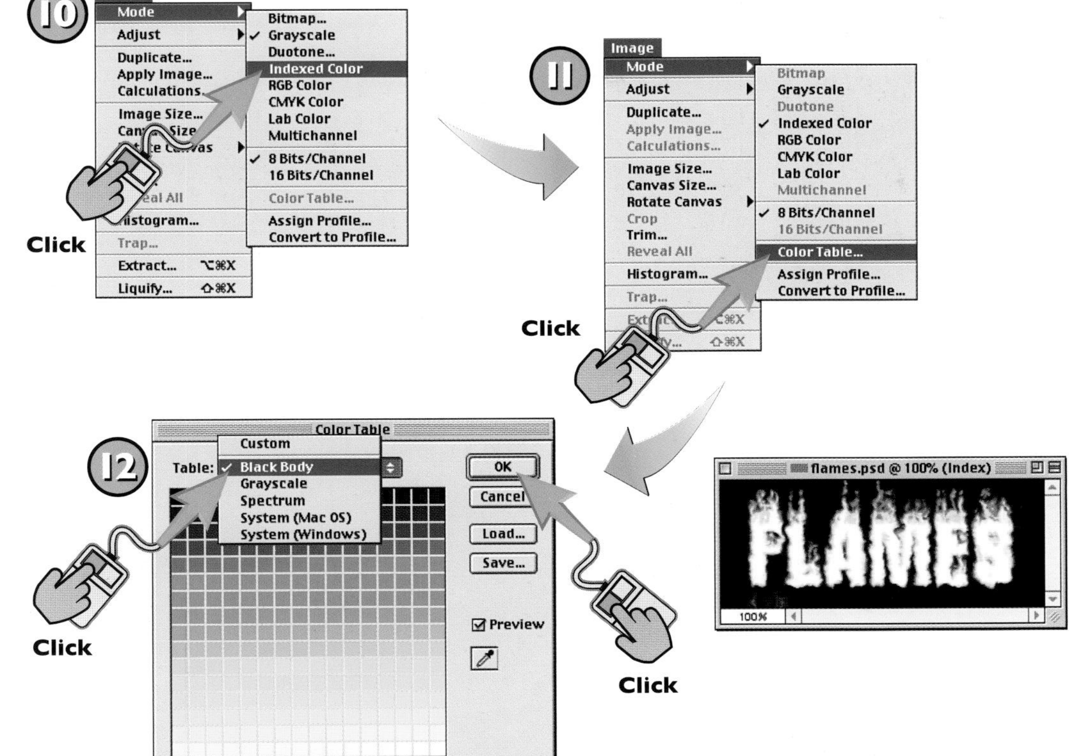

If the colors don't look right when you are finished, your image probably wasn't in Grayscale mode before step 10.

If you like this effect, create an Action to apply these steps to any type with one click. (See Part 1, Task 16, "Automating a Series of Steps," for information on making actions.)

Your results will vary depending on the resolution of the image and the size of the type; the images shown here were created with 45-point Futura Condensed Bold type in a 150-ppi image.

10 Choose **Image**, **Mode**, **Indexed Color**.

11 Choose **Image**, **Mode**, **Color Table**.

12 Choose **Black Body** from the **Table** pop-up menu and click **OK**.

PART 10

Creating Special Effects

Playing with Photoshop's filters is probably the most fun you'll have using the program. Adobe includes dozens of plug-in filters with Photoshop, ranging from purely functional (Unsharp Mask, for example) to truly unusual (Polar Coordinates). But each one has a useful function—the challenge is to keep working until you find it.

Photoshop's filters are arranged in logical groups; for example, all the filters in the Distort submenu apply some kind of distortion effect to an image, such as rippling or twirling it. This part shows you how to use several of the most useful filters, both for creating new effects within an image and for cleaning up flaws such as blurriness or dust. Also included in this part are instructions for fading the effects of a filter after it's been applied.

Tasks

Task 1: Adding Noise

"Noise" is an electronic term more than it is a photographic one; it refers to randomly colored pixels added throughout an image. Photoshop's Add Noise filter enables you to insert colored or monochrome noise and determine how it's placed in the image.

Start Here

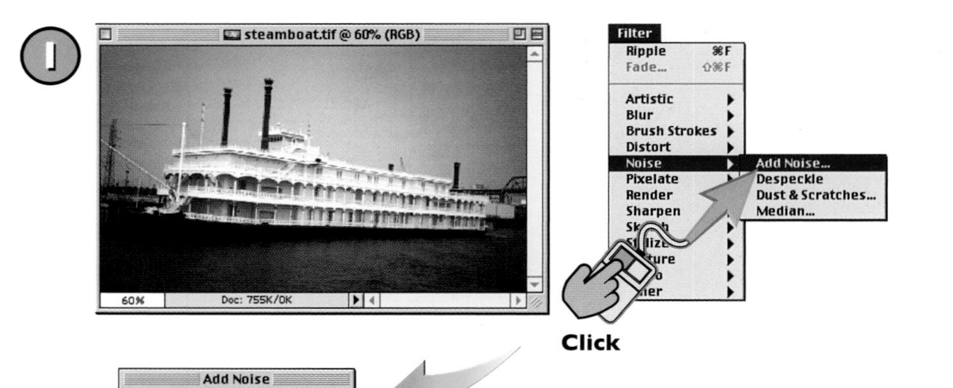

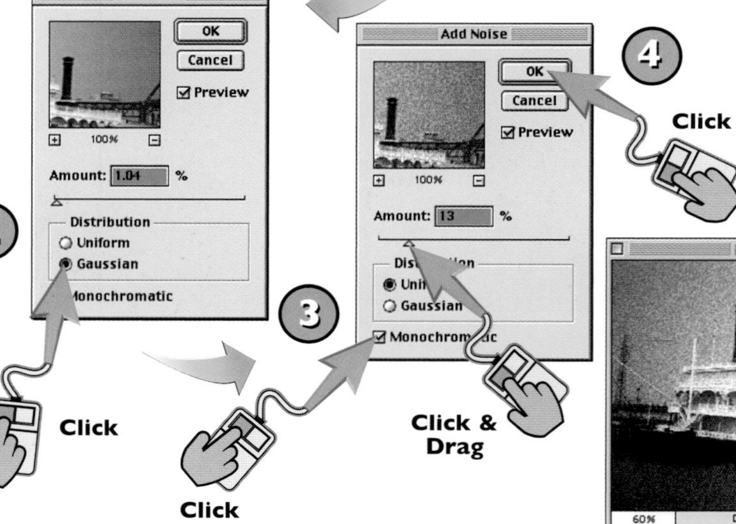

✓ Adding noise is a good starting point for many special effects, and it's a quick fix for boring, flat images. If you're creating a background pattern for a Web page or other use, try a plain color with a little noise added—subtle and classy.

1. Choose **Filter**, **Noise**, **Add Noise**.
2. Click **Uniform** for a noise pattern or **Gaussian** for random distribution.
3. Click **Monochromatic** for black-and-white noise, or click it off for colored noise.
4. Choose an **Amount** and click **OK** to apply the filter.

Task 2: Blurring a Selection or Layer

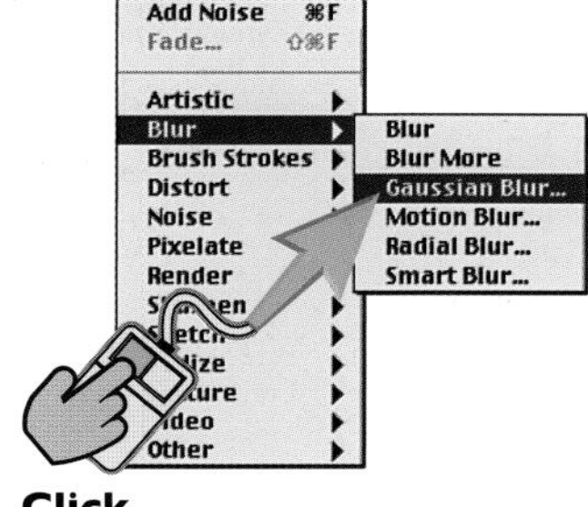

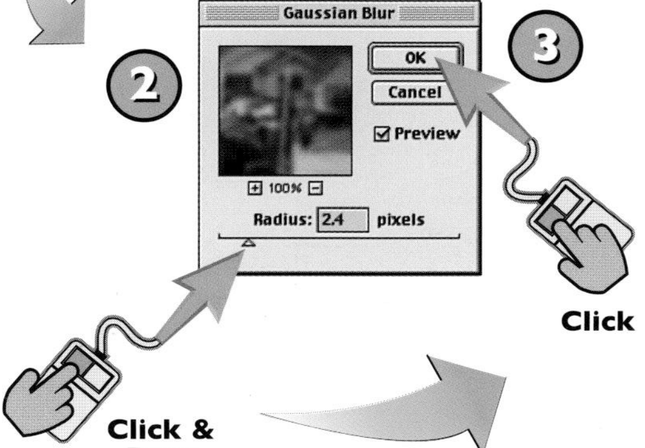

Blurring gets rid of detail by softening transitions between different colors. You can blur entire images for a soft-focus effect, you can blur backgrounds to point up the foreground, and you can blur to remove details by "averaging" colors.

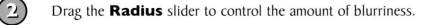

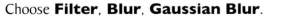

1. Choose **Filter**, **Blur**, **Gaussian Blur**.
2. Drag the **Radius** slider to control the amount of blurriness.
3. Click **OK** to apply the change.

Radius refers to the distance from each color transition that the blur effect is applied; smaller **Radius** settings result in less blurring.

Task 3: Sharpening a Selection or Layer

Sharpening works by "hardening" the transitions between one color and another. Although sharpening can't correct a photo that was blurry before it was scanned, it's a good way to correct some of the inevitable image degradation that comes from scanning an image and using that second-generation copy.

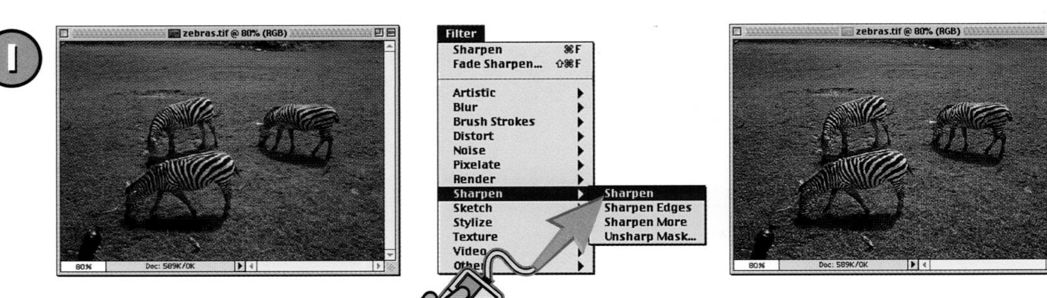
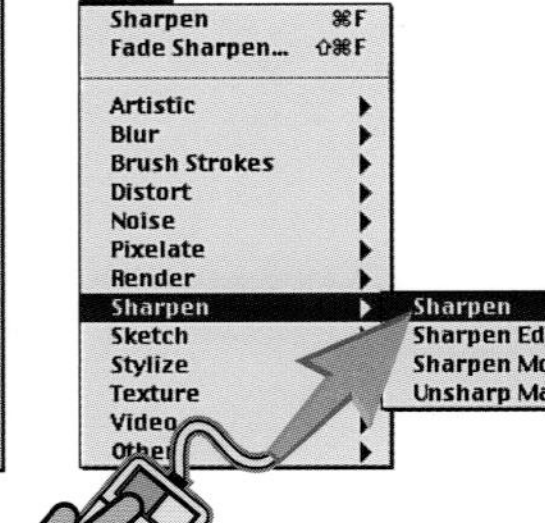
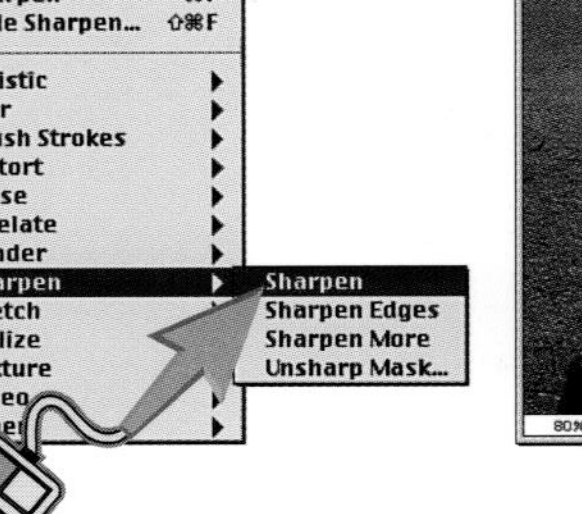
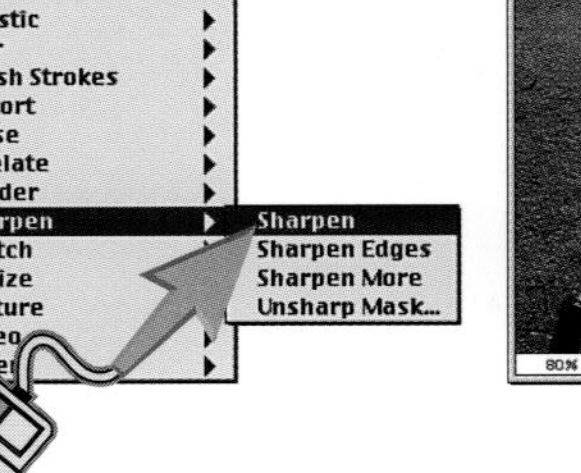
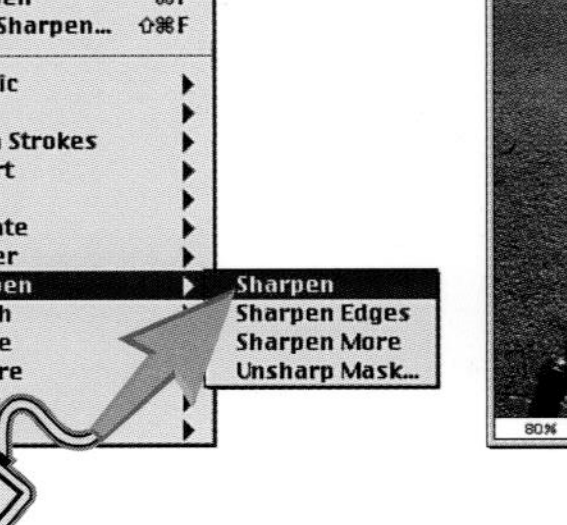
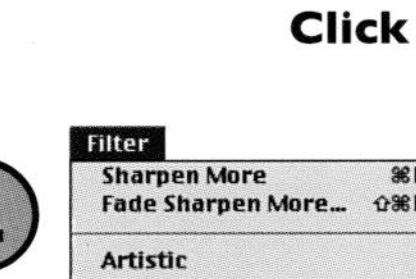
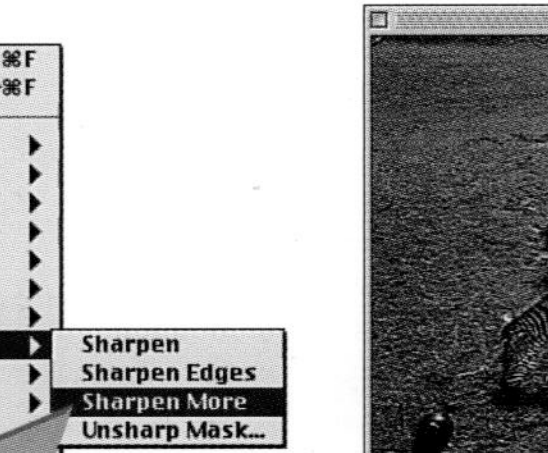

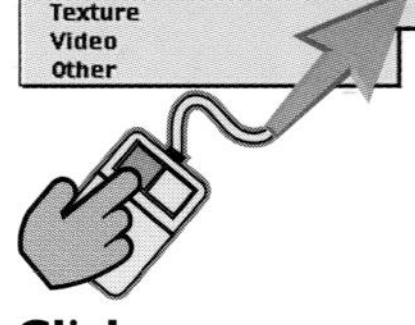

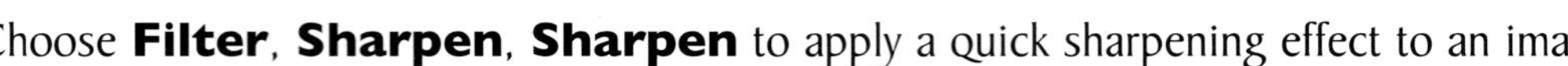

1. Choose **Filter**, **Sharpen**, **Sharpen** to apply a quick sharpening effect to an image.
2. Choose **Filter**, **Sharpen**, **Sharpen More** for more sharpening.
3. Choose **Filter**, **Sharpen**, **Unsharp Mask** to apply a variable amount of sharpening.

✓ Use a light touch with the Unsharp Mask filter; it's better to go back and sharpen more than to sharpen too much at one time.

Next Step

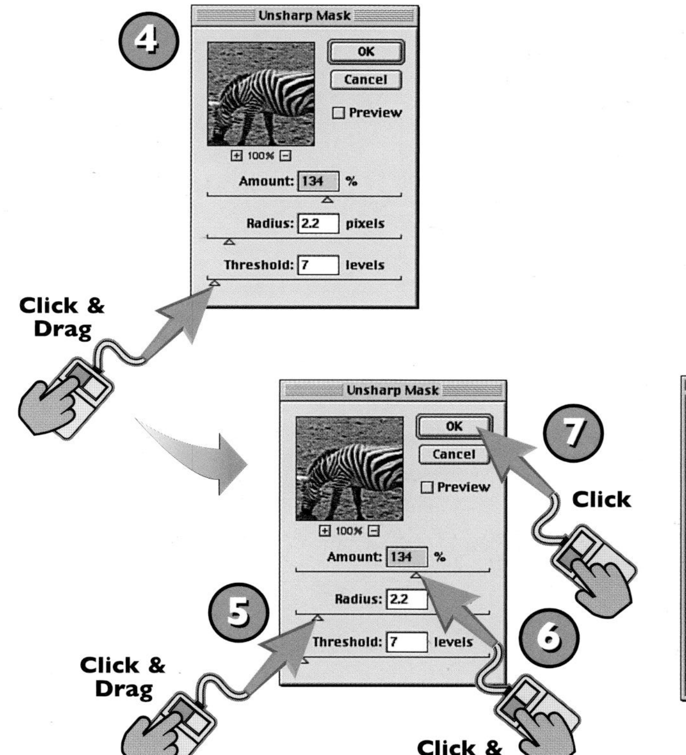

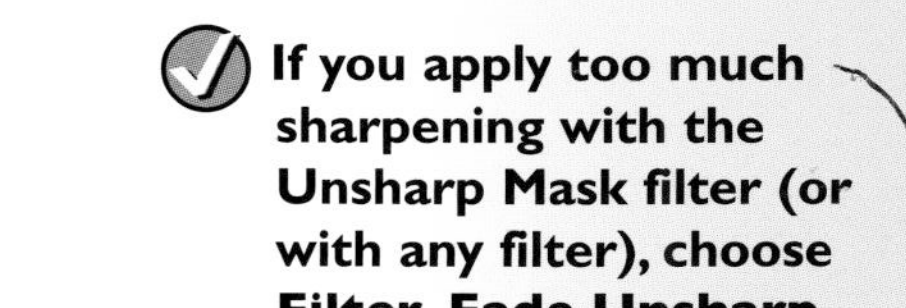

4 Drag the **Threshold** slider to control how different colors must be for their edges to be affected.

5 Drag the **Radius** slider to control how much of the area around transitions is sharpened.

6 Drag the **Amount** slider to determine how much sharpening is applied.

7 Click **OK** to apply the filter.

If you apply too much sharpening with the Unsharp Mask filter (or with any filter), choose Filter, Fade Unsharp Mask and drag the Opacity slider to reduce the impact of the filter.

The Unsharp Mask filter takes its name from a darkroom technique that involves combining multiple negatives to create the final, sharper image.

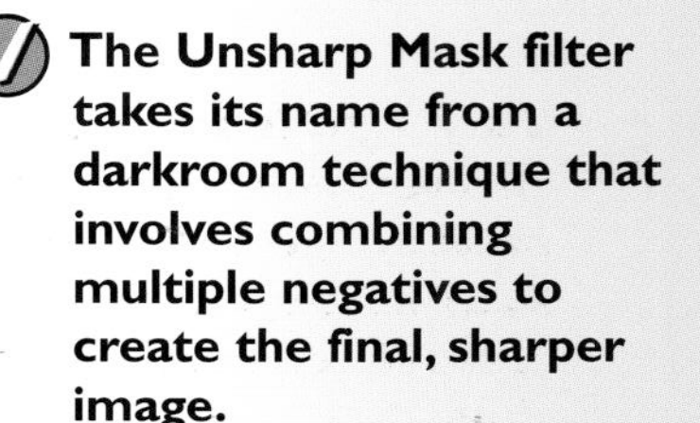

Task 4: Removing Dust and Scratches from a Scan

Even with the best of intentions and lots of rubbing alcohol, it's not always possible to keep images and scanner beds clean. Although it's possible to retouch each dust mote or scratch individually, the Dust & Scratches filter tackles them all at once.

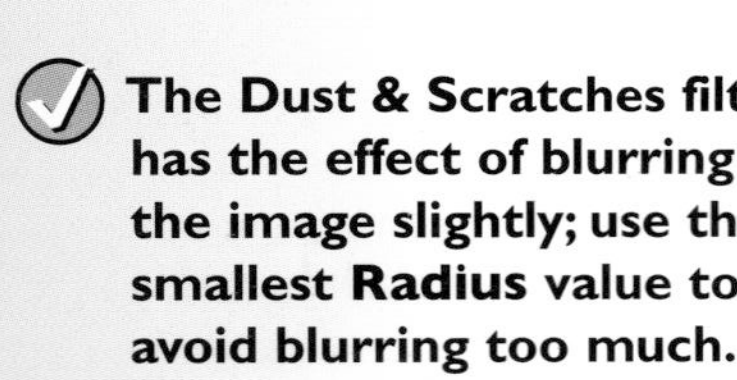

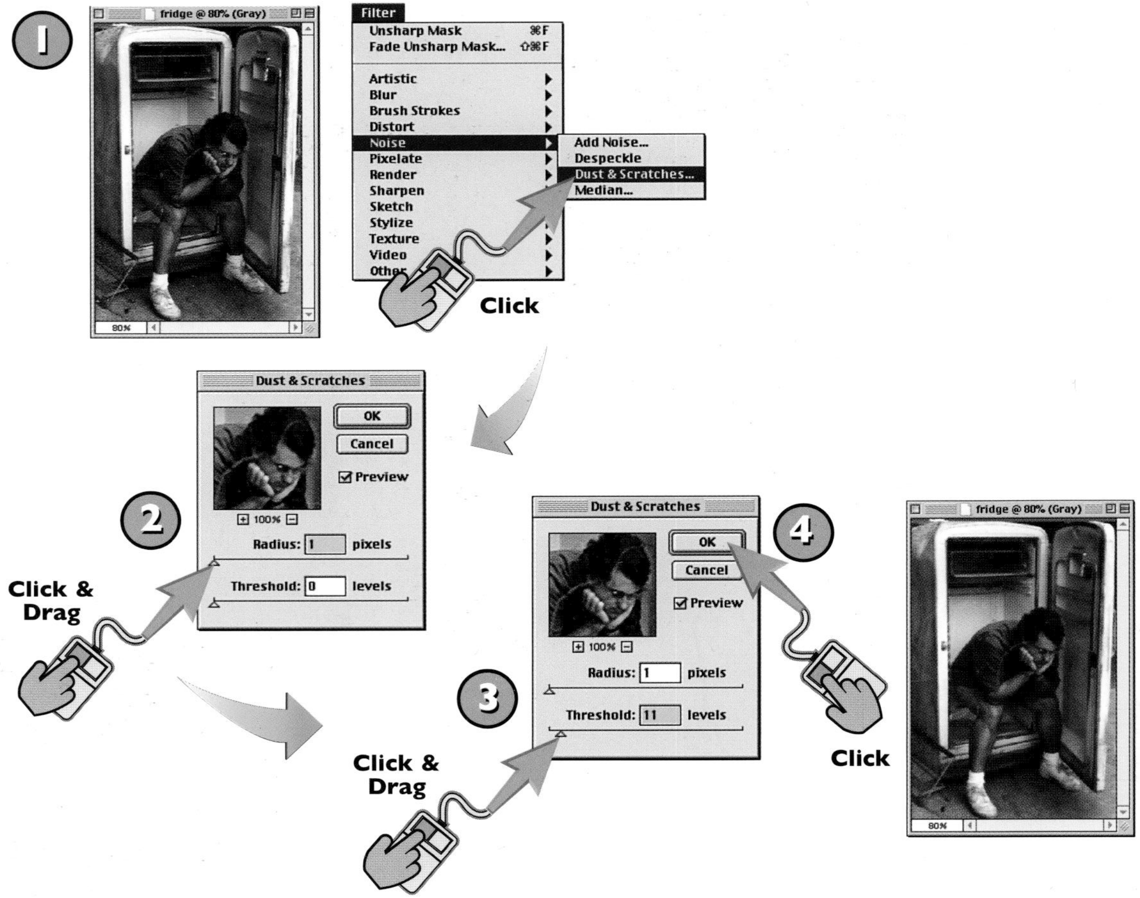

- **The Dust & Scratches filter has the effect of blurring the image slightly; use the smallest Radius value to avoid blurring too much.**
- **If you do decide to go after dust and scratch marks individually, the best tool to use is the Rubber Stamp. You can clone nearby areas to cover up stray marks—this is especially effective in sky areas.**

1. Choose **Filter**, **Noise**, **Dust & Scratches**.
2. Drag the **Radius** slider to determine the size of dust to be eliminated.
3. Drag the **Threshold** slider to determine the contrast level at which dust is "noticed."
4. Click **OK**.

Task 5: Rippling an Image

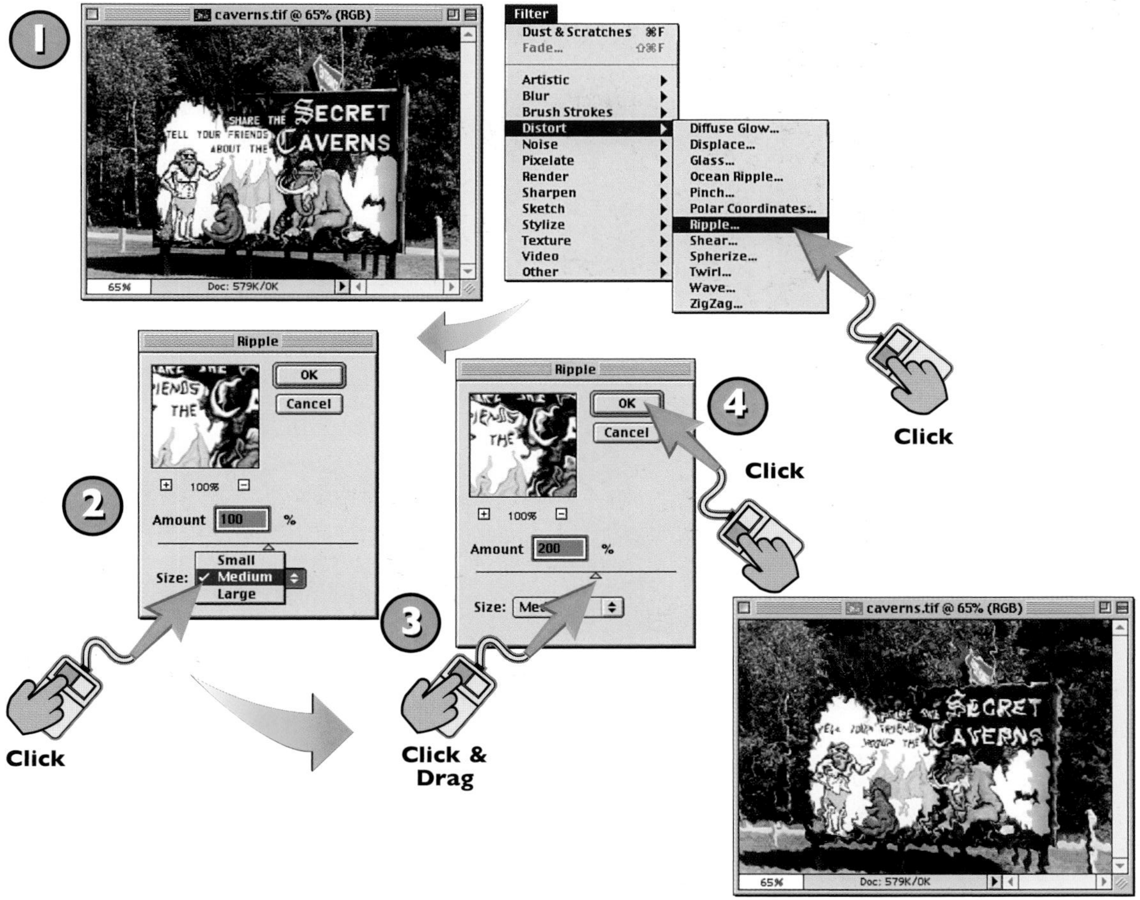

Among Photoshop's Distort group of filters, Ripple is perhaps the most useful. It gives an image or type a pleasant hand-drawn feeling by rippling any straight lines in the image.

1. Choose **Filter**, **Distort**, **Ripple**.
2. Choose a **Size** for the ripples.
3. Drag the **Amount** slider to raise or lower the ripples.
4. Click **OK** to apply the changes.

Related to Ripple are Wave and Ocean Ripple, also in the Distort filter group. Wave offers a similar effect to Ripple but with more control. Ocean Ripple creates shapes like the ripples you see reflected on the sea floor.

Task 6: Pinching an Image

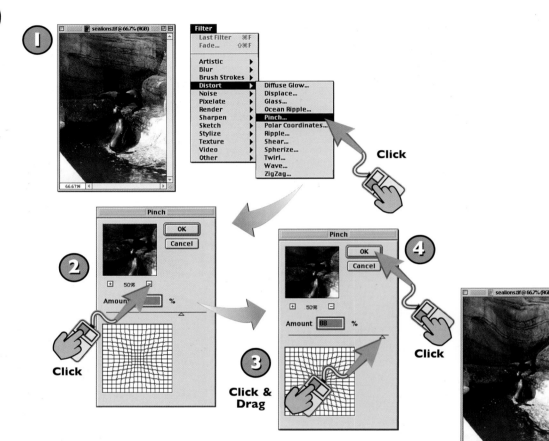

The Pinch filter does just that: It squishes an image's center so it looks as though you'd pinched together the paper on which it's printed (or the screen on which it's displayed). It's similar in operation to the Spherize filter—both look as though they're performing a 3D action on a 2D image.

Start Here

To save time, preview filters such as Pinch by selecting a small portion of the image before applying the filter. This will give you an idea of what the filter will do, but it takes less time than applying the filter to the entire image—just in case you don't like the effect.

1. Choose **Filter**, **Distort**, **Pinch**.
2. Click the plus and minus buttons to enlarge or reduce the preview.
3. Drag the **Amount** slider right to push the image inward, left to pull it outward.

4. Click **OK** to apply the filter.

Task 7: Shearing an Image

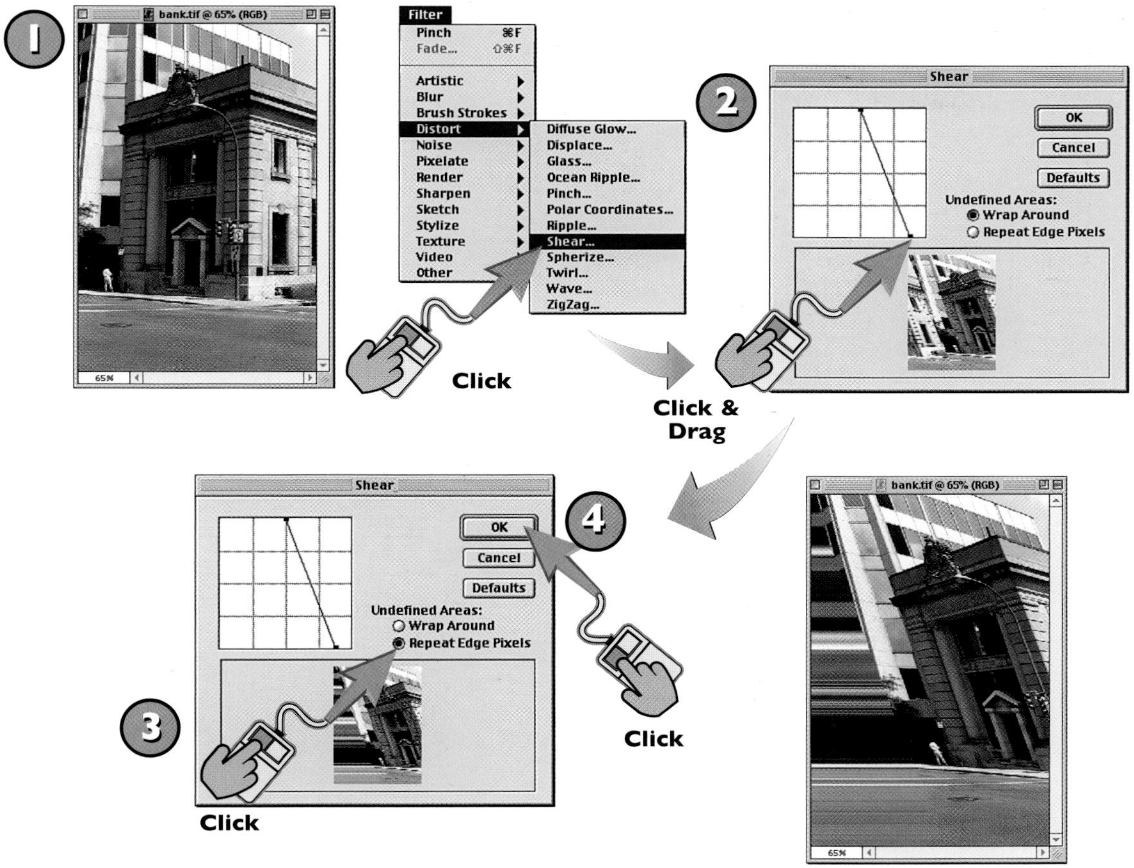

Shearing is what other programs call skewing. The image is tilted but its base remains in place. The result is a distorted image that can wrap around or disappear off the edge of the window.

1. Choose **Filter**, **Distort**, **Shear**.
2. Drag either end of the line to adjust the shear angle.
3. Click **Wrap Around** or **Repeat Edge Pixels**.
4. Click **OK** to apply the filter.

When using the Shear filter, don't forget that you can drag both ends of the line—you're not restricted to one at a time.

This effect is similar to that of the Skew transformation (choose Layer, Transform, Skew), but the Skew command doesn't offer the choices of wrapping around or repeating the edge pixels.

Task 8: Twirling an Image

To imagine the effect of the Twirl filter, picture the image floating on the surface of a bowl of pudding. Now stick your finger in and drag it in circles. At high settings, Twirl wreaks havoc on an image; at low settings, it applies a rather psychedelic curvy distortion.

Start Here

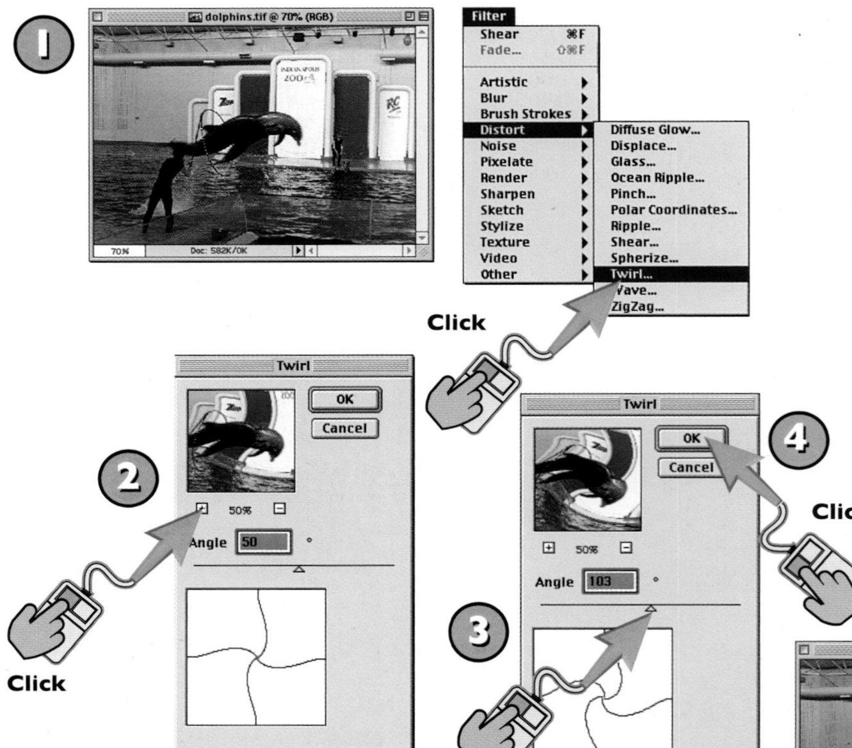

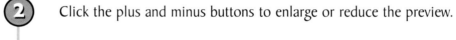

1. Choose **Filter**, **Distort**, **Twirl**.
2. Click the plus and minus buttons to enlarge or reduce the preview.
3. Drag the **Angle** slider right to twirl to the right, left to twirl to the left.
4. Click **OK** to apply the filter.

For an unpredictable twirling of just an object's interior, apply the Twirl filter once and then apply it again using the opposite setting (for example, 135° and –135°). The outlines of the object will return to their original shape, but some of its interior will still be twirled.

End Task

Task 9: Switching Image Coordinates

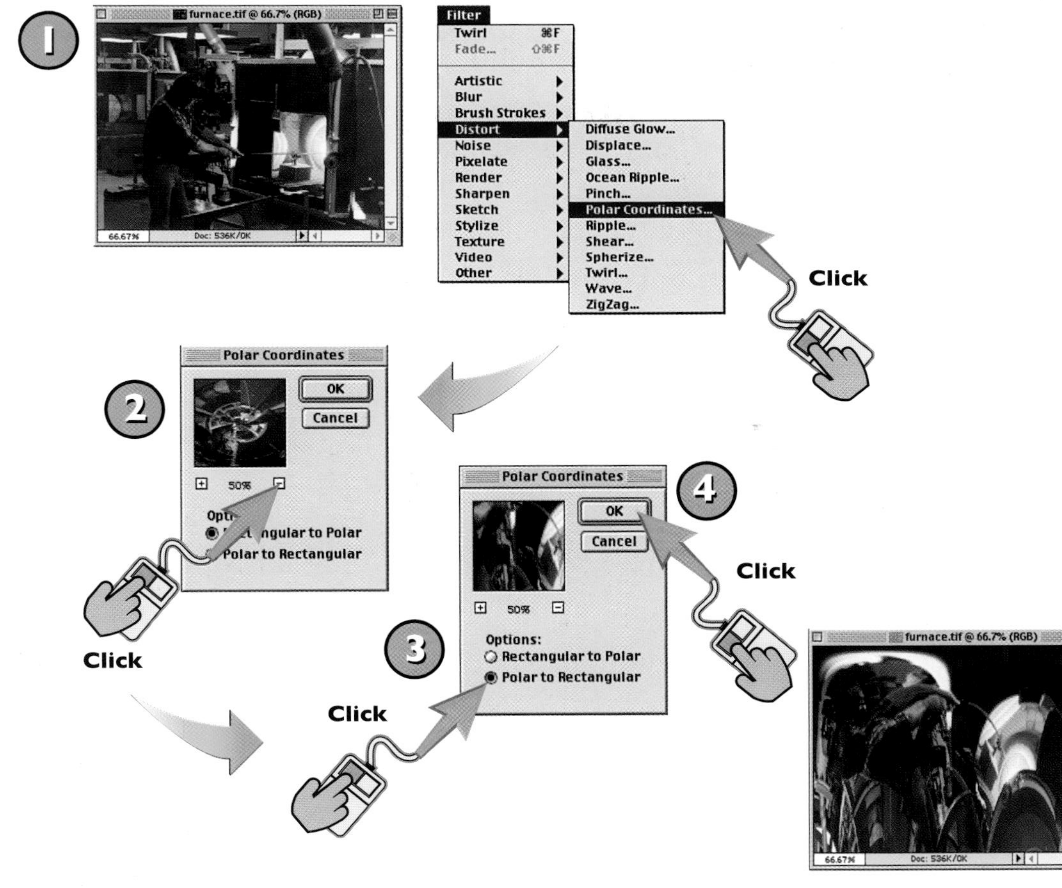

The Polar Coordinates filter remaps an image by converting each pixel's Cartesian coordinates into polar coordinates. The effect is difficult to describe, but it distorts an image about as much as you possibly can and still recognize it.

1. Choose **Filter**, **Distort**, **Polar Coordinates**.
2. Click the plus and minus buttons to enlarge or reduce the preview.
3. Click **Rectangular to Polar** or **Polar to Rectangular**.
4. Click **OK** to apply the filter.

Unlike most of the Distort filters, you can undo the effects of Polar Coordinates by applying it again, with the other option chosen the second time.

The Glass filter makes your image look as though it's behind a glass shower door. You have a choice of glass textures to use with it, including glass blocks and frosted glass.

Start Here

Task 10: Applying a Glass Distortion Effect

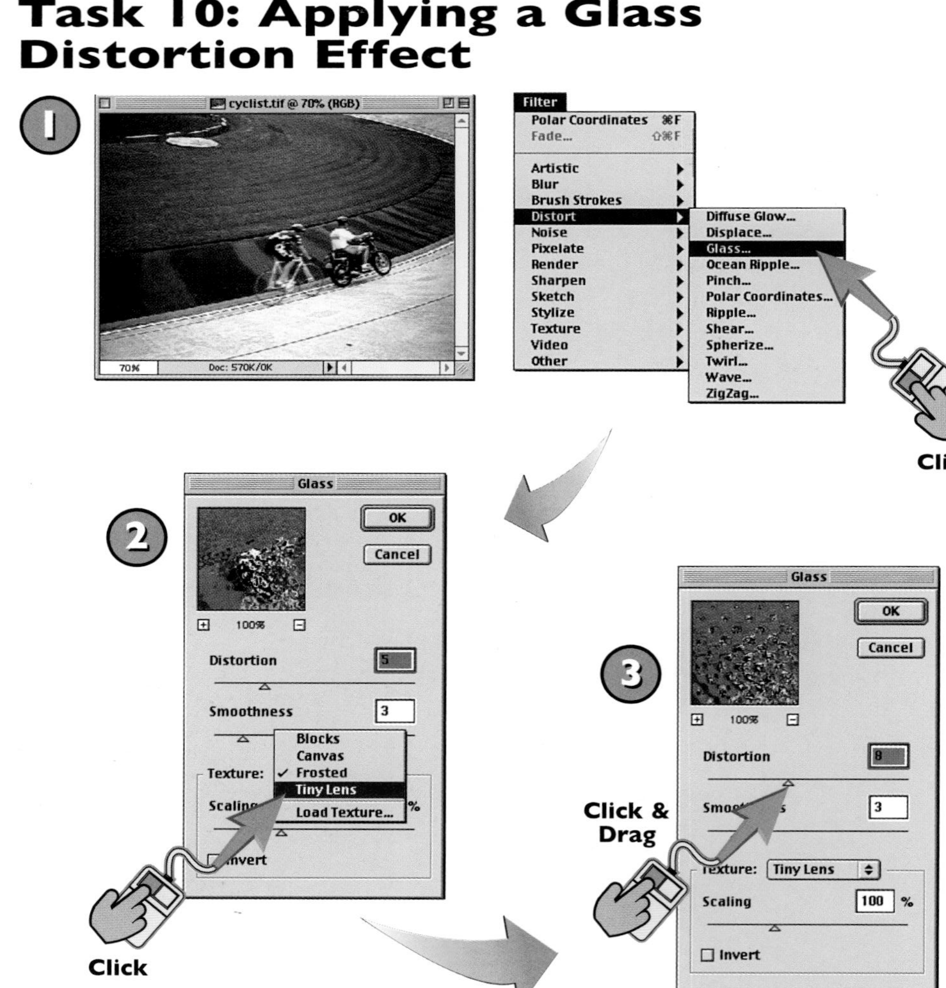

1 Choose **Filter**, **Distort**, **Glass**.

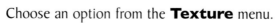

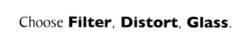

2 Choose an option from the **Texture** menu.

3 Drag the **Distortion** slider to adjust the texture's effects on the image.

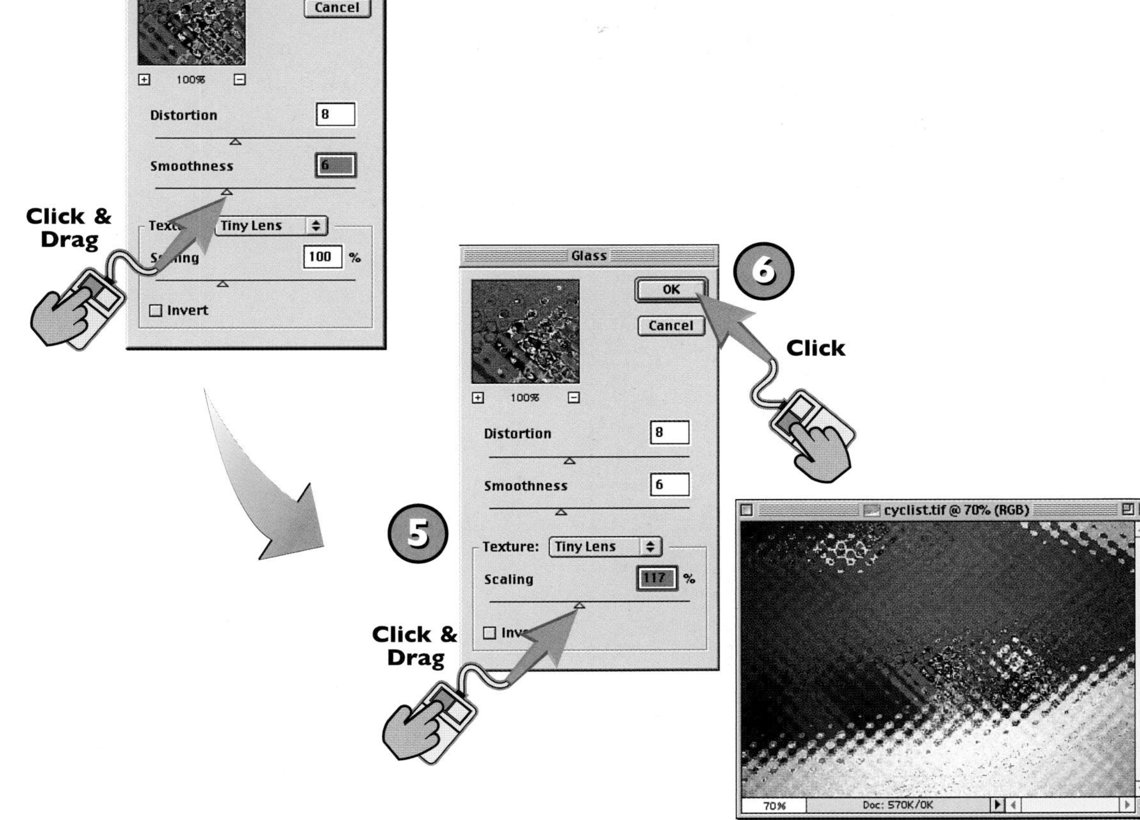

4 Drag the **Smoothness** slider to adjust the texture's effects on the image.

5 Drag the **Scaling** slider to scale the texture.

6 Click **OK** to apply the texture.

You can make your own textures to use with the Glass filter; save them as grayscale files in Photoshop format. Choose Load Texture from the Texture pop-up menu to use them.

Task 11: Creating Clouds

The Clouds filter obliterates any existing image, filling the window with a cloudy texture by using the foreground and background colors. You can't start with a transparent layer, though; the filter must have some pixels on which to work.

Start Here

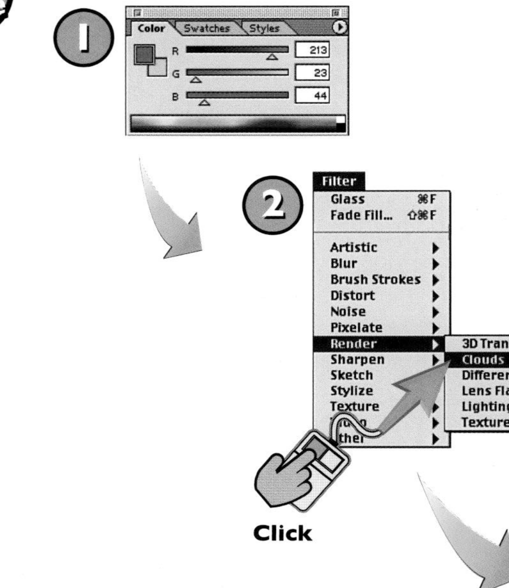

Difference Clouds is a related filter that does operate on the image's existing colors. If you run the filter again, it inverts the colors it used the first time. Use Difference Clouds repeatedly on a white background to get rainbow colors.

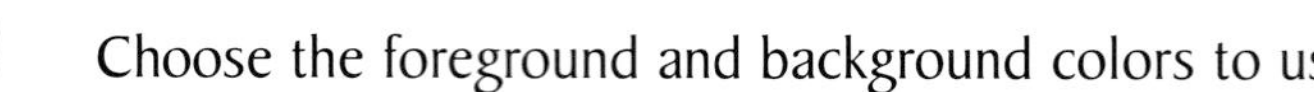

1. Choose the foreground and background colors to use.

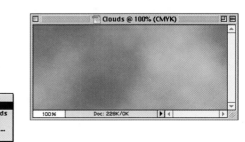

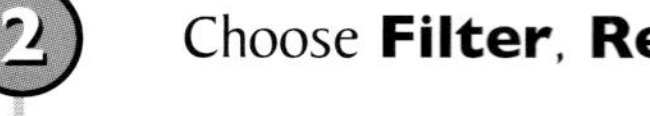

2. Choose **Filter**, **Render**, **Clouds**.

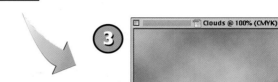

3. Press **Cmd+F/Ctrl+F** to apply the filter again to change the cloud pattern.

End Task

Task 12: Adding a Lens Flare

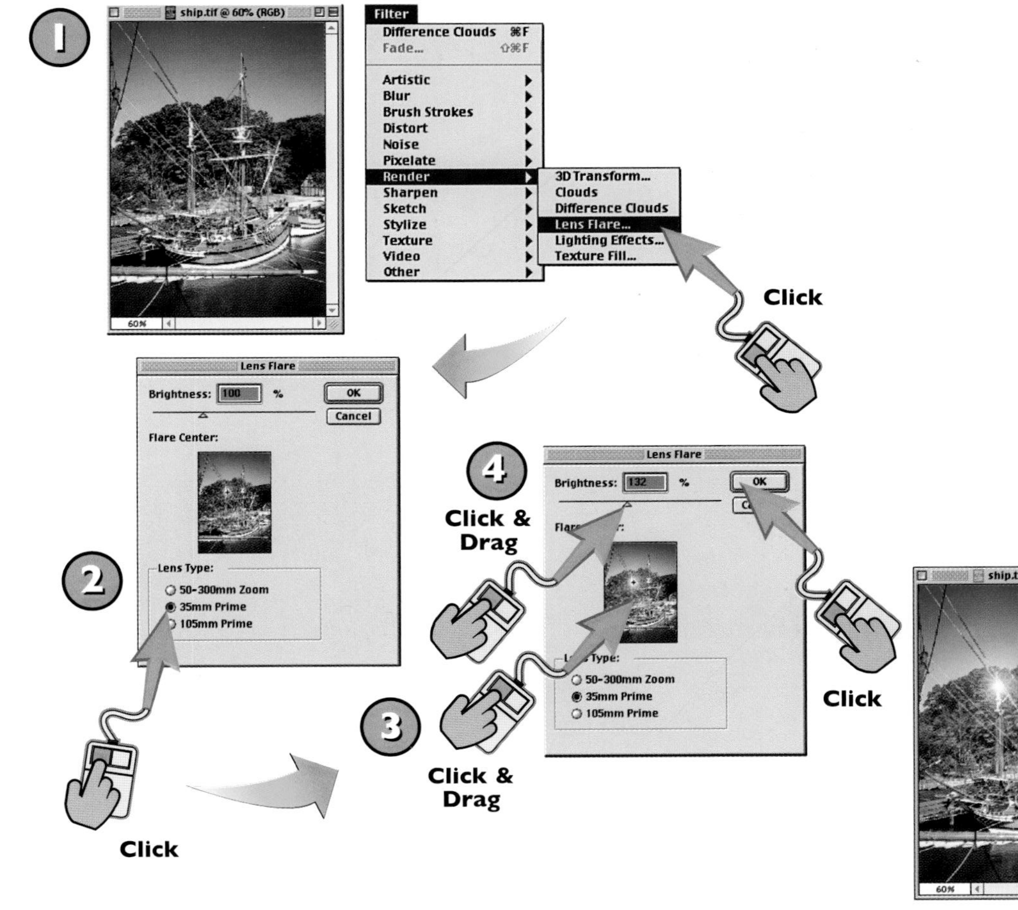

You can spice up your photos by adding an effect that photographers sometimes get accidentally: a lens flare. This bright flare of light can add a twinkle to chrome bumpers in scans of antique autos, among other things.

1. Choose **Filter**, **Render**, **Lens Flare**.
2. Choose a **Lens Type**.
3. Drag the cross in the preview window to move the flare.
4. Drag the **Brightness** slider to set the flare's intensity, and then click **OK**.

✓ The three lens types, from top to bottom, make successively larger flares, but they have other differences too. Try all three for variety!

There are several ways to achieve a pop art–style halftone effect—in other words, a halftone screen with dots so large they actually form an element of the image. This method produces a two-color halftone that uses the foreground and background colors.

Task 13: Applying a Stylized Halftone Pattern

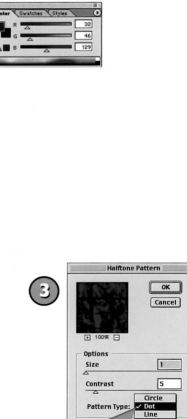

Start Here

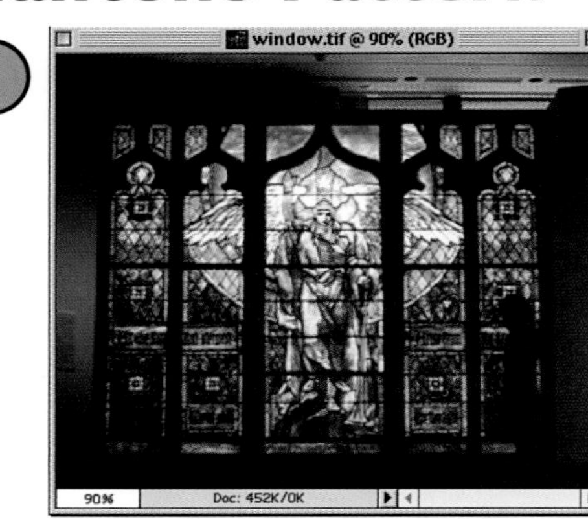

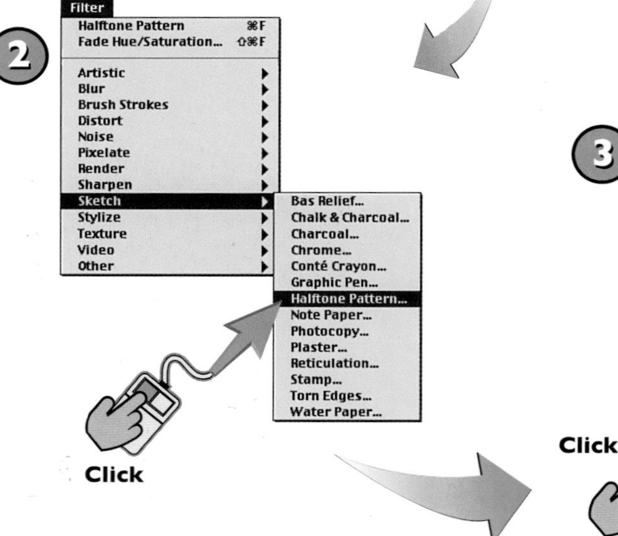

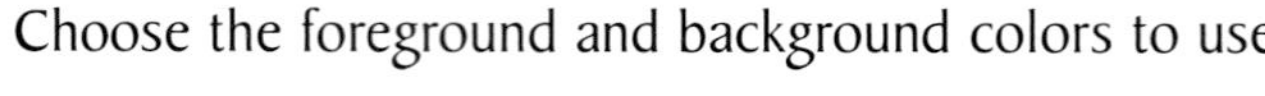

1. Choose the foreground and background colors to use.
2. Choose **Filter**, **Sketch**, **Halftone Pattern**.
3. Choose a **Pattern Type** from the pop-up menu.

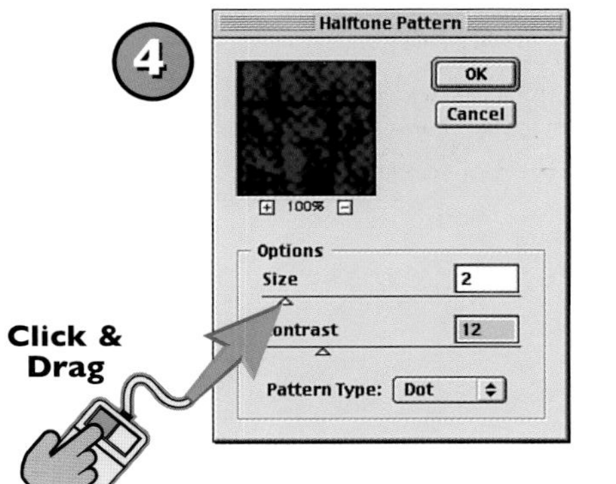

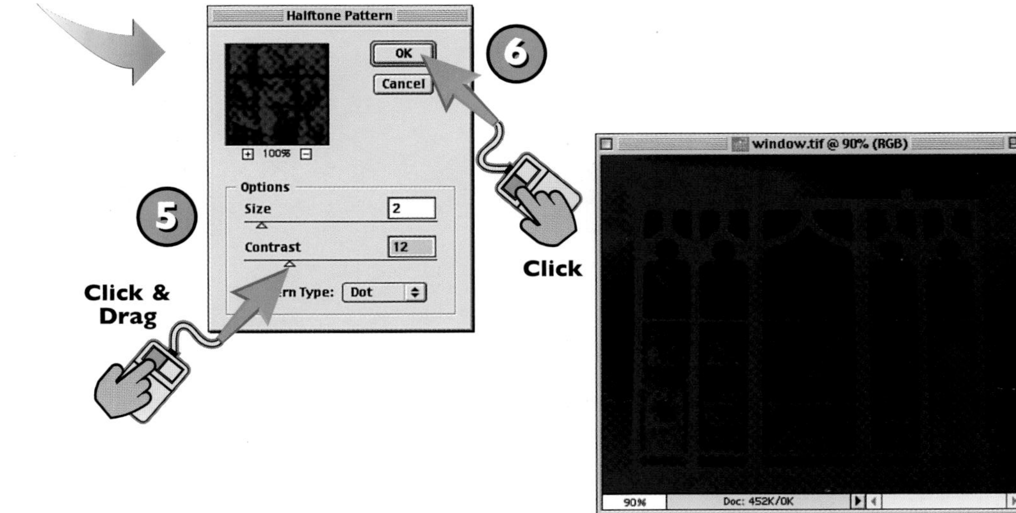

4. Drag the **Size** slider to adjust the image.
5. Drag the **Contrast** slider to adjust the image.
6. Click **OK**.

The Color Halftone filter in the Pixelate group of filters also creates a halftone effect, but it uses the image's basic colors—red, green, and blue; or cyan, magenta, yellow, and black.

Task 14: Applying Texture

Want to make a photo look as though it's printed on the side of a brick wall? The Texturizer filter is your solution. It includes four built-in textures and enables you to create your own and load them into the Filter dialog box.

Start Here

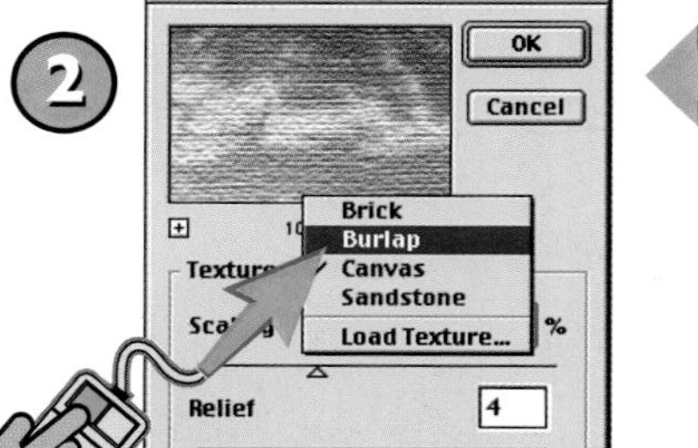

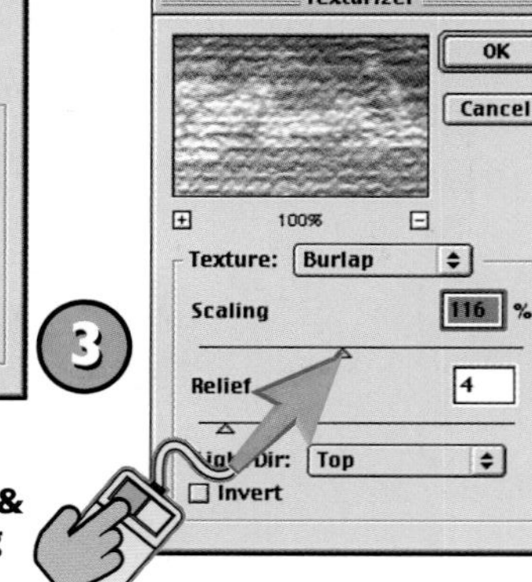

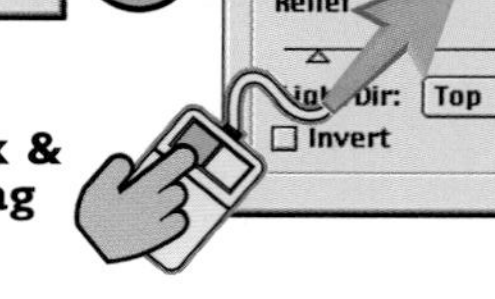

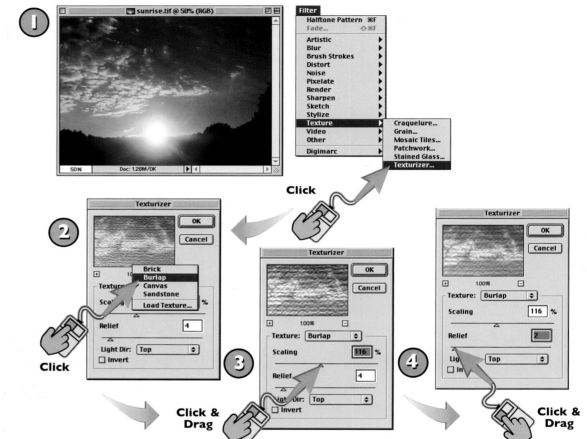

1. Choose **Filter**, **Texture**, **Texturizer**.
2. Choose an option from the **Texture** pop-up menu.
3. Drag the **Scaling** slider to enlarge or reduce the texture.
4. Drag the **Relief** slider to determine the height of the texture.

Next Step

Choose an option from the **Light Dir:** pop-up menu.

Click **Invert** to reverse the high and low areas of the texture.

Click **OK** to apply the texture.

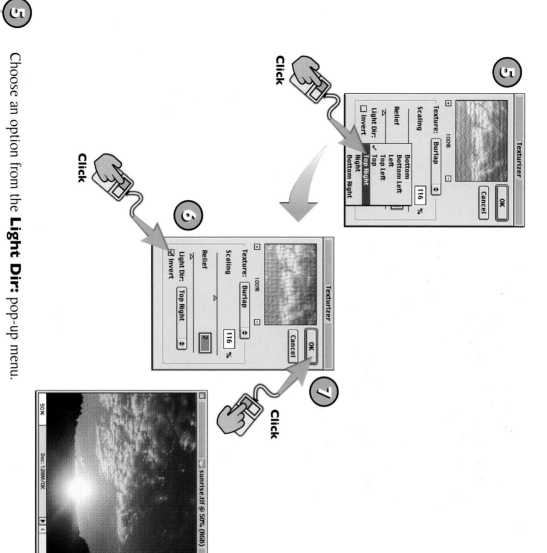

If you're creating your own textures, be sure to save them in Photoshop format. Choose Load Texture in the Texture pop-up menu to use your own texture.

For a 3D effect, save your image in Photoshop format, and then choose Load Texture and select the image on which you're working. It's applied to itself as a texture, making all the light areas jump forward and the dark areas recede.

The Glowing Edges filter applies brightly colored edges to an image, darkening the image enough that any other details are effectively lost. It works best with high-contrast images.

Task 15: Converting an Image to Glowing Edges

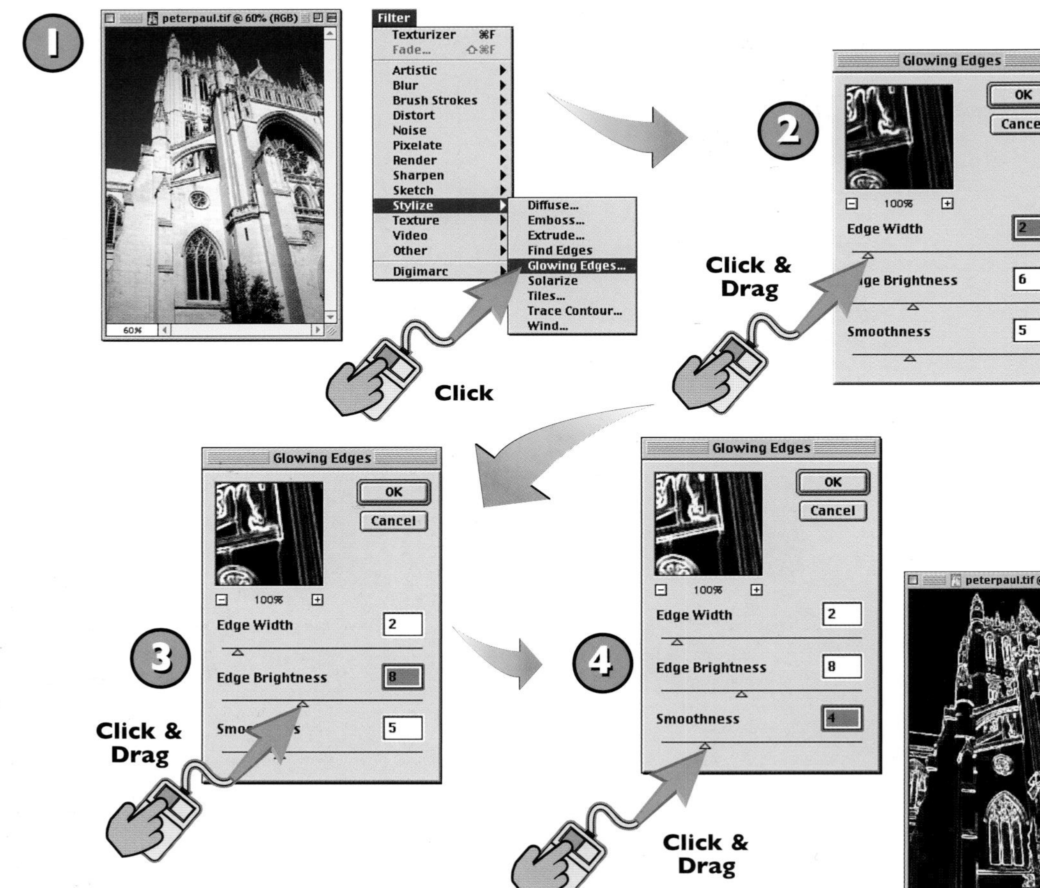

1. Choose **Filter**, **Stylize**, **Glowing Edges**.
2. Drag the **Edge Width** slider to widen the edges.
3. Drag the **Edge Brightness** slider to make the edges brighter or dimmer.
4. Drag the **Smoothness** slider to add or remove detail from the edges and click **OK**.

Apply Glowing Edges and then choose Filter, Fade Glowing Edges for just a suggestion of glow. Drag the slider to reduce the opacity of the glowing edges.

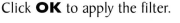

Task 16: Applying a Windblown Effect

The Wind filter makes an object look as though it's being blown away by the wind, bit by bit. It works best with an object on a plain background.

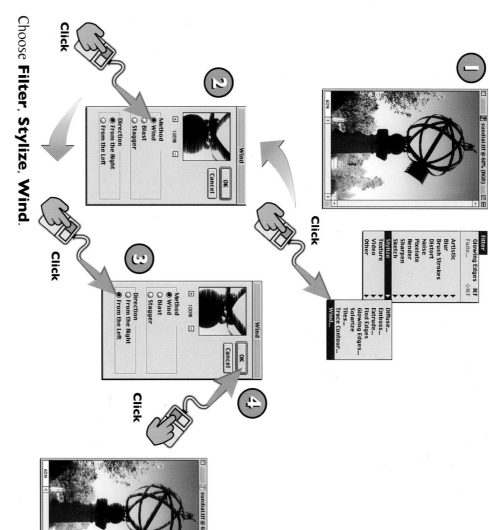

1. Choose **Filter**, **Stylize**, **Wind**.
2. Click a **Method**.
3. Click a **Direction**.
4. Click **OK** to apply the filter.

✓ The **Method** choices increase in intensity from top to bottom.

✓ For a fun effect that uses the Wind filter, see Part 9, Task 5, "Creating Flaming Type."

Task 17: Creating Contour Lines

Here's an easy way to convert a normal photograph into something that looks like one of those geological survey maps with all the contour lines. This filter finds the edges in an image and draws lines along them. The simpler the image, the better Trace Contour works.

Start Here

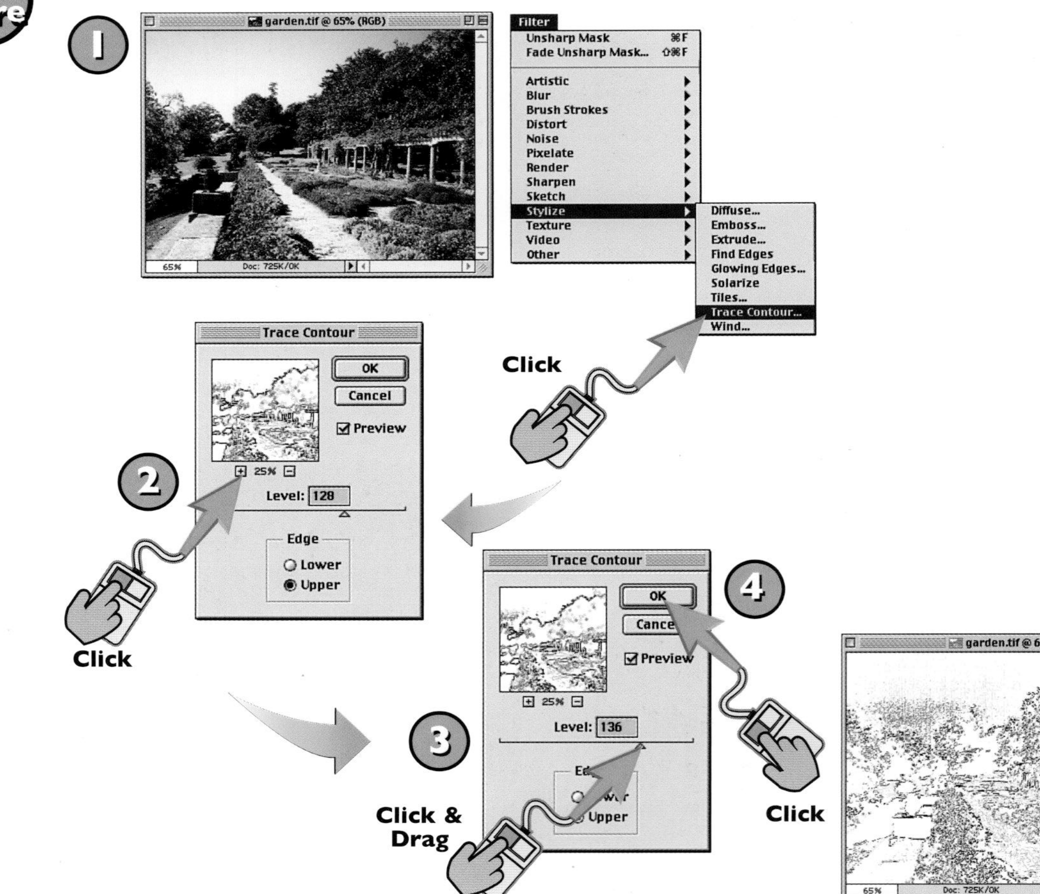

1. Choose **Filter**, **Stylize**, **Trace Contour**.
2. Choose an **Edge** to be traced.
3. Drag the **Level** slider to determine what brightness level is traced.
4. Click **OK** to apply the filter.

For an interesting effect, apply the Trace Contour filter and then press Cmd+F/Ctrl+F to apply it again—Photoshop traces the edges of the edges.

Task 18: Applying a Neon Glow

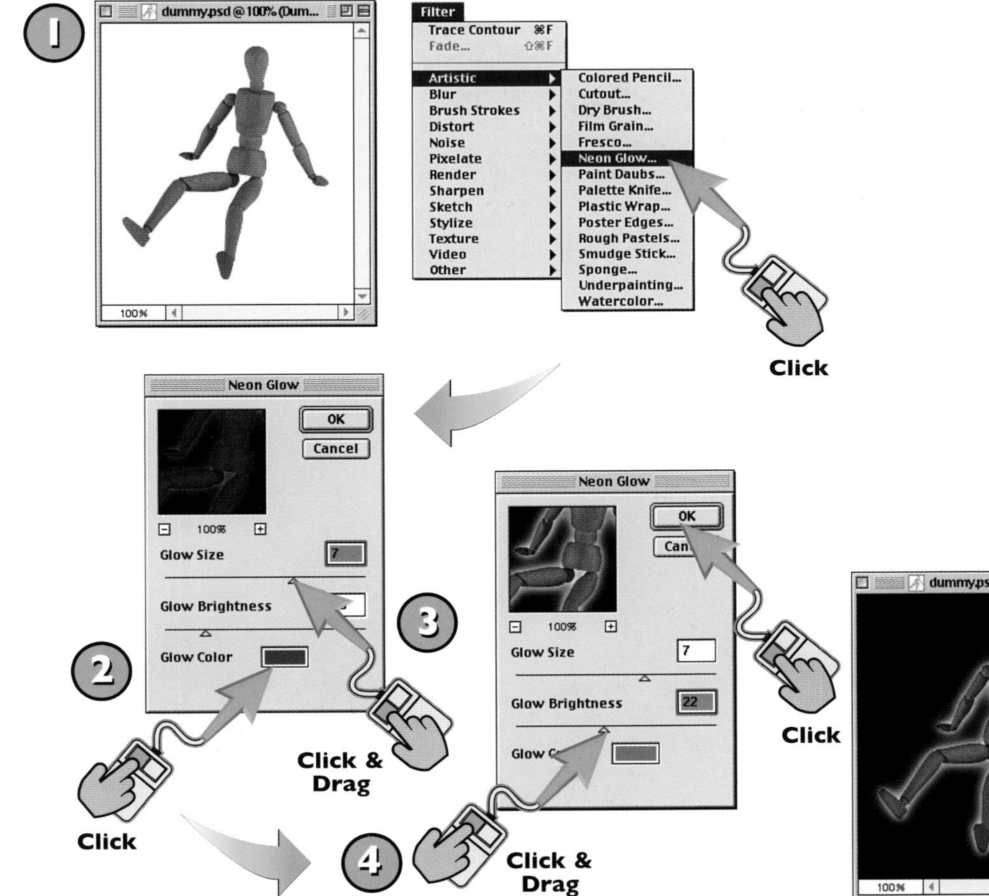

Unlike Glowing Edges, Neon Glow leaves image detail fairly intact, although it obscures image colors. This filter works best with an object on a plain white background, which will turn black.

1 Choose **Filter**, **Artistic**, **Neon Glow**.

2 Click the color swatch to choose a color.

3 Drag the **Glow Size** slider to adjust the extent of the glow.

4 Drag the **Glow Brightness** slider to make the glow brighter or dimmer, and click **OK** to apply the filter.

✓ **Negative values on the Size slider place the glow inside the object; positive ones place the glow outside it.**

Start Here

Task 19: Diffusing an Image

The Diffuse filter is similar to a blur filter in that it shuffles pixels around the edges of objects in an image. But instead of blurring them, Diffuse spreads them around to give a sort of crumbly effect. It's a good quick fix for blurry images that can't be sharpened any further.

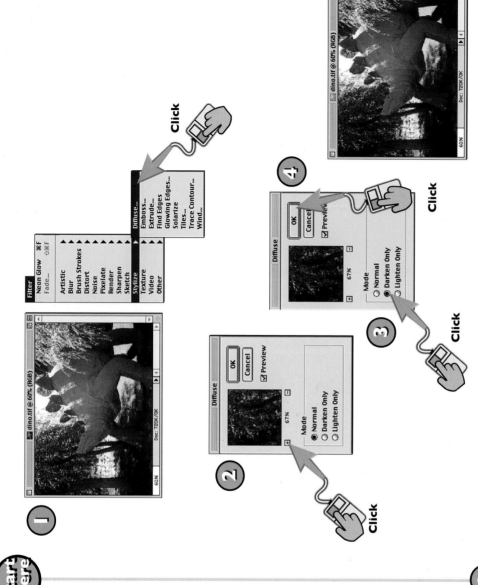

1. Choose **Filter**, **Stylize**, **Diffuse**.
2. Click the plus and minus buttons to enlarge or reduce the preview.
3. Click a **Mode**.
4. Click **OK** to apply the filter.

The Darken Only and Lighten Only options show only the "shuffled" pixels that darken or lighten the image, respectively. The result is that they produce a less fuzzy image that's either darker or lighter than the Normal mode.

Task 20: Adding a Motion Blur to an Image

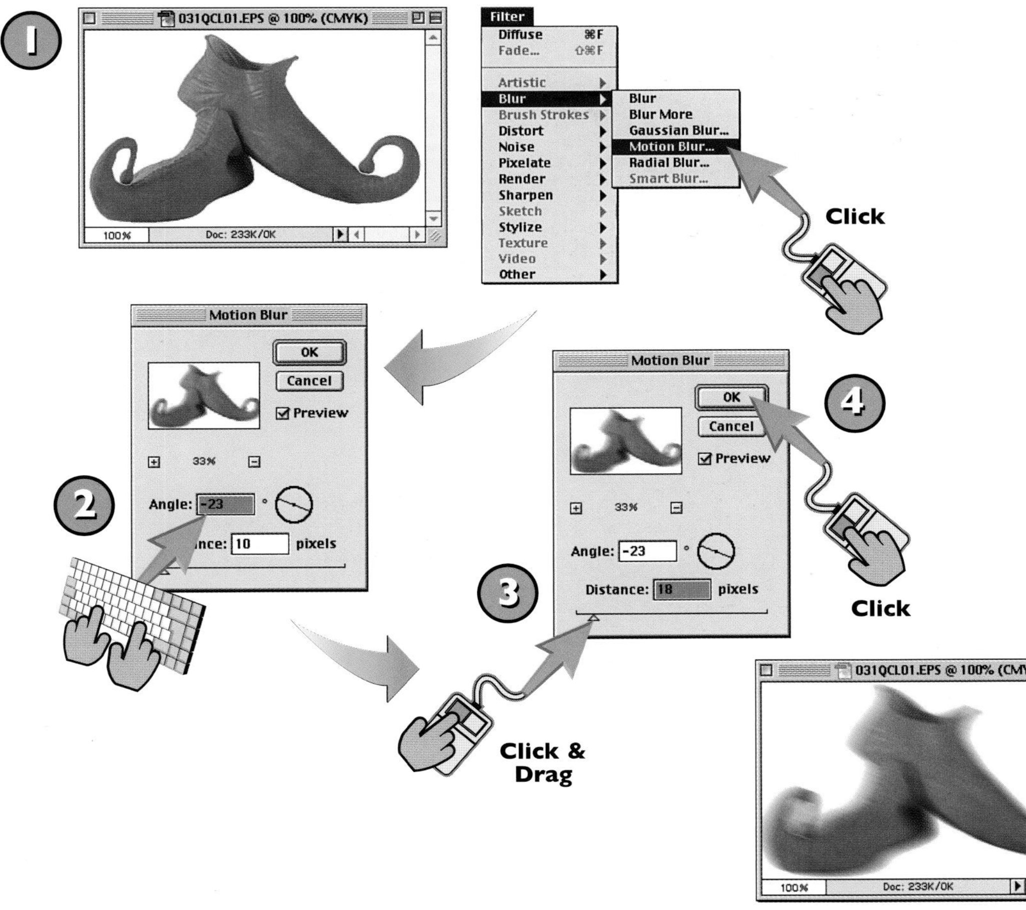

Motion Blur produces the same effect you get when you use slow film to photograph something that's moving fast—the image is blurred in the direction from which the object is moving. Photoshop enables you to control both the amount of blur and its direction.

1. Choose **Filter**, **Blur**, **Motion Blur**.
2. Choose an **Angle** by entering a value or dragging the circle.
3. Drag the **Distance** slider to set the size of the blur.
4. Click **OK** to apply the filter.

Applying the Motion Blur filter in two different directions gives a general blurry effect.

Task 21: Adding Lighting Effects

One of Photoshop's most complex filters, Lighting Effects enables you to define the lighting that illuminates the image. You can also choose a channel to be added to the image's surface as a texture.

Start Here

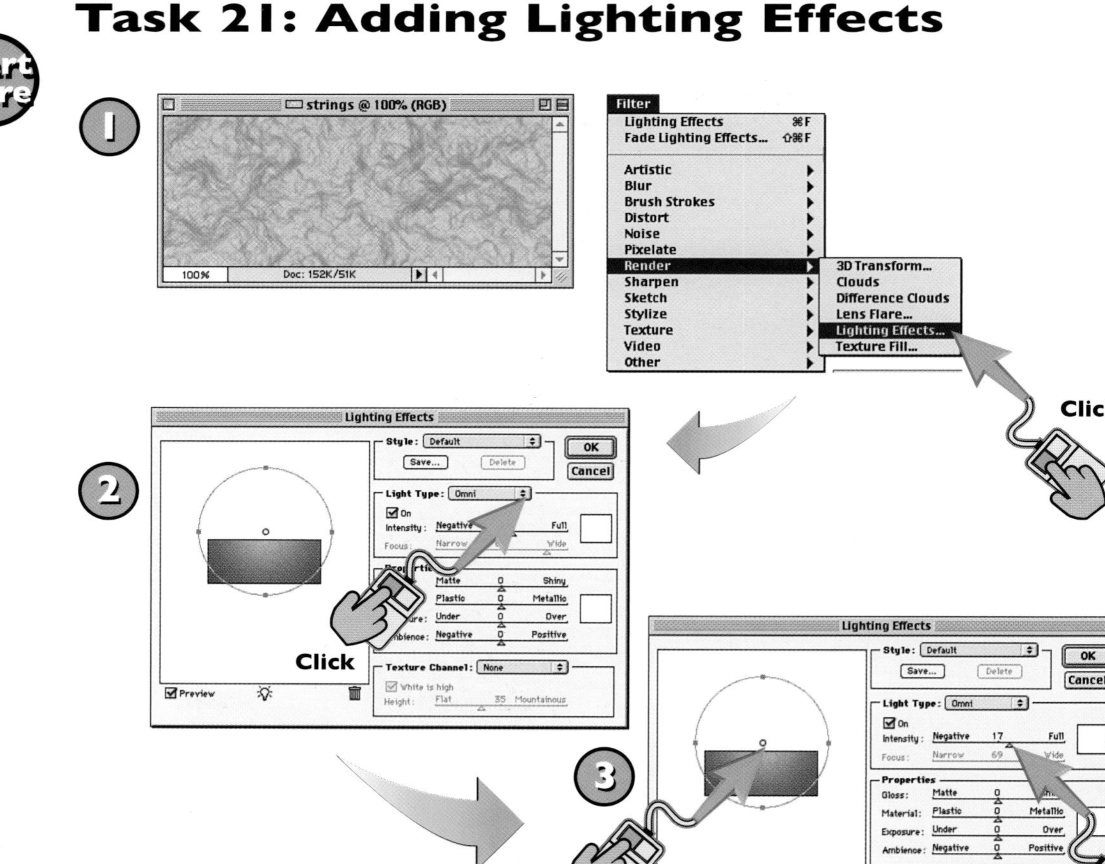

1. Choose **Filter**, **Render**, **Lighting Effects**.
2. Choose a **Light Type** from the pop-up menu.
3. Drag to position the light in the preview window.
4. Drag the **Intensity** slider to brighten or dim the light.

The Lighting Effects filter uses a lot of memory (RAM). If you see an alert saying that there's not enough RAM to run the filter, choose **Edit, Purge, All.** You'll lose the History of the image, but you'll probably clear out enough memory to run the filter.

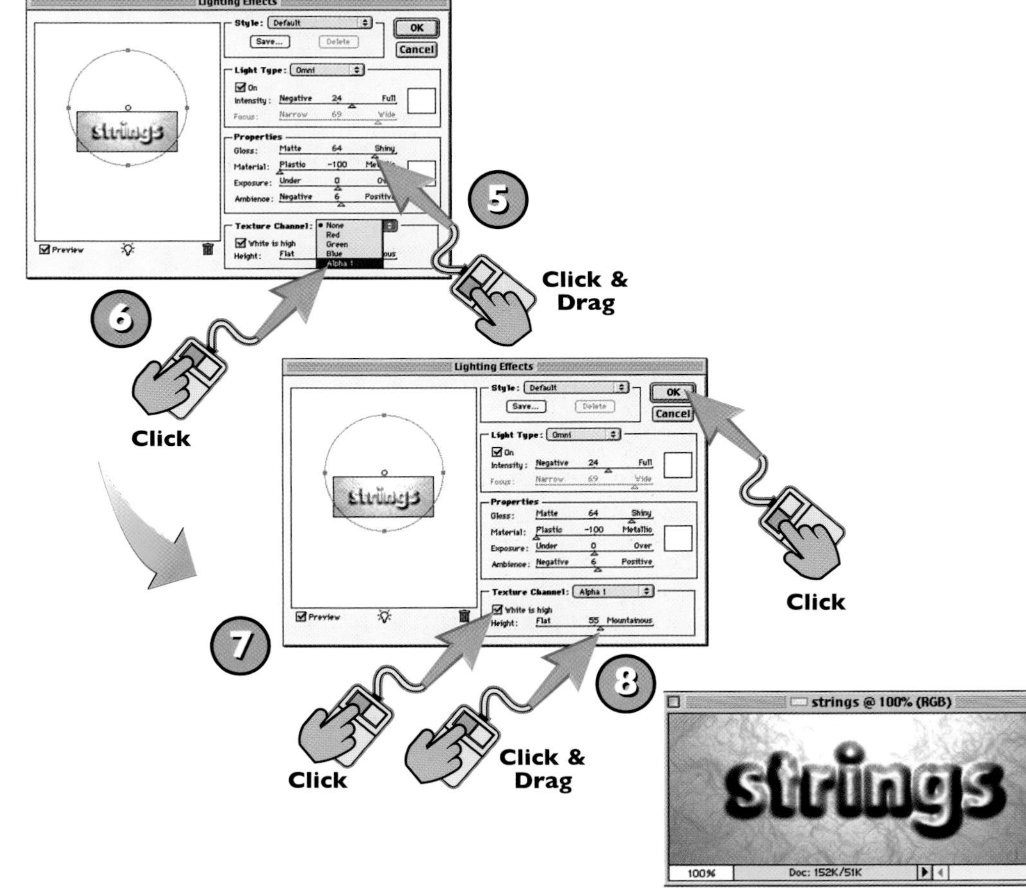

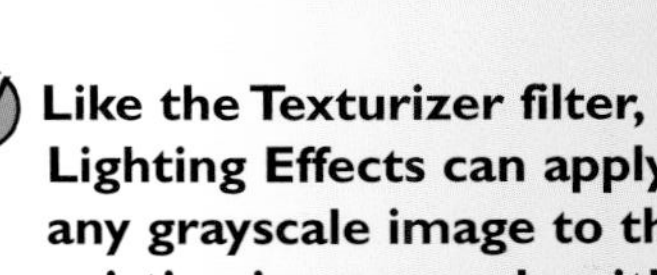

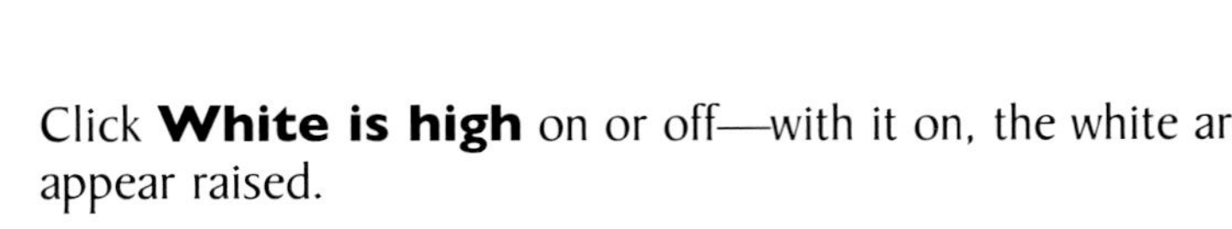

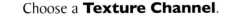

5. Drag the **Properties** sliders to change the surface appearance of the image.

6. Choose a **Texture Channel**.

7. Click **White is high** on or off—with it on, the white area of the texture channel will appear raised.

8. Drag the **Height** slider to adjust the texture's depth, and then click **OK**.

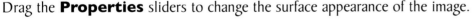

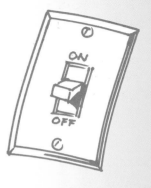

Like the Texturizer filter, Lighting Effects can apply any grayscale image to the existing image—only with a lot more control over surface and lighting properties. To create an image to be applied by using Lighting Effects, store it in an alpha channel of the image and choose that channel from the Texture Channel pop-up menu.

Task 22: Crystallizing an Image

The Crystallize filter, like all the Pixelate filters, turns an image into chunks of pixels all the same color. In this case, the resulting image looks as though it's made of rock candy.

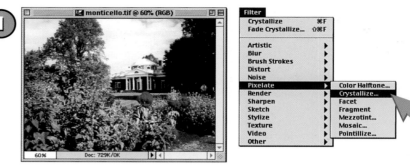

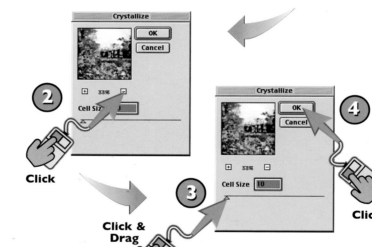

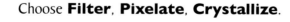

Start Here

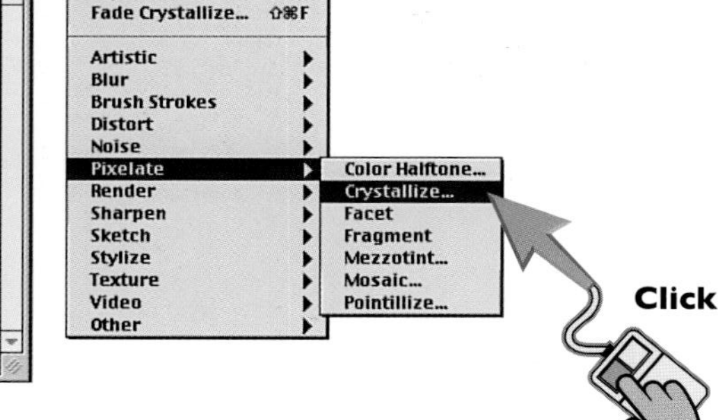

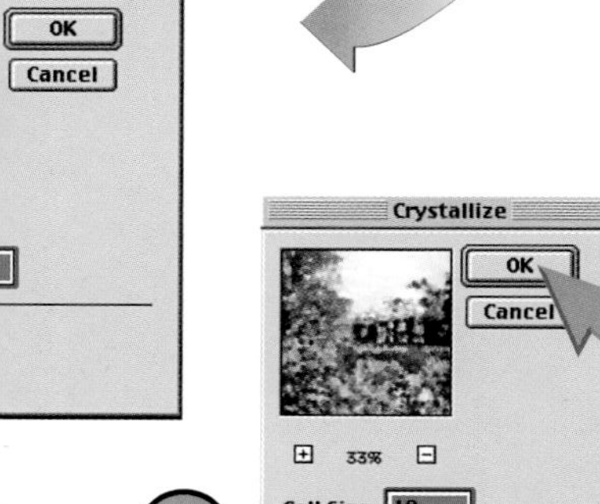

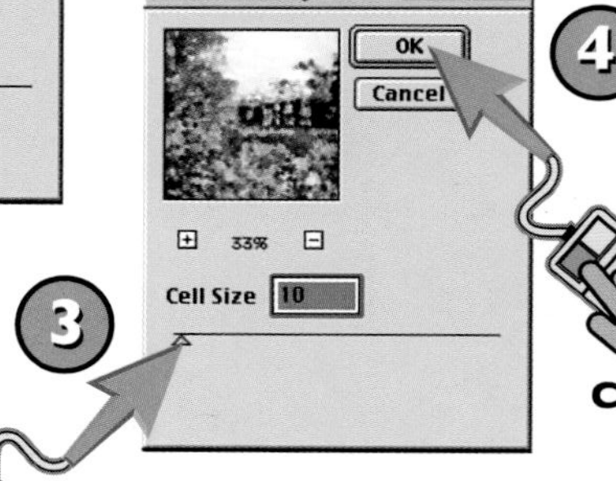

1. Choose **Filter**, **Pixelate**, **Crystallize**.
2. Click the plus and minus buttons to enlarge or reduce the preview.
3. Drag the **Cell Size** slider to adjust the size of the crystals.
4. Click **OK** to apply the filter.

The Pointillize filter works similarly to the Crystallize filter, but it produces round blobs instead of angular ones.

End Task

Task 23: Fading an Effect

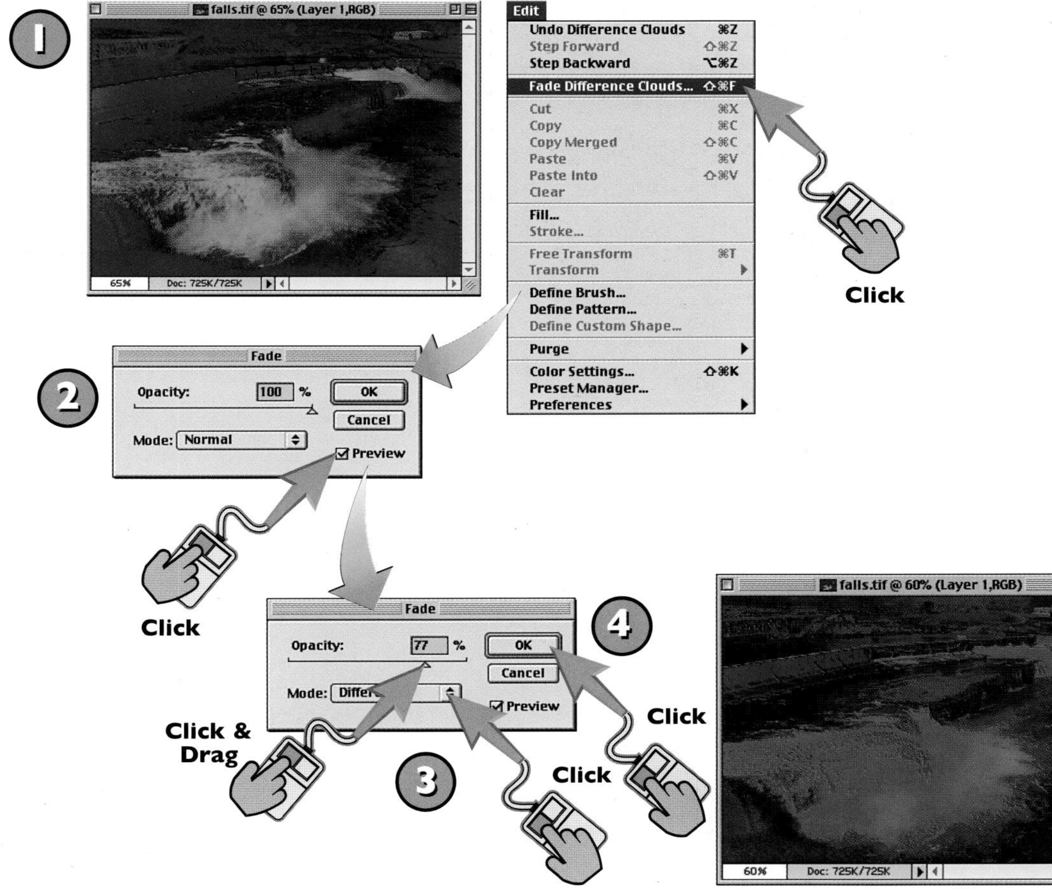

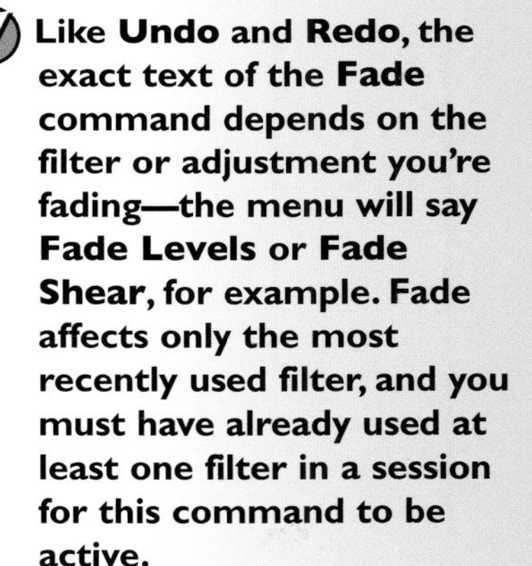

Fading a filter leaves the filter's effects in place but reduces its opacity so you can see the original image underlying the filtered image. It's usually not quite the same as using a lower intensity setting in the filter.

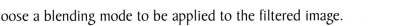

1. Choose **Edit**, **Fade [command]** or press **Cmd+Shift+F/Ctrl+Shift+F**.
2. Click **Preview** to show the effects of the **Fade** command as you work.
3. Choose a blending mode to be applied to the filtered image.
4. Drag the **Opacity** slider to fade the filter, and then click **OK**.

✓ Like **Undo** and **Redo**, the exact text of the **Fade** command depends on the filter or adjustment you're fading—the menu will say **Fade Levels** or **Fade Shear**, for example. Fade affects only the most recently used filter, and you must have already used at least one filter in a session for this command to be active.

✓ The **Fade** command also works with image adjustment commands such as **Hue/Saturate**, **Levels**, and **Selective Color**.

PART II

Creating Artistic Effects

The other half of Photoshop's split personality—image editor versus paint program—takes the fore in the program's collection of artistic filters. These filters simulate effects ordinarily achieved by fine artists by using natural media such as oils, watercolors, chalks, pencils, crayons, and plaster. You can use Photoshop's more artistic filters on their own or combined with other filters to extend the range of possible effects. Many controls used by the artistic filters are similar; for example, several filters include texture controls so that you can apply a background texture such as canvas or burlap along with the "brushstrokes" or other effects.

Part II shows you how to use the controls for several of Photoshop's most popular artistic filters, including Watercolor, Rough Pastels, and Craquelure.

Tasks

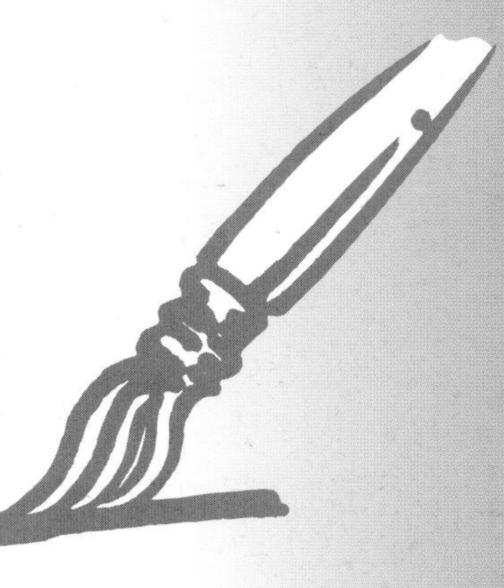

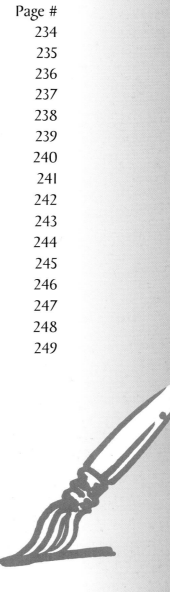

Task 1: Applying a Pen-and-Ink Effect

Photoshop's Ink Outlines filter creates the effect of an ink drawing with a watercolor wash. Details are outlined in black "ink" and colors are softened and blurred. You can control the amount of detail retained in the effect, as well as how much of the image's original color is preserved.

Higher Stroke Length settings decrease the image's detail. Higher Dark and Light Intensity settings increase the image's color saturation; lower settings allow a "rainbow" color effect to show through the image's colors.

Start Here

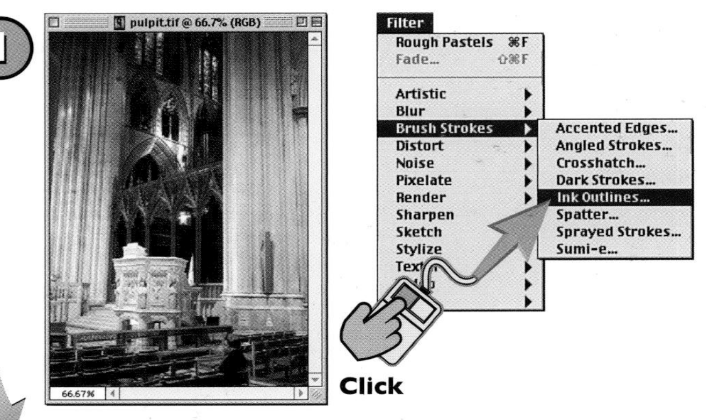

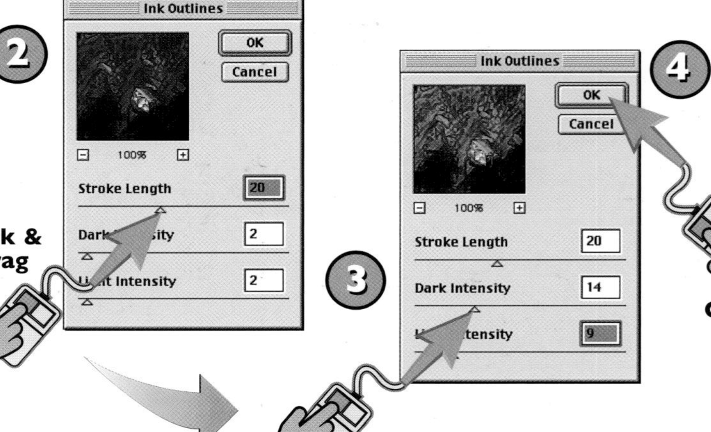

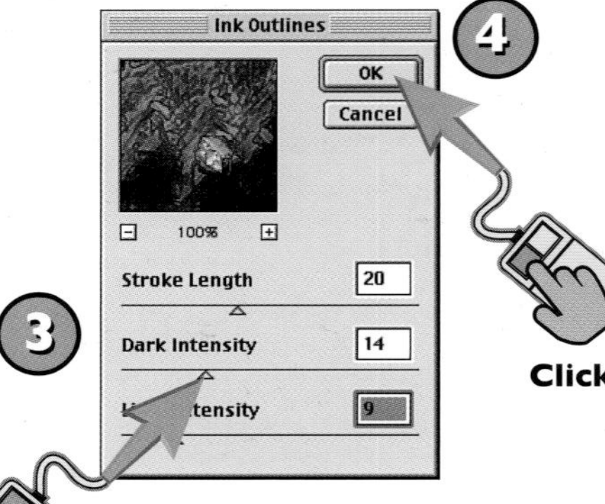

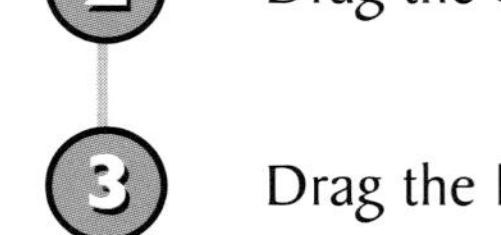

1. Choose **Filter**, **Brush Strokes**, **Ink Outlines**.
2. Drag the **Stroke Length** slider to adjust the amount of detail.
3. Drag the **Dark Intensity** and **Light Intensity** sliders to adjust the color intensity.
4. Click **OK** to apply the filter.

Task 2: Applying a Crayon Effect

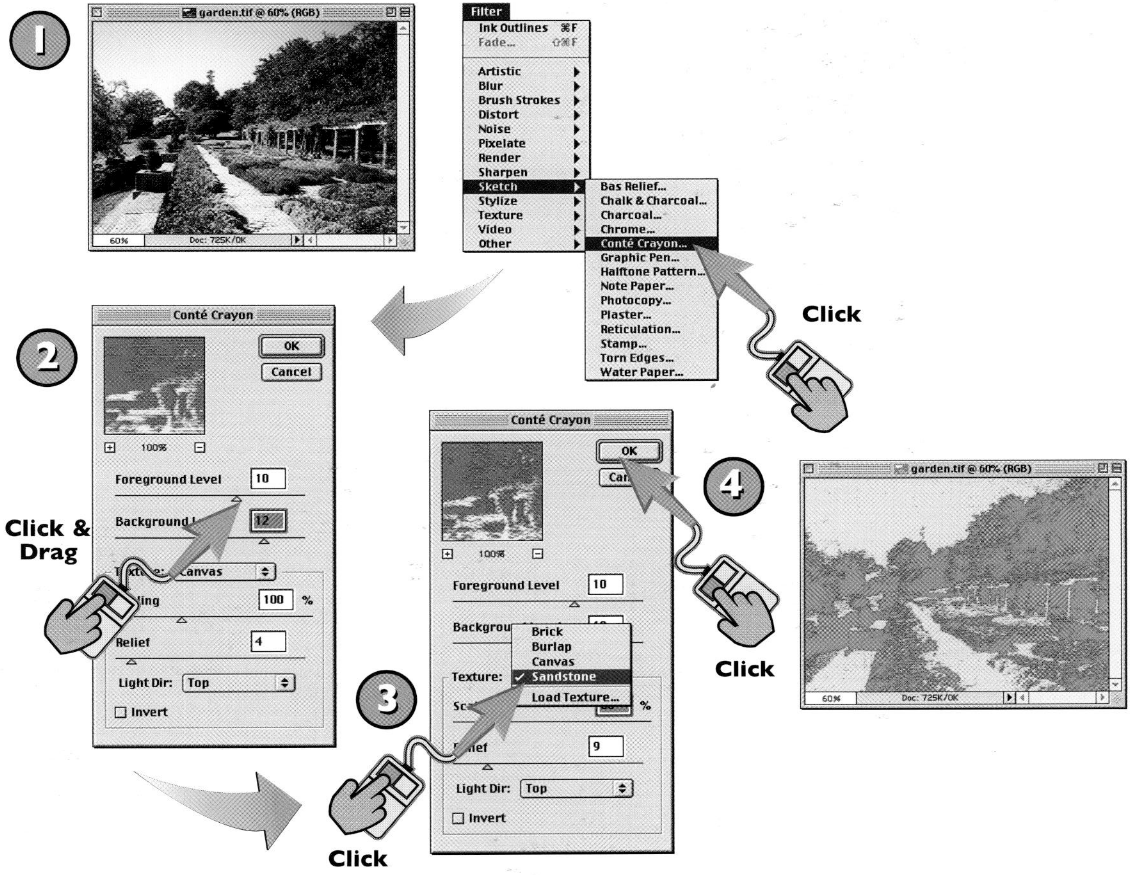

The Conté Crayon filter creates an effect similar to that of a crayon rubbing, with a choice of "paper" textures. The filter uses the foreground and background colors, combined with a neutral gray, to create the image.

1. Choose **Filter**, **Sketch**, **Conté Crayon**.
2. Drag the **Foreground Level** and **Background Level** sliders to adjust the amount of color used.
3. Choose a **Texture** from the pop-up menu.
4. Click **OK** to apply the filter.

The Conté Crayon filter's Texture settings are the same as those used in Part 10, Task 14, "Applying Texture."

Included in the Artistic filter group is the Watercolor filter, which is supposed to simulate the effect of a medium-sized watercolor brush, very wet, with lots of paint. Don't expect to get light, frothy pastel images from this filter—it tends to produce rather dark colors.

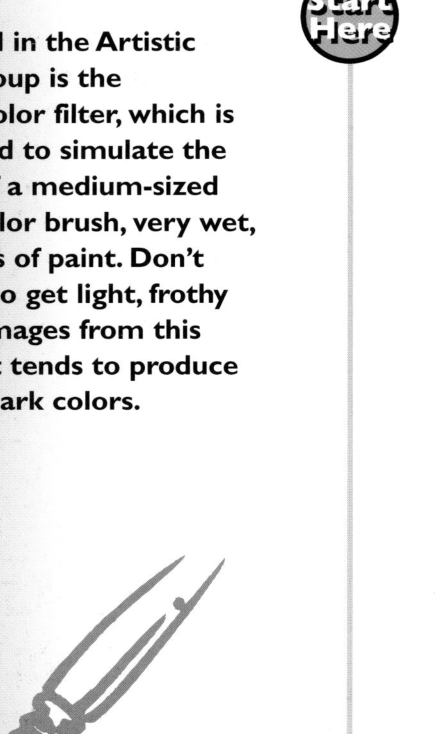

✓ Dragging the **Texture** slider to the right "simplifies" the colors in the image, making them brighter and clearer.

Task 3: Applying a Watercolor Effect

Start Here

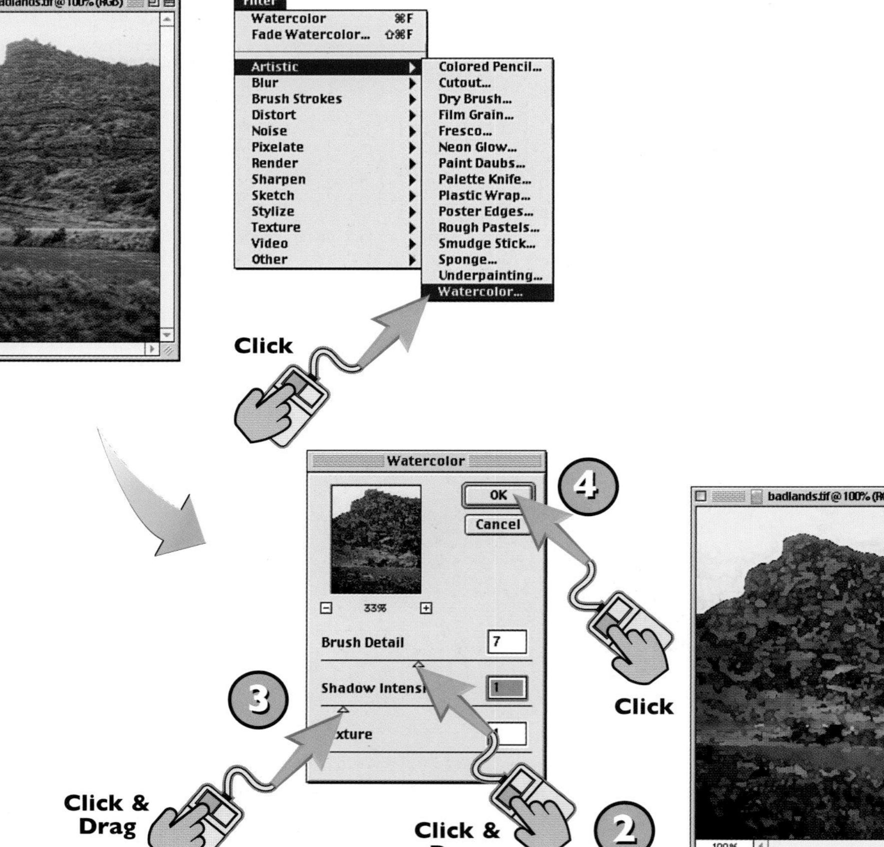

1. Choose **Filter**, **Artistic**, **Watercolor**.
2. Drag the **Brush Detail** slider to adjust the amount of image detail that is preserved.
3. Drag the **Shadow Intensity** slider to lighten or darken shadows.
4. Click **OK** to apply the filter.

Task 4: Applying a Rough Pastels Effect

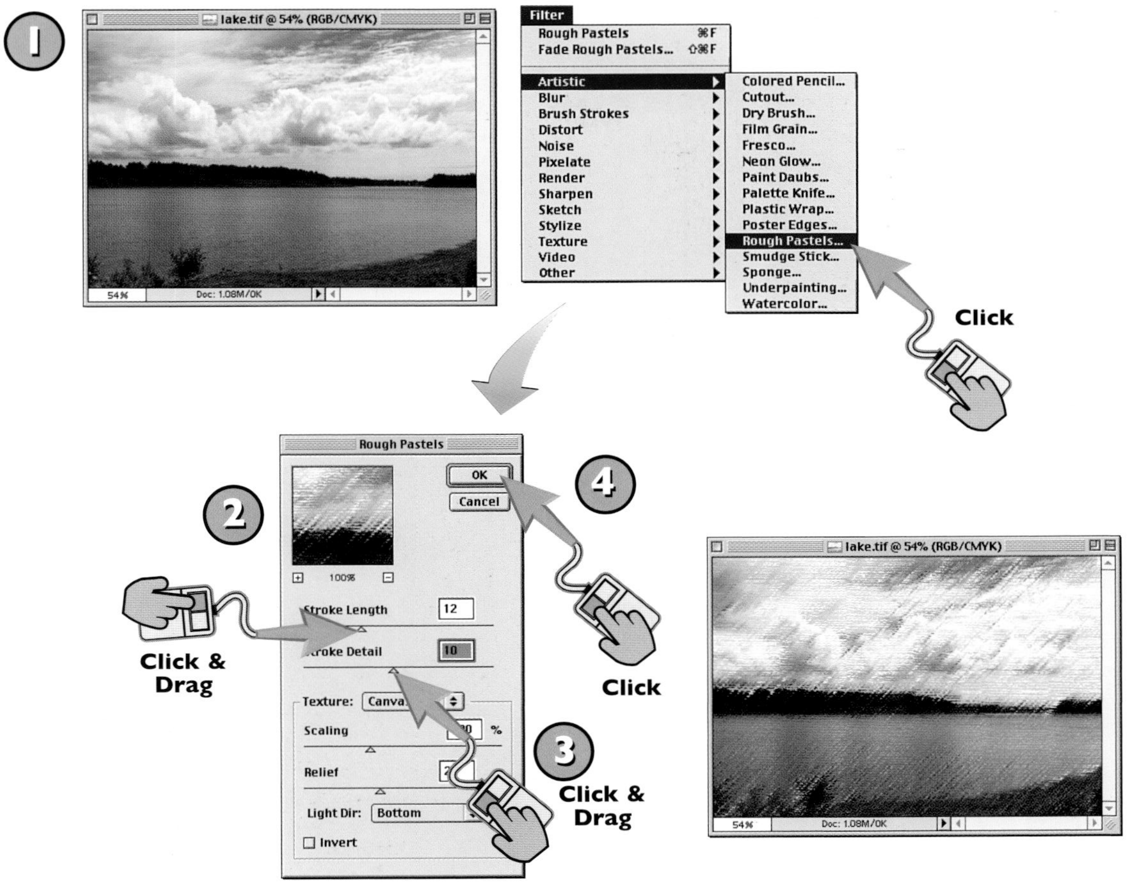

Some of Photoshop's Artistic filters are more convincing than others. Although Rough Pastels produces an interesting effect, it doesn't actually make an image look as though it's been drawn with pastels—the result is more like a chalky texture laid over the existing image.

1. Choose **Filter**, **Artistic**, **Rough Pastels**.
2. Drag the **Stroke Length** slider to adjust the length of the chalk strokes.
3. Drag the **Stroke Detail** slider to control how much image detail is preserved.
4. Click **OK** to apply the filter.

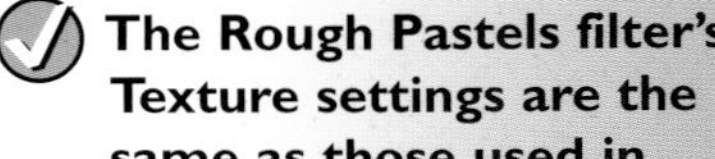

The Rough Pastels filter's Texture settings are the same as those used in Part 10, Task 14, "Applying Texture."

Task 5: Applying a Colored Pencil Effect

Start Here

Photoshop's Colored Pencil filter does a credible job of producing an image that looks as though it's been done with colored pencils, except for the fact that you have no control over the angle of the pencil strokes. You can control how much the paper shows through and how bright the paper is.

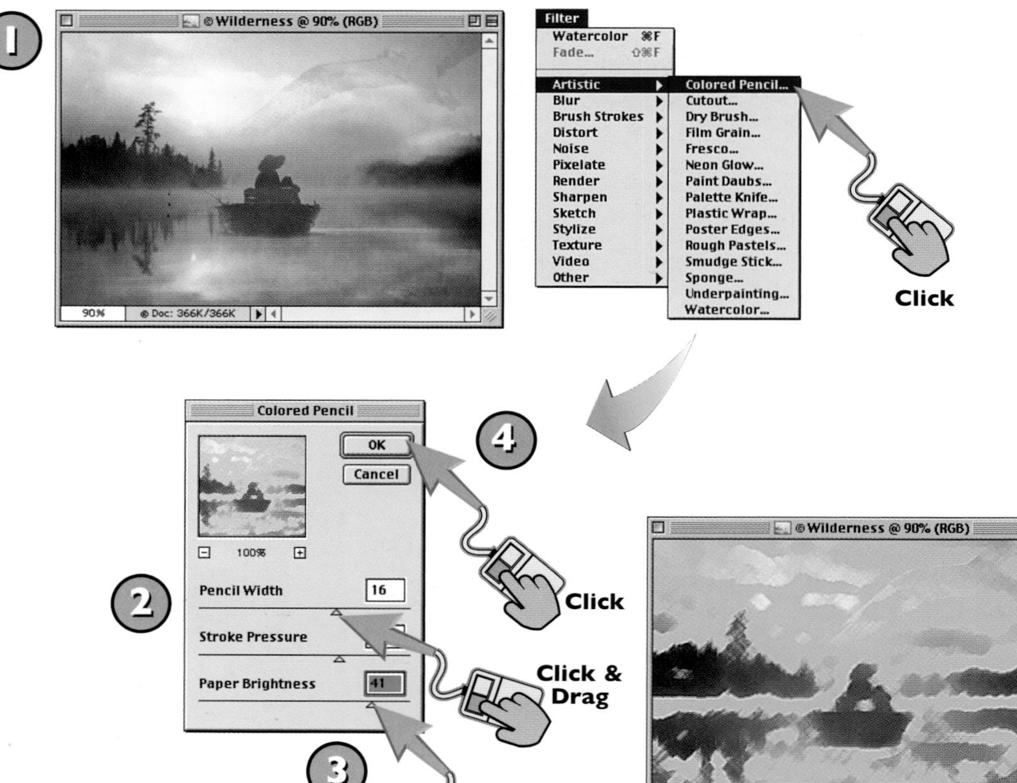

1. Choose **Filter**, **Artistic**, **Colored Pencil**.
2. Drag the **Pencil Width** and **Stroke Pressure** sliders to control the "pencil strokes."
3. Drag the **Paper Brightness** slider to lighten or darken the "paper."
4. Click **OK** to apply the filter.

Photoshop uses the current background color for the color of the paper when applying the Colored Pencil filter.

Task 6: Applying a Photocopy Effect

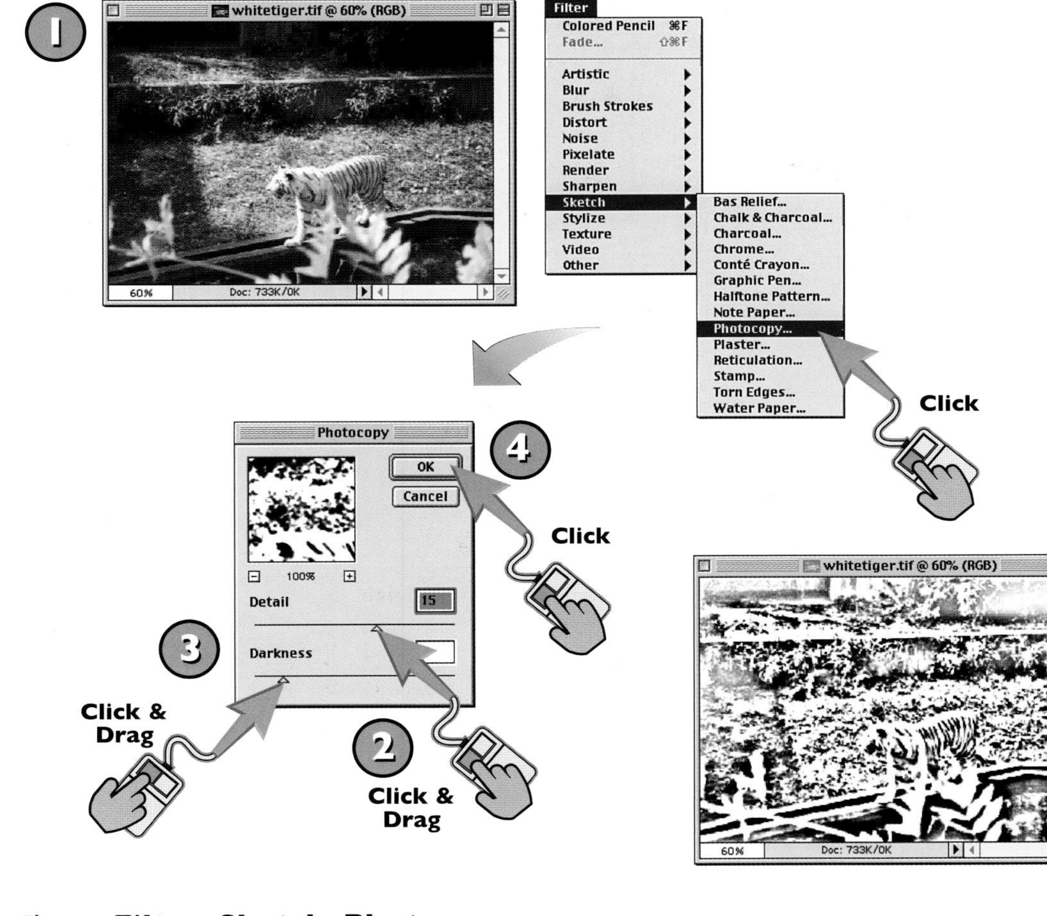

The Photocopy filter has one big advantage over using a real photocopier to create images—it works in color, converting an image by combining the current foreground and background colors. Like a real photocopier, the filter enables you to adjust the brightness of the copy.

1 Choose **Filter**, **Sketch**, **Photocopy**.

2 Drag the **Detail** slider to control the amount of image detail that is preserved.

3 Drag the **Darkness** slider to lighten or darken the image.

4 Click **OK** to apply the filter.

Photoshop uses the current foreground color for dark areas and the current background color for light areas when applying the Photocopy filter.

Task 7: Applying a Bas Relief Effect

Photoshop can simulate three-dimensional effects with several filters, including Bas Relief. This filter "raises" light areas of the image, "lowers" dark areas, and replaces the image's colors with the current foreground and background colors.

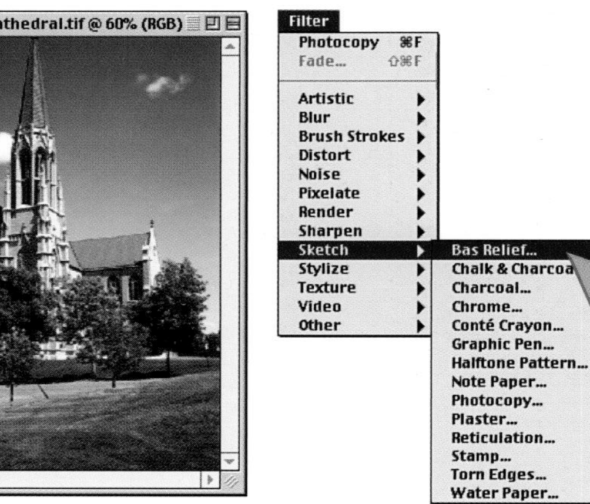

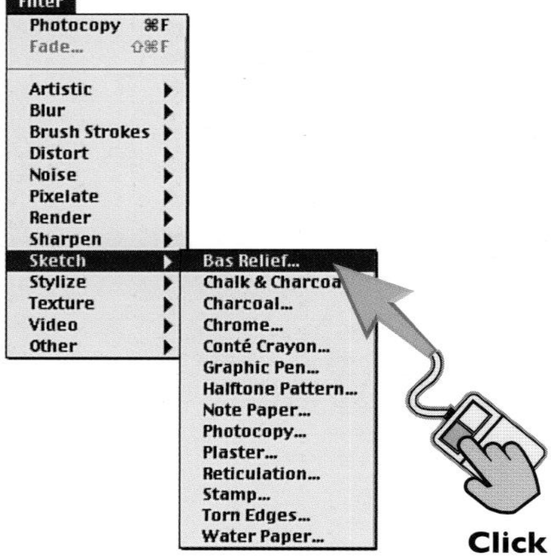

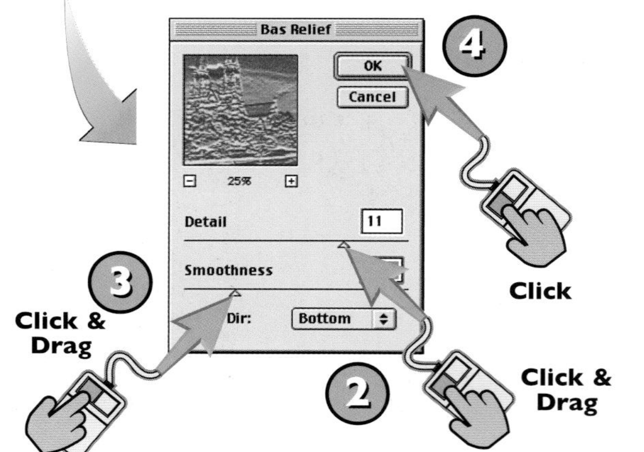

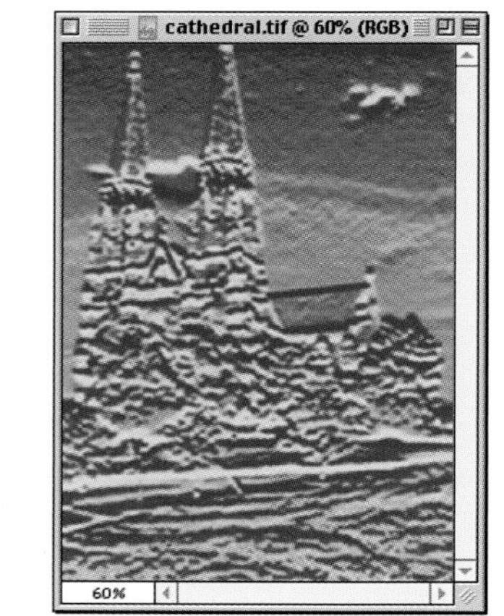

1. Choose **Filter**, **Sketch**, **Bas Relief**.
2. Drag the **Detail** slider to control the amount of image detail that is preserved.
3. Drag the **Smoothness** slider to control the image's surface texture.
4. Click **OK** to apply the filter.

✓ Photoshop uses the current foreground color for dark areas and the current background color for light areas when applying the Bas Relief filter.

Task 8: Applying a Craquelure Effect

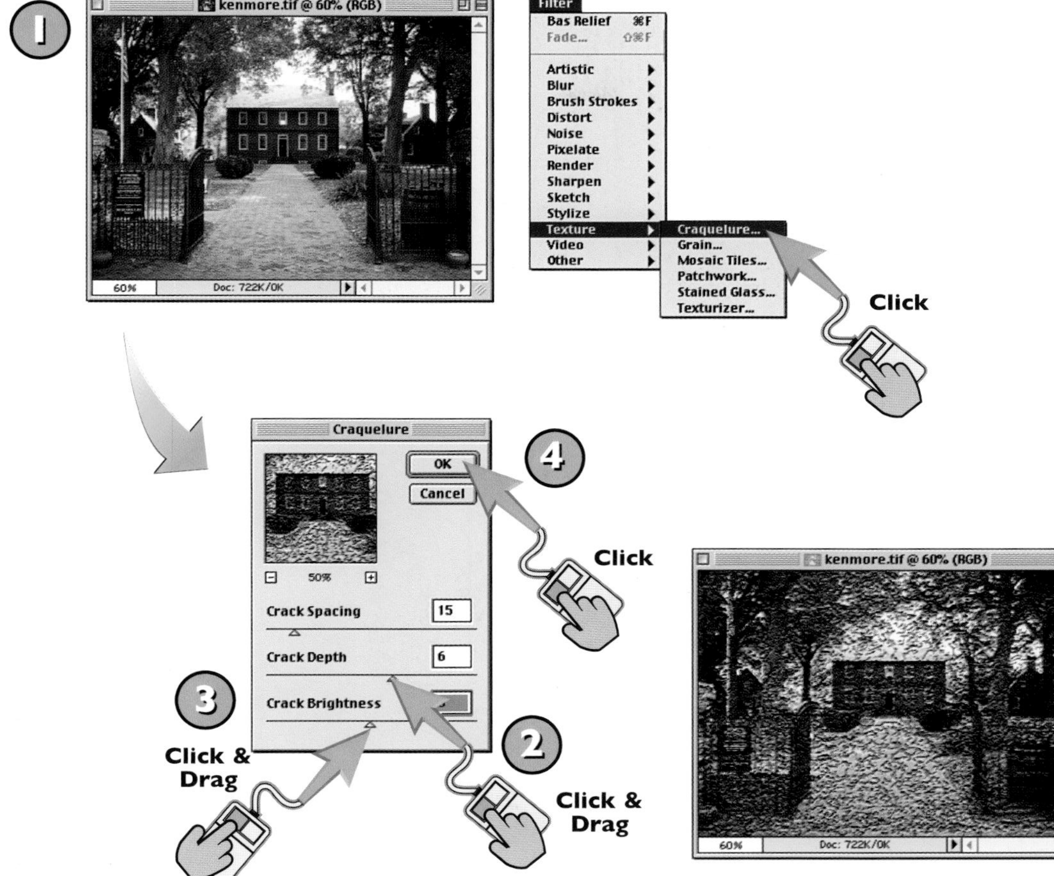

In craquelure, images are painted on highly textured plaster surfaces with many tiny cracks. Photoshop's Craquelure filter produces an attractive embossed effect with as much cracking as you want (or as little).

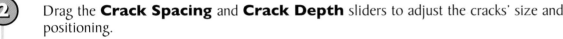

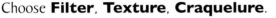

1. Choose **Filter**, **Texture**, **Craquelure**.
2. Drag the **Crack Spacing** and **Crack Depth** sliders to adjust the cracks' size and positioning.
3. Drag the **Crack Brightness** slider to make the cracks brighter or darker.
4. Click **OK** to apply the filter.

Like most filters that incorporate an embossing effect, the Craquelure filter raises light areas of the image and sinks dark areas.

Task 9: Applying a Film Grain Effect

The Film Grain filter is similar to the non-Gaussian version of the Add Noise filter, except that it applies different noise patterns to the highlights of an image and to the darker areas. It simulates the film grain you can see when you overenlarge a slide.

Start Here

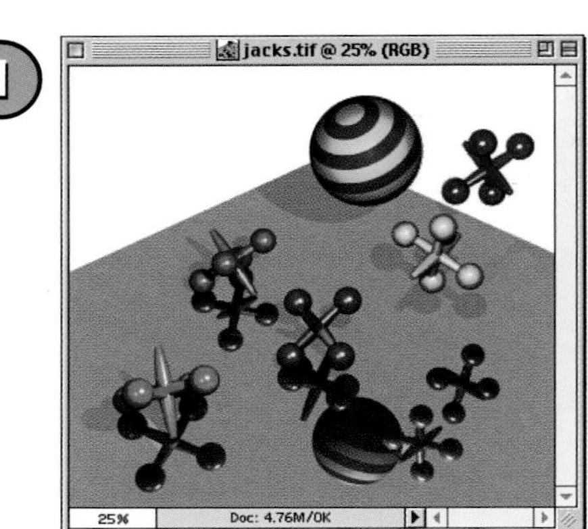

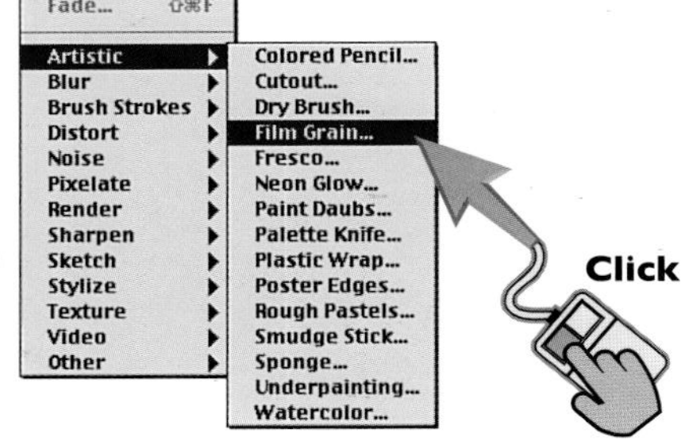

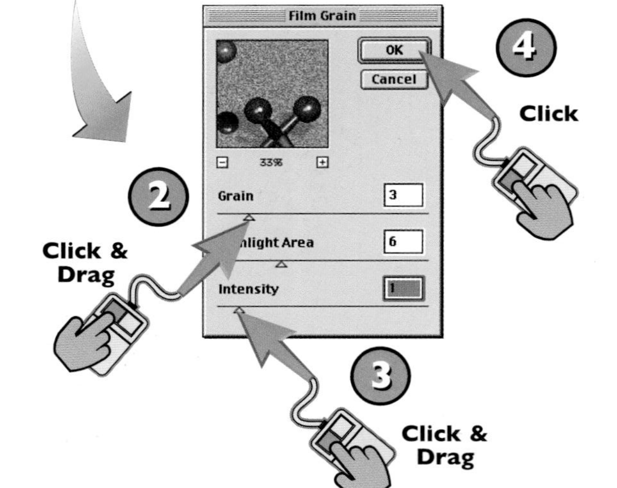

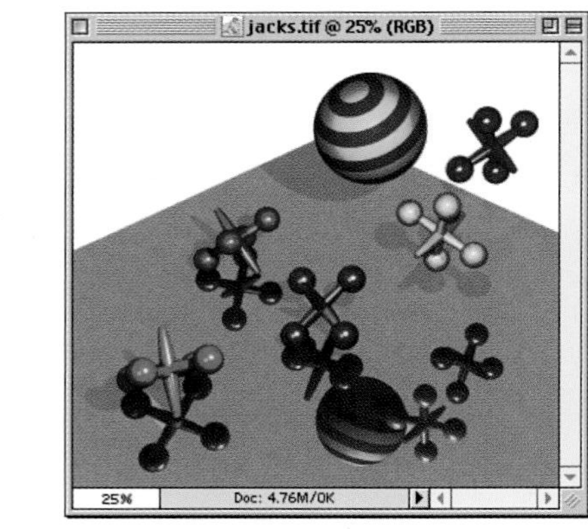

1. Choose **Filter**, **Artistic**, **Film Grain**.
2. Drag the **Grain** slider to adjust the amount of grain added.
3. Drag the **Intensity** slider to adjust the intensity of the image's colors.
4. Click **OK** to apply the filter.

The Highlight Area slider controls how much of the image's lighter areas are considered highlights for the purposes of adding grain—a different pattern is used for grain in highlight areas.

To apply noise to an image, see Part 10, Task 1, "Adding Noise."

Task 10: Applying a Stained Glass Effect

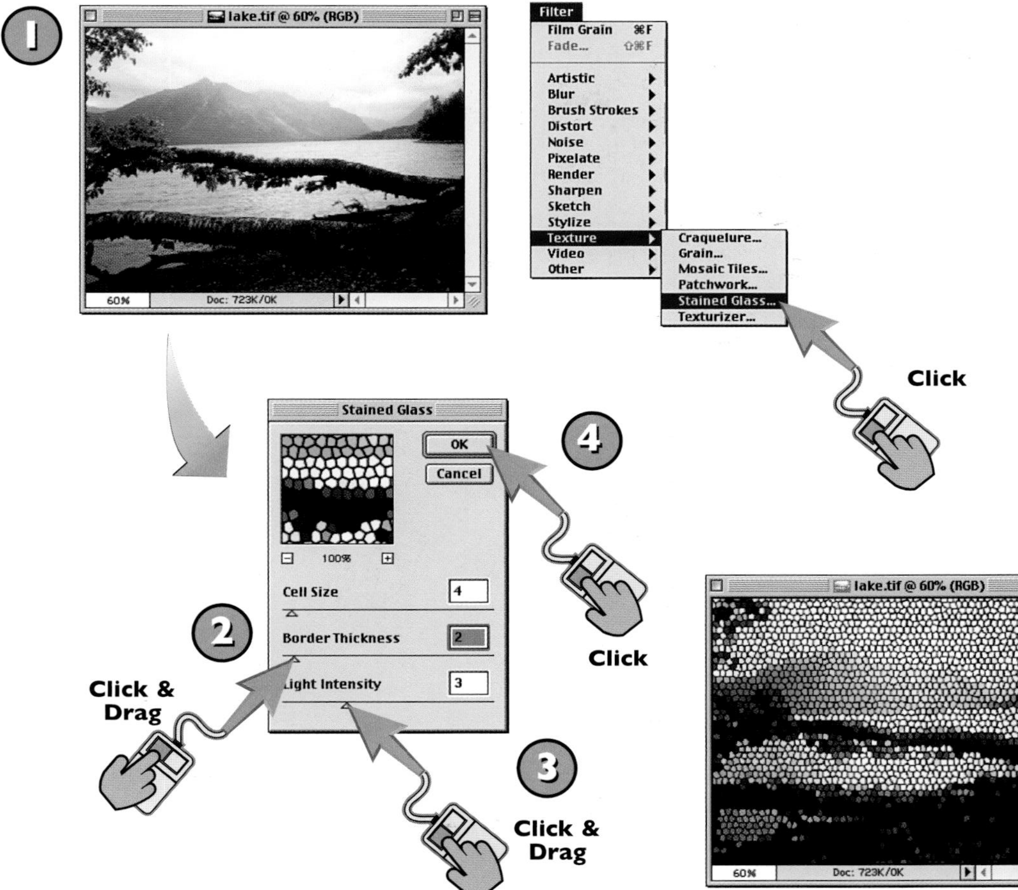

Do the results of Photoshop's Stained Glass filter look like stained glass? Not really, but this filter can be useful nonetheless. It produces a honeycomb effect with a single color in each "cell." The Stained Glass filter works best with large, simple images.

1. Choose **Filter**, **Texture**, **Stained Glass**.
2. Drag the **Cell Size** and **Border Thickness** sliders to adjust the cells and the space between them.
3. Drag the **Light Intensity** slider to control the image's brightness.
4. Click **OK** to apply the filter.

The current foreground color is used for the "lead" between the pieces of colored glass.

Task 11: Applying a Mosaic Effect

The Mosaic Tiles filter doesn't produce a traditional mosaic effect; instead, it creates images that look as though they've been painted on top of irregularly shaped tiles. You can control the size and spacing of the tiles, but they're always based on a square grid.

Start Here

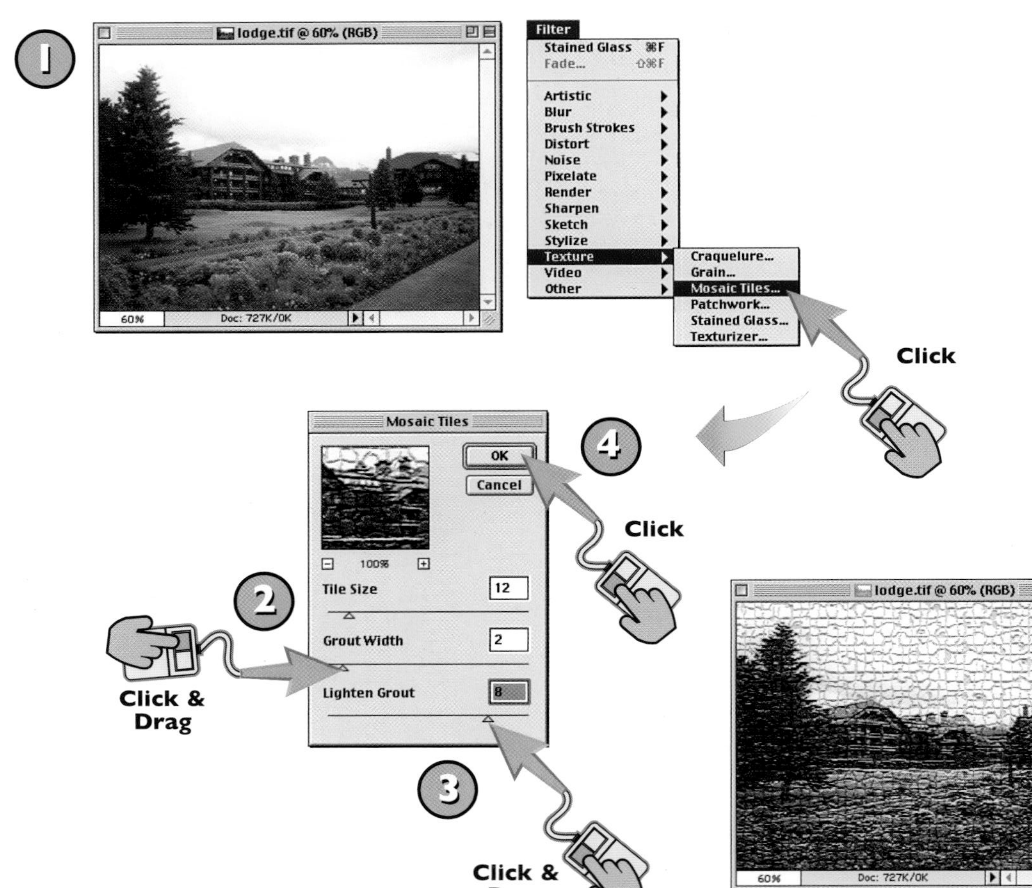

1. Choose **Filter**, **Texture**, **Mosaic Tiles**.
2. Drag the **Tile Size** and **Grout Width** sliders to adjust the tiles' size and spacing.
3. Drag the **Lighten Grout** slider to control the brightness of the spaces between tiles.
4. Click **OK** to apply the filter.

The results of the Mosaic Tiles filter are much improved by following the filter with a light application of noise. To apply noise to an image, see Part 10, Task 1, "Adding Noise."

Task 12: Applying a Stamped Effect

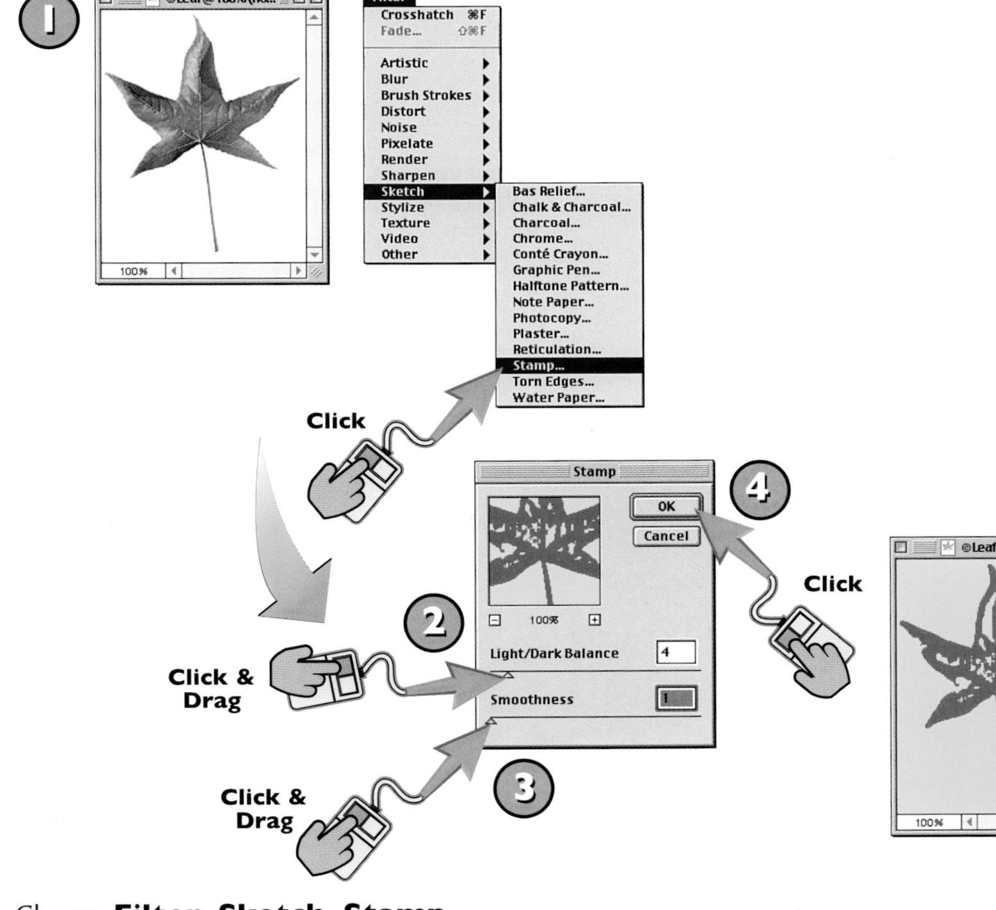

The name of this filter is somewhat misleading—the effect is really more like a silkscreen print. Using the foreground and background colors, the Stamp filter converts the image to a somewhat abstract representation of its former self that resembles the results of the Photocopy filter.

1. Choose **Filter**, **Sketch**, **Stamp**.
2. Drag the **Light/Dark Balance** slider to adjust the ratio of the two colors.
3. Drag the **Smoothness** slider to smooth or roughen the image's edges.
4. Click **OK** to apply the filter.

Photoshop uses the current foreground color for dark areas and the current background color for light areas when applying the Stamp filter.

Task 13: Applying a Plaster Effect

Start Here

The Plaster filter molds your image onto a plaster wall by using the current foreground and background colors to indicate highlights and shadows. The effect is three-dimensional and works best on simple images without a lot of small details.

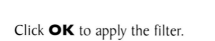

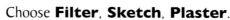

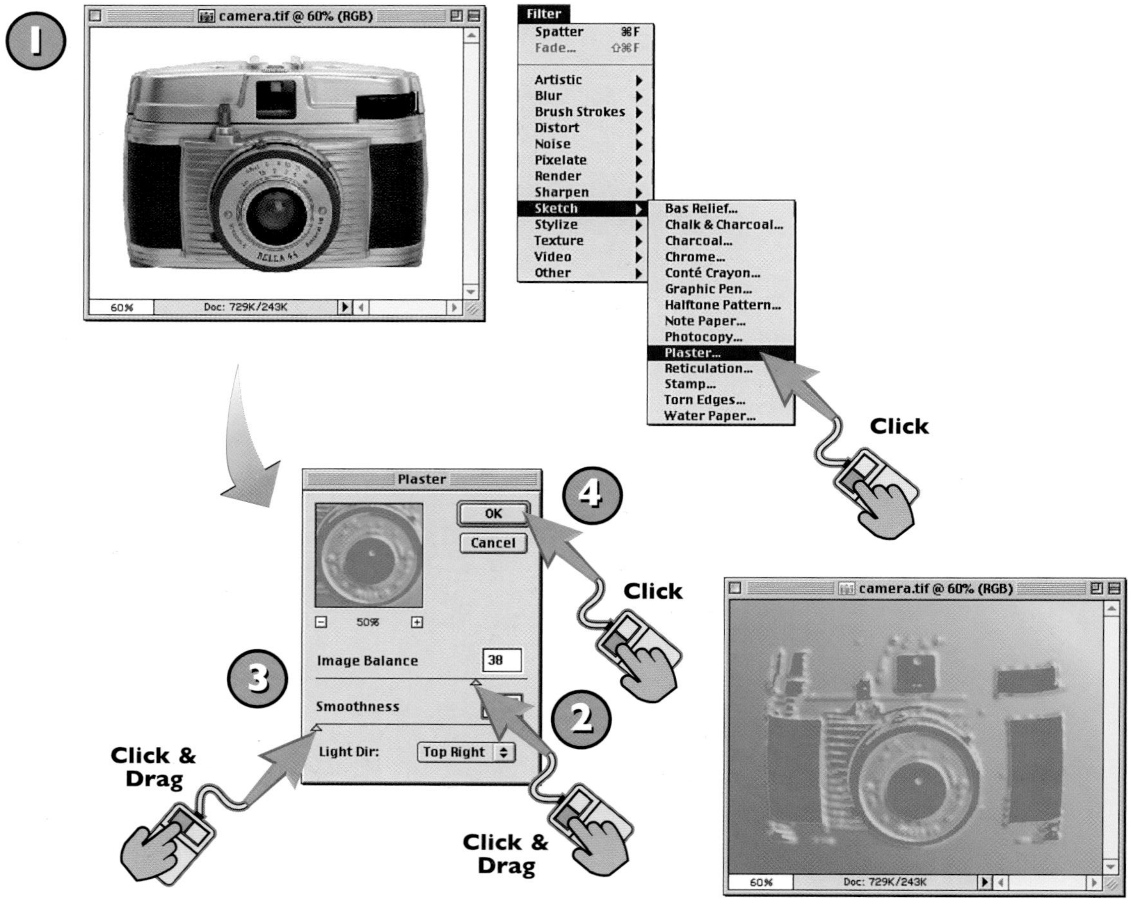

1. Choose **Filter**, **Sketch**, **Plaster**.
2. Drag the **Image Balance** slider to control the light and dark areas.
3. Drag the **Smoothness** slider to determine the "cragginess" of the plaster.
4. Click **OK** to apply the filter.

The Light Dir. pop-up menu controls the direction of the light casting the shadows in the plaster image. Changing this setting can make a big difference in which details show up in the final image.

End Task

Task 14: Applying an Extruded Effect

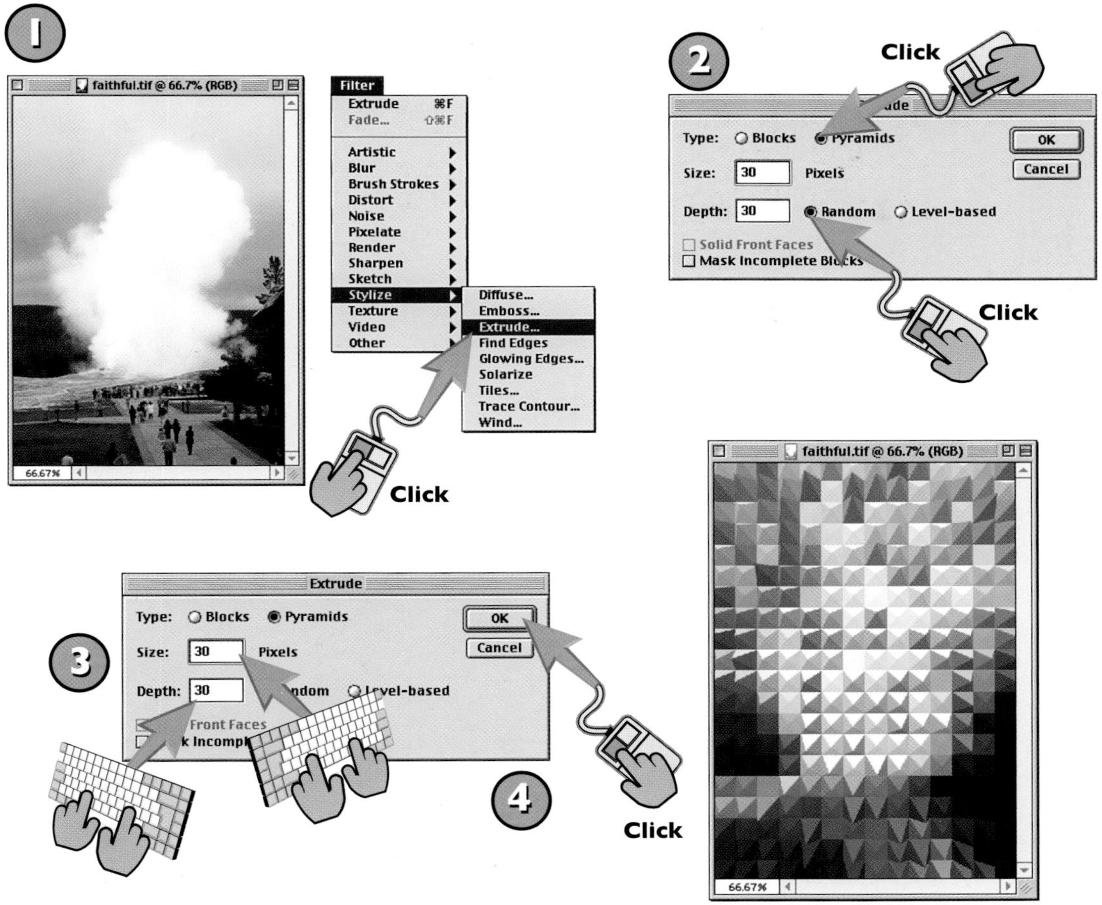

How about creating a picture from stacks of colored blocks or pyramids? That's the effect the Extrude filter produces. You can choose the size and depth of the blocks, but they always appear to be stacked from below your feet to over your head.

1. Choose **Filter**, **Stylize**, **Extrude**.
2. Click a **Type** option, and click **Random** or **Level-based**.
3. Enter a **Size** setting and a **Depth** setting.
4. Click **OK** to apply the filter.

✓ The **Solid Front Faces** option makes each block or pyramid a solid color, which works best with large simple images and smaller block sizes.

Task 15: Applying a Spatter Effect

The Spatter effect turns a photo into an impressionist painting—sort of. You can control how far from its original location each pixel is spattered, and you can control the overall amount of spattering. The effect preserves image colors and is fairly attractive.

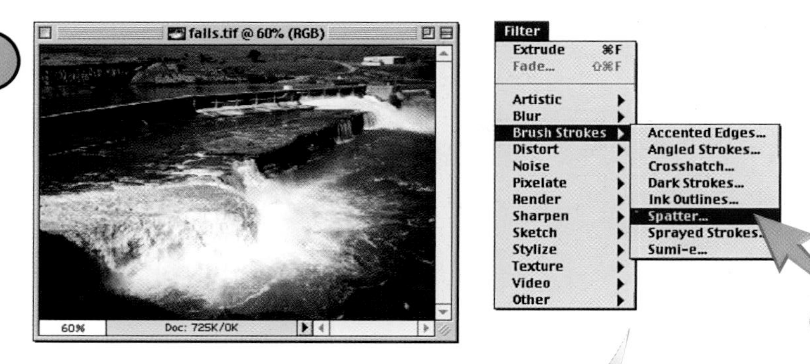

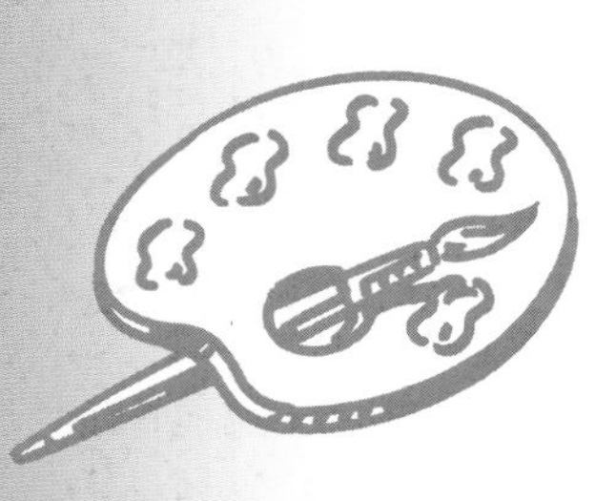

1. Choose **Filter**, **Brush Strokes**, **Spatter**.
2. Drag the **Spray Radius** slider to spatter each pixel less or more.
3. Drag the **Smoothness** slider to determine how much spattering takes place.
4. Click **OK** to apply the filter.

To minimize the spatter effect, drag **Spray Radius** all the way to the left and **Smoothness** all the way to the right. This is a good place to start—from there, move the sliders back toward the middle to add more spattering.

Task 16: Applying Crosshatching

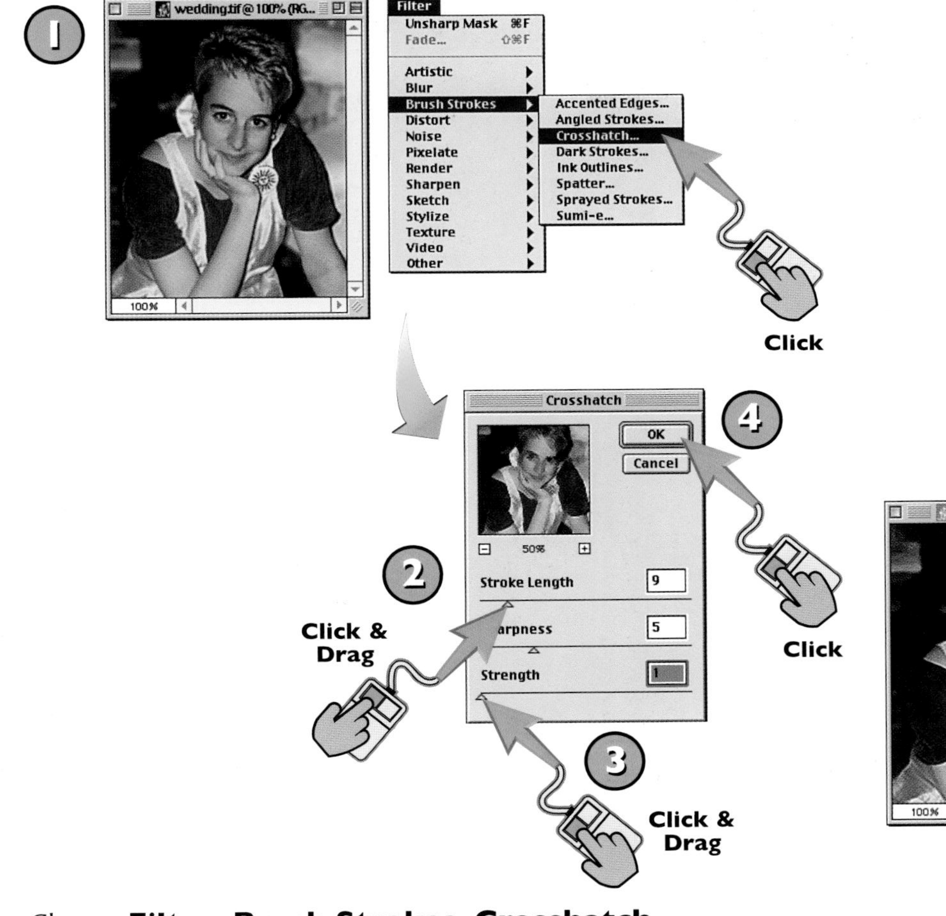

Don't confuse Photoshop's version of crosshatching with the pen-and-ink technique by the same name. The results of the Crosshatch filter are soft and chalky, with distinct diagonal "strokes." This is another way to achieve a "fine art" effect with little effort.

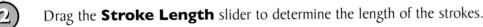

1. Choose **Filter**, **Brush Strokes**, **Crosshatch**.
2. Drag the **Stroke Length** slider to determine the length of the strokes.
3. Drag the **Sharpness** and **Strength** sliders to adjust the strokes' prominence.
4. Click **OK** to apply the filter.

✓ The higher the **Strength** setting, the more the crosshatching strokes obscure the image.

End Task

PART 12

Creating Images for the Web

Since the Web's birth, Photoshop has been the premier image editor for online graphics—with its pinpoint control over color and resolution, combined with its capability to save images in just about any file format you can think of, why would Web artists use any other program? Photoshop 6 introduces several new features, and a new partnership with a program called ImageReady, that make Photoshop a better choice for creating Web images than ever before.

In Part 12 you'll learn how to divide an image into several sections for quick loading and for special effects, how to create rollovers and animations, how to adjust an image to look great on other platforms, and how to save images you plan to use on the Web.

Tasks

Task 1: Slicing Images into Sections

Slices have many functions. For example, you can use them if you want to replace part of an image with a blank area to hold text or if you want to create a rollover effect that makes part of the image change when the cursor is placed over it. When you slice an image in Photoshop, you can automatically save the image into several component image files.

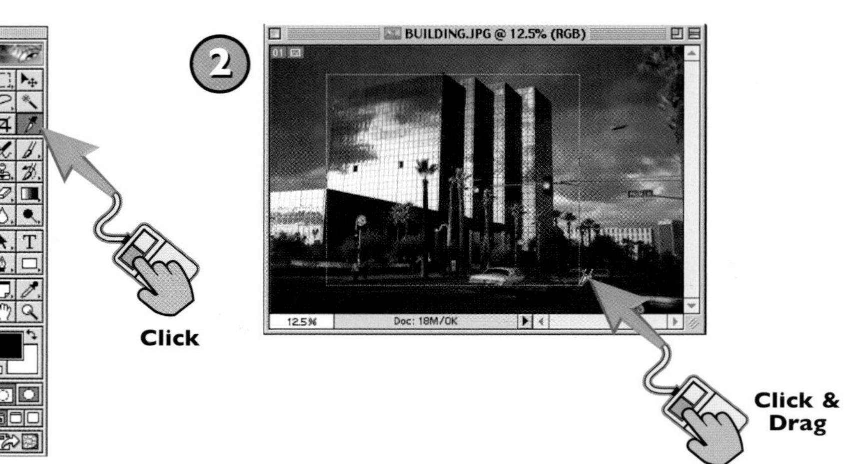

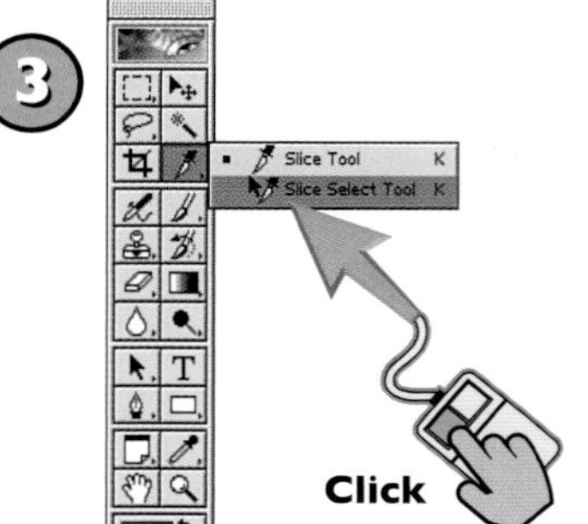

When you save a sliced image, Photoshop creates the multiple image files and the HTML file that references them, with the images placed in an HTML table to form one large image. See Task 9, "Saving Web Pages," to learn how to save sliced images.

1. Click on the **Slice** tool in the **Tool** palette.
2. Drag in the image window to select a rectangular area for your first slice.
3. After you've created all your slices, click on the **Slice** tool in the **Tool** palette and slide the cursor out to switch to the **Slice Select** tool.
4. Adjust the shapes of slices as necessary by dragging their corner points.

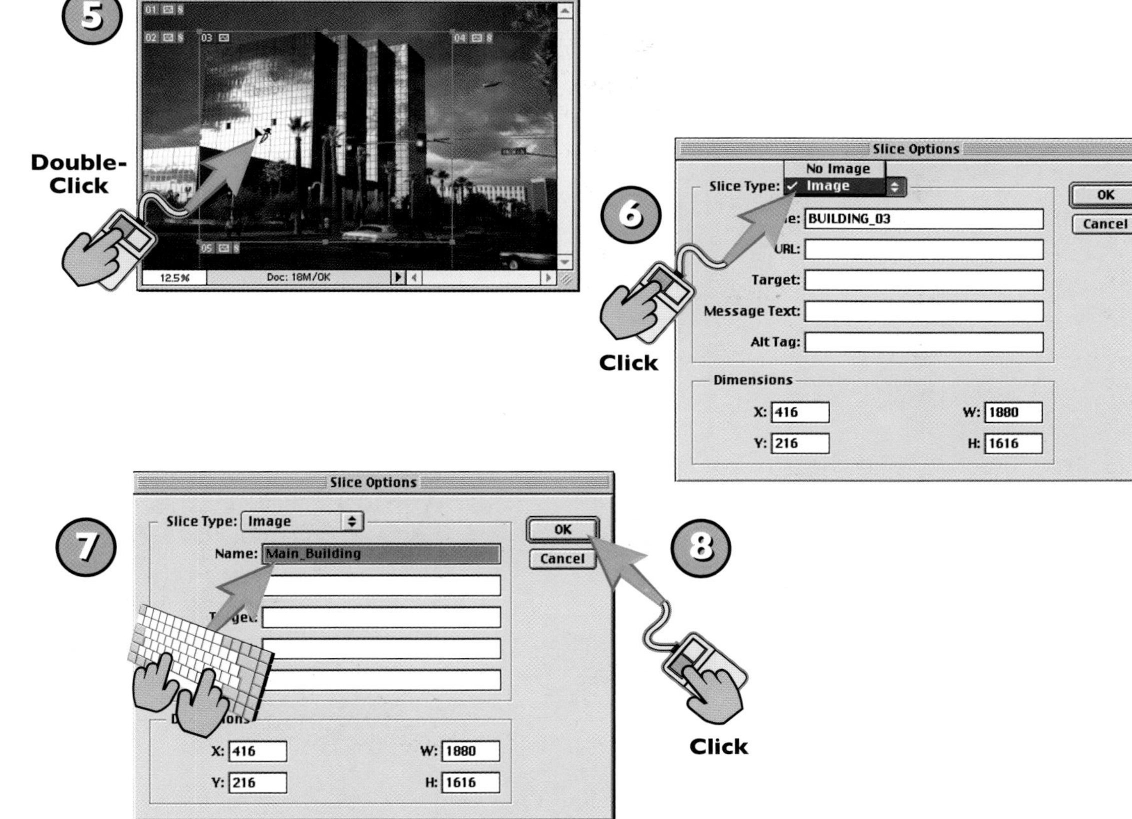

5 Double-click anywhere in a slice to bring up the **Slice Options** dialog box.

6 Choose a **Slice Type** from the pop-up menu: **Image** keeps this part of the image or **No Image** deletes it and substitutes text or another image.

7 If you chose **Image**, give the image a name; if you chose **No Image**, enter the HTML code in the **HTML** field.

8 Click **OK** to save your changes to the slice.

One handy way to use slices is for creating several slightly different versions of the same image, such as a page-top banner head with different heading text on different pages. Use the Slice tool to define a slice that encompasses only the text; Photoshop will create slices for the rest of the image. Then, after you've saved the HTML and images, you can open just the image file with the text and create different versions of that file for the different page headers.

Task 2: Creating Animations

Photoshop's companion program, ImageReady, can be used to create Web animations in the form of animated GIF images. These image files actually contain multiple images that are displayed in sequence when the image is loaded as part of a Web page.

Start Here

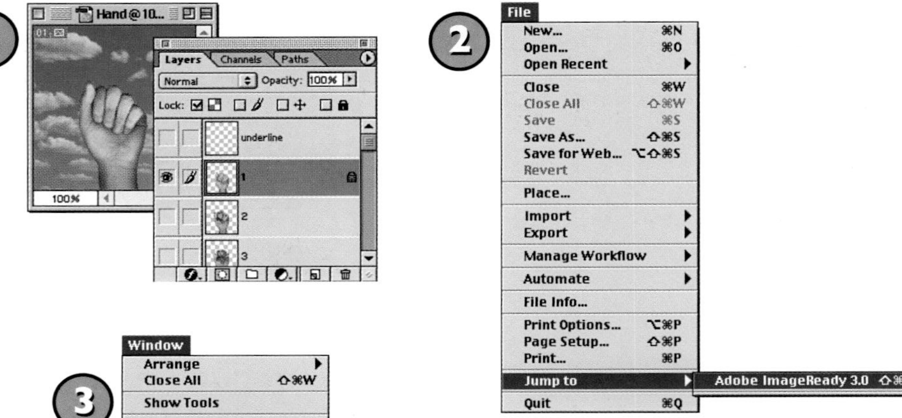

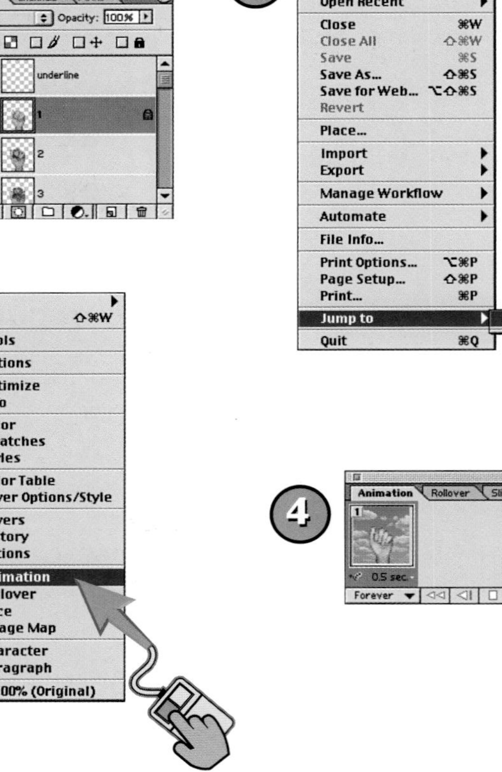

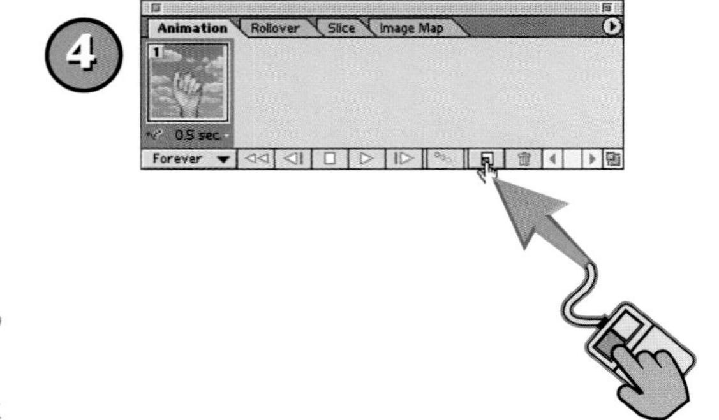

1. In Photoshop, create an image with separate layers for each element that will move, appear, or disappear in your animation.
2. Switch to ImageReady by choosing **File**, **Jump to**, **Adobe ImageReady 3.0**.
3. Choose **Window**, **Show Animation** to display the **Animation** palette.
4. Click the **New Frame** button to create a new frame of the animation containing the same layers as in the first frame.

To preview an animation, click the Play button at the bottom of the Animation palette.

Next Step

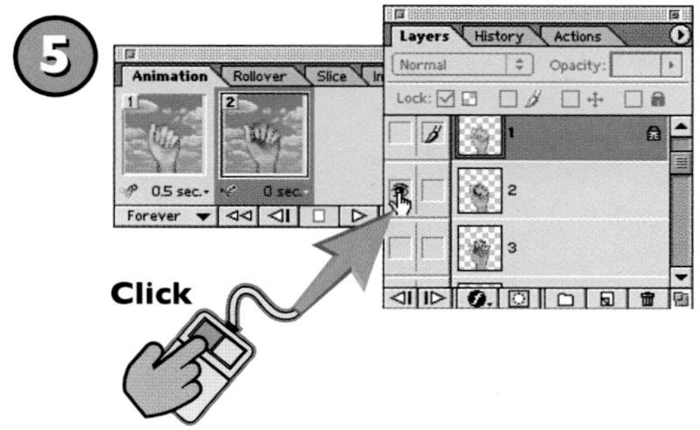

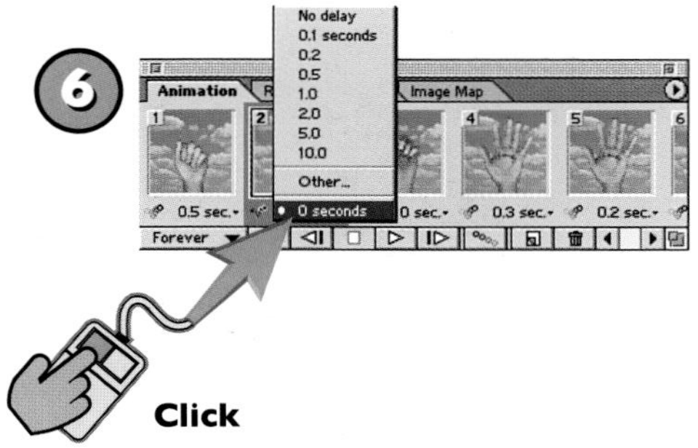

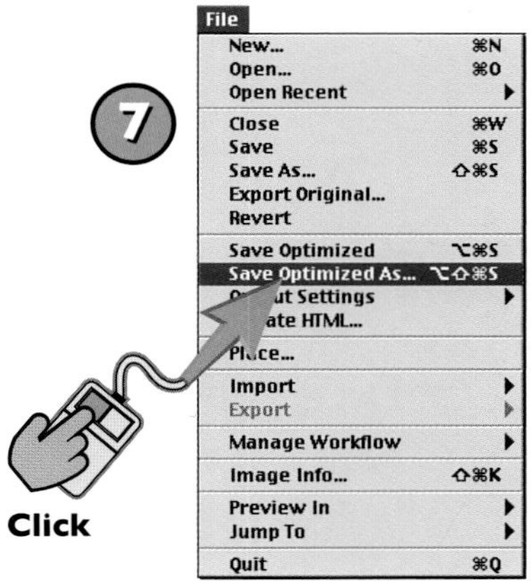

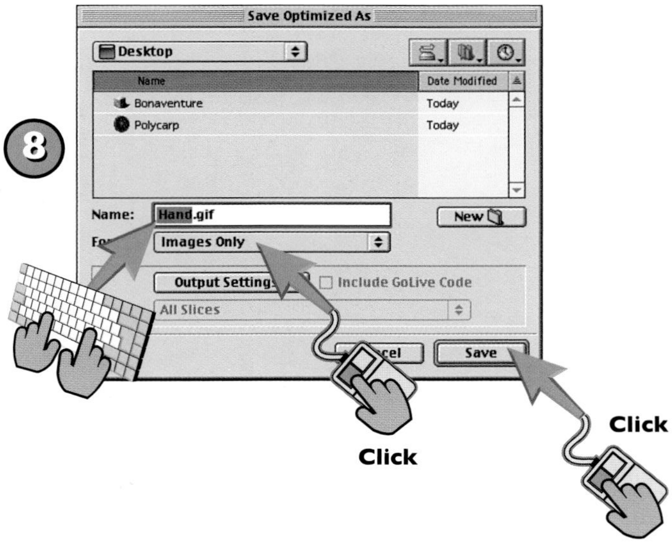

5. In the **Layers** palette, hide layers containing objects that you want to disappear in the second frame, and then create more frames and repeat this step for each.

6. Click on each frame in the **Animation** palette and choose an amount of time for that frame to display from the pop-up menu.

7. Choose **File**, **Save Optimized As**.

8. Choose **Images Only**, give the file a name, and click **Save**.

You can also save animations as QuickTime files by choosing File, Export Original and choosing QuickTime Movie from the Format pop-up menu. To view QuickTime movies, users must have QuickTime installed on their computers; all Macs come with QuickTime, but Windows users might have to download it from `www.apple.com`.

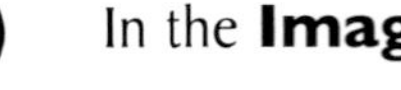

Task 3: Creating Image Maps

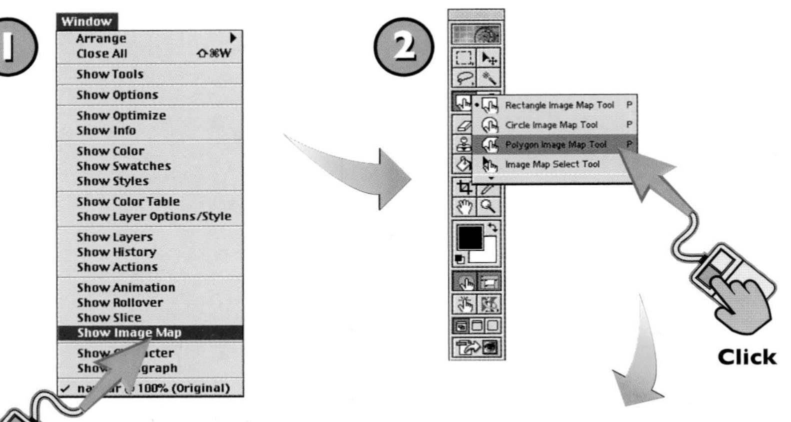

An *image map* is a Web image that's divided into multiple zones, or *hotspots*, each of which is a hyperlink to another page or file. Hotspots can be any shape, and they're easy to create with ImageReady's Image Map tool.

1. In ImageReady, choose **Window**, **Show Image Map**.
2. To draw a hotspot, click on any of the **Image Map** tools in the **Tool** palette.
3. Click and drag in the image window to create a hotspot.
4. In the **Image Map** palette, enter a URL.

To activate the hotspots in an image, you must save it as a Web page; see Task 9, "Saving Web Pages."

To change the settings or size of a hotspot, switch to the Image Map Select tool. You can reshape a hotspot by dragging its corner points; to change its settings, just click on it and make the desired changes in the Image Map palette. You can temporarily access the Image Map Select tool by holding down Cmd/Ctrl when any Image Map tool is active.

Task 4: Creating Image Maps from Layers

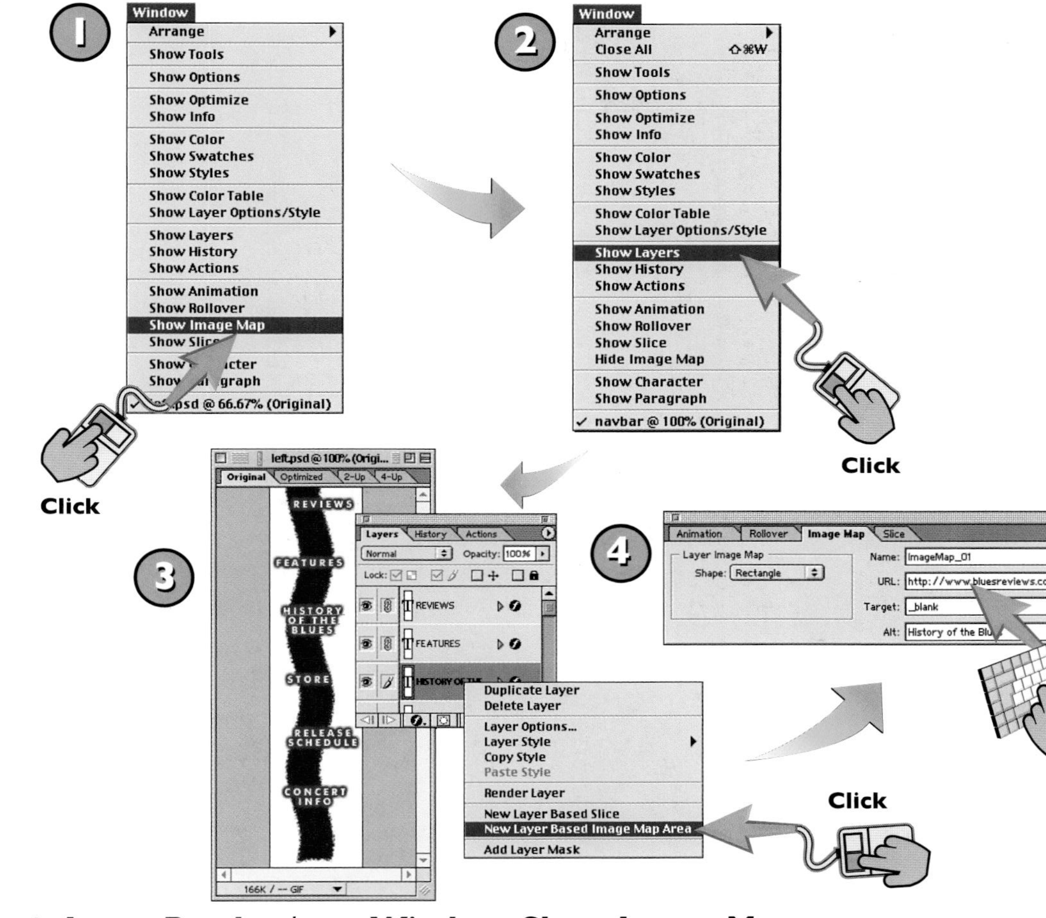

If the image elements that you want to make into hyperlinks exist on individual layers, you can define each layer as a hotspot rather than draw each one with the Image Map tool. This time-saving technique is especially useful when you're creating an image by combining other images—just drag each image into the main file with the Move tool so that it's on its own layer, and you're all set!

1. In **ImageReady**, choose **Window**, **Show Image Map**.
2. Choose **Window**, **Show Layers**.
3. Right-click on the layer you want to use, and choose **New Layer Based Image Map Area** from the contextual menu.
4. Enter a URL in the **Image Map** palette.

If you want the hotspot's link to open in a new window, choose **_blank** from the **Target** pop-up menu in the **Image Map** palette.

Task 5: Creating Rollovers

A rollover is an image that changes in some way when you move your cursor over it. On the Web, rollovers are created using JavaScript, but with Photoshop you don't have to know a word of JavaScript—Photoshop will do all the coding for you. All you have to do is create the original view of the image and the changed view and tell Photoshop which is which.

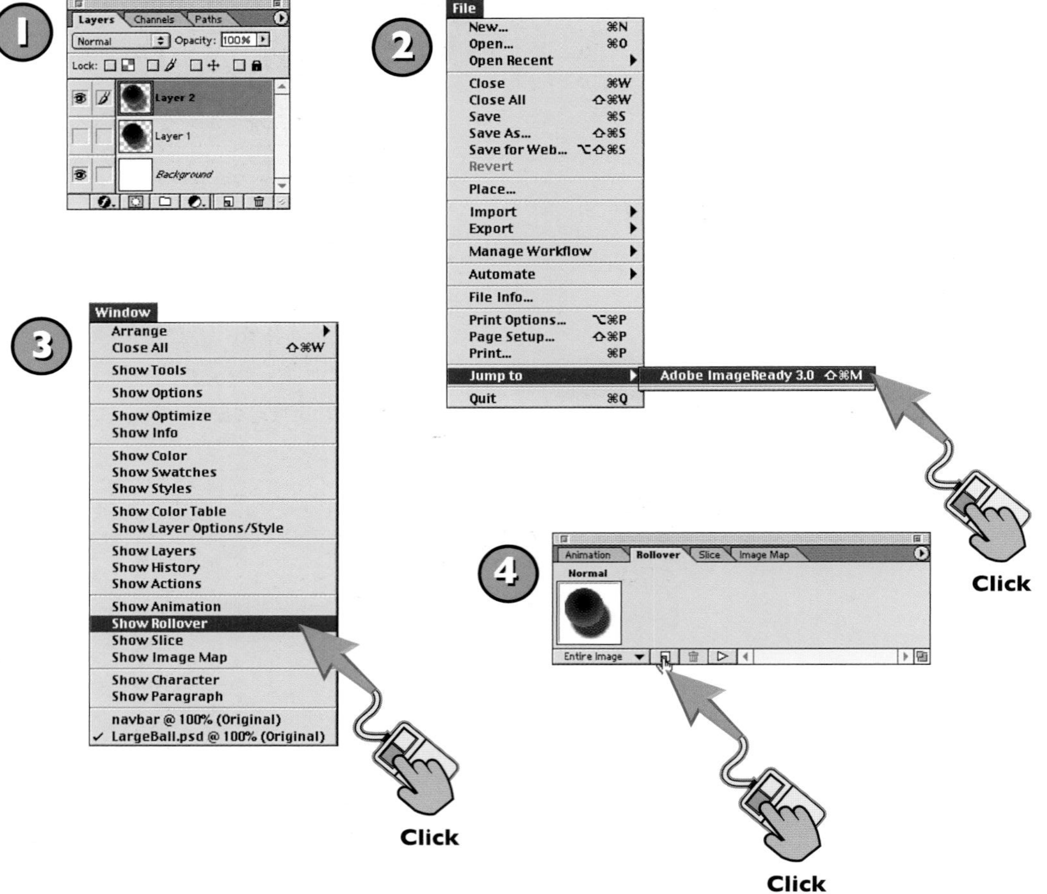

1. In Photoshop, create an image with separate layers for each element that will change in your rollover.
2. Switch to ImageReady by choosing **File**, **Jump to**, **Adobe ImageReady 3.0**.
3. Choose **Window**, **Show Rollover** to display the **Rollover** palette.
4. Click the **New Rollover** button to create a new rollover state containing the same layers as in the first state.

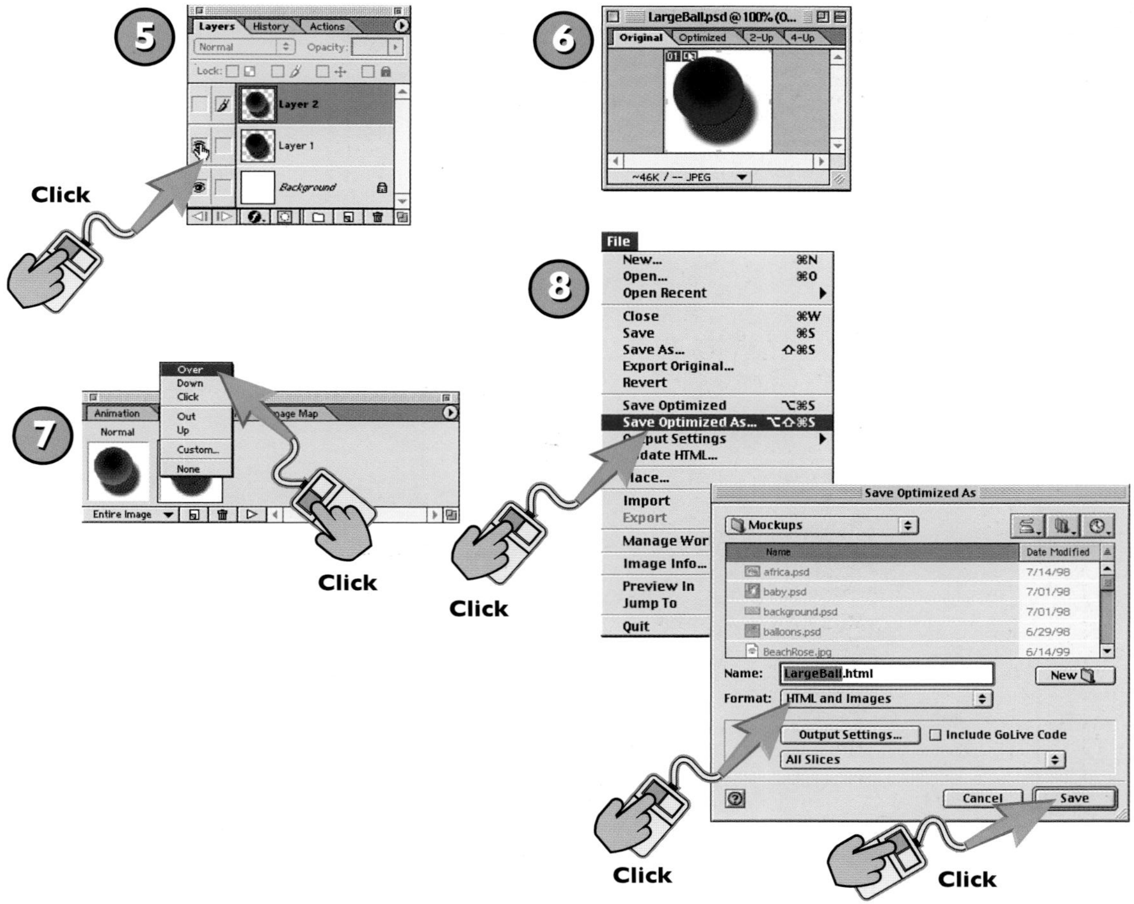

5 In the **Layers** palette, hide layers containing objects that you want to disappear in the rollover state.

6 Edit the remaining layers to move or delete objects as necessary.

7 Click on each added state in the **Rollover** palette and choose a mouse action to activate the rollover from the pop-up menu.

8 Choose **File**, **Save Optimized As**, then choose **HTML and Images** and click **Save**.

Saving HTML and Images gives you an HTML file containing the JavaScript code that creates the rollover effect, as well as the multiple images created by slicing the images and the alternative images displayed in the rollover effect.

Task 6: Previewing an Image in a Web Browser

As you work on an image, it's important to make sure it looks the way you think it will in an actual Web browser. ImageReady's Preview In command gives you a chance to do a spot check at any time while you're editing an image.

Start Here

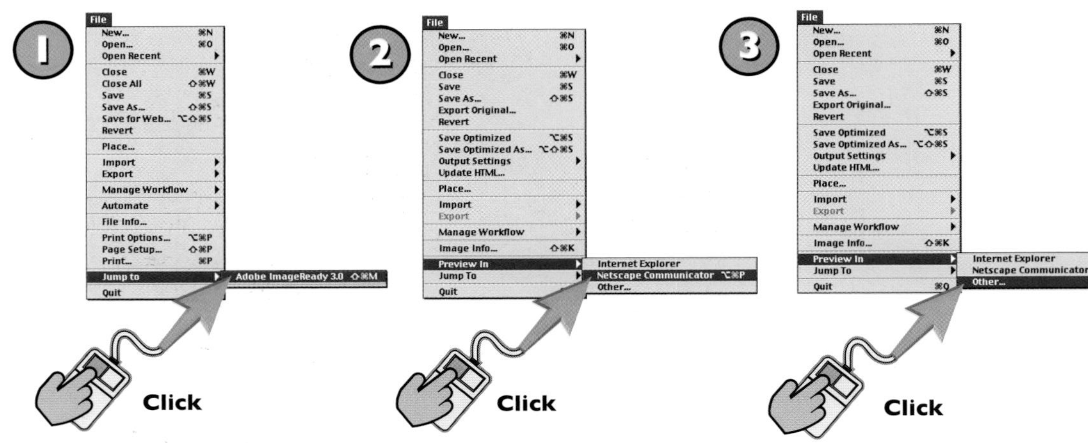

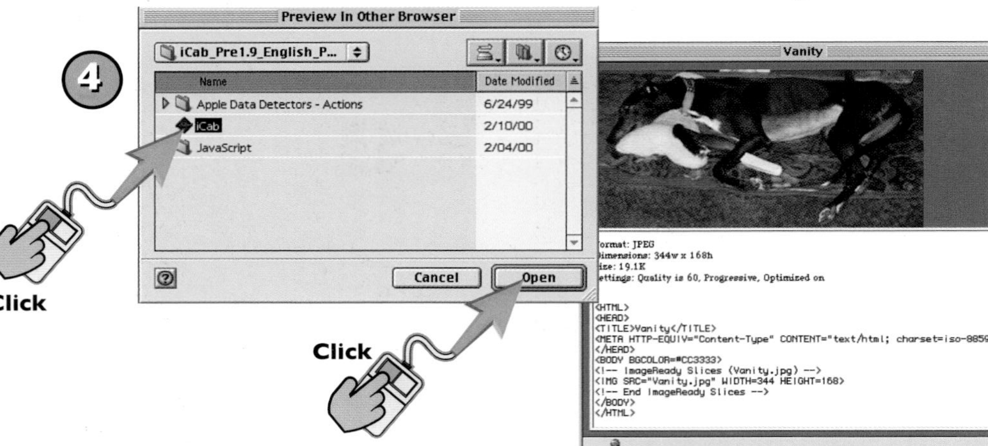

1. Switch to ImageReady by choosing **File**, **Jump to**, **Adobe ImageReady 3.0**.
2. Choose **File**, **Preview In** and choose a browser from the submenu.
3. To use a browser that isn't in the list, choose **File**, **Preview In**, **Other**.
4. Locate the new browser and click **Open**.

In addition to displaying the image in the Web browser, Photoshop shows you information about the image, including its file size, dimensions, and associated HTML code.

End Task

Task 7: Adjusting an Image's Gamma Value

Gamma refers to the standard monitor brightness on a particular computer platform—the same image typically appears darker on Windows computer monitors than it does on a Macintosh computer monitor. By previewing an image's gamma, you can determine whether it needs an automatic gamma adjustment to display well on both platforms.

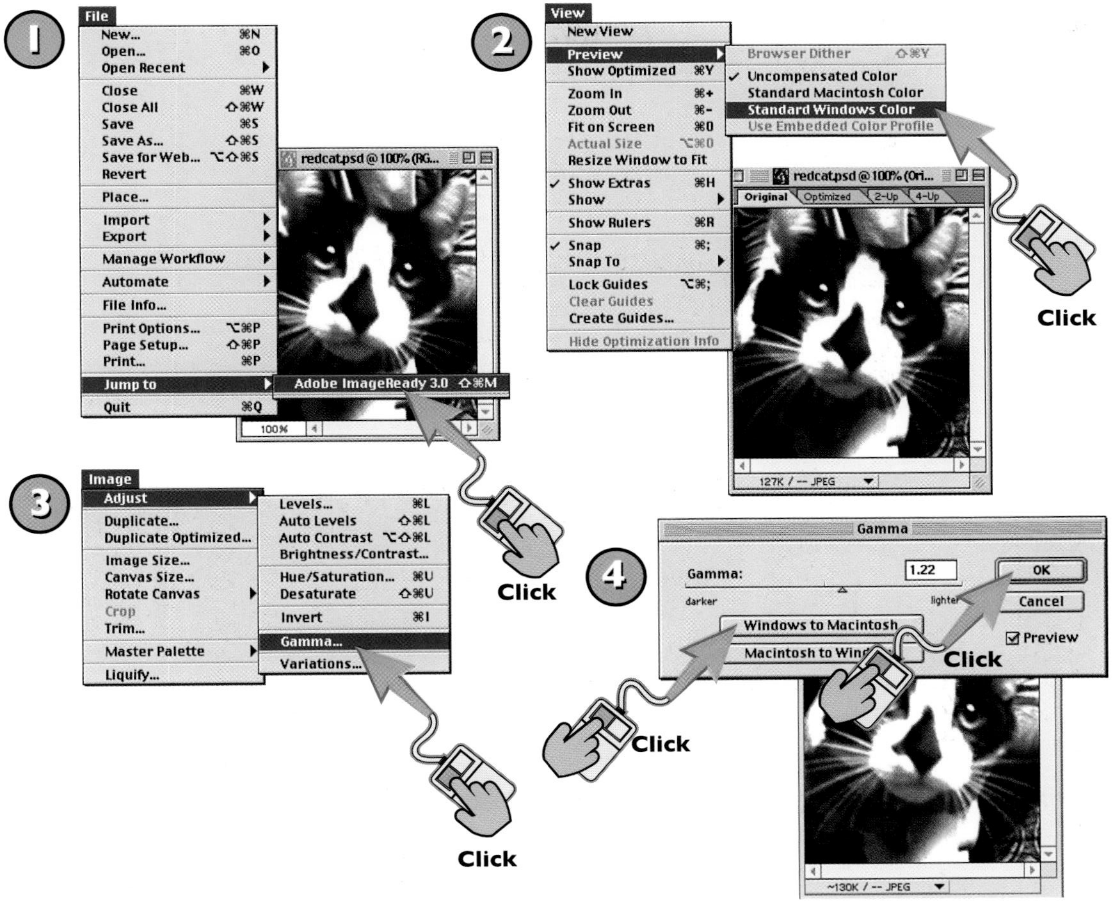

1. Switch to ImageReady by choosing **File**, **Jump to**, **Adobe ImageReady 3.0**.
2. To see how your image will appear on the opposite platform, choose **View**, **Preview** and select **Standard Macintosh Color** or **Standard Windows Color**.
3. If the image is too dark or too light in the opposite-platform preview, choose **Image**, **Adjust**, **Gamma**.
4. Click on **Windows to Macintosh** or **Macintosh to Windows**, and click **OK**.

Some images are never going to look perfect on both platforms. For these images, either choose the one platform on which the image is most likely to be viewed and adjust for that gamma value, or try to strike a balance somewhere in the middle by adjusting the image's overall lightness—just drag the gamma slider until you reach a good compromise.

Task 8: Saving Images for the Web

Ordinarily when you save an image, you just choose a format in the Save As dialog box and off you go. With the Save for Web command, though, you can do a lot more than just save an image—Photoshop enables you to reduce the image's file size by reducing the number of colors in it and previewing the results as you choose different options.

Start Here

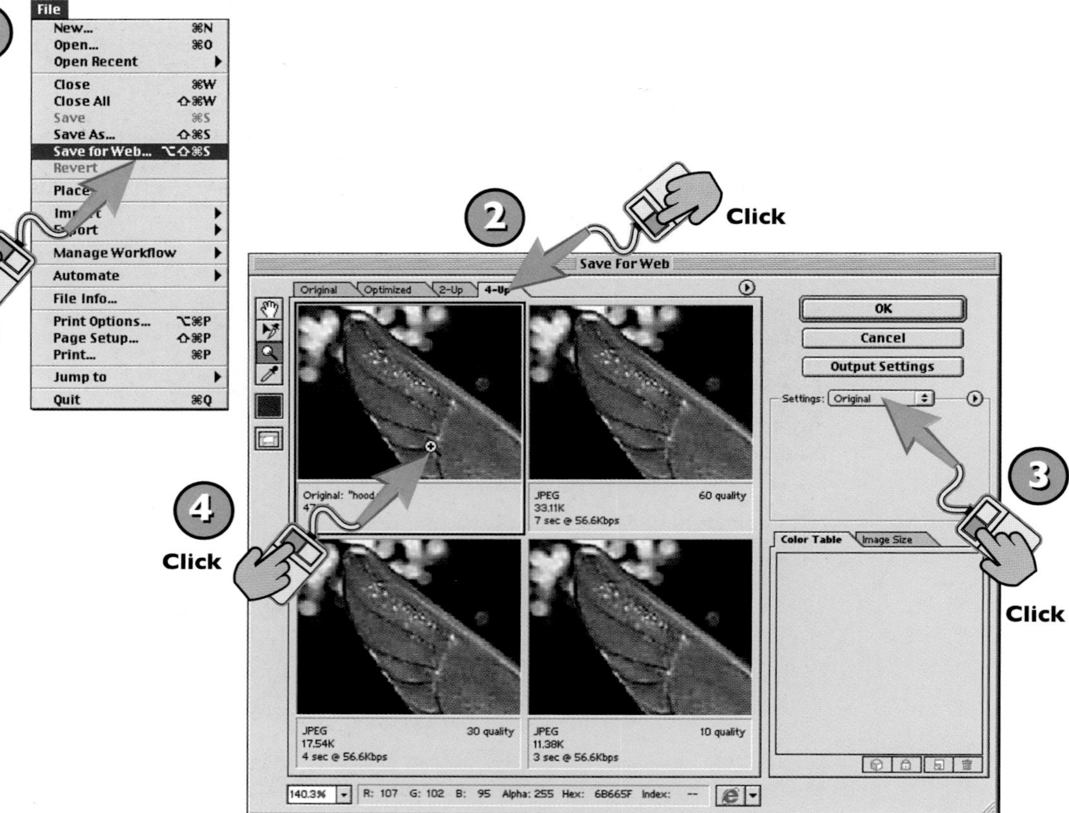

1. Choose **File**, **Save for Web**.

2. Click on the **4-Up** tab to show four image previews.

3. Click on each preview and choose an option from the **Settings** pop-up menu.

4. Use the **Zoom** tool to zoom in on the image previews and the **Hand** tool to move the previews around in the window.

The Settings options are all variations on GIF and JPEG formats, with different amounts of compression and *dithering*. For photos, use JPEG; for other artwork, use GIF.

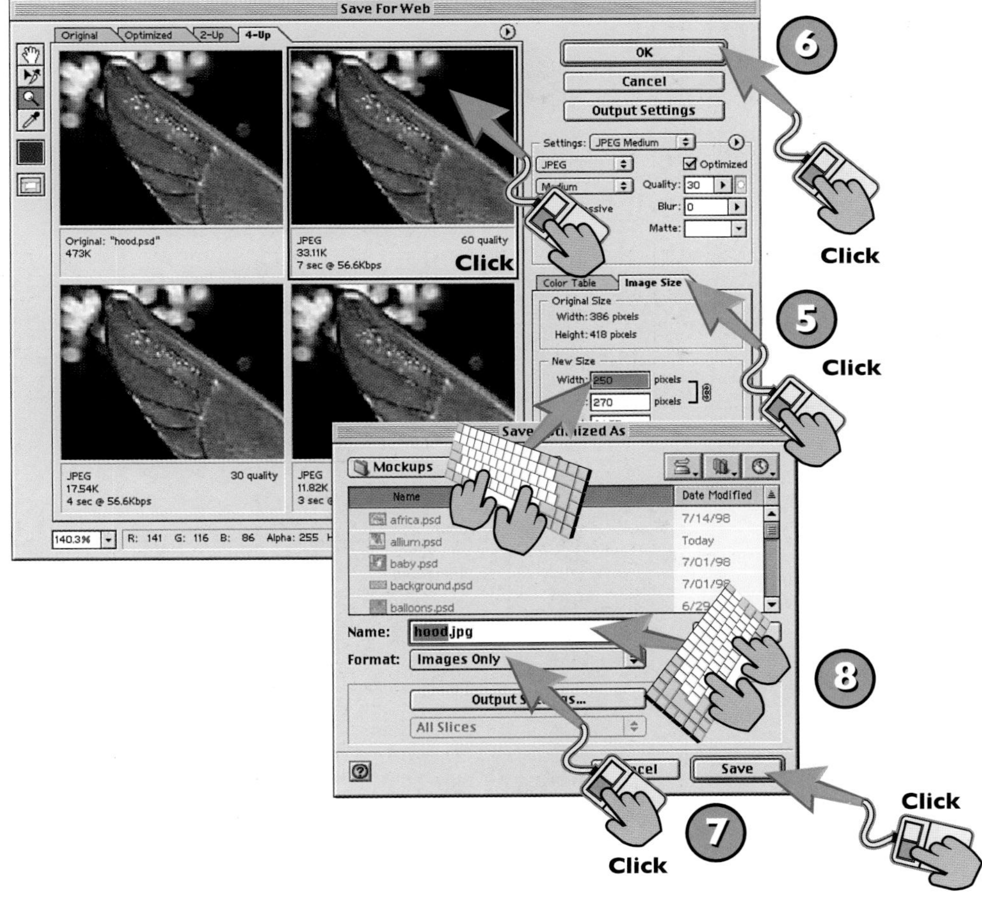

5 To resize the image as it's saved, click on the **Image Size** tab and enter a new size.

6 Click on the preview you prefer and click **OK** to continue saving the file.

7 In the **Format** pop-up menu, choose **Images Only**.

8 Enter a filename and choose a location, and then click **Save**.

When using JPEG, watch out for compression artifacts—you'll be able to see distortions that look like heat mirages when you zoom in on the image. The lower the JPEG quality level, the more likely you are to see these flaws. When saving JPEG images, you must balance your desire for a small file size with the effect that artifacts have on the image.

Task 9: Creating Background Images

HTML enables you to specify an image to be placed behind all the other text and images on a Web page. Usually, background images are tiled—repeated so that a small image can fill an infinitely large window. Creating such an image is easy with ImageReady's Tile Maker filter.

Start Here

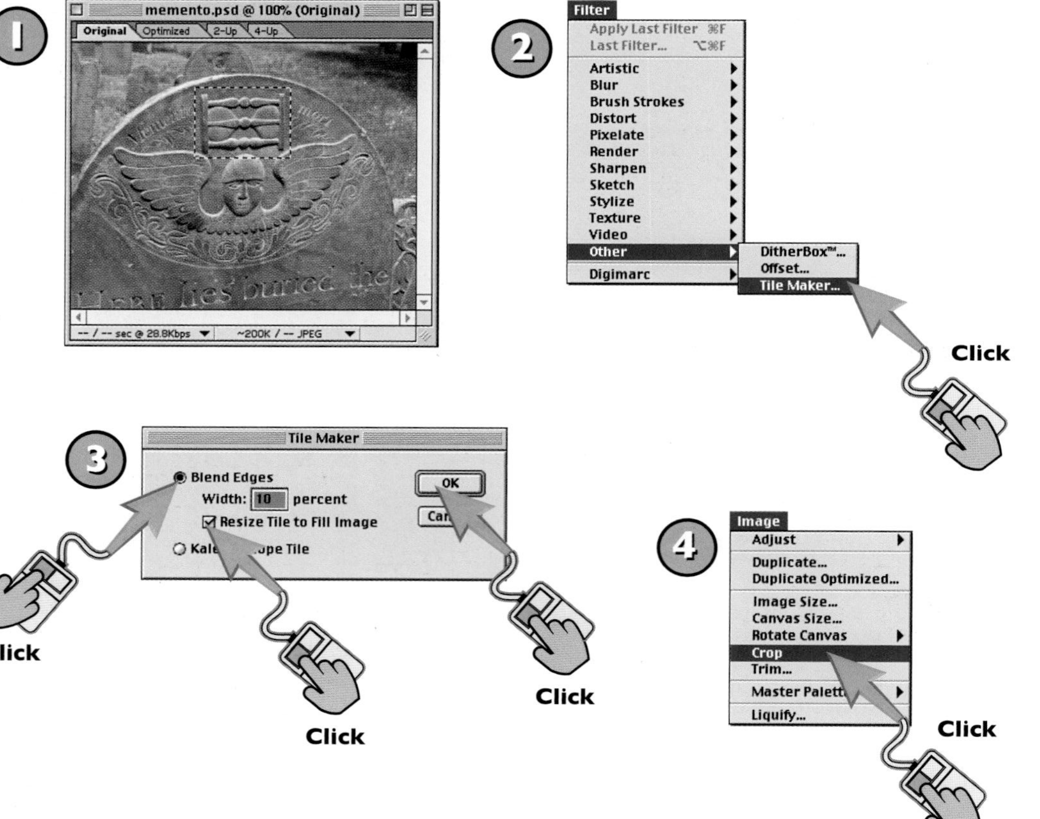

For an interesting effect that completely alters the original look of the background image, try clicking on Kaleidoscope Tile instead of Blend Edges—this flips the tile vertically and horizontally in on itself so that it looks as though you're viewing the image through a kaleidoscope.

1. In ImageReady, select the area of the image that you want to use as a background.
2. Choose **Filter**, **Other**, **Tile Maker**.
3. Click on **Blend Edges** and **Resize Tile to Fill Image**, and then click **OK** to create the tile.
4. Choose **Image, Crop** to delete the rest of the image.

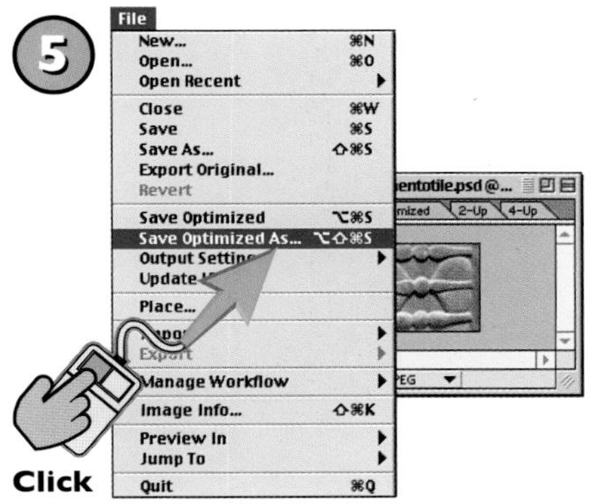

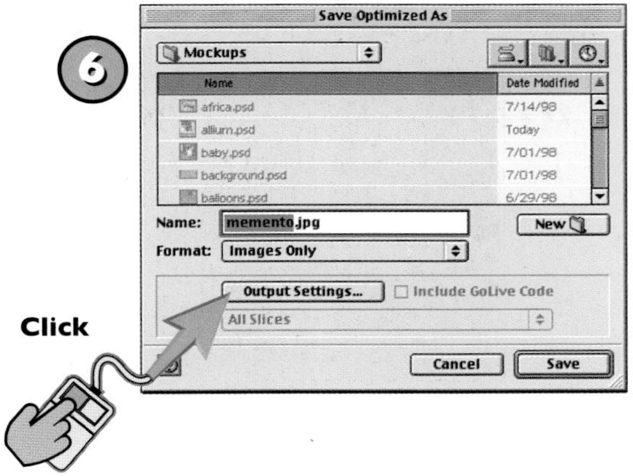

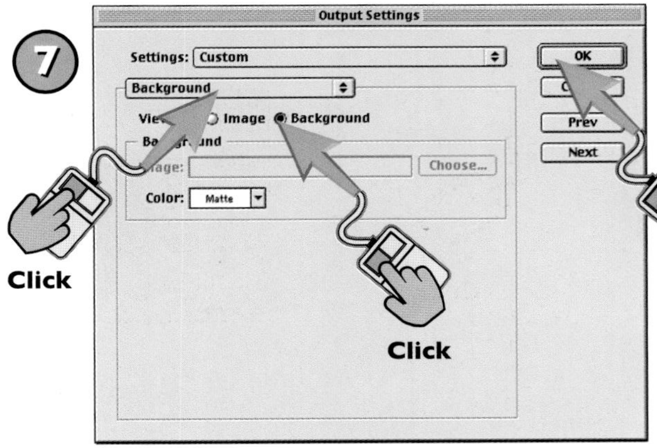

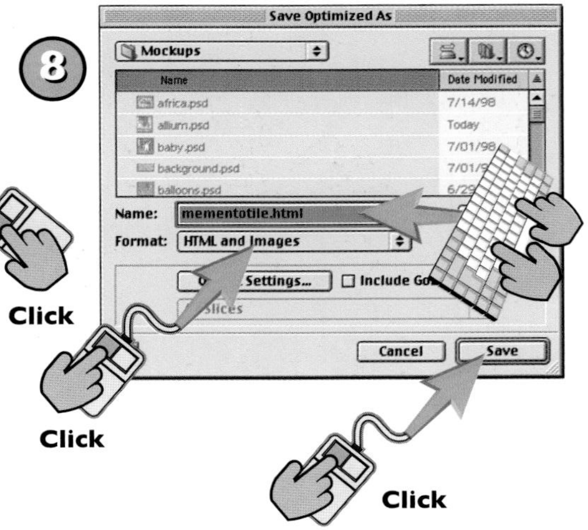

5 Choose **File**, **Save Optimized As**.

6 Click on **Output Settings** to bring up the **Output Settings** dialog box.

7 Choose **Background** from the unlabeled pop-up menu at the top of the dialog, click the **Background** radio button, and then click **OK**.

8 Give the image a name and choose **HTML and Images** from the **Format** pop-up menu, and then click **Save**.

Saving the background image results in a GIF file—the background image itself—and an HTML file that uses the GIF as its background. To use the background image in another Web page, you can copy and paste the BODY tag, which will look something like this: `<BODY BGCOLOR=#FFFFFF BACKGROUND="sunset.gif">`.

Task 10: Saving Web Pages

New to Photoshop 6 is the capability to create entire Web pages, not just the images referenced in them. You can specify HTML text, a background color or image, and even an image sliced into sections that are automatically reassembled in an HTML table in your Web page.

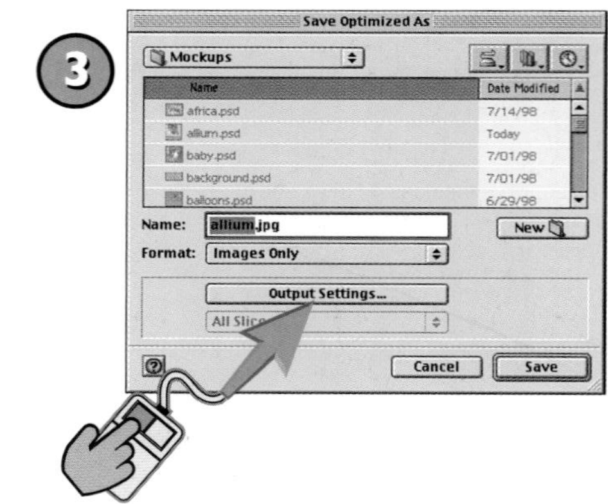

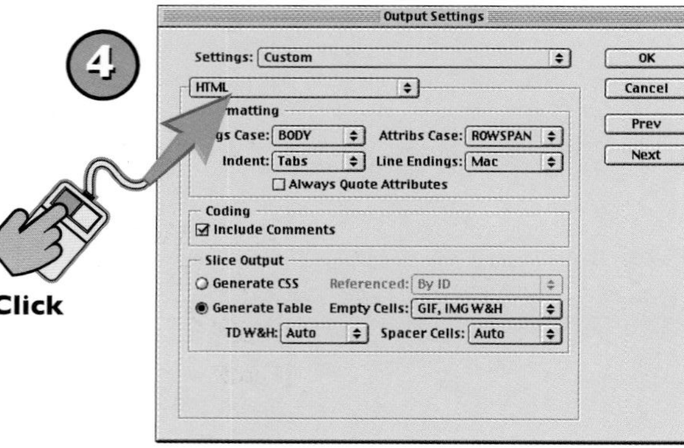

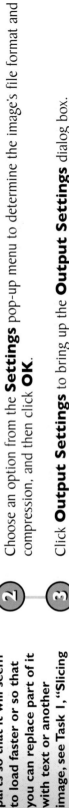

1. Choose **File**, **Save for Web**.

2. Choose an option from the **Settings** pop-up menu to determine the image's file format and compression, and then click **OK**.

3. Click **Output Settings** to bring up the **Output Settings** dialog box.

4. To specify HTML options, choose **HTML** from the pop-up menu and choose **Formatting** options.

To break an image into parts so that it will seem to load faster or so that you can replace part of it with text or another image, see Task 1, "Slicing Images into Sections."

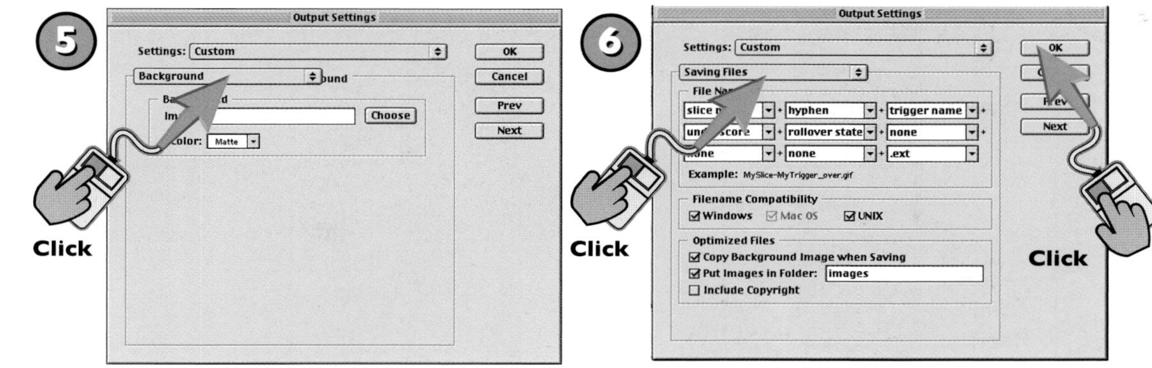

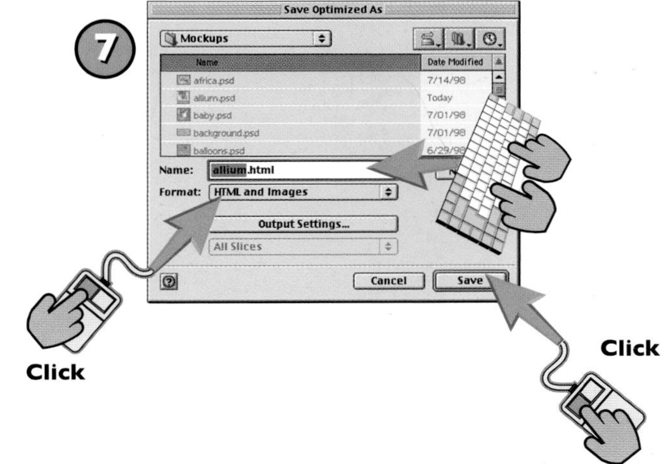

5 To assign a background color or image, choose **Background** and specify the color or image in the **Background** tab.

6 To specify file and folder names for the files you're creating, choose **Saving Files** and enter the names you want to use, and then click **OK**.

7 Give the image a name and choose **HTML and Images** from the **Format** pop-up menu, then click **Save**.

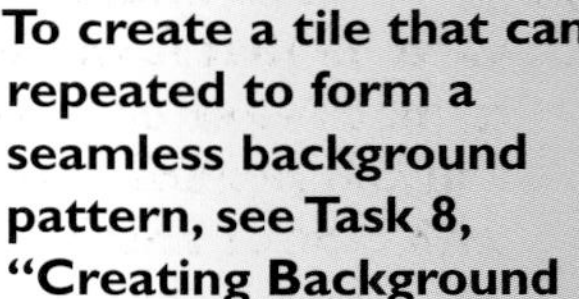

To create a tile that can be repeated to form a seamless background pattern, see Task 8, "Creating Background Images."

Glossary

Action A named series of Photoshop commands that can be executed by simply invoking the Action.

alpha channel A channel that contains a mask image, as opposed to a color channel.

anti-aliasing Smoothing the edges in an image by adding pixels of intermediate colors between contrasting pixels.

batch processing Applying changes to a specified group of images automatically through the use of Actions.

Bézier path A path in which each curve is defined by three points, one indicating position and the others indicating direction. Used in drawing programs such as FreeHand, CorelDraw, and Illustrator and also in Photoshop's paths.

bicubic The highest-quality method of interpolation.

bilinear The moderate-quality method of interpolation.

bitmap mode Photoshop's term for a black-and-white (as opposed to grayscale) image.

bitmapped image An image created from colored, gray, or black pixels, each occupying a predetermined position on a grid.

blending mode A mathematically based way of combining colors on two or more layers or in a new element and an existing one; the most commonly used blending mode is Normal.

BMP The bitmapped file format commonly used on PCs.

burn To intensify by darkening the image details.

channel A component of an image; each file contains several color channels (such as red, green, and blue channels) and potentially several alpha channels used for masking portions of the image.

clipping path A path that is used to mask portions of an image that lie outside the path's boundaries.

CMYK Cyan (light blue), magenta (bright pinkish-red), yellow, and black—the four colors used in process printing to create full-color images.

color mode A way of defining color within Photoshop, such as CMYK, Grayscale, or Bitmap.

color model Another term for color mode that is more commonly used when not referring to Photoshop.

color-separated Broken into component images that reflect the amount of ink required from each ink color to produce a full-color printed image. A color-separated file contains separate grayscale images for each of the four process ink colors.

compression A method of encoding image data more efficiently to decrease file size.

crop To delete any portion of the image that lies outside a rectangular cropping selection.

curve handles Imaginary points that can be moved to define the shape of a Bézier path.

DCS Desktop Color Separation, an EPS file format option that creates five files to form a preseparated color image (one for each process color and one containing a full-color preview).

dither To simulate missing colors in an image by clustering pixels of other colors together to "mix" a new color

dodge To de-emphasize by lightening image details.

EPS Encapsulated PostScript; a file format used for both bitmapped images, as in Photoshop, and vector images, as in drawing programs like Illustrator.

feathered Refers to a selection that "fades out" around the edges for a specified distance. In a feathered selection, the outer pixels are only partially selected, and any change made to that selection will be only partially applied to those pixels.

filter A command that changes the appearance of an image by applying a mathematical equation to each pixel in the image.

gamma Monitor brightness.

gamut The range of colors that can be reproduced by a particular device or process.

Gaussian Refers to a mathematical method of redistributing pixels randomly; used to blur and add noise to images in Photoshop.

GIF Graphic Interchange Format, a file format originated by CompuServe and widely used on the Internet.

Grabber Hand A tool that moves the image within the window. To access the Grabber Hand, press the spacebar, and then click and drag.

gradient A color fill that shades from one color to another. Gradients can include multiple colors and even transparency.

grayscale Composed completely of shades of gray.

grid Non-printing rows and columns that can be used to position objects within an image more precisely.

guides Non-printing lines that can be placed anywhere within an image.

highlights The brightest (closest to white) points in an image.

hotspot A clickable area in an image map that links to a Web page or file.

HSB A method of defining colors in terms of hue (color), saturation (purity), and brightness (intensity).

image map A Web image divided into clickable areas, each linking to a different Web page or file.

imagesetter A high-resolution printing device that prints on coated paper (used for paste-up) or film (used for making printing plates).

interlaced Refers to an image whose data is saved in an order that will allow the image to be displayed in a low resolution, even before all the image data is delivered to the viewing computer; commonly used on the World Wide Web.

JPEG Joint Photographic Experts Group—a compression method and lossy file format that allows for extremely high compression levels.

layer Part of an image that can lie above or below other parts of the image and that can be modified without affecting the rest of the image.

layer mask A grayscale image that determines what parts of a layer are visible and what parts do not show.

lossless compression A compression method that does not affect the quality of the image compressed.

lossy A compression method that reduces the quality of the image compressed.

LZW Lempel-Ziv-Welch—a lossless image compression method used in the TIFF format.

marching ants The common term for the moving selection marquee.

midtones The middle (between white and black) tones in an image.

nearest neighbor The lowest-quality (but quickest) method of interpolation.

path See ***Bézier path***.

PDF Portable Document Format—the format used by Adobe's Acrobat software.

Photo CD A file format used to store multiple resolutions of an image within one file.

pixel A "picture element," a square portion of an image that can be only one color.

PostScript A page description language that defines images in mathematical terms; used by printers and imagesetters. PostScript fonts are defined in terms of their character outlines.

preview A low-resolution version of an image stored within the image file so that the image can be viewed in programs into which it is imported, such as page layout applications.

process color One of the four ink colors used to print CMYK images; that is, cyan, magenta, yellow, or black.

progressive Refers to an image that displays at gradually higher resolutions as more image data is downloaded to the viewer's computer.

RAM Random Access Memory—the computer memory in which currently active programs are stored.

rasterize To convert from Bézier paths to pixels.

resample To add or delete pixels and rearrange existing pixels to resize or change the resolution of an image.

resolution The number of pixels per measurement unit; usually measured in pixels per inch or pixels per centimeter.

resolution-independent Stored in a format that can be printed at any size or resolution.

RGB Red, green, and blue, the colors displayed by computer monitors and combined to create the illusion of full-color images.

RIP Raster Image Processor—the "brain" of a printing device; usually used in reference to high-resolution imagesetters.

rulers The measurement guides along the top and left edges of the image window.

selection The currently active area of the image, to which any changes will be applied; indicated by "marching ants" along the outer edges of the selection.

shadows The darkest (closest to black) points in an image.

spot color Printed color that will be reproduced by a single ink rather than by a combination of the four process ink colors.

spot color channel The channel that contains image data to be printed with a spot color rather than with the process colors.

swatchbook The book of printed ink samples showing what common colors look like on paper rather than onscreen.

TIFF Tag Image File Format; bitmapped file format commonly used in prepress applications.

transform To modify an image by rotating, skewing, or otherwise reshaping it.

transparency mask The selection that includes all non-transparent pixels on a layer.

vector image An image created from points, lines, and fills and defined in terms of the mathematical characteristics of those elements. Drawing programs such as Illustrator, CorelDraw, and FreeHand create vector images.

work path The currently active path.

Index

F

J-L

M

N

O

P

Q

R